S0-CAA-209

*A Comprehensive Guide to Buying,*
*Owning, and Selling Your Power or Sail Boat*

# BOATING

# FOR

# LESS

## Second Edition

## STEVE HENKEL

 **INTERNATIONAL MARINE PUBLISHING**
**CAMDEN, MAINE**

Published by International Marine

10  9  8  7  6  5  4  3  2  1

Copyright © 1990/1992 International Marine, an imprint of TAB BOOKS. TAB BOOKS is a division of McGraw-Hill, Inc.

All rights reserved. The publisher takes no responsibility for the use of any of the materials or methods described in this book, nor for the products thereof. The name "International Marine" and the International Marine logo are trademarks of TAB BOOKS. Printed in the United States of America.

**Library of Congress Cataloging-in-Publication Data**

Henkel, Steve.
    Boating for less: a comprehensive guide to buying, owning, and selling your power or sail boat / Steve Henkel. —2nd ed.
      p.    cm.
    Includes bibliographical references and index.
    ISBN 0-87742-315-6
    1. Boats and boating—United States—Costs.    I. Title.
VM320.H46  1991
623.8'223—dc20                              91-28391
                                                  CIP

Questions regarding the content of this book should be addressed to:

International Marine Publishing
P.O: Box 220
Camden, ME 04843

Typeset by Maryland Composition Co., Glen Burnie, Maryland
Printed by Hamilton Printing, Castleton, New York
Design by Meredith Lightbown
Illustrations on pages 1, 35, 111, and 189 by Richard Gorski

# CONTENTS

# Acknowledgments

This book is full of facts and figures that could not have been assembled without the existence of the rich literature available in the boating field. Of particular use have been the boating newspaper *Soundings*, the magazines *Yachting, Boating, Power & Motor Yacht, Sail, Small Boat Journal* and *WoodenBoat* (in which portions of chapters on insurance and financing were originally published), and the newsletter *Practical Sailor*. Books of particular value included Arthur Beiser's *The Proper Yacht, Skene's Elements Of Yacht Design, Ted Brewer Explains Sailboat Design* and the many catalog annuals published by the magazines, a full list of which appears in this book's Appendix 2. To the writers, editors and staffs of these publications I extend my thanks.

Jon Eaton, editor-in-chief at International Marine Publishing Company, not only invited me to write this book in the first place (for which I am very grateful), but provided many valuable suggestions on the book's development, content and form. In addition to the improvements brought about by Jon's deft editorial touch, the book is better as a result of the efforts of Jim Payne of Cannell, Payne & Page, yacht brokers in Camden, Maine, and Michael A. Smith, senior editor at *Power & Motor Yacht*, both of whom kindly agreed to read the manuscript and offer comments. To these perceptive and candid individuals and to Claire Cramer, who read the manuscript line by line and contributed much to the book's readability, I offer my sincere thanks.

To the staff at the Darien Public Library, and especially to research librarian Irene Delor for her ever-smiling responses to some pretty uncommon questions, go my special thanks.

Also on hand as I collected material for use in these pages were naval architects Craig Walters of Craig Walters Yacht Designs, Alan Gilbert of Sparkman & Stephens, and Evan Marshall; Jules Fleder of the Westlawn School of Yacht Design; yacht broker Jake Leo of Lion Yachts; Bill McDonough of Connecticut Marine Sales; Greg Clement, Bill Beke, and Stan Wetreich of Rex Marine; Ed Rogers, Mal Watson, Walt Reynolds, Gaeton Andretta, and Jack Quigley at the Small Boat Shop in Norwalk, Connecticut; Mark Smith of *American Sailor* magazine; Mimi Dyer of USYRU; Wally and Jean Ross of Sonar International; Greg Proteau of the National Marine Manufacturer's Association; Wells M. Pile of Key Financial Services Inc.; and numerous others who were helpful in my quest for information. To all these, and to the many individuals who design, produce, sell, repair, store, finance and insure boats, engines and accessories, who have generously taken the time over the past dozen and more years at their places of business and at boat shows all over the country to try to answer my probing questions about their products, I also offer my sincere thanks.

My admiration for a job well done goes to Dick Gorski, who created the amusing and decorative drawings that introduce the four parts of the book.

Finally, to my wife Carol, and to my two sons Charlie and Laird, I give my love and my appreciation for their constant and continuing patience, understanding, and support.

Steve Henkel
Darien, Connecticut
March 15, 1988

To the above I would like to add thanks to Richard Thiel, editor of *MotorBoat* and more recently of *Power & Motor Yacht*; to Freeman Pittman at *Sail*; to Tim Cole at *Powerboat Reports*; and to the folks at *Boat Journal*, *Boating Digest*, and *Great Lakes Sailor*, for writing assignments that came in handy when updating this Second Edition.

Again I offer my thanks and admiration to the research team at the Darien Library, especially to Maura Ritz and Blanche Parker, for their help.

Between the first and second editions the kids flew the coop, so they no longer have to put up with my idiosyncrasies while I write; but I continue to be grateful for my wife Carol's outstanding patience, understanding, and support.

Steve Henkel
Osprey, Florida
June 1, 1991

# INTRODUCTION

# 101 Ways to Save Money on Boating

This book is about money — your money — and how to get the biggest possible bang for your bucks when you're buying, using, or selling a boat.

Friends and acquaintances, knowing I am interested in such things, occasionally ask for advice when they're considering buying a new or used boat. While their individual questions are specific ("Which do you think I should buy, a Mako or an Aquasport?"), there is a recurring pattern to their inquiries. They all boil down to eight questions, which go like this:

1. What general type of boat should I buy?
2. What specific brand and model should I buy?
3. What are the advantages and disadvantages to buying Brand X/Model X instead of Brand Y/Model Y, which is similar?
4. What version of Brand X/Model X should I buy (new or old, equipped or bare, shiny or shopworn)?
5. I know what brand and model I want, and even what version, but where should I look to buy the best boat for the lowest cost?
6. How much should I pay for the boat I want — including equipment?
7. After I buy, how much will I have to budget for annual costs?
8. How can I save money on all of this?

The way I figure the situation, there are literally hundreds of ways to save money in the process of buying, owning, and selling a boat. The remainder of this introduction lists 101 of them.

## When you're deciding on what general type of boat to buy . . .

1. Don't even think about buying a boat you won't enjoy owning at least three years. Generally speaking, the longer you keep her, the lower your ownership cost per year.
2. Before you buy, shop the market thoroughly and in as wide a geographical area as you can; leave no bargain-buying opportunity unrecognized.
3. Think about buying used rather than new, to avoid high early-years depreciation.
4. Think about building your boat from a kit; you can save 20% to 30% compared with buying ready-made.
5. Choose a "cult boat" — a design that enjoys unusually intense popularity among its owners — if you can find one you like. She'll hold her value better and be easier to sell.
6. Don't buy a "dog" — a bad boat, one that can't get out of her own way, is singularly ugly, or is so sloppily constructed that she'd be dangerous at sea. You may enjoy her for awhile, but eventually, almost inevitably she'll become tiresome, and you'll want to sell her. Then you're likely to have trouble finding a buyer — at any price.
7. Look for boats with relatively low maintenance requirements (e.g., light rather than dark topsides).
8. Try to choose a brand whose builder is likely to stay in business. "Orphaned" boats are harder to sell.

## When you're budgeting for a boat . . .

9. Try to buy a quality boat; depreciation is lower, resale value is higher.
10. Look for boats designed by firms with a good reputation; resale values tend to be higher.
11. If buying a one-design sailboat, look for a class with an active association, preferably one that publishes a newsletter.
12. Buy traditional or classic styling, which is more likely to survive changes in market taste.
13. Look for brands and models that are popular in your geographical area.
14. Decide on your budget — for both first cost and upkeep — and don't buy beyond it.
15. Know how to "fair price" a new boat — and be sure the new-boat price compares favorably with competitive used-boat prices before buying. We'll explain how.
16. Know how to "fair price" a used boat — and don't spend more than what's fair. Again, we'll explain how.

17. Use your boat enough to justify the investment you're making. The more you use her, the less your cost per hour of use.
18. Consider chartering your boat to help defray ownership costs.
19. Swap with a friend's boat off-season, thus gaining boating time at zero incremental cash cost.
20. Try co-owning with one or more individuals to cut your costs in half or better.
21. Think about joining a co-op boat club (i.e., co-own with a whole crowd).
22. Investigate "creative ownership packages" that provide an income to you in return for use of your boat by a charter company.
23. Know precisely what you want in the way of features and benefits from your new boat, and why you want them. List your wants and needs in order of priority. Buying the boat that satisfies the "top 10" priorities on your list will yield maximum value for your money.

## When you're inspecting possible candidates for purchase, and before you start to negotiate in earnest . . .

24. Shop for boat insurance before you commit to buying a specific boat. Don't let yourself get caught with an uninsurable boat.
25. When you shop for boat insurance, don't accept the first offer you get. Insurance rates can vary widely for the same coverage.
26. Become familiar with the range of market prices for the specific type of boat you're after, so you'll know what's a bargain and what isn't.
27. Conduct a do-it-yourself minisurvey among other owners of the same model of your potential dreamboat.
28. Make a list of what extras come with each candidate boat — before beginning price negotiations.
29. Check if the boat is really the seller's to sell. Don't be the victim of a scam.
30. Check the trailer, if any, to determine if it's road-legal and roadworthy.
31. Examine the engine yourself. Smell it; touch it; listen to it run. If it doesn't feel, smell, or sound perfect to you, hire a mechanic to tell you what's wrong, if anything.
32. Consider asking a mechanic to do a compression test on the engine, or do one yourself.
33. Consider asking a mechanic to arrange for an oil and fuel analysis on the engine, or arrange for one yourself.
34. Check fuel consumption; avoid fuel-guzzlers.

35. Don't forget the sea trials if you can arrange a time when the harbor isn't frozen in. And the rougher the weather, the better.
36. Take an expert with you when on your final shopping run.
37. Time your purchase wisely; buy in the buying season, not in the selling season, if possible.
38. Study foreign exchange rate fluctuations if you are considering importing your purchase, new or used; time your move to come out ahead.
39. Try to speak to the person who owned the boat before the present owner about any features, positive or negative, he thinks are significant. Ask his advice on whether he would buy if he were you. The answers might surprise you.
40. Avoid the temptation to buy on impulse, before thoroughly exploring your options . . . and don't get carried away by a fast-talking "closer."

## When you're negotiating the purchase . . .

41. Early on, identify the seller's goals as well as your own.
42. Establish a rapport with the seller. Negotiate by aiming for full cooperation to achieve his goals as well as yours, creatively bringing together any divergent interests.
43. Don't get too emotionally involved with any one boat; always be willing to walk away from a deal if common sense tells you you should.
44. Use time as a negotiating tool.
45. Use a professional surveyor, if warranted. We'll explain how to decide whether one is needed.
46. Check any warranties; be sure they're in writing, crystal-clear, and either unbiased or favorable to the buyer, not the seller.
47. In any negotiation, be sure to verify all your assumptions. Strive to avoid surprises.
48. Avoid or minimize brokerage commissions if you decide you don't need brokerage services.

## After you sign on the dotted line . . .

49. Do your own documentation paperwork.
50. Don't overspend on equipment or fix-up for a boat whose value is limited.
51. Don't move the boat until she is fully insured.
52. Insure your boat and equipment only up to her fair market value, not more. If repair is costlier than replacement in kind, you should negotiate with the insurer to replace in kind.
53. Insure for as high a deductible as you can absorb.
54. Buy only the insurance coverage you need, and take full advantage of all discounts available.

## When you're planning maintenance and repair . . .

55. During the on-season, keep sails from premature deterioration by protecting from sun and caked salt spray when not in use, and from unnecessary flogging at all times.

56. Also during the on-season, give your engine a visual check at regular intervals while you're underway, to be sure it's not overheating, leaking fluids, or developing other problems. Avoid an "out-of-sight, out-of mind" attitude.

57. Plan a regular systematic schedule of preventive maintenance — and stick to it — to defer inevitable replacements of gear and equipment as long as possible.

58. Perform routine maintenance and repairs yourself, rather than contracting it to a boatyard; avoid using yards that don't welcome do-it-yourselfers.

59. If yard rules permit, lend a hand when work is being done on your boat and you can replace paid hands with your own "free" hands, such as when stepping or unstepping the mast. If appropriate, notify the yard of your intention to participate in advance, so you can be there when needed.

60. Protect the boat in the off-season: faithfully cover the hull, service the engine, drain or treat fluids to prevent freezing and protect spars and equipment from the weather.

61. Use those long winter evenings to perform maintenance on equipment.

62. Take an engine troubleshooting and repair course to become thoroughly familiar with your powerplant. Doing your own engine maintenance and repair will not only save you money, but will give you peace of mind when underway, knowing you can deal with engine failure.

63. If you have a boatyard do the work, give them your work orders early in the off-season; this could yield better as well as less costly results.

64. For work to be done by the yard, get an estimate in advance and negotiate until it's satisfactory to you. If the quote seems high, don't be shy; find out why before the work is done.

65. Set limits on any "open cost" work you agree to be done by the yard and insist they discuss the situation with you *before* the limits are exceeded.

66. In anticipation of major maintenance or repair (engine or sail replacement, fairing and painting the hull), start to accumulate a "replacement fund" to which you regularly contribute, thus avoiding a financial crunch requiring costly loan interest payments when replacement time comes.

## When you're thinking about dockage and storage . . .

67. Store the boat in your own backyard rather than a boatyard, if possible.

68. If you keep your boat in the water, use a mooring rather than a marina slip — preferably your own mushroom and chain, not a rental mooring.

69. If you decide to keep your boat in a boatyard, look for one that caters to do-it-yourselfers.

70. If you're thinking of buying a dockominium to save money in the long run, study the economics before making your move. Maybe you'll save, and maybe you won't. Compare alternatives by running a discounted cash flow analysis first, using the "present value" techniques presented in Chapter 15, and the table in Appendix 4.

## When you're buying additional gear and equipment . . .

71. Don't buy at list price if possible; shop for discounts.

72. Buy used gear rather than new when the price is right and condition is acceptable.

73. Try to plan ahead, and accumulate lists of items needed. Then buy in bulk, and ask for a discount for quantity.

74. Order new sails at the end of the sailing season; sailmakers give special discounts then.

75. If you're racing in a one-design sailboat fleet, organize a "buying syndicate" among your fleet friends to get an additional discount for group purchases.

## When you're selling . . .

76. Advertise in media that produce multiple responses; avoid those that don't.

77. Don't use a broker if you have the time, energy, skills and inclination to sell on your own.

78. Advertise at the right time of year to maximize responses.

79. When prospects call, be available. Prospects gravitate toward sellers who answer the phone when called, and can show the boat at the convenience of the prospect.

80. Unload all excess equipment and loose clutter before showing the boat. When the prospect is appraising the boat, neatness counts.

81. Clean, buff, polish, oil, varnish, and deodorize the boat before showing her. Like neatness, shine and sparkle count, too.

82. Decorate the interior with "boat show props."

83. Leave a take-along brochure on board for each prospect to keep.

84. Hang a For Sale sign on the boat, and place the boat in a high-traffic location.

85. Don't forget word-of-mouth advertising.

86. Keep records of prospect calls — and follow up.

87. When the buyer is ready to buy, be sure you're ready to sell. Don't hem and haw. Be decisive.
88. Accept cash, certified checks, or cashier's checks only.
89. Cancel your insurance immediately after the sale is final.
90. Consider running the sale through your new-boat broker to save state sales taxes.
91. Keep all paperwork for at least a year.
92. Set your asking price slightly below the advertised market to attract the maximum number of prospects.
93. Make some equipment optional to keep the base price low.
94. Avoid being in the position of *having* to sell.
95. Accentuate the positives and eliminate the negatives in your sales pitch.
96. As when buying, establish rapport with each prospect; tune in on his wavelength and stay tuned in.
97. Concentrate on selling your boat's unique features and benefits. Every boat has them.
98. Be sure you're selling in the right geographic area.
99. Look for special limited-time opportunities to display your boat wherever prospects might gather.
100. If possible, time your sales campaign to coincide with start-of-season or end-of-season buyer interest.
101. If you just can't sell your boat, donate her and get a tax deduction.

And that's not all.

The rest of the book expands these and other ideas in detail, to help you save as much money as possible while enjoying the incomparable thrill of owning and using your own boat.

# PART ONE

# Thinking About Buying a Boat

**Can You Afford to Buy a Boat?**
**Alternatives to Buying a Boat "the Regular Way"**
**Recognizing Your Motivations**

# CHAPTER 1

# Can You Afford to Buy a Boat?

Anyone can afford a boat.

J.P. Morgan once said that if you have to ask the price of a yacht, you can't afford to own it. Well, it ain't so, J.P. Any boat used for pleasure qualifies as a yacht, and there's a boat to fit everyone's budget, even if the budget is zero. Sure, you can pay $3,000,000 or more for a 125-foot custom-designed and custom-built megayacht. But you can also pay nothing at all to acquire broken but usually fixable small craft such as Boston Whalers, Marshall 22 catboats, or Alcort Sunfish, to take a few examples from my personal experience. Figures 1-2 and 1-3 show typical boat prices by length on deck (LOD).

## Some boats cost nothing, or close to it

If you don't want the bother of fixing up a worn or damaged boat, but still want something for free, you can sometimes find it by faithfully scanning the boat ads. But you have to act quickly.

For example, an ad in a recent issue of *WoodenBoat* magazine read: "Free: beautiful 19' traditional gaff schooner, excellent maintenance and condition, 7 sails including topsail and fisherman, very able, exceptional for coastal waters, want good owner." The ad wasn't a gag; the owner's name and home and office telephone numbers were listed. I called; the owner told me he had received 372 phone calls responding to the ad, from as far away as Alaska. He found someone he felt would be a good owner (an educational institution in Massachusetts) on the morning of the first day the magazine was distributed.

Sometimes you can buy a boat for next to nothing, apply a little elbow grease to fix her up, and end up with both a nice yacht and a

FIGURE 1-1
**A megayacht. Length: 125
feet. Cost: $3,000,000.
(Drawing courtesy
Sparkman & Stephens)**

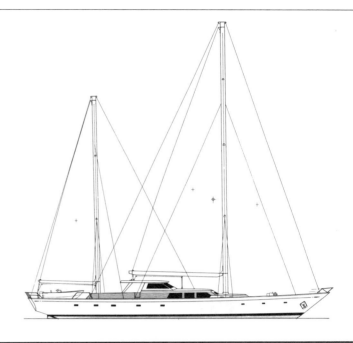

goodly profit when you want to sell her and move up. The cheapest sailboat I ever bought (aside from several free boats I've acquired over the years) was a half-sunk wooden Beetle Catboat for which, in 1962, I paid $25 initially. I say "initially" because my wife and I put a significant amount of additional funds, to say nothing of our own labor hours, into fiberglassing the hull to stop the persistent leaks, making a new sail (on a sewing machine we bought for the purpose), renewing worn lines and fittings, and sanding, painting, and varnishing to make our pride and joy gleam.

We didn't really mind the work. For us, fussing with boats for the most part has always been recreation rather than work, so we don't resent the time it takes. We get a feeling of accomplishment and pride of craftsmanship, and almost always learn something from the do-it-yourself approach, even when we've gone through more or less the same procedure before. And sometimes there can be a small financial reward when you do the work yourself, since you add value to the boat without spending much money to do it.

In the case of the Beetle Cat, we ended up putting around $300 worth of materials into the project (not including $50 for the sewing machine, bought used), but after a couple of years of sailing the finished product, decided to move on to bigger and better things. We chose a South Coast 23 which, partly because of the confidence gained in fixing the Beetle Cat, we decided to build from a kit. We sold the catboat for $600, a profit of $300 before considering our no-charge labor cost, or inflation.

# THINKING ABOUT BUYING A BOAT

FIGURE 1-2
**Typical powerboat prices by LOD (length on deck). Source: manufacturers' price lists, classified sections of boating periodicals, author's estimates.**

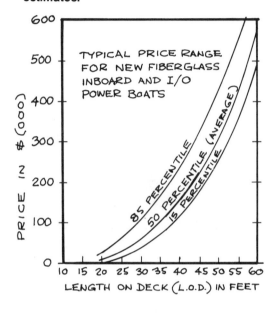

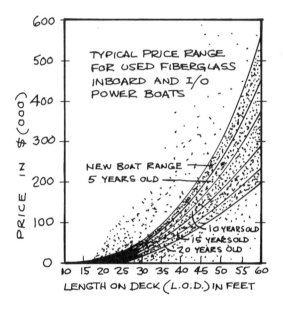

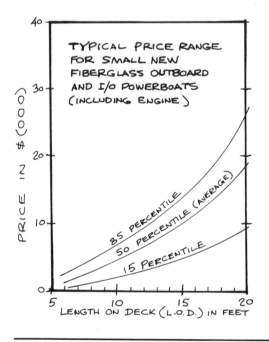

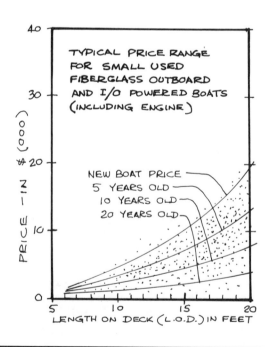

FIGURE 1-3
**Typical sailboat prices by
LOD. Source: same as for
Figure 1-2.**

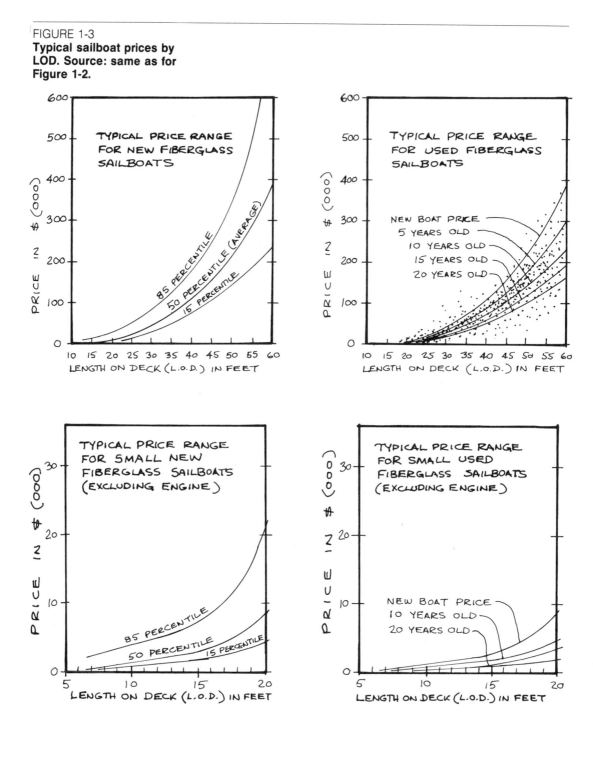

# THINKING ABOUT BUYING A BOAT

FIGURE 1-4

**A good value. Cost: nothing. This schooner was advertised in the May/June 1987 issue of *Wooden Boat* Magazine. (Courtesy *Wooden Boat*)**

BEAUTIFUL 19′ TRADITIONAL GAFF SCHOONER. Excellent maintenance and condition. 2′9″ draft. 7 sails, including topsail and fisherman. Very able. Exceptional for coastal cruising. Want good owner. Call Pierre Wagner: business, 212-869-1720; home, 718-423-1136.

As already mentioned, there are boats that people are willing to give away for nothing, just to get rid of them. Over the years, I've acquired a 13-foot Boston Whaler, a Marshall 22 cruising catboat, and two Sunfish that way. All four boats were molded fiberglass (a material that's relatively easy to repair), all were free (again, *initially*), and all had some defects that their previous owners didn't want to bother fixing, or didn't have the knowledge to fix. All were bound for the city dump if I hadn't hauled them away to my backyard instead. Some had major problems, such as a gaping hole in the starboard side of the Marshall 22; but some problems were minor, such as a split along a seam on one of the Sunfish, fixable with a couple of hours' work using fiberglass and polyester resin.

All the boats I acquired free were the result of chance meetings with their owners or mutual friends who knew I was a "fixer." Some others who like to fix things advertise for damaged boats in the boating magazines and boats-for-sale columns in newspapers. You could take that approach, too, if you yearn for a fix-up project but nothing seems to be coming your way.

Insurance adjusters are another good source of leads —though usually at least a little money will be needed to acquire even a "constructive total loss."

Free wooden boats are usually easier to find than their plastic sisters, since wooden craft require more sophisticated skills to fix and

FIGURE 1-5
**A Beetle Cat, one of the author's former boats. Purchase price: $25. Sale price: $600. (Courtesy Norman Fortier)**

therefore command a smaller market. The schooner ad in *WoodenBoat* (see Appendix 2 for magazine addresses in case you want to subscribe) isn't unique. In almost every issue of *WoodenBoat*, you'll find "Boats For Free" ads in the classified section. Besides the schooner, recent issues have listed a 16-foot lapstrake lifeboat and a 30-foot launch in Massachusetts, a 30-foot plywood trawler sheathed in fiberglass in Arkansas, a 16-foot Thompson utility with a 50 h.p. Johnson in New Jersey, a 25-foot sloop and a 30-foot Richardson sportfisherman in Connecticut, and others — all absolutely free.

If you can find a way to haul a boat to your backyard to fix it up, and your neighbors don't mind the ensuing view, you too can have a bit of fun and learn something worthwhile while creating a yacht for yourself, even if your finances are severely restricted. So don't say, "I can't afford it." Where there's a will, there's a way.

FIGURE 1-6
**A "free" Marshall 22.**

## How much to budget: rules of thumb

How much to budget for your boating activities depends to a great extent on how much in the way of savings and discretionary income (income left over after paying for the necessities of living, including food, shelter, clothing, taxes, etc.) you have to spend, and how much of it is already committed to other competing recreational and non-recreational activities. It also depends on your personal priorities and, usually, those of the other members of your family.

The planning that goes into the purchase of a boat should involve a meeting of all the family members to get their input. Dad may want to go fishing; mother may dream of cruising for weeks at a time; older son may want to water-ski; younger son may want to learn how to sail; older daughter might like a boat she can take her boyfriend out on; younger daughter, perhaps, doesn't want any part of boating. How much each member of the family — and the family as a whole — will use the new boat should be a major consideration in deciding how much to allocate for her purchase and upkeep. The greater the potential use, the bigger the budget that can be justified.

There may be conflicting priorities among family members, and it may take many conferences to work things out to everyone's satisfaction. Take the Jones family's dilemma, for instance, depicted in Figure 1-7.

FIGURE 1-7
**Calculating disposable
and discretionary income
available for the Jones
family boating budget.**

| BUDGET ITEM | | JONESES' AMOUNT | YOUR AMOUNT |
|---|---|---|---|
| Gross salary | | $45,000 | _____ |
| Taxes | | 8,000 | _____ |
| Disposable income | | $37,000 | |
| | | | |
| *Less* necessities of life: | | | |
| Housing costs (including utilities, etc.) | $6,000 | | _____ |
| Food | $6,000 | | _____ |
| Clothing | $1,500 | | _____ |
| Auto loan payments | $5,400 | | _____ |
| Home and auto insurance | $2,400 | | _____ |
| Life insurance | $1,200 | | _____ |
| Medical costs | $1,200 | | _____ |
| Other necessities | $3,600 | | _____ |
| Total necessities of life | | 27,300 | _____ |
| | | | |
| Discretionary income | | $9,700 | _____ |
| | | | |
| *Less* for non-boating activities: | | | |
| Kids' education fund | $2,400 | | _____ |
| Family vacation fund | $2,400 | | _____ |
| Kids' dancing classes | $600 | | _____ |
| Kids' allowances, etc. | $400 | | _____ |
| Mink coat for wife | $1,800 | | _____ |
| New motorcycle for husband | $2,000 | | _____ |
| Miscellaneous other | $100 | | _____ |
| Total for non-boating activities | | $9,700 | _____ |
| | | | |
| Left over for boating | | 0 | _____ |
| | | | |
| Or, alternatively . . . for boating: | | | |
| Loan payments on boat | $5,000 | | _____ |
| Boating club dues, fees, dinners | $400 | | _____ |
| Insurance on boat | $500 | | _____ |
| Fuel cost for boat | $300 | | _____ |
| Dockage for boat | $800 | | _____ |
| Winter storage for boat | $600 | | _____ |
| Maintenance, repair, and replacement | $1,200 | | _____ |
| Equipment additions and improvements | $600 | | _____ |
| Other | $300 | | _____ |
| Total for boating | | $9,700 | _____ |
| | | | |
| Left over for non-boating discretionary activities | | 0 | |

The Joneses obviously have some heavy family negotiating to do, if their boating dreams are to be realized.

Sometimes the uses of a prospective boat are so varied that the family ends up buying more than one boat. For example, my family and I once owned 10 different watercraft at the same time:

- a 22-foot Aquasport center console outboard for family use watching sailboat races, short-range exploring, general "tooling around," and occasional fishing
- a 17-foot Cape Cod catboat for author and wife to use for daysailing and occasional short cruises
- a 16-foot Fireball for both sons to use in class racing
- a 15-foot Laser II for younger son to participate in National Youth Sailing Championship racing
- a 14-foot International 420 sailboat for both sons' use in organized racing
- two 12-foot Windsurfers for family use sailing around off the local beach
- two 8-foot Dyer Midget sailing dinghies for family use in frostbiting (local winter dinghy racing), as a tender for the catboat when cruising, and general utility use
- a 6-foot rowing dink that weighs only 35 pounds and fits on the deck of the catboat

If you decide on several boats instead of one, you should think of the total budget for all of them in the same way as if they were a single boat. For the family of six with varied ambitions described above, some grouping of interests probably could be agreed upon. That might result in the purchase of, say, a 25-foot Boston Whaler outboard runabout with a powerful engine and a cuddy cabin with a couple of berths, so mom can go cruising, dad can fish, and the water-skiing son can do his thing, too. When cruising in the Whaler, an 8-foot Dyer Midget sailing dink lashed aboard or towed behind the "big boat" (if cruising speeds are kept low) would be nice, and could be used by the younger son (or the whole family, for that matter) to learn to sail. The older daughter could teach her boyfriend to sail too, if she wished.

Additionally, if faraway vacations were appealing, a Whaler trailer could be added to the budget; and so could a suitable tow vehicle (such as a full-size trailer-tow-package equipped station wagon or utility vehicle).

Before you get too far along in deciding what to buy, however, you should have a fairly good idea of the limitations of your budget. You can start by referring to Figure 1-8 and Figure 1-9 for some rules of thumb on discretionary income allocated to boating and other recreational acivities.

The rules of thumb in Figure 1-8 are guidelines only, of course. The level of individual savings and other factors could mean your particular situation warrants a wholly different set of numbers. For instance, you may be retired and have only a relatively small income

FIGURE 1-8
**Rules of thumb for
estimating boating
budgets by gross income
and discretionary income.**

| GROSS ANNUAL FAMILY INCOME | TYPICAL AFFORDABLE CAPITAL VALUE OF BOATS* | TYPICAL ANNUAL DISCRETIONARY INCOME ALLOCATED TO BOATING OR OTHER RECREATION** |
|---|---|---|
| $10,000 | $1,000 | $350 |
| 20,000 | 2,000 | 700 |
| 30,000 | 3,000 | 1,100 |
| 40,000 | 6,000 | 1,800 |
| 50,000 | 12,000 | 2,300 |
| 60,000 | 18,000 | 3,500 |
| 70,000 | 25,000 | 5,300 |
| 80,000 | 38,000 | 7,000 |
| 90,000 | 50,000 | 13,000 |
| 100,000 | 62,000 | 18,000 |
| 120,000 | 85,000 | 23,000 |
| 150,000 | 120,000 | 32,000 |
| 200,000 | 200,000 | 42,000 |
| 300,000 | 350,000 | 63,000 |
| 500,000 | 700,000 | 100,000 |
| Over 500,000 | See your financial advisor | See your financial advisor |

   * Total capital value of boats includes basic boat or boats, sails, engines, equipment, etc. and is estimated by the author, based on net worth, level of savings, and personal priorities of typical individuals having gross incomes as shown. Net worth and accumulated savings can vary widely for different people with identical gross incomes, so the figures in the "Affordable Capital Value" column are *typical only* and are *not* specific limits. See Figure 1-9 for examples.
   For financing your boat, banks and finance companies sometimes use the following rules of thumb: (1) your total debt including boat loans, home mortgages and consumer debt should not exceed 2.5 times your annual income; (2) you should have an amount equal to 15% to 20% of any boat loan in liquid assets; and (3) you should have a net worth of at least twice the value of the boat loan. Financing of 80% of the boat's purchase price is typical; 100% financing is possible if you have "blue ribbon" credit and the ratios are all in line.
   ** Total typical annual allocation to boating includes amortization of capital costs as well as interest payments on boat loans, dockage or mooring, dry storage, maintenance, repair, insurance, taxes, dues at yacht clubs, etc. These annual expenditures might run in the neighborhood of 10% to 40% of the total capital value of the boat or boats plus equipment.

but very large savings, some of which you could use to buy a boat without jeopardizing your financial well-being. Or you may have a high income, but have many financial commitments. Then you may feel that boating and other recreational activities should take a back seat to, say, educating your ten children, playing the horses, or making your annual safari to the Elks' convention in Pittsburgh. Whatever your needs and wants, only you can decide how to allocate your discretionary funds.

## Some boat-budgeting examples

If you need help visualizing how different folks with different financial circumstances can plan out how much they can afford when buying a boat, check out the analysis in Figure 1-9. It covers three different age groups with varying economic circumstances. You can jot down your own numbers in the right-hand column as you read along.

Figure 1-10 examines the income and expenditures of each group to show how much is left for boating after the necessities are taken care of.

Let's assume that each group wants to finance at least a portion of the cost of their new boat. (According to the NMMA, about 75% of all boat purchases are paid for on monthly installment plans). Figure 1-11 shows how the bank or finance company will view the situation.

## Justifying the purchase: a matter of trade-offs

If your budget is limited (as it is for most of us), you probably will have to settle for less boat than you might ultimately prefer if money were no object. However, you can justify increasing your boat budget if you reduce some other discretionary expense. For example:

- Plan to eliminate or reduce spending on other vacation and recreational activities that were included in your budget before

---

FIGURE 1-9
**Three examples using the rules of thumb of Figure 1-8.**

|  | MR. GRAY & MS. GREEN | THE JONES FAMILY | DR. AND MRS. J. PIERPONT SMITH | YOU |
|---|---|---|---|---|
| Approximate age and family status of group: | Both in twenties, no kids or other dependents | Both in late thirties, two kids in teens | Both in early fifties, kids finished school and on their own | _____ |
| Gross income | $25,000 | $45,000 | $110,000 | _____ |

. . . per Figure 1-8, a typical affordable capital value of boat is:

| Suggested average | 2,500 | 9,000 | 73,000 | _____ |
|---|---|---|---|---|

. . . and a typical annual discretionary income allocated to boating is:

| Average | 900 | 2,050 | 20,500 |  |
|---|---|---|---|---|

---

FIGURE 1-10
**Income, expenditures,
and net worth for Gray &
Green, Jones, and Smith.**

|  | GRAY & GREEN | JONES | SMITH | YOU |
|---|---|---|---|---|
| Gross salary | $25,000 | $45,000 | $110,000 | _____ |
| Taxes | 3,500 | 8,000 | 25,000 | _____ |
| Disposable income | $21,500 | $37,000 | $85,000 | _____ |
| *Less* necessities of life: |  |  |  |  |
| Housing costs | $4,000 | $6,000 | $12,000 | _____ |
| Food | 5,000 | 7,000 | 10,000 | _____ |
| Clothing | 500 | 1,500 | 2,500 | _____ |
| Auto loan payments | 2,500 | 4,400 | 9,000 | _____ |
| Home and auto insurance | 1,500 | 2,400 | 4,000 | _____ |
| Life insurance | 600 | 1,200 | 2,500 | _____ |
| Medical costs | 600 | 1,200 | 4,600 | _____ |
| Other necessities | 2,700 | 3,600 | 9,900 | _____ |
| Total necessities | 17,400 | 27,300 | 54,500 | _____ |
| Discretionary income | $4,100 | $9,700 | $30,500 | _____ |
| For non-boating activities: |  |  |  |  |
| Kids' education fund | 0 | 2,100 | 0 | _____ |
| For savings | 1,000 | 1,000 | 10,000 | _____ |
| Reserves, vacations, misc. | 600 | 900 | 4,000 |  |
| Left over for boating | $2,500 | $5,700 | $16,500 | _____ |

| Boating budget details | Outboard runabout | Small power cruiser | Cruising sailboat | Your Choice |
|---|---|---|---|---|
| Loan payments on boat | $1,000 | $2,200 | $ 7,000 | _____ |
| Boating club dues, etc. | 0 | 400 | 1,000 | _____ |
| Insurance on boat | 200 | 400 | 3,500 | _____ |
| Fuel cost for boat | 300 | 1,100 | 100 | _____ |
| Dockage for boat | 0 | 600 | 2,000 | _____ |
| Winter storage for boat | 0 | 100 | 800 | _____ |
| Maintenance, etc. | 500 | 400 | 700 | _____ |
| Additions, improvements | 300 | 300 | 900 | _____ |
| Other | 200 | 200 | 500 | _____ |
| Total boating budget | $2,500 | $5,700 | $16,500 | _____ |
| Typical savings in cash, securities, other liquid assets | $1,000 | $40,000 | $300,000 | _____ |
| Real estate and other assets, net of loans, etc. | 1,000 | 100,000 | 500,000 | _____ |
| Net worth | $2,000 | $140,000 | $800,000 | _____ |

FIGURE 1-11
**The bank's rules of thumb
for considering boat loans
for Gray & Green, Jones
and Smith.**

| | GRAY & GREEN | JONES | SMITH | YOU |
|---|---|---|---|---|
| Bank's rule of thumb on maximum total debt including mortgages, consumer debt, and anticipated boat loan (2.5 × income per footnote to Figure 1-8) | $60,000 | $110,000 | $275,000 | _____ |
| *Less* debt except boat debt: | 0 | 90,000 | 100,000 | _____ |
| *Equals* maximum amount bank might authorize for boat loan, based on above data and assuming the buyer wants 80% financing | $60,000 | $20,000 | $175,000 | _____ |
| Bank's second rule of thumb on maximum loan permitted (based on requiring a net worth of at least twice the loan per footnote to Figure 1-8) | $1,000 | $70,000 | $400,000 | _____ |
| Bank loan based on above two rules of thumb | $1,000 | $20,000 | $175,000 | _____ |
| Probable interest rate based on bank's perceived risk | 16% | 12% | 10% | _____ |
| Probable suggested loan term | 3 yrs. | 5 yrs. | 7 yrs. | _____ |
| Payment required to amortize $1,000 in period indicated, assuming no points or fees: | | | | |
|     Per month | $35.16 | $22.25 | $16.61 | _____ |
|     Per year | $422 | $267 | $199 | _____ |
| Amount budgeted for annual loan payment on boat (see Figure 1-10) | $1,000 | $2,200 | $7,000 | _____ |
| Value of boat that can be purchased with loan: | | | | |
| Amount paid from loan proceeds (see Note 1) | $2,369 | $8,239 | $35,176 | _____ |
| Paid from savings | 500 | 5,000 | $40,000 | _____ |
| Total capital value of boat targetted | $2,800 | $13,000 | $75,000 | _____ |

Note 1: "Amount paid from proceeds" is calculated as follows:

$$\text{Amount from loan proceeds} = \frac{\text{Annual loan payment} \times \$1,000}{\text{Annual payment to amortize } \$1,000} \text{ ; therefore}$$

$$\text{for Dr. \& Mrs. Smith, proceeds} = \frac{\$7,000 \times \$1,000}{\$199} = \$35,176.$$

the boat bug bit you. Naturally, you won't need to rent that cottage on Cape Cod in July next year; you'll be on your boat. And you can skip the week-long winter pilgrimage to the Virgin Islands this year; that could pay for the new engine your boat needs, and you can spend the time at home instead, poring over charts for next summer's cruise. The time and expense you devoted to golf, tennis, and other recreational activities similarly can be cut down, until you reach a comfortable equilibrium. That point should occur just before you begin to feel that boating is becoming an unwanted drain on your time and resources, and you're not having fun anymore.

- Convince your wife (or husband) she/he really doesn't need that new fur coat/set of golf clubs. (Have you ever noticed all the boats named *Mom's Mink*?)
- Put off, for a year or two, buying that new car you planned to get next year (unless, of course, it's the one you need to tow the new boat).
- Instead of hiring painters to redecorate your house, do it yourself and put the savings into boating.

And so on, ad infinitum. The possibilities are only limited by your own sense of priorities, and by the strength of the objections (if any) of the other members of your family.

## Summary

Anyone can afford to own some kind of boat, even if their boat-buying budget is a big fat zero. It's really a question of what you want, why you want it, and how much money, time and effort you are willing to invest in order to attain the benefits you're looking for.

# CHAPTER 2

# Alternatives to Buying a Boat "the Regular Way"

OK, you're serious about owning a boat. But, as you ponder the question of whether you can afford the boat of your dreams, you should remember that there are some alternatives to normal, everyday sole ownership. You can buy the boat of your dreams "the regular way," as most people do, by looking at ads, maybe inquiring to a few brokers and dealers, and letting nature take its course. Or you can charter her from some other owner, enter into a buy/lease or other creative ownership arrangement, join a co-op group, co-own her with a few friends, build her with your own two hands, swap her for something you have that somebody else wants, or borrow somebody else's boat and use her without any financial obligation, provided that you can convince the owner it's appropriate for you to do so. This chapter discusses the ins and outs of these alternatives, plus a few variations on them.

***Try chartering from others.***   You can always charter somebody else's boat if, for instance, you want a 40-footer but can't swing the $100,000-plus price tag or don't have the time to justify sinking that much capital into a boat. A typical 40-foot sailing bareboat charter (i.e., no captain; you run it, you provision it) goes for around $2,000 to $3,000 per week; powerboats tend to be priced slightly higher. Gas or diesel fuel, which is extra, can add up to a significant additional cost on a powerboat burning up a gallon of fuel every one or two miles. Hired captains generally cost an extra $100 to $150 a day; you'll need one unless you can prove you've had sufficient experience running a boat of the same size and type. (It'd be hard to lie on this matter; you must be skipper on a checkout run with the owner or charter company representative before you're given permission to use the boat without a captain.) If you don't have the time or inclination to spend more than a couple of weeks a year on the water, chartering is the way to go. The cost of the charter is likely to be significantly less than 10% of the capital value of the vessel, which is roughly how much you'd pay just for annual loan interest if you owned her and financed her through a bank.

Where can you find a charter boat that suits your needs? Sailboat charter ads abound in the boating magazines. The majors have special charter sections in mid-summer issues (*Cruising World* in July, *Sail* and *Yachting* in August). Some powerboat charters are also listed, but they're relatively rare compared to sailboats. A big, fast powerboat can be a dangerous toy in the hands of an inexperienced operator. Hence, high insurance rates preclude wider availability.

***Buy a creative ownership package.*** You'll find that a variety of choices are offered by a multitude of yacht management firms. You buy a boat from a yacht charter outfit, then lease it back to them. They pay you a portion of the charter fees they earn. This arrangement is fine provided that you don't mind a few wrinkles:

- Other people will be using your boat by chartering her, which can tend to produce considerably more wear and tear than if you only used the boat yourself.
- You'll have to sink a considerable amount of cash into the management firm's program, which is typically non-liquid (i.e., you can't get the money out for several years after you put it in). Your investment in a typical program would have some prospect of a cash return, but not as good (and not as liquid) as if you invested the same amount in stocks or bonds.
- A resident manager or management group will look after your boat for you, doing all the repair work, maintenance and cleaning, and you'll have to trust in their competence.
- You'll usually have to travel to wherever the management company happens to operate the boat (which is usually in a major boating location with a desirable climate, such as the Caribbean, Chesapeake Bay, etc.), rather than having it where you want it. However, there are some charter companies in the Caribbean willing to deliver your boat to northern waters in the spring and pick it up again in the fall, enabling you to use it during the summer.
- There is some risk of losing most or all of your investment if, for instance, the management company folds. (If you're thinking seriously of getting involved in such a venture, read any proposed contract carefully and check up on the company's financial condition and operating history before plunking down any money.)

Most charter firms offer creative ownership packages. Check the charter sections of the boating mags for ads.

***Look into time-sharing and purchase-leaseback-swap-charter deals.*** A new trend a few years ago was "yacht timesharing" or "interval ownership." It works like this: you buy one week (or more) of cruising time per year, on a specific boat usually located in a resort area. You then "own" this week, usually one of 50 (the remaining two weeks in the year are typically used for maintenance turnaround: haulout for bottom cleaning, fumigation, engine overhaul etc.). You own the week—and 1/50 of the boat—forever, or until you sell your share to someone else, or the boat is sold, sunk, or taken to the old-age home for boats.

Of course, you might not want to be tied down to going to the same place year after year to sail your boat. Until recently you could arrange to exchange your owned week for a week elsewhere by joining Resort Condominiums International (known in the trade as "RCI"). This is a business organization that serves as a "vacation exchange" clearinghouse for its 700,000 members, who own a week in one property but want to swap it for an equivalent week somewhere else. For an annual membership fee of around $50, plus another per-swap fee of around $50, you could arrange to swap your week on your yacht for someone else's week at a plush resort of your choice. RCI gave you a choice of 1,400 other resort areas in 50 countries worldwide. The details were a bit complex: For instance, not all weeks at all resorts are of comparable value, and you couldn't trade up.

I thought the idea had merit. However, the current economic recession has forced charter companies to pull in their horns, and at this point RCI no longer has any charter outfits in its group. Perhaps they'll add some at a future date; you can check status with them toll-free at 1-800-338-7777.

Purchase-leaseback-swap-charter has some of the advantages of a timeshare, in that you own a piece of the action (a charter boat), lease it back to a charter company, and then get to use either it or a similar boat at a different location for a specified time each year. The Moorings, a large, multi-location charter outfit, offers this arrangement. Call them for details at 1-800-535-7289.

***Join a "co-op" boating club — or organize one.*** This type of organization owns and shares the use of several boats. They may or may not have a clubhouse; some co-ops exist only on paper and in the living rooms of the members, and, of course, on board the clubs' boats. In commercial co-op clubs (such as are listed in Appendix 2) the members don't get equity in the boats or facilities; the organizers own the physical assets.

Right now, only a few of these clubs, scattered around the country, have been publicized; the concept is a good one, and there should be more, but for some reason co-op clubs haven't caught on in a big way yet. Membership can be anywhere from a few friends who get together and contribute to a boat fund (in effect, an expansion of a two- or three-owner partnership) to hundreds of participants. The groups are usually composed of men and women in their twenties, thirties, and early forties, looking for a way to meet others with similar interests and to go sailing without committing a lot of capital. You can always quit a co-op boating club, and you don't have to go through the hassle of selling your boat when you do (though you may have to pay some sort of penalty fee). Membership costs vary, depending at least partly on facilities and types of boats available. Contact individual clubs for details (see Appendix 2 for list).

For some reason, there are at least a few sailing co-op clubs but not a single powerboat co-op that I've heard of. Some co-ops seem to come and go, as the membership gains or loses interest.

***Go into partnerships with friends.*** You can look for a partner or partners to own a boat jointly with you, making it a kind of small-scale co-op deal. This is an increasingly popular alternative to swinging the expense of a yacht all by yourself, since with even one partner your capital outlay and your operating expenses are cut in half, with two partners they're cut by two thirds, and so on. There are some catches, of course:

- If you're spending only one-third of the cash, you'll probably get use of the boat for only a third of the time. Often this will fit right in with your desires anyway, particularly if you and your partners run your lives on different wavelengths. For instance, if you're setting up a partnership for a cruising boat and you love to cruise in June, Partner A prefers July, and Partner B's favorite time is August, you'll be all set, with no need for squabbles or drawing straws. Sometimes everyone wants July, though; that can cause problems that can be awkward for all concerned.

- If one of your partners wants out, you'll probably all have to agree to sell the boat and try for a new, different partnership, unless you or the departing investor can find a replacement partner. In any case, breaking out of such a partnership is often time-consuming and a nuisance.

- Unless you and your partners are identical in philosophies, attitudes and habits, members of the group are likely to experience some petty annoyances if not major squabbles. For example, suppose that you discover your partners aren't as neat and tidy as you are, and you have to keep picking up after them when they disembark and you board your jointly owned boat. That may gradually gnaw away at you. Or your partners aren't handy, and you end up doing a lot more than your share of maintenance on the boat. Sure, you could have the yard do it, but you and your partners have agreed to do such work yourselves. They aren't holding up their end of the bargain, but they just shrug it off. That can cause blow-ups too.

Moral: unless you know your partners extremely well, and know they'll honor to the letter the detailed written contract which they all agree to sign, you should ponder such an arrangement long and hard before entering into it. When composing the contract, try to imagine every conceivable eventuality, and reach written agreement as to what the partners will do in each case. Then, when unexpected but not unanticipated problems arise, there won't be needless arguing or unpleasantness.

*Build your own.* When my wife and I were crossing the age threshhold from our twenties to our thirties in 1964, we began shopping for a new fiberglass cruising sailboat in the 22-foot to 24-foot range. But we were reluctant to commit our modest savings to purchasing a boat that size, which sold in the neighborhood of $3,000 or $3,500 at that time. Used models, if you could find them, weren't much less, since fiberglass boats hadn't been produced in quantity before around 1960. So you just couldn't buy an "old" fiberglass boat.

Then we saw an ad for a 23-foot sloop, advertised in *Yachting* magazine by South Coast Seacraft. She was pretty as a picture, a Carl Alberg design, very traditional, very seaworthy; just our style. Best of all, she was available in kit form for a mere $1,375, not including lead ballast, sails, rigging, hardware, and wood trim. We wrote for a brochure, got a Dun & Bradstreet credit report on the company to make sure they weren't about to go bankrupt, looked at a few kits that had been delivered to the New York metropolitan area and spoke to their builders-to-be. After some agonizing (Would we have the time? The skills? The persistence?) we decided that we could and should build one. The price was right: we guessed the boat, complete with sails and equipment, could be finished for around $2,500. (Our guess was on the low side, but only by a couple of hundred dollars or so). We decided on the color combination and other details, and in October 1964 we mailed off a deposit check. Just before Thanksgiving Day, a truck backed into our yard and slid off the unfinished hull, which was on a cradle. We completed *Pipit* over the winter, launched her the following June, and never regretted the time and effort we put into the project.

If you have the time and space in your yard, and are reasonably handy with tools, you can save 20% to 30% by building from a kit. A list of boats available in kit form, both sail and power, appears annually in *Boat Journal*. Write them for the latest listing. (See Appendix 2 for *BJ*'s address.)

*Look for swap deals.* Check the ads in the boating mag classifieds. You're sure to find at least one person who wants to swap his ten acres of land in Maine, his ranch in Arizona, or his antique Stutz Bearcat automobile for a live-aboard cruising boat. Almost always, the advertiser wants a boat, and has land, a house, a house trailer, a car, or what-have-you to trade for it. Chances of connecting with someone who has what you want (presumably a boat, not a car, house trailer or land), and convincing him that you have what he wants, are slim. But

FIGURE 2-1
**Our 23-foot kit boat awaits completion in our backyard.**

sometimes it works. If the potential of a swap appeals to you, keep looking at the ads, and maybe you'll connect.

Another swap arrangement — and one that's usually more workable — occurs when two owners with the same or similar boats in different parts of the country get together and trade vessels for some period of time. For example, a couple with a Catalina 30 in Florida wants to spend their vacation period in the northeast in the summer. They meet another couple with a Catalina 30 or similar boat on Cape Cod, and agree to loan their Florida boat to the Cape people for a week or two in February or March. In return, they get the Cape boat for the same period in July or August. Usually it's a friendly deal, with no money changing hands. Of course, you have to own a boat to work this type of swap, but it does "extend" your ownership, increasing the overall return on your investment, and costs nothing extra.

One way to find others to swap with is to place an ad in *Soundings* or the other widely-distributed boating periodicals. If you have a popular class sailboat, you may be able to find a swap through your class association newsletter, if one exists. If none does, you could consider starting one; the boat's manufacturer will love you for it, and may even offer to help out financially. You'll be in a position to meet a lot of people with similar interests, some of whom are probably just itching to swap boats with you.

A list of addresses for 50 of the most popular sailboat class associations appears in Appendix 2. I haven't heard of any powerboat

FIGURE 2-2
**There's always someone who wants to swap something he's got for a boat. (Source: *Soundings*)**

## TRADE

**SMALL OCEANFRONT CONDO,** Sarasota, FL Bay, + cash for 30ft.+ cruising sailboat. (617) 862-7349. (0052775)

**WANTED: WHITEWATER SAILBOAT** 35'+. Trade: Congregate home of 3300, $169,000. or 1-1/3 acres Bayou-Sarasota or 40 acres-Minnesota or Colorado business lot. (813) 951-1619. (0053002)

## TRAILERS

**CUSTOM BUILT** boat trailers. Give us the specifications and the

class associations that operate as the sailboat groups do; powerboat manufacturers would do well to promote such organizations.

*Use other people's boats.* The people who do this, when asked what kind of boat they sail, say "OPB" ("Other People's Boats"). This can be a satisfactory alternative to owning your own, particularly if you don't want the responsibilities or commitments that ownership usually entails.

You stand a better chance of being invited to go along on OPBs if you have at least some on-the-water experience. That may mean you'll need to own some kind of boat for awhile, just to get started.

For cruising sailors who prefer OPB, there's even a nationwide organization, the Corinthians, that helps put crew and skippers together (see Appendix 2 for how to make contact). If your cup of tea is sailboat racing, many of the one-design class associations listed in Appendix 2 would also welcome you as a volunteer crew, no doubt. The Corinthians and one-design classes are for sailboat people only. Again, as far as I know, there are no comparable powerboaters' organizations.

Meeting and making friends with lots of owners helps, too. You might want to join a local boating or fishing club, look into sailing lessons, take a Power Squadron course or two, or otherwise try to find a way to rub shoulders with current or prospective boat owners who might invite you to go out with them. (For directions on how to locate your nearest Power Squadron representative, see Appendix 2).

*Charter to others.* Chartering your boat to others will help defray your costs of ownership. Some owners advertise the availability of their boat for charter in the boating publications; others try to work through a charter broker. Either way, don't expect a hoard of applicants rushing to use your boat, particularly right away, unless your asking price is significantly below the normal market or your boat happens to be located in a very high-demand, low-supply chartering area. A one-boat charter business can take years to build up, with repeat customers contributing most of the business. So be prepared to wait a while before you become well established.

Another thing you'll find out if you put your boat up for charter is that it's hard work. As with any business, there's a lot of organizing to do: insurance to be arranged, the boat to be cleaned and tanks topped off, the charterers to be checked out, and so on. There's risk, too. What if your charterers have driven hundreds of miles to get to you, but they don't check out to your satisfaction when you take them out for a test run? Or what if they bring the boat back with damage that can be repaired, but which will mar the looks of your boat forevermore, regardless of how much is paid in insurance claims? What if they use the boat and bring it back, pay you, and then their check bounces? All these "what ifs" are not far-fetched theoretical possibilities; they actually happen. Nevertheless, putting your boat up for charter may be just what you need to balance your long-range boating budget. If so, you may be willing to spend the necessary time and effort to make chartering a success.

## Summary

If you don't want to sink a large amount of capital into buying a boat, but are willing to make certain sacrifices, you still might swing a deal to get the boat you want. Maybe not for every day of the boating season. Maybe not where you want it, when you want it. And maybe you'll need to spend some extra time and effort — "sweat equity" — to get your boat. But if you can't or don't want to buy and own a boat "the regular way," don't despair. You can still go boating, one way or another. Where there's a will, there's a way.

# CHAPTER 3

# Recognizing Your Motivations

If you already know what kind of boat you want, and are sure you know why you want it, you can skip the rest of this chapter and go on to "The Seven Basic Rules of the Boat-Buying Game." But if you're new to boating, or have owned boats but haven't been entirely satisfied with your previous choices, some suggestions on choosing the right general type of boat to fit your needs might be appropriate.

## What is your true motivation for wanting a boat?

The key move you should make when considering what kind of boat you want — and can afford — is to think seriously about your motivations. It'll help you decide if you'd be better off with power or sail, big or small, basic or fancy, cruiser or racer, day boat or live-aboard. To get you started on the necessary soul-searching exercise, here's a checklist of possible motivations:

- Investment for resale?
- Acquiring prestige?
- Exploration and adventure?
- Getting close to nature?
- Getting away from it all?
- Waterskiing?
- Catching fish?
- Sailboat or powerboat racing?
- Experiencing the thrill of power and speed?

Investment with the expectation of buying low, selling high, and making a wagonload of money in the process may be your prime motivator. Sure, it's possible to make money if everything goes right, including the timing of purchase and sale. If profit is your main goal, and if you have a boat budget of up to $10,000 or so and don't mind shopping for bargains or spending the necessary time and work to fix up a poorly maintained boat, have at it. But you'd almost certainly make more on the stock market or in real estate if your budget is $10,000 to $20,000 or more and you have a natural sense of investment timing. Figure 3-1 shows how prices have appreciated in the last 10 years for relatively liquid investments like stocks (using the Dow Jones Industrial Average as an indicator) and for boats. The chart shows that, comparatively, most used boats aren't spectacular investments, even if the main consideration is financial appreciation.

A brief explanation of Figure 3-1 may be useful. The first column lists some representative boats. The second column shows the original 1980 prices of these boats, without any adjustment for the effects of inflation (i.e. prices in "current" terms, as reported at the time sales were being made). The third column shows these prices adjusted to 1990's economic level, thus eliminating the effects of inflation on purchasing power. When these "real" values are compared with 1990 used prices, it becomes clear that, because of the shrinking value of the dollar, investing in a boat wouldn't be the best choice for you if profit is what you're after. The stock market, to take one of many alternative examples, would have been a much better bet.

As this is written in the spring of 1991, the DJIA stands at around 2,950—an 81% gain compared with a loss for every one of the boats listed. In fact, the Dow would have to decline all the way down to 850 to equal the best investment value among the boats, namely the Catalina 30. Furthermore, in this analysis we haven't considered that stocks provide income from dividends, which aren't included in the Dow market values—while the boats would incur storage charges, fuel bills, and maintenance costs.

In summary: Most people, even if they think of their boat as an investment, plan to keep her and use her, at least for a season or two, after they go to the trouble of purchase and fix-up. Unless inflation at some specific time happens to be rising considerably faster for boats than it is for the economy as a whole, using a boat is more likely to reduce its value than increase it. So unless you're a do-it-yourselfer who would just as soon be working on a boat in your backyard as taking her out for a ride, try not to think of your boat as an investment, any more than you think of your car as one.

You can still think in terms of getting the biggest possible return on your investment, but remember that return can be measured in terms of happiness and relaxation as well as cold cash. If you buy low, sell high, and spend wisely while intensively enjoying the use of your boat in between, you'll be maximizing your return.

FIGURE 3-1

| Price appreciation for boats and stocks, 1980–1990. CHOICE OF "INVESTMENT" | ORIGINAL 1980 PRICE | ORIGINAL PRICE ADJUSTED FOR INFLATION TO 1990 LEVEL | AVERAGE USED MARKET PRICE IN 1990 | GAIN OR (LOSS) COMPARED WITH ADJUSTED PRICE | |
|---|---|---|---|---|---|
| | | | | $ | % |
| Powerboats | | | | | |
| Bertram 33 dsl | $104,600 | $166,300 | $83,800 | $(82,500) | (50)% |
| Carver 28 gas | 34,800 | 55,300 | 17,500 | (37,800) | (68) |
| Mako 17 | 4,600 | 7,300 | 1,850 | (5,450) | (75) |
| Boston Whaler 13 | 2,100 | 3,300 | 850 | (2,450) | (74) |
| Sailboats | | | | | |
| Tartan 37 | 66,700 | 106,000 | 60,000 | (46,000) | (43)% |
| Sabre 30 | 37,800 | 60,100 | 26,600 | (33,500) | (56) |
| Catalina 30 | 26,700 | 42,500 | 27,700 | (14,800) | (35) |
| Catalina 22 | 5,000 | 8,000 | 3,400 | (4,600) | (58) |
| DJ Industrial Average | 825 | 1,312 | 2,950 | 1,062 | +81% |

Notes: Mako and Whaler prices do not include engine; all others do. The CPI-U was used to adjust for inflation. During the period 1980 to 1990 the CPI-U increased by 59%.

## If your prime goal is investment for resale . . .

- **Aim to buy a popular, sought-after, used stock fiberglass model to keep your investment liquid.** Avoid custom designs, odd-ball materials (i.e., any material other than fiberglass), and anything more than six to eight years old. Don't buy brand new, either; the first week's depreciation can be 10% or more.
- **Don't buy too big.** The market is very thin for large boats, as Figure 3-2 shows.
- **Look for scruffy, apparently poorly maintained boats that you can fix up with a little elbow grease.** If engine and other basic equipment is serviceable but dirty and unkempt, the market price at which the seller will be able to interest typical potential buyers will be below average, often lower far out of proportion to fix-up expenses. If you are willing to tackle the fix-up work that the seller isn't, you may acquire a genuine bargain. Watch out, though; sometimes a sloppy owner will ignore required maintenance on the engine, significantly shortening its life or requiring major fix-up expenses. Then the boat is no bargain.
- **Time your purchase to take advantage of seasonality.** Buy in the fall, sell in the spring (or, in subtropical climates like southern Florida where the boating seasons are reversed, buy in

FIGURE 3-2
**Number of boats of
different sizes and types
sold in 1990. Source:
NMMA reports, author's
estimates.**

| | NUMBER OF BOATS OWNED IN 1990 (000) | NUMBER OF BOATS PURCHASED IN 1990 (000) | | AVERAGE COST IN 1990 ($000) | |
| --- | --- | --- | --- | --- | --- |
| | | NEW | USED | NEW | USED |
| Outboard runabouts, bass boats, etc. | 8,030 | 227 | 1,300 | 7 | 4 |
| Inboard/outboard boats | 1,559 | 97 | 200 | 18 | 12 |
| Houseboats | 38 | 2 | 6 | 30 | 15 |
| Open deck and pontoon types | 225 | 10 | 30 | 8 | 5 |
| Jet drive boats | 104 | 4 | 20 | 6 | 3 |
| Inboard-powered runabouts | 140 | 5 | 24 | 18 | 10 |
| Inboard-powered cruisers | 280 | 10 | 40 | 184 | 70 |
| TOTAL POWERBOATS | 10,376 | 355 | 1,620 | NA | NA |
| | | | | | |
| Non-powered sailboats: | | | | | |
| under 16′ except sailboards | 1,000 | 15 | 100 | 2 | 1 |
| 16′ and up except sailboards | 298 | 4 | 30 | 3 | 2 |
| | | | | | |
| Powered sailboats (auxiliaries): | | | | | |
| to 25′ | 100 | 3 | 10 | 25 | 14 |
| 26′ to 39′ | 50 | 1 | 7 | 80 | 50 |
| 40′ and over | 15 | 1 | 3 | 150 | 80 |
| TOTAL SAILBOATS | 1,463 | 24 | 150 | NA | NA |
| | | | | | |
| Miscellaneous watercraft: | | | | | |
| Canoes and kayaks | 2,200 | 75 | 400 | 1.2 | 0.5 |
| Inflatables | 200 | 26 | 40 | 1.5 | 0.8 |
| Sailboards | 500 | 42 | 40 | 1.0 | 0.5 |
| Other, including rowboats and non-motorized dinghies | 1,800 | 70 | 350 | 0.6 | 0.3 |
| TOTAL MISCELLANEOUS | 4,700 | 213 | 830 | NA | NA |
| | | | | | |
| TOTAL ALL RECREATIONAL BOATS | 16,539 | 592 | 2,600 | NA | NA |

the late spring, sell in the late fall — after hurricane season — or early winter). That way, you'll buy when demand is low, keeping prices down and values up. And when you sell, you may be able to avoid in-season storage costs and haulout charges, as well as take advantage of higher seasonal demand.

- **Don't plan to use the boat extensively.** Ideally, don't use her at all except to demonstrate to prospective buyers. The longer you keep her and the more you use her, the lower will be your return on investment — excluding, of course, the return in terms of pleasure you get from using the boat, which would be a secondary consideration for you since investment for resale is your main goal.

Prestige may be what you think you're after when you decide to own a boat. Some people think you can buy personal prestige just by spending oodles of money on gleam and glitter; others (the author included) disagree. True, if your yacht is big enough, you'll get plenty of stares and waves from dockside — but not necessarily all admiring. On the other hand, whether you own an ocean liner or a small, inexpensive boat, if she is elegant and shipshape, you're likely to get genuine expressions of admiration, at least from knowledgeable boat people. The message: you can enjoy prestige by owning a yacht, but normally you have to do more to earn it than just throw cash around. And it helps to have some knowledge of seamanship and a sense of what constitutes good taste.

Anyway, if spending a lot of cash makes you feel good, and you have the money to do it, go ahead. Just make sure you buy the best — which isn't always easy to tell from second best. And remember: even millionaires have budgets (though they may not talk about them). If you want the most and the best for your money, this book will help you make some crucial choices in the right direction.

## If your prime goal is acquiring prestige. . . .

- **Be prepared to keep your yacht in topflight condition,** whether she is a megayacht or a kayak. Make her sparkle.
- **Fancy fittings and exotic equipment can add to the lustre of a prestigious yacht (and also to her expense).** Go ahead and splurge if you value prestige as your first priority. But remember, you'll never get your money back on all that fancy equipment when selling time comes.
- **Pick a boat designed by a "prestige" firm.** There's no universal agreement on which naval architects qualify for this honor and which don't. If you're into prestige, you've probably formed your own opinions anyway.

Exploration and adventure is the goal of some boat buyers. A few dream of ocean voyages and dancing girls in Tahiti. Most of us are satisfied to think in terms of taking our boat to quiet coves nearby, or at most going off for a week or a month of cruising in territory new to us, but not too distant in time or space. Whether you're weekending or world-girdling, you can do plenty of exploring, and get your share of adventure in the process, in a wide variety of craft. Luckily, size and cost aren't prime factors if exploring or adventure is your main thing. You can sometimes see more in a 20-foot Mako or Aquasport than you can in a megayacht. (Millionaire Malcolm Forbes knew; he carried a Donzi and a Cigarette—as well as a Harley Davidson motorcycle and a helicopter—on the deck of his 151-foot motor vessel *Highlander II*, and used them for exploring shoal waters inaccessible to his "big boat.") My friends Linc and "T" Jewett have trailered their 19-foot Aquasport from Canada to Florida and explored up and down the Mississippi and the waters around scores of ports along the east coast. They've even made a crossing from Florida to the Bahamas. Cruising accommodations can't be highly luxurious in a trailerable outboard boat; the Jewetts sleep under a canvas dodger in the forward half of the boat, and use a bucket for a head. The basic nature of their accommodations doesn't bother them at all, since their prime objective is exploration and adventure, not living at sea in the lap of luxury.

## If your prime goal is exploration and adventure . . .

- **Pick a boat with powerplant and equipment that have a reputation for reliability.** If you're going to the remote corners of your part of the earth—or water—you'll want to be sure you can get back in one piece. Check with independent brokers or other unbiased sources to determine which manufacturers have the best reputations for building reliable products.

- **Strength and hull shape are important.** Look for a sturdily built hull that's not likely to puncture or crack if you go aground in uncharted waters, and perhaps a flattish bottom to permit the boat to take the ground without significant listing if you're exploring particularly shallow waters. If a powerboat, look for good prop protection. For extremely shallow water, consider a jet drive or even an airboat, which can plane on a heavy dew. If a sailboat, think about a centerboard model that will open up shoal water cruising grounds not accessible to deeper keel boats. Three feet of draft will make a noticeable difference compared to four feet. Two feet will be noticeable compared to three feet, particularly in very shoal water areas such as Florida Bay or Nantucket Sound.

- **Plan on budgeting for good navigational instruments.** For a small boat, this could mean just a compass, a depth sounder, binoculars, and maybe a VHF radio and a radio direction finder. For a larger boat, you might want to add Loran, radar, and possibly sonar, weatherfax and SatNav.

- **Consider speed and comfort.** If you're especially impatient to get where you're going, check out the boat's top speed and her comfort at that speed, particularly in rough water. But remember, extra miles per hour in a powerboat costs money in terms of fuel consumption. Recognize this before you buy, and be sure you can afford the higher operating costs that almost always go with greater speed.

Getting close to nature is the primary appeal for some. Most fishermen fit into this category. So do some cruising people — both powerboaters and sailors.

## If your prime goal is getting close to nature . . .

- **Consider a wind-powered or human-powered vessel.** They're quiet, and more in tune with nature than powerboats. If you're a "nature freak" in the Thoreau vein, you may even want to buy an engineless sailboat, a rowing shell, or a paddle-powered canoe or kayak.
- **Go for simplicity.** A compass is always a good idea, but think about eliminating electronics and other space-age gear (although I'd keep a VHF as a safety item, along with electric running lights).
- **Think about space aboard.** Be sure that your final choice of boat has enough space for the gear you'll need to totally appreciate your natural environment: scuba diving stuff, bird-watching binoculars, etc.

Just relaxing and getting away from it all — your job, your house or apartment, your workaday environment, perhaps even your mother-in-law — is the goal of a great many boat people. If this is your bag, you couldn't go far wrong by using the checklists applicable to "getting close to nature" and "exploration and adventure" above.

Waterskiing may be your dream, as it is for more than a million others in the U.S. alone. The absolute minimum rig for this purpose would be a 13-foot planing powerboat with a 20 or 25 h.p. engine. That's barely enough power to plane a small boat at around 16 m.p.h. with two people aboard (one to drive and the other to act as "safety observer," facing backwards to watch the skier) while towing a skier. For faster action or more than two people aboard while towing, a larger motor (and preferably a larger boat) would be required.

## Boat requirements for waterskiing

- **The boat must be big enough.** The absolute minimum is around 13 feet long, with a 5-foot beam. Wider beam is preferable; it keeps the boat more stable on turns, and provides space to contain ski equipment, vests, towlines, etc. as well as driver, on-board observer, and one or two skiers when they're not in the water. Ideal boat size is around 17 feet long, with a 7-foot beam.

- **Low freeboard is also desirable,** since it makes it easy for skiers to climb onboard and off, and improves driver visibility.
- **Forward helm position,** with a wheel and forward-facing seat, gives the driver the good visibility he needs. Stern-steered outboards should be avoided for waterskiing use.
- **The engine must be big enough.** Minimum size is 20 to 25 horsepower or more, depending on boat size and load carried. Below 20 h.p., the boat may not have power to lift a skier onto plane (which happens at around 15 to 20 miles an hour). For competition skiing, 36 m.p.h. is needed, meaning bigger boats and larger engines. For a 17-foot ski boat, 200 h.p. to 250 h.p. is not too much power. But caution: transom must be specially designed to take unusually big engines — plus the tug of skiers. Check manufacturers' specs.

Catching fish is what millions of Americans like to do best. If feeling the tug of a tuna or a trout at the end of a fishing line turns you on, owning a "fishing machine" that lets you go where the big ones are may be the main reason you want a boat. If so, you should look for a platform specially designed for fishing. You'll have a tremendous range of choices; there are literally thousands of types to choose from, from canoes and aluminum rowboats to huge sea-going sportfishing machines that can roam the oceans looking for swordfish and marlin. The only limitations are the type of fishing you like to do, the type of waters you fish, and of course, your budget.

## If your prime goal is catching fish . . .

- **Look for a fish boat.** Try to home in on the types of boats used by those who do your kind of fishing. If you don't know how to go about doing this, ask around. Read the fishing mags (list in Appendix 2); attend "fishing expos" and boat shows (listed in Chapter 5); talk to the folks selling boats and gear. Usually they love to give advice.
- **Look for stability and capacity.** It's nice to fish with a friend or two.
- **Buy a boat that'll get you there fast.** Look for high speed and a comfortable ride in a chop, especially if your favorite fishing grounds are some distance away. Alternatively, aim for an easily trailered boat (up to 22 feet long or so if your tow vehicle is big enough) to get close to the fishing hot spots by road rather than by water. The comfort of an air-conditioned car will usually beat a rolling, pitching boat in choppy seas. And speaking of comfort, having some sort of shelter on board where you can stroll — or at least crawl — in out of the rain is nice, too.

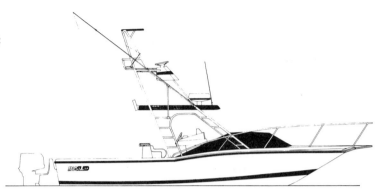

FIGURE 3-3
**A "fishing machine." This one is a Sea Sled, 29 feet LOA. She features twin OMC 140 h.p. Seadrives, two helm stations, and a tower to help spot fish.**

Sailboat and powerboat racing are popular pastimes, offering comradeship, competition at a variety of levels, and a chance to "accomplish something" while soaking up the rays (and the spray).

## If your prime goal is sailboat racing or powerboat racing. . .

- **Contact people in the sport.** Friends are the usual source of introductions. Call the people who are involved in racing, tell them you'd like to learn more about it with an eye to possibly buying a class boat, and ask them to help. If you don't know anybody involved, contact the USYRU or the APBA (addresses in Appendix 2) and ask them to help.
- **Attend some regattas as a spectator** to check out boats of the type you might like to race. Talk to the contestants; see if you like the lifestyle.
- **Join a frostbite group.** There are lots of small informal groups of sailors who "frostbite" (i.e. sail in 6-foot to 15-foot dinghies in the off-season). It's a great way to meet sailors and learn racing strategy without having to make a huge investment. Typically, dues are $20 to $50 a year, and the boats might cost $300 to $3,000 each.

Thundering power off the race course appeals to people who just like the thrill of skimming across the water at ultra-high speed. And you don't necessarily have to pay a bundle to go fast. In fact, the fastest boat may be one of the smallest, with one of the lowest prices. And for less than 10 grand, you can scoot along at better than 35 m.p.h., which for many people is plenty fast enough, especially in a 17-foot boat.

The fastest sailboats are multihulls (catamarans and trimarans), which can zoom along at 20-plus m.p.h. in a good breeze, and sailboards, which under ideal conditions can go even faster. Some multihull and sailboard classes have active one-design class organizations (listed in Appendix 2).

## Summary

Whether you want to make money at boat-owning, enjoy the prestige of the yachting scene, go for adventure, explore, get close to nature, get away from it all, or just go fishing or waterskiing, somewhere out there there's just the boat for you. Pondering the fundamental reasons behind why you want to buy a boat can help in clarifying what kind of vessel is your best choice.

# PART TWO

# The Seven Basic Rules of the Boat Buying Game

*Rule One: Know What You Want*
*Rule Two: Comb the Market Thoroughly*
*Rule Three: Know What You're Buying*
*Rule Four: Time Your Purchase Intelligently*
*Rule Five: Be a Strong Negotiator*
*Rule Six: Be Willing to Walk Away From a Deal*
*Rule Seven: Buy Low, Sell High*

# CHAPTER 4

# Rule One: Know What You Want

The first thing to do when preparing to buy a boat is to figure out exactly what kind of a boat you want to own. For most people, especially those new to boating, this is not an easy task. You may need to search the depths of your soul for the right answers.

**You have a large number of choices.** Every year something like 150,000 used sailboats and over 1,600,000 used powerboats in the U.S. change hands (about 10% of the floating population for sailboats, 20% for powerboats), and normally around 40,000 new sailboats and 500,000 new powerboats are sold. (Less are sold in recession years like 1990.) Brands and models abound; for every boat buyer there are literally thousands of choices. But by using the checklists and worksheets in this chapter to help you approach a decision, you can quickly eliminate 99% or more of these choices.

**Begin with the fundamentals, keep your family involved, and be systematic.** Start by examining your basic motivations regarding boats, as outlined in Chapter 3. Be sure to include your family, if any, in any planning you do. The boating magazine polls indicate that men make most of the boat-buying decisions in this country. That may be so, but I know a number of men who have ended up alone, single-handing their boats because they couldn't or wouldn't convince their wives or families to join them. Perhaps it's no worse than taking off every weekend for golf with your buddies, leaving your spouse behind. But I think it's sad to see these people alone on their boats on a gorgeous weekend, and to imagine their wives (or, occasionally, husbands) and families sitting at home, missing the fun of being on the water and the joy of participating in joint family activities.

If you're the type who likes to surprise your spouse with new toys you've bought, forget it. You're better off considering the needs and desires of your spouse and family before you buy, rather than trying to sell them on the boat you've picked after the deal is closed.

A few lucky people instinctively find a way to focus instantly on a specific boat, buy her, and live happily ever after.   But they are the exception. Most of us are vastly more indecisive. I know many boat-owners who seem to be forever buying and selling, and buying again, apparently never fully satisfied with their latest choice. Powerboaters, especially, seem to trade boats every two, three, or four years, the way some people trade automobiles. On the other hand, sailboat people as a group seem to take forever to make up their minds on what they want, but once decided, they usually stick with their choices, typically for five to ten years or longer. Why there is such a difference between the habits of powerboaters and sailors is an unsolved mystery; it would make an interesting investigation for some nautically-inclined psychologist.

Whether you're a powerboat nut, a sailboat nut, or haven't yet decided what you are, if you want to avoid chronic indecisiveness, you can systematically analyze your specific situation with the help of the material that follows. It will speed you to a conclusion on what *kind* of boat you want, giving you more time to look for specific boats of the type you decide on.

**Homing in on the right boat for you.**   To help you define precisely which size, type, style, age — and even color — you like best, you can start with the worksheet contained in Figure 4-1, which addresses the questions of *who, what, when, where, and how much?* Answering these questions will lay the groundwork for your choice of boats, so they should be addressed with due diligence and care. Write down your answers for your own review and possible amendment later. Date the checklist to give yourself a permanent record of your desires at that time, the better to understand your motivations later, when they change.   (Yes, most people's desires do change as time goes by, much to the delight of boat brokers.)

**Who will use her with you?**   How much privacy, how many berths, how big a saloon, how many cabins?—all this is partly determined by the way you answer the questions.

**What will you use her for?**   At the risk of explaining the obvious, your answers will determine, to a great extent, the size and shape of your boat. For example, if you want a boat mainly for relaxing alone or with your spouse, it might be nice to have just a small cockpit and a small cabin, to be easy to maintain and to discourage unwanted visitors. Small scale — an overall length of around 20 feet to 35 feet — makes for easier operation, too. You'll understand why if you've ever

# THE SEVEN BASIC RULES OF THE BOAT BUYING GAME

FIGURE 4-1
**Worksheet for deciding what kind of boat you really want. (Note: See text for explanation of specific questions.)**

## General

Purpose of Boat _____ _____ _____
                                (primary)         (secondary)      (other)

Persons on Board _____ _____ _____
                                 (family)          (guests)    (men/women)

Type of Use: all year _____; seasonal _____; day trips _____;

overnight _____; cruising _____; partying _____;

fishing _____; racing _____; waterskiing _____;

living _____; trailering _____; other _____.

Where Used: lakes _____; rivers _____; harbors _____;

bays _____; ocean _____; warm climate _____;

cold climate _____.

Total Est. Yearly Usage (days): day trips _____; overnight _____;

cruising _____.

Money in Your Budget: Initial cost of boat itself _____;

annual related expenses _____.

## Desired Specifics

Type of Boat (see Appendix 1): _____

Size: _____ Age: _____ Color: _____

Condition (see Figure 4-3): _____

Design style: _____ Brand: _____

Equipment: _____

Construction material: _____

Minimum Top Speed: _____ Max. Fuel Consumption: _____

Displacement (see Figure 4-10): _____

tried to bring a 40-footer alongside a pier single-handed in a strong crosswind.

On the other hand, if you're planning to do a lot of entertaining at the dock, a huge cockpit (to host the crowds in good weather) and a huge cabin (for rainy weather) is indicated. And assuming performance at sea isn't an important consideration, a houseboat might be your cup of tea. Otherwise a large inboard powerboat might be indicated.

**When will you use her?** The more you plan to use her, the bigger the vessel you can justify acquiring. And if you'll use her only for day trips, you'll want lots of space on deck, where the action usually is, rather than down below.

**Where will you use her?** Your boat's most frequent environment will have a major bearing on her size, shape, and type. For example, you don't usually see many 50-foot sportfishermen on small freshwater lakes. Except in Texas maybe, where anything can happen.

**How much will you use her each year?** This question should make you stop and think about all that money that you're getting ready to put into a new boat. On the basis of dollars per year you'll spend divided by days of use, is it going to be worth the cost? Only you can decide. But the more days you plan to use your boat, the lower the cost per day, and the bigger the benefit to you.

That might tempt you to overestimate the time you say you'll use her. But if you do, you'll only be fooling yourself. Indicate the probable number of days per year you will actually use her. Don't count days to be spent aboard fitting out, fixing up, or putting her to bed for the winter.

As you figure your time, remember that there are 365 days in a year, and 91 days in each of the four seasons. There are 104 weekend days (26 of which fall in each season), about 15 holidays, and 10 to 50 days of vacation for most of us, exclusive of weekends and holidays. And don't forget you have to stay home and cut the lawn or weed the garden some days, and other days will be so stormy you won't want to go out on the water.

Surveys indicate the average U.S. pleasure boat is used less than 150 hours a year. Assuming four hours per trip on the average, that amounts to 37 days a year of use.

**How much money are you willing to commit to her?** Consult Chapter 1 for rules of thumb and tips on estimating an amount appropriate to your specific circumstances. But remember: These are rules of thumb, not hard-and-fast requirements. In the end, you'll have to use your own judgment as to how much you want to spend on boating and how much you can afford.

**What type, size, age, design style?** Now you're ready for another group of questions that define some of the major characteristics of the boat you're looking for:

- What general type of boat is best for the particular use you have in mind?
- What size boat is appropriate for your intended use?
- How old a boat would you prefer?
- Do you have a preference for her general condition?
- What design style suits you best?
- What is your preference for specific brand and model, if any?
- Are you willing to settle for a "dog" to get more size and space?
- What do you require (or prefer) in the way of specific equipment types, quantity, quality, and age?

You should be aware that conflicts may develop between what you specify here. For example, suppose you want a 30-foot boat, not a "dog," no more than 5 years old and in excellent condition. Suppose further that $20,000 isn't enough to buy any boat that meets your criteria. When such conflicts develop, you'll have to alter one or more of your original choices. In this example, you'd either have to increase your budget, reduce the size of the boat, or settle for an older model, a dog, or a boat in considerably worse than average condition.

Compromises are almost always necessary when matching your needs to what's available. But having done your homework with the checklists, you'll be facing compromise decisions with full awareness and knowledge that your decision will be the best one for you.

Although you may plan to use your boat for more than one purpose, try to envision the boat's primary use, and focus your efforts on finding the best type for that use.

As far as type of power, there are pluses and minuses to each of the various choices. For example:

*Maintenance.* Some boat owners think it's easier to do their own maintenance work on outboards than inboards or I/O combos. But new outboards are getting more complicated and often require special tools; for anything except routine maintenance, I'd give an outboard to a knowledgeable mechanic to fix. In this, outboards have the advantage: certainly it's easier and generally less expensive to bring an outboard motor to a shop than it is to bring in an inboard (or to pay a mechanic to come to the boat to do the work, at $30 to $60 an hour.

*Smooth-running reliability.* Inboards and I/Os are sometimes considered to be quieter, more fuel-efficient, smoother-running, and more reliable than outboards, but I've seen some pretty smooth-running outboards and some gas-guzzling, rough-running inboards too. Reliability of both types of engines today is very high if they're well cared for.

Also, I would say that inboards have the edge on longevity; it's not unusual to see a 20-year-old gasoline inboard engine in a sailboat or lightly used powerboat. Diesel engines last even longer if they're heavily enough built. Outboards typically turn faster (5,000 r.p.m. for outboards versus 3,500 r.p.m. full-ahead cruising speed for inboards), so outboards tend to wear out faster.

*Economy.* Diesels became popular when a gallon of gasoline was a lot more expensive than the same amount of diesel fuel, and engine builders devised ways to lighten the heavy diesel for yacht use (largely by modifying small Japanese tractor engines, using high-strength aluminum alloys in place of cast iron, and adding turbochargers to jam more fuel and air into the combustion chamber in a shorter space of time, thus boosting power without enlarging the engine). However, in some places around the U.S. these days, diesel fuel is around 50% more expensive per gallon than gasoline, and since diesel engines burn about two-thirds as many gallons per hour or per mile in an equivalent service, the fuel costs per mile of boat operation can sometimes be close to the same for either fuel. So the highly touted fuel economy of diesel engines may not be a major factor in some locations.

On the other hand, the first cost of buying a diesel is considerably higher than for a similar-size gasoline inboard, especially in the larger sizes. Outboard engines have the lowest cost per horsepower, and I/Os are in between outboards and inboards in cost.

*Safety.* Diesels usually are considered to be safer than gasoline models, since diesel oil is less volatile than gasoline. Nevertheless, there are numerous Coast Guard-approved gasoline engines still being installed on brand new boats—at least on powerboats. New sailboats builders, unlike powerboat builders, have almost all gone to diesel, citing safety. Safety is a consideration, but the main reason is probably more a matter of sailboat manufacturing economics. The Universal Atomic 4, a 30-h.p. gasoline engine specifically designed for sailboats, was installed on the lion's share of new sailing inboard auxiliaries in the 1960s and early 1970s, but was discontinued in the early 1980s due to lack of demand brought on by higher gas prices and the advent of the new lightweight diesels. With only 3,000 or 4,000 new inboard auxiliaries being built each year, and strong competition from the new lightweight diesels, the incentive to keep manufacturing just wasn't there.

Incidentally, if you still want a new gasoline engine for your sailboat, you can get it. Westerbeke introduced a whole new line of small-sized gasoline auxiliary engines (mainly for repowering older sailboats) in 1986. First cost is a lot lower than an equivalent diesel engine.

On balance, I'd go for an outboard if my boat were under 25 feet or so, and if I was seeking first-cost economy, easy maintenance, and the ability to easily disentangle weeds and flotsam from the prop. I'd pick an inboard for boats 25 feet and up, and if my top priorities were safety (and hence diesel rather than gas), relatively quiet power, and plenty of power in difficult conditions (where a deeply buried inboard prop is less likely to pop out of the water in waves, causing "cavitation," over-revving and loss of thrust). And I might try an I/O combo if I wanted to combine some of the best features of each and was willing to accept the negatives (not lowest first cost, more expensive to repair and replace).

***What horsepower?*** There are many factors that help determine a planing powerboat's top speed, among others being shape and smoothness of the immersed portion of the hull while on a plane; area of the wetted surface; fore-and-aft trim; windage of hull, cabin, and equipment; and — according to some authorities — waterline length (though when a boat is planing, the water can't "see" much of her at-rest waterline). However, the two biggest determinants of a planing boat's maximum speed are her weight and the horsepower of her engine.

To get a rough idea of the relationship between these two factors and maximum speed, refer to Figure 4-2, which shows lines of "constant horsepower" plotted against displacement and maximum speed, using the equation:

$$\text{Maximum MPH} = \frac{160}{\sqrt{0.85 \ (\text{displacement/HP})}}$$

The basic equation is known as "Crouch's Formula":

$$\text{Maximum MPH} = \frac{C}{\sqrt{(\text{displacement/HP})}}$$

where C is a constant, usually derived from trial data of existing boats of the same type. I've stretched this usual practice a bit with, it would seem, satisfactory results.

Note that in Figure 4-2, speed is shown in land miles per hour; to translate to knots, divide by 1.15.

Since Figure 4-2 concentrates on horsepower and weight and ignores the other speed-affecting factors mentioned above, its accuracy isn't perfect. Still, most pleasure craft should fit the chart within plus or minus 5 m.p.h. or so, as is intimated by the examples plotted in on the chart.

If you care about money and/or performance, you'll want to know how much power your hull can safely handle, what it will give you in terms of speed, and what it will cost. If you buy a boat with plenty of horsepower for her size, she'll go like a bullet but your initial cost as well as your fuel bills will be higher. If you skimp on power, you'll save on first cost and fuel, but performance will suffer. You pay your money and take your choice.

***What size boat (length overall)?*** What length boat you choose mainly depends on end use, the size of your pocketbook, where you plan to keep her, and how comfortable you feel about running a big boat vs. a little boat.

Incidentally, a boat isn't necessarily easier to handle just because she's small. In fact, very often the opposite is true for boats up to around

FIGURE 4-2
**How horsepower and
weight affect speed.
(Note that boat lengths
indicated are load
waterline lengths
assuming a D/L
ratio of 200.)**

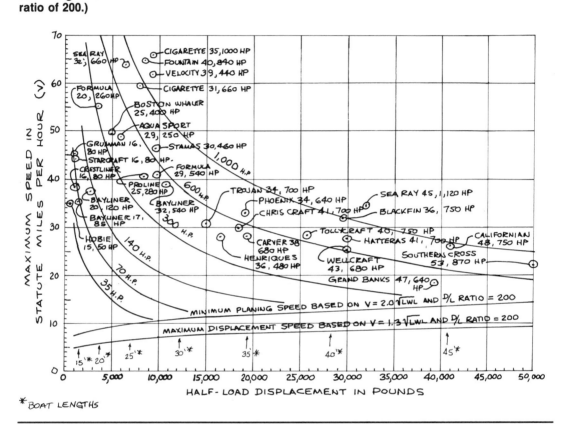

\* BOAT LENGTHS

30 feet in length. I once owned a 17-foot Picnic sloop (no longer manufactured) that was an absolute dog in all but the lightest wind conditions. She was tender (tippy), required constant attention to the helm,
and was slow. When I sold her and moved up to a South Coast 23 sloop
(eventually converted to a yawl), I was amazed at how much easier
the bigger boat was to sail. I could single-handedly sail the 23 up to a
dock or mooring with absolute confidence. With the Picnic, though,
a second crewmember always had to be stationed at the bow to grab
the mooring pickup buoy before the boat drifted off course.

A well-designed boat (sail or power) in the 18- to 26-foot range
makes an ideal adult beginner's training vessel. For kids, a smaller first
boat, in the range of 8 feet (for a 7- or 8-year-old) to 14 feet (for a 12-
to 14-year-old) is better.

I recommend that everyone learn to sail, and keep a small sailboat

8 feet to 10 feet long, even those planning to buy a powerboat. If you're just starting out in boating, you'll learn more and learn faster about how to handle a boat. If you're experienced in powerboats but not sailing, you'll find out how much fun sailing is, and you can use the dinghy as a tender for your "big" boat.

For single-handing by an experienced boatman, any well-designed boat up to about 30 feet is a comfortable maximum size. Beyond that, the gear (such as the anchor and the sails) gets heavier and more awkward to lug about, and the deck is long enough from end to end to make it harder to single-hand into a dock and tie up without rushing around in an unseemly manner, particularly if maneuvering room is limited or when the wind is blowing the boat off the pier.

Beginning at about 30 feet, you can feel confident about sailing or powering most boats long distances, such as from Maine to Florida, and perhaps across to the Bahamas or the West Indies, without swamping or being extremely uncomfortable. Provided, that is, that you've had sufficient experience in more protected waters to develop competence, and provided you watch the weather and stay in port when it's stormy. And of course it's prudent to have someone to accompany you if you go offshore in a boat this size.

A man and his wife might find it difficult to run a yacht larger than 40 feet without the help of power devices such as electric sheet winches and an anchor windlass. Given enough hydraulic or electric power, two experienced boatmen can handle a vessel up to 50 or 60 feet in most reasonable conditions, and three or four might handle up to 120 feet or so. (When there's wind, though, any boat over 30 feet may need an extra hand when being maneuvered in close quarters, especially if the boat has a lot of windage aloft.)

*How old a boat?* A brand-new boat has its attractions, principal among them being the gleam and glitter that mark any object on which no other owner has left his fingerprints. In addition, it's sometimes easier to get financing and insurance. And if defects show up after the sale has been consummated, it's easier to convince the builder to fix them without charge than to get action out of a former owner who, 99 times out of 100, will plead honest ignorance, usually sincerely.

But buying new has its disadvantages, too. A big depreciation in market price occurs the moment a new boat is sold, when it becomes "used," just like a new car. And the first owner must find and exterminate the "bugs" that infest practically any new boat. This may mean forfeiting use of the boat while it's back in the shop being fixed. Boatbuilders usually don't offer "loaners" under these circumstances, since keeping an extra inventory of high-priced boats for that purpose is just too expensive.

Old boats are significantly less expensive than new, but have disadvantages of their own. For example, as boats get older, they require more maintenance, look less up-to-date and command a lower market price when it comes time to sell.

As a boat approaches 10 years in age, insurance companies begin to take a different view regarding her insurability. Whether logical or not, some companies won't insure boats more than 10 years old. If that happens, banks and finance companies won't loan money with the boat as collateral. The demand for such boats falls off, as do prices compared to more easily insured boats.

Not all insurance companies discriminate against old boats. I bought a 17-year-old sailboat in 1986 and have had no trouble insuring her each year since. Of course, I've been insuring all my boats with the same insurance agency for over 20 years, and have never had a major claim. "Bundling" your home-owner, auto, and boat insurance so that the insurer gets some attractive business along with the nuisance items (such as looking for a company that is willing to underwrite your old sailboat) can help if you're having difficulty finding proper coverage. (See Chapter 14 for what to do when you just can't find insurance.)

When any sailboat passes its twentieth anniversary, its market price tends to level off and remain virtually static from then on, at least as the market stands today. That is, for example, a 1967 Tartan 27 yawl and a 1971 Tartan 27 yawl may be priced at the same dollar value in the marketplace in 1991, assuming the same level of condition, equipment, etc. This is a peculiarity of the marketplace presumably brought about because many buyers don't perceive any difference between a 20-year-old fiberglass sailboat and, say, a 25- or 30-year-old boat. That may be so today, but it may not be so next year, or the year after, as perceptions change.

Powerboat prices behave somewhat differently, tending to decline in value more rapidly than sailboats. In general they're more like cars: their engines wear out, their mechanical systems suffer due to the constant vibration, and their owners seem to want to keep up with changing styles on a more intensive basis—a characteristic that power-boat manufacturers are quick to exploit.

What condition you're looking for — or are willing to settle for in order to get the most boat for the money — depends on how much work you are willing to do yourself. There are plenty of "bargains" going begging these days, and the worse the boat's condition, the lower the price. There just aren't that many handymen out there looking for a boat to fix up. The handyman specials often never get sold; they get carted to the dump instead, or are given to "fixers" like me free of charge.

The other side of the coin is that, very often, the asking price of a boat in better-than-average condition will be inflated out of propor-tion to the money needed to change an average boat into one in ex-cellent condition.  So, if you want to get the most for your money, look for a boat in average or not too bad condition, not a very good or excellent specimen. Refer to the definitions in Figure 4-3.

***What design style do you prefer?***  Style is an elusive concept, difficult to describe with mere words. There are boats with classic clipper bows and gaff rigs still being launched today; and there are powerboats for which the word futuristic might seem inadequate.

# THE SEVEN BASIC RULES OF THE BOAT BUYING GAME

FIGURE 4-3
**Preferred condition
of the boat**

_____ **Gold-plater.** Typically maintained professionally, stored indoors, never in salt water, never raced, used lightly by perfectionist. Very hard to tell boat or equipment from brand new; sometimes better than new, since "bugs" have been worked out

_____ **Brand new.** Right off the showroom floor

_____ **Excellent.** As if brand new

_____ **Very good.** Everything works; may have a few scratches and dings, but nothing irreparable; gelcoat in excellent condition; no pinholes

_____ **Pretty good.** Above average condition, but not up to *very good* standards

_____ **Average.** In-the-middle physical condition for her age

_____ **Not too bad.** A couple of weekends of elbow grease will put her in at least average condition. If painted fiberglass, job will have been done professionally, using spray

_____ **Pretty bad.** Needs a lot of work, but problems are cosmetic in nature; can be used as is if you don't mind an occasional derogatory remark from passersby. May have gelcoat crazing; may need paint or may be fiberglass already painted by previous owner, using brush rather than spray

_____ **Handyman special.** Must be fixed before using; would be unsafe, or at least very unseamanlike, to use before fixing

FIGURE 4-4
**Classic designs are
evoked by fiberglass
replicas of styles from the
1930s or earlier — vintage
quality that is outdated
but still admired. Pictured
are Eastland Yachts'
*Escort*, a 30-foot
powerboat, and a 17-foot
Cape Cod Shipbuilding
catboat.**

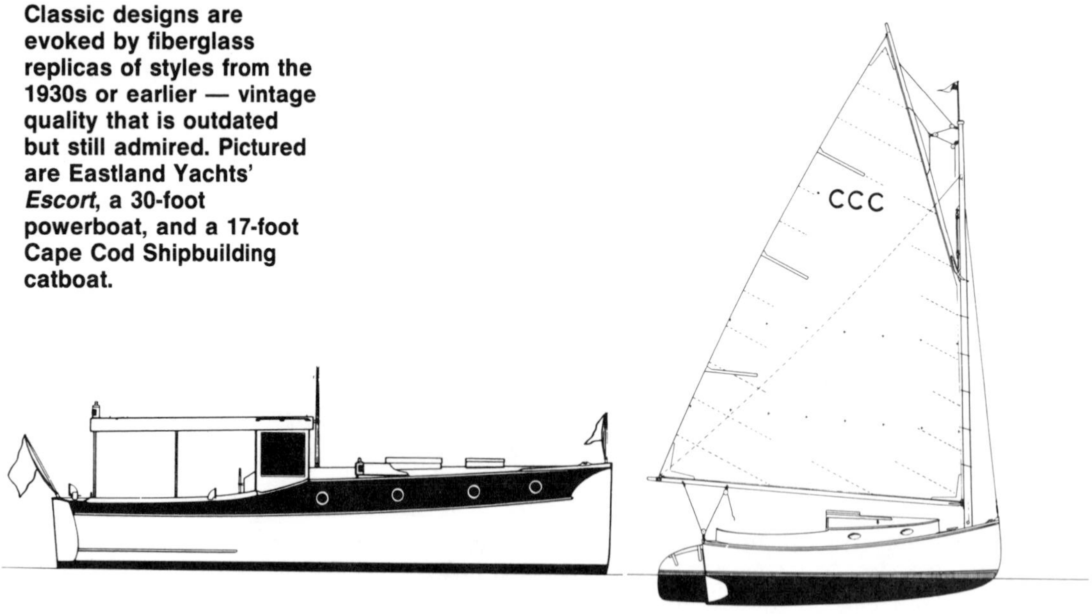

CCC

FIGURE 4-5
**Traditional styling from the 1940s through the 1960s moved along with the times somewhat, and those qualities are still sought by a considerable number of today's dyed-in-the-wool-traditionalists who have no desire to go modern. Pictured are a Morris 36 sailboat and a Wilbur 38 flying bridge sportfisherman.**

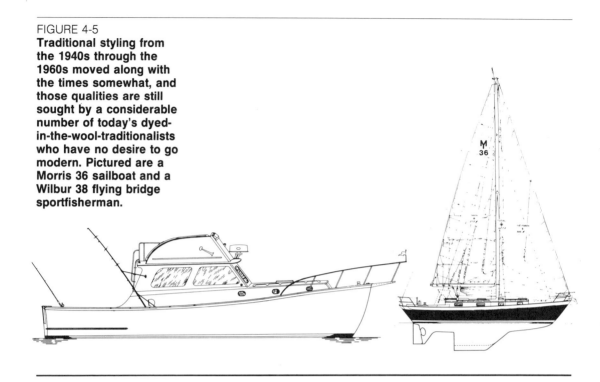

Figures 4-4 through 4-9 give a general sense of what is meant by terms such as classic, traditional, contemporary, modern, and futuristic.

*Homing in on a specific brand and model.* To start, try to come up with at least three brands and models you especially prefer — and six or seven if you can, at least on a preliminary basis. Study of details for a larger initial group of boats will make it less likely that you'll miss any "perfect" boats for you. And by the time you narrow the field to one or two models after studying what boats are available, you'll be more knowledgeable about details, and thus in a better position to bargain.

Read the boating mags; visit the boat shows; ask your friends what they'd recommend (assuming they know what your preferences are as recorded on the questionnaire in this chapter); visit boat brokers and show them your answers to the questionnaire. From these discussions and your answers to the questionnaire, you should be able to come up with an initial "cut list" of a half dozen or so top choices.

*Are any special "dog" models acceptable or "cult" models preferred?* The main point here is that you should think about your boat's future resale value. A dog may be hard to sell at any price; a cult boat is usually easy to sell, unless the group of people forming the cult is very small, or it disbands during your period of ownership.

FIGURE 4-6
**Contemporary/traditional yachts build in the thinking of the 1970s and '80s: they are conventional, wholesome and non-sexy, but enjoy wide acceptance among conservative yachtsmen. Profiles are of a Bertram 28 flybridge cruiser and a Sabre 36 sloop.**

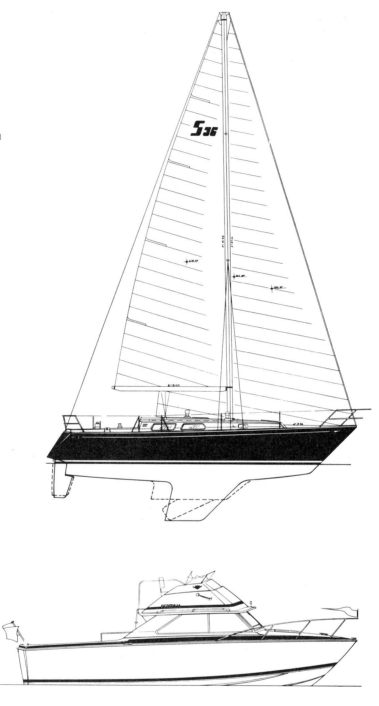

FIGURE 4-7

**Contemporary modern design is the look of the mid-1990s—up-to-date but solid and comfortable, not quite modern in the uninhibited sense. Shown are a Black Watch 30 power cruiser and an O'Day 322 sloop.**

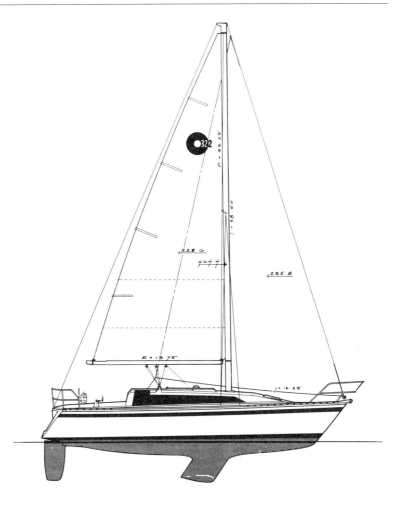

# THE SEVEN BASIC RULES OF THE BOAT BUYING GAME

FIGURE 4-8
**Modern styling builds in a slightly startling avant-garde look recognizable as the latest thinking. It pushes the boundaries of what's acceptable, but still is sufficiently connected to yesterday to be familiar and friendly. Shown are a Topaz 39 flying bridge fishing machine and a Sweden Yacht sloop.**

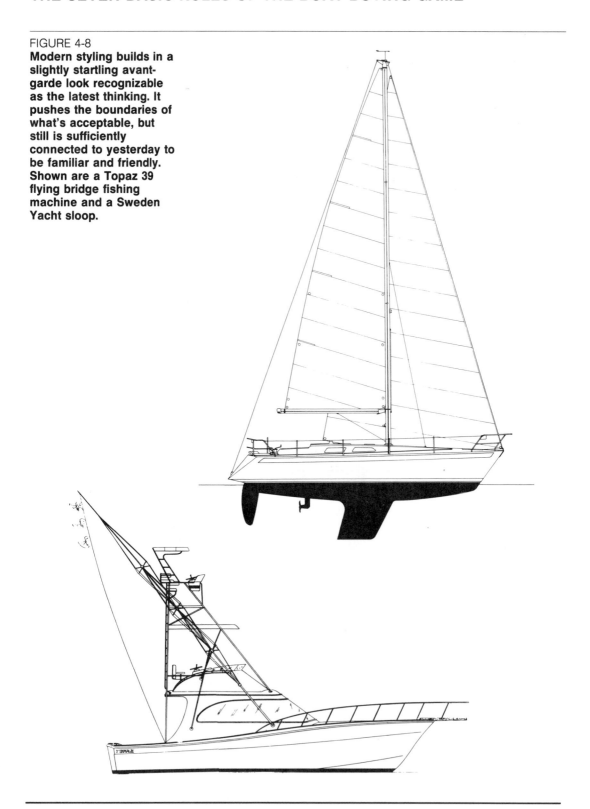

FIGURE 4-9
**Futuristic yachts reach beyond the 1990s for styling concepts; they are viewed as sleek, sexy, daring and experimental. The Gentry Eagle and Hoyt Delta 26 illustrated here show the bold thinking required for such designs.**

You should be aware that even the best cult designs gradually lose favor over the years, as other similar but more up-to-date designs develop cult status of their own. The Pearson Triton and Tartan 27, both super boats in their day with well-deserved cult status, might fall into this category, as might Boston Whalers, Makos and Aquasports more than, say, 15 or 20 years old. And among big powerboats, for example, wood cruisers such as Huckins and Post had their moments of glory in the 1950s, before the advent of mass-production fiberglass construction. Today, some wood powerboats are still cult boats, but prices ain't what they used to be.

***Is any specific equipment type, quality, or age preferred?*** Think of all the items of equipment you might want, using the list in Appendix 6 as a guide. Then decide which of the items you might want are "must haves" and which are "like to haves" (if your budget will stand it, there's room on board, your spouse doesn't object, it doesn't add too much weight, etc.)

Decide, too, what equipment quality level you're willing to live with. If you prefer top quality brands, that usually — though by no means always — means paying high prices. You might also decide that average quality is acceptable, as long as all equipment is in good working order. Or you may decide that the quality — or even the presence — of equipment on board is not important.

The equipment's age also might or might not be important to you. If you prefer new or almost-new equipment, you'll pay a premium to get it. For most people, most equipment is acceptable if it is the same age as the boat, unless the boat is very old. For example, the VHF on my Tartan 27 was installed in 1967 when the boat was new. It was a crystal-cartridge model with six channels, which was the standard in the old days. Now a good VHF may only cost around $150 to $200 after discounts (about the same in current dollars as my 1967 model) but can receive 40 or more channels instead of six. I wouldn't hesitate to opt for a new VHF if I were buying my old Tartan today.

***Now you're ready to start shopping.*** At this point, you have more or less all the information you'll need to begin the process of preliminary shopping. You can start by browsing through the boats listed in Appendix 1, checking out the annual boat catalogs listed in Appendix 2, looking at ads in the magazines, attending a few boat shows, and wandering through a few marinas in your neighborhood, if such exist.

It's probably premature at this point to contact boat brokers or dealers, unless you're prepared to spend a lot of unnecessary time explaining why you don't want to buy the particular boats they have to offer. Not that you shouldn't contact certain brokers and dealers later — it'll be part of your buying strategy. But you have some more homework to finish before doing so.

***Some little details that could be important.*** By now you've addressed all the "big" questions raised earlier in this chapter. But there are certain details — some would say inconsequential details — that might make the difference between loving and hating your new boat. For example, the color of the topsides and deck, the quality of the construction, the relative weight of the boat for her size, all may turn out to be major factors in your decision, even though many people hardly give them a second thought when shopping.

My family and I have owned two black boats (a home-built 17-foot sailing cruiser and a South Coast 23 sailboat), a navy blue boat (Tartan 27 yawl), a lime green boat (Optimist dinghy), and two light blue boats (Blue Jay and Fireball one-design racing sailboats). All the rest of the boats we've owned, which is around 30 different types, mostly fiberglass, have had white topsides and white or off-white cabins and decks. And I'll probably never own another non-white boat. Why?

First of all, dark colors are hot, since they absorb heat from the sun. Sleeping aboard our blue Tartan 27, I used to be awakened by the hot interior wall of my quarter berth, as the early morning sun's radiation became absorbed by the dark topside color outside. The fiberglass skin heated to well over 100° Fahrenheit on a sunny day, on the inside. The outside was even hotter.

The deck of our South Coast 23 was colored a nifty-looking light tan, and was designed to prevent glare reflecting into the eyes of the crew back in the cockpit. But on a sunny day, particularly when the wind was light, the deck could be painfully hot to walk on barefoot. And who wants to wear shoes on a hot day on a hot boat in zero air?

Second of all, colors fade. Sure, builders talk about non-fading colors or special techniques (such as repainting every few years with Awlgrip or Imron), but in my experience, even non-fading colors fade, eventually.

Third, because of fading, colors are hard to match when a repair must be made. By the time a new fiberglass hull has been out of the mold a few months, or in sunny climates even a few weeks, it fades. For this reason, some manufacturers automatically paint their new hulls for easier color-matching later, rather than pigmenting the gelcoat. That's okay if the paint is as durable as the fiberglass gelcoat. Sometimes it is, and sometimes it isn't.

And fourth, white boats command higher resale prices, because more people prefer white boats than any other color, for the very reasons mentioned above. Higher demand translates to higher prices.

I recommend white.

***Quality of construction.*** It's easy to be enticed by a boat with super-high construction quality. Hinckley, Little Harbor, Baltic, Nautor-Swan, Morris, and Able Marine among sailboats, and Post, Huckins, Rybovich, Hatteras and Lee Wilbur among powerboats are examples of the best. The best costs money and they are priced, when new, accordingly. Moreover, to maintain their value, they must be coddled like royal princesses, which costs more money.

At the other end of the scale is the el-cheapo boat that may or may not sink in the middle of your next voyage.

I'd pick a quality level somewhere in between, unless you have a big bank account and love your boat enough to literally treat her royally.

***Displacement.*** The displacement/length ratio (D/L Ratio) is generally used in connection with sailboat hulls. A different ratio, relating displacement to horsepower, is more useful when comparing powerboat hulls (as shown graphically in Figure 4-2).

$$\text{D/L Ratio} = \frac{\text{Displacement in pounds} \div 2240}{(0.01 \times \text{waterline length in feet})^3}$$

# THE SEVEN BASIC RULES OF THE BOAT BUYING GAME

If you're worried about having to deal with this complicated formula, don't. A computer has already done the work for you, and the D/L ratios for any length boat from 8 feet to 50 feet are given in Figure 12-5, in Chapter 12. You can interpolate numbers between lines if necessary.

What good is the D/L Ratio? A glance at Figure 4-10 explains.

Sailboats with high D/L ratios tend to heel less under heavy wind conditions for a given sail area, assuming a well-designed hull with relatively firm rather than slack bilges. That can give comfort and a feeling of security in adverse sea conditions. But a high D/L ratio means relatively high inertia, which reduces acceleration and deceleration. In accordance with Newton's First Law, a stopped boat wants to stay stopped, and a moving boat wants to keep moving. Thus you have to have more patience to coax a heavy boat into or out of a dock, as compared with a light boat. A heavy boat also tends to burn more fuel per mile travelled, compared to a light boat with the same size engine.

Besides the advantage of more comfort at sea, a boat with a big D/L can accommodate more cargo, more people, gear, stores, what have you. That can be a big advantage when you're starting on a long cruise and want to take along lots of food, clothes, and sea-going toys. It can also help if you're crossing an ocean or other body of water without a

FIGURE 4-10
**The implications of the displacement/length ratio for sailboats**

| RANGE OF RATIOS | TYPE OF HULL | PLANING ABILITY | TYPICAL MOTION IN A SEAWAY | TYPICAL ACCELERATION |
|---|---|---|---|---|
| 0–100 | Ultralight | Planes very easily. | Very "corky" and uncomfortable. | Excellent. |
| 100–200 | Light displacement | Planes if sufficient power is applied. | Quick motion. | Very good. |
| 200–300 | Medium displacement | Ordinarily non-planing. | Moderate motion. | Average. |
| 300–400 | Heavy displacement | Non-planing. | Typically slow and comfortable motion. | Fair. |
| Over 400 | Very heavy displacement | Non-planing. | Typically very slow and very comfortable. | Slow. |

chance to refuel or take on water. You can have bigger tanks, and thus be self-sufficient for longer periods of time.

The cost of a boat tends to vary more or less in direct proportion to her weight (all other things being equal), and therefore boats with higher D/L ratios tend to cost more (and be priced higher) than their lighter weight sisters.

A relatively low D/L, of course, gives opposite characteristics: relatively tender (i.e. tippy) hulls, lots of bouncing around in a seaway, exciting acceleration (and, in a sailboat race, heart-stopping deceleration), less load-carrying capacity and relatively lower cost.

## Other questions to be answered

There are other questions that may pop up. For example, do you prefer wood, steel, aluminum, or ferrocement to fiberglass? Some may prefer these other materials, even though most boats today are made of "glass," there is greater demand for glass than for other materials, and the resale market for glass boats is therefore by far the most liquid. Follow your heart if you can, but don't ignore your pocketbook while doing so.

Used wood, steel, aluminum or ferrocement boats are sometimes (but not always) priced lower than glass boats of similar size and type. An owner may feel (often with justification) that he's forced to ask a lower price in order to develop interest from prospects in a thin marketplace. In the era of strong, easy-to-care-for, no-rot, no-rust fiberglass, a lower interest in alternative materials is understandable. Let's take a closer look at each type.

*Wood.*  Many folks fear wood as a boatbuilding material. Some don't have the appreciable skills needed to properly maintain a wooden vessel and have no interest in learning. For some, it's the horror stories they've heard: rot in the keelson or the stem, electrolyzed plank fastenings, rusted keelbolts or fungus-ridden canvas, all requiring months or years of restoration time, vast surgery, and vast funds to match. (Such stories are sometimes true, but are rarer than many people assume.) For some, it's the rumor they've heard that insurance is impossible to obtain. (It's not; see Chapter 14.)

Whatever the reason, a large group of boat buyers won't consider wood, and that makes the market thin. The result is that a wooden boat is blessed and cursed at the same time. Blessed because a well-found wooden boat has a special aesthetic quality all her own that makes her a pleasure to use and to look at; she's often sturdier and easier-riding than her fiberglass or metal counterparts; and she tends to be quieter and more comfortable below because of wood's natural insulating qualities.

But there are special risks attending wooden boats that are not present with the less noble but eminently practical fiberglass, and therein lies her curse. A wooden boat owner must inspect and maintain with an intensity not needed with a fiberglass boat. If he doesn't, the rumored horror stories may come true. Conclusion: unless you're wealthy enough not to have to worry about extensive yard bills, or unless you're a do-it-yourselfer with the time, the energy, and/or the money to spend fixing up and maintaining, I'd shy away from wood.

*Aluminum and steel.* The plus side is that aluminum usually stands up well in fresh water, as does steel if diligently protected with modern zinc-rich epoxy coatings and inspected thoroughly and often. The minus side is that even a hairline scratch through the "corrosion barrier" (surface coating) to the bare metal can start dangerous corrosion in steel, and under some circumstances in aluminum, too. I'd worry about both steel and aluminum in salt water, unless you're willing to commit to a maintenance program that calls for frequent and regular effort, considerably in excess of what a fiberglass hull demands.

*Ferrocement.* Ferrocement had its day in the 1970s, but developed a reputation for problems. There may be a few good ferrocement boats around, but you'd probably have trouble finding a surveyor competent to inspect them. And the market is very thin; you'd almost certainly have trouble selling a ferrocement boat — at any price. I'd avoid the material.

In summary: unless you have some special reason to do otherwise, stick with fiberglass.

Another question you may want to address now is how much of the maintenance and repair work on your new boat you plan to do yourself (and have the skills to do), and how much you're willing (or forced) to pay others to do. Your answer will have a bearing on whether or not you'll be better off limiting your choice to especially easy-to-care-for craft. Generally, the less wood and the more glass, the easier the maintenance. That's true down below as well as on deck. But an all-glass, no-wood boat is spurned by some as a "Clorox bottle" or a "floating bathroom" — too antiseptic.

Still another question is where you'll keep the boat, both in and out of the water. You'll see in Chapter 11 that, unless she's in your own backyard, garage, or closet, storing your boat out of the water can be quite expensive. On the water, it can cost even more. And if you live a fair distance from the shore, you'll find it costly not only in storage fees, but also in terms of your personal time spent driving to and from the dock. Nevertheless, if you love boats enough, you'll either accept the long trek, or do what my wife and I finally did: buy a house in a coastal town, and then buy a boat.

## Summary

Before you buy, one of the most important steps is to do enough research and soul-searching to develop a good idea of what type of boat you want to buy. Then you can narrow the field down to a half dozen or fewer brands and models that you think would fit all your needs.

Presumably these few will be very similar in size and general type. You may even narrow down to a single choice. If so, it'll help make the rest of the buying process a lot easier, since your search in that case will involve making fewer inquiries, answering fewer ads, and so on.

In any case, you should now be ready to take your completed worksheet in hand, and begin seriously shopping for your dreamboat.

# CHAPTER 5

# Rule Two: Comb the Market Thoroughly

This can be one of the most enjoyable — and occasionally one of the most frustrating — aspects of your involvement in the world of boating. Hunting for the right boat is your excuse to roam the boatyards and to "talk boats" with others who love to do so. You've got money jingling in your pocket (or potentially available at the bank) and the world of sellers awaits you with open arms. It's a great feeling.

To comb the market thoroughly without making it a career, your best bet is to get organized for the task. Here are some suggested actions you can take.

*Set a schedule.* Give yourself enough time to do a proper job of finding the right boat for your needs and pocketbook. If possible, start at least six months before, and preferably a year before you want to sign the papers for your new boat (see Figure 5-1). That'll give you enough time to decide exactly what you want and to check out what's available. It'll also give you time to spread the word to friends, selected brokers, dealers and manufacturers that you're in a buying mode. You won't have to work so hard once the word has spread; other people will come to you with leads, some good, some not so good, but all a result of your having spread the word to your network of associates.

A year may sound like a long time to find your dreamboat, but when time is on your side, you're likely to get the best deal.

*Start a notebook.* List all candidates for purchase. Devote a full page to each boat, noting everything about her: when and where she

FIGURE 5-1
**Suggested schedule for
buying your boat.**

| APPROXIMATE POINT IN TIME (VARIES SOMEWHAT DEPENDING ON LOCATION) | TIMING RELATIVE TO BOATING SEASON | ACTIVITY OR EVENT |
| --- | --- | --- |
| First month | Start-of-season seller's market begins. | Start your search: spread the word, begin regularly calling brokers, combing ads, visiting boatyards. |
| Second month | | |
| Third month | | Keep looking, but don't buy yet. |
| Fourth month | | Keep looking, still don't buy. |
| Fifth month | In-season buyer's market begins; seller's market ends. | Inspect and test a variety of boats. Visit many dealers and brokers. Write to manufacturers. Attend at least two large boat shows. |
| Sixth month | | |
| Seventh month | | Narrow your choice to two or three boats and begin negotiating with sellers. |
| Eighth month | End-of-season seller's market begins; buyer's market ends. | Keep looking too—maybe you missed a better choice. |
| Ninth month | | |
| | Off-season buyer's market begins; seller's market ends. | |
| Tenth month | | Keep negotiating. |
| Eleventh month | | Finish negotiating and sign on the dotted line. |
| Twelfth month | | |

Note: This schedule assumes you don't have a boat to sell or trade in on a new one. If you do own a boat, you should aim to complete selling it before the sixth month.

first came to your attention, what you liked or didn't like about her, how to get in touch with the broker or owner, etc.

*Begin combing ads for used boats.* Check newspaper and magazine ads in everything from your local "bargain news" tabloids (generally for small, low-priced boats) to *Yachting* magazine (generally confined to big, expensive boats). Appendix 2 includes a list of national, regional and even international publications for you to start with.

In addition to commercial publications, check bulletin boards at yacht clubs, marine stores and marinas, and class association newsletters.

# THE SEVEN BASIC RULES OF THE BOAT BUYING GAME

If you're new to the boat-ad scanning game, you may need a program to understand all the abbreviations. Figure 5-2 tells you what they mean.

*Make lists.* Keep track of places you want to visit, people you want to call, write or visit to enlist their aid in your search, bulletin boards where you want to post "wanted" signs. Keep the list in the front of your notebook, and refer to it often.

*Check with brokers.* When people sell their boats, some use yacht brokers, others don't. But you won't have a full grasp of what's out there if you don't contact at least a few brokers.

Yacht brokers are middlemen who spend their days and sometimes their nights trying to bring buyers and sellers together. Compensation for their efforts almost always comes exclusively from the seller as a commission on the sale — usually 10% of the sale price. There are something like 5,000 full-time yacht brokers in the U.S., so if you're anywhere near water, it shouldn't be too hard to find a few to talk to.

Every yacht broker has three main selling features which may serve to distinguish him from his competitors. These are: (1) his particular collection of listings of boats for sale, which may be specialized or a hodge-podge, sail or power or both, mostly big or mostly small; (2) his following of repeat clients, often on both the buying and the selling side; and (3) his personal skill at matching a buyer's dreams against the boats he has listed or thinks may be available (i.e., a boat that's not yet listed but might be if a hot prospect were to be found). Hence, a good broker spends a fair amount of time pursuing new leads — leads on boats for sale, and leads on people looking to buy. His stock in trade is his listings.

A listing is generally one of three types. An *open listing* is placed by the owner with many brokers, and the owner also retains the right to sell the boat himself if he can, with no compensation to any broker if he does.

An *exclusive listing* (not a very common arrangement in these days of computerized multiple-listing techniques) gives a single broker the selling rights. This generally limits exposure in the marketplace, though the listing broker is supposed to be extra-aggressive if he has an exclusive. The exclusive rights may be of limited duration, so if time drags on and the boat remains unsold, the owner may switch to a different broker or listing arrangement. One drawback of the exclusive arrangement is that the broker customarily receives a commission — usually the full amount — even if the owner sells the boat privately.

A *central listing* usually splits the commission, 3% of the sale price going to the listing broker and 7% to the selling broker (though the split may vary somewhat depending on the relative effort contributed by each party to making the sale). If the owner sells the boat privately while there is a central listing on her, a commission usually

FIGURE 5-2
**How to read boat ad abbreviations.**

### POWERBOAT TYPES

AC = aft cabin
C/C or CC = center console
COMBI = combination (e.g., cruiser and sportfisherman combined)
CONV = convertible
CR = cruiser
DC = double cabin
EX = express
FB = flying bridge
FD = flush deck
MY = motor yacht
OC = ocean cruiser
PH = pilot house
SED = sedan
SF = sport fisherman
SKI = ski boat
TR = trawler
T-TOP = fixed sunshade over a center console
TTWR = tuna tower

### SAILBOAT TYPES

BR = brigantine
CB = centerboarder
CTR = cutter
GF = gaff rigged
KL = keel
KTCH = ketch rigged
SL = sloop rigged
YWL = yawl rigged

### TYPE OF CONSTRUCTION

AL = aluminum
CE = ferrocement
FB = fiberglass
STL = steel
WD = wood

### TYPE OF POWER

AT 4 = Universal Atomic-4 brand engine
CAT = Caterpillar brand engine
CHRYS = Chrysler brand engine
CMDR = Commander brand engine
CRSDR = Crusader brand engine
CMNS = Cummins brand engine
DD = Detroit Diesel brand engine
DSL = diesel
ENG = engine
IB = inboard
I/O = inboard/outboard
MERC = Mercury brand engine
OMC = Outboard Marine Corp. brand engine (makers of OMC, Evinrude, and Johnson engines)
T-340 = twin engines of 340 h.p. each
NANNI = Nannidiesel brand engine

### MISCELLANEOUS WORDS

AC = air conditioning
COND = condition
DEMO = demonstration model
DF or DS = depth finder or depth sounder (they're the same)
EQPD = equipped
GEN = auxiliary electric power generator
140% GEN = 140% genoa jib
HCPW = hot and cold pressure water
KM = knot meter

M&J = mainsail and jib
MJGS = main, jib, genoa, and spinnaker
PROF MAINT = professionally maintained
SL or SLPS = sleeps
SPEEDO = speedometer
SPIN = spinnaker
ST = self tailing (winches)
VHF = very high frequency two-way radio
WS = wind speed instrument
WD = wind direction instrument

Note: see Chapter 19 for more ad talk defined

is still due, with the amount depending on the details of the listing agreement. Usually the seller pays the 3% the listing broker is entitled to. But note: The seller may be able to save even that 3% by giving the listing broker 30 days' written notice. More on this in Chapter 13.

Since yacht brokers ordinarily receive a commission based on the selling price of the boat, they'll make more money if they deal exclusively in relatively new, large — and therefore expensive — boats than if they attempt to serve the entire boat market. After all, 10% of $100,000 is $10,000; 10% of $10,000 is only $1,000. So it's only natural that many brokers won't touch boats costing less than $20,000 or $25,000, or boats older than 15 years or so. Not only is the commission lower, but the buyers and sellers involved in small transactions tend to be less sophisticated and need more hand-holding, and older boats are often a hassle, what with surveyors likely to come up with long lists of problems that need correction or that must be negotiated in price adjustment, and insurance and financing that may be hard to find. It doesn't take long for many brokers to decide they have better things to do with their time than deal in older, smaller, less expensive boats.

Still, some brokers will handle smaller or older boats, banking on the idea that if they do a good job for someone with $10,000 to spend this time around, they might get another chance to do business with the same client a few years down the road, when higher stakes might be involved. It may be difficult to find brokers willing to handle small boats as well as large, but they're out there, and some will work hard for you.

Where do you find the right broker to work with? The big-boat brokers (handling craft over 25 or 30 feet) usually advertise in the national yachting press, and that's the most convenient place to look when developing your initial broker list if you're in the market for a larger boat.

Boat brokers who handle mostly "small" boats (under 25 or 30 feet) usually can't afford to place big-bucks display ads in the national boating press, but you may find their ads in back-of-the-book classified sections, or in the specialized magazine *Boat Journal*, or in *Soundings*. Besides these sources, you're most likely to find small-boat brokers listed in the Yellow Pages of your telephone book, or in regional boating publications such as *Eastern Boating* or *New England Offshore* in the Northeast, or *Latitude 38* or *48° North* on the West Coast. See Appendix 2 for a more extensive list of regional publications.

You'll have to visit brokers, or at least talk to them on the telephone, to determine whether they're right for your needs. Here are some questions you'll want to ask the brokers during your initial screening:

- **Does he have a lower limit on price, below which he's not interested?** If so, be sure his limit is a minimum of 20% or 30% below what you expect your dream boat to cost.

- **Does he specialize in the type of boat you're looking for?** He should have a number of listings for boats you might be interested in — a dozen or so listings would not be too many — and should have sold at least one or two during the last month, or have a good reason not to have done so.
- **Is he well informed?** Obviously, it would be awkward to ask him this question directly, but you can try to gauge how much he knows about the subject he's hired to help you with. Think of a relatively difficult technical question, and ask it of several brokers. You don't have to know the right answer — hopefully you'll learn it by talking to the brokers in your screening process, and learn something about the competence of the brokers at the same time. For example, if you're after a small powerboat, you could ask about the advantages and disadvantages of a flat bottom vs. a V-bottom at the stern. At a recent boat show, I asked several brokers this question. One said, "A flat bottom aft will give you lower gas mileage and be harder to get up on a plane, but will provide a more comfortable ride in rough water." Two other brokers responded with an exactly opposite answer: a flat bottom aft provides better gas mileage and is easier to get onto a plane, but is less comfortable in rough water. Which is the right answer? You can guess. After all, it's two against one.
- **Can you trust him?** Again, you can't ask this question directly and expect to get an answer that means anything. But you can get a feel for it by visiting his office and chatting. Start with small talk; ask about what boats he's sold recently and what he liked and didn't like about them. Draw him out; then you can at least judge if you like him, and if you like him, you'll probably trust him.

  Then ask about his procedures. If you give him a deposit, will he put it into an escrow account? What bank does he use? Would he mind giving you some references to call? (Ask for references from a couple of clients and from a couple of other brokers who know him. If you decide you want to use him and there is any doubt in your mind about him, call the references and call his bank as well.) How long has he been in business? Are things going well now? Is being a broker fun for him?

  While you're chatting, look around his office. Is the phone ringing? If it's not, maybe business is bad (or, on the other hand, it may be just a lull while you're there, or a receptionist elsewhere in the building is answering it, or an answering machine is taking the calls). If the phone *is* ringing, is somebody answering it? (If you send him a $1,000 deposit and call to see if he got it, will somebody answer?)
- **Will he photocopy any of his listings that you might find attractive, and give or send them to you?** His answer will be

one indicator of whether he's willing to spend the necessary time and effort to help you. To a broker, time is money, so don't be surprised if he resists giving you full cooperation and the attention you think you deserve. If he resists, just cross him off your list and look elsewhere. If he promises to send you material, check up on his follow-through. If he fails to send a simple brokerage listing, how can you expect him to handle more complicated things, like helping you find a good boat?

In summary, a good broker can show you listings and detailed descriptions for hundreds and sometimes thousands of boats (some of which you might otherwise never discover in your search), can steer you toward the best boat to suit your needs, can help in negotiation, can ease your paperwork burden and find sources of financing and insurance, and can generally save you time.

On the other hand, if you buy privately you may (or may not) save around 10% of the boat's price as a reward for spending the extra time to hunt on your own. You'll never really know exactly how much you'd have saved, if anything, if you buy the do-it-yourself way, since the broker's commission is presumably built into the final selling price — and the final price may have ended up lower — or, conceivably, higher — than if a broker were negotiating on your behalf.

***Visit dealers.*** Dealers are agents for manufacturers of specific boats. Often, they are used boat brokers as well. Some dealers accept trade-ins, which they then fix up and sell, with procedures very much like auto dealers. They can be a good source of reasonably priced used boats, since they usually don't like to carry a big inventory of used boats; after all, their main business is selling new boats.

***Write to manufacturers.*** This will expand your knowledge of any boats you might be interested in for which you can't find a conveniently located dealer. Express an interest in learning more about their offerings. Do this even if you think you want to buy a used boat. Why? There are several reasons. For one thing, a manufacturer will probably try to convince you to buy new rather than used, and may give you sufficient incentive to justify accepting his offer. For another, some manufacturers carry inventories of used boats, either recent trade-ins or demo models. They'll want to be sure you're aware of these.

When contacting manufacturers, be sure to mention any boat shows you may be interested in attending. This may result in free or heavily discounted tickets, if the exhibitor thinks you are a serious prospect, and will give the exhibitor a chance to prepare a pitch designed specifically for you.

***Schedule at least one or two boat shows into your plans.*** Boat shows give you a chance to see a broad range of offerings, close up. Boat shows are going on somewhere in the U.S. all year long, but the big ones (Newport, Annapolis, Long Beach) are mostly in September and October (except New York, which is in January and Miami, in February). You might consider combining a vacation with the boat show in Miami in February; the weather there is usually in the seventies and eighties at that time of year, and it's a 20-minute walk from the hotels along Miami Beach. See Figure 5-3 for a sampling of shows.

***Check other sources.*** Boat listing services such as *Admax* and *American Boat Listing Ltd.* maintain computerized lists of boats showing price, size, type, and owner's name. Generally they charge a flat fee for both buyers and sellers. See Appendix 2 for list.

Finance company or bank "repos" (repossessions of vessels on which loans are in default) are a possibility, as are bankruptcy auctions. Call a couple of the larger marine finance companies (see any boating publication or your telephone book Yellow Pages for their ads) and ask them if they'll send you a list of their current repos. If they have none, ask for leads. They may be in a position to steer you in the right direction.

Some brokers advertise repos, presumably being marketed by them on behalf of banks and finance companies. They may or may not be bargains. But sometimes financial institutions are willing to settle for less than a private owner would be. It's worth checking.

If you're an ardent do-it-yourselfer, you may want to search for a damaged but repairable boat and fix her up. Some boats in this category are classified by insurance companies as "constructive total losses" even if they're repairable. That's because the professional labor (at $30 to $50 an hour or more) plus materials to fix them would cost more than the total insured value. The insurer pays off the policyholder and then owns the boat, which he may either scrap or sell as is if he can find a buyer. Call your favorite insurance agent to get the names and numbers of nearby claims adjusters. Contact the adjusters to see what's available. If nothing is available at the moment, describe the type of boat you're after and get the adjuster to call you when something comes in.

***Map out your territory.*** Make your exploration area as large as possible. For very big boats, 60 feet and up, it's not uncommon for a potential buyer to search worldwide, since doing so will increase the number of possible choices by leaps and bounds, and the cost of seeing boats in the Caribbean and even in Europe or the Far East is minuscule compared with the ultimate capital cost of the boat itself.

Even for smaller boats, it may pay to shop offshore. Would-be long distance voyagers often begin a round-the-world cruise and change their minds along the way. When they do, they often need cash and are ready to sell cheap to attract quick bidders. Popular yachting cen-

FIGURE 5-3
**Boat shows are an all-
year-round institution.**

| NAME OF SHOW | LOCATION | APPROXIMATE DATE | TYPE OF SHOW |
|---|---|---|---|
| International Boat Show | San Francisco CA | Early January | All types |
| Southern California Boat Show | Los Angeles CA | Early January | All types |
| Anaheim Boat Show | Anaheim CA | Early January | All types |
| Seattle Boat Show | Seattle WA | Early January | All types |
| Houston Intnl. Boat, Sport, & Travel Show | Houston TX | Early January | All types |
| London Intnl. Boat Show | London, England | Early January | All types |
| Worcester Boat Show | Worcester MA | Mid January | All types |
| Nashville Boat & Sports Show | Nashville TN | Mid January | All types |
| Chesapeake Bay Boat Show | Baltimore MD | Mid January | All types |
| Cape Cod Boat Show | Hyannis MA | Mid January | All types |
| New York Natl. Boat Show | New York NY | Mid January | All types |
| Toronto Intnl. Boat Show | Toronto Ontario, Canada | Mid January | All types |
| Paris International Boat Show | Paris, France | Mid January | All types |
| San Francisco Boat & Sport Show | San Francisco CA | Mid January | All types |
| Oklahoma City Boat Show | Oklahoma City OK | Late January | All types |
| Mid-America Boat Show | Cleveland OH | Late January | All types |
| Birmingham Sport & Boat Show | Birmingham AL | Late January | All types |
| Westchester Boat Show | White Plains NY | Late January | All types |
| Rhode Island Boat Show | Providence RI | Late January | All types |
| Fort Worth Boat Show | Fort Worth TX | Late January | All types |
| Austin Boat, Sport, and Motorcycle Show | Austin TX | Late January | All types |
| Connecticut Marine Trades Assoc Boat Show | Hartford CT | Late January | All types |
| Intnl. Boat Show | Dusseldorf, West Germany | Late January | All types |
| The Boat Show | Minneapolis MN | Late January | All types |
| Seattle Intnl. Boat Show | Seattle WA | Late January | All types |
| Dallas Boat Show | Dallas TX | Early February | All types |
| Atlanta Boat Show | Atlanta GA | Early February | All types |
| Mid Atlantic Boat Show | Charlotte NC | Early February | All types |
| Washington DC Boat Show | Washington DC | Early February | All types |
| Philadelphia Boat Show | Philadelphia PA | Early February | All types |
| Boston Powerboat Show | Boston MA | Early February | Power only |
| Chicago Boat, Sports & RV Show | Chicago IL | Early February | All types |
| Copenhagen Intnl. Boat Show | Copenhagen, Denmark | Early February | All types |
| Barcelona Intnl. Boat Show | Barcelona, Spain | Early February | All types |

*continued*

FIGURE 5-3
*continued*

| NAME OF SHOW | LOCATION | APPROXIMATE DATE | TYPE OF SHOW |
|---|---|---|---|
| Helsinki Intnl. Boat Show | Helsinki, Finland | Mid February | All types |
| Jersey Coast Boat Show | Asbury Park NJ | Mid February | All types |
| Detroit Boat & Fishing Show | Detroit MI | Mid February | All types |
| Miami Intnl. Boat Show | Miami FL | Mid February | All types |
| Long Island Boat Show | Uniondale NY | Mid February | All types |
| New Orleans Boat Show | New Orleans LA | Late February | All types |
| Salon Nautique | Montreal, Quebec, Canada | Late February | All types |
| Grand Center Boat Show | Grand Rapids MI | Late February | All types |
| Swiss Boat Show | Zurich, Switzerland | Late February | All types |
| Stockholm Intnl. Boat Show | Alvsjo, Sweden | Late February | All types |
| Amsterdam Intnl. Boat Show | Amsterdam, Netherlands | Early March | All types |
| Colorado Sports, Boat & Travel Show | Denver CO | Early March | All types |
| Tacoma Dome Boat Show | Tacoma WA | Early March | All types |
| Augusta Boat Show | Augusta ME | Early March | All types |
| Knoxville Boat Show | Knoxville TN | Early March | All types |
| Utah Boat, Sports, & Travel Show | Salt Lake City, UT | Mid March | All types |
| Fort Worth Sports & Vacation Show | Fort Worth, TX | Mid March | All types |
| Atlantic City Boat Show | Atlantic City, NJ | Mid March | All types |
| Suncoast Boat Show | Sarasota FL | Mid March | All types |
| New Hampshire Boat Show | Manchester NH | Mid March | All types |
| Milwaukee Sentinel Sports, Travel and Boat Show | Milwaukee WI | Late March | All types |
| Boston Boat Show | Boston MA | Late March | All types |
| Maine Boat Show | Portland ME | Late March | All types |
| Palm Beach Boat Show | Palm Beach FL | Late March | All types |
| Northwest Sports Show | Minneapolis MN | Late March | All types |
| Newport Used Boat Show | Newport CA | Late March | All types |
| Newport Sailboat Show | Newport CA | Early April | Sail only |
| Iowa Sports, Boat & Vacation Show | Des Moines IA | Early April | All types |
| Barnegat Bay/Mooring Boat Show | Point Pleasant NJ | Early April | All types |
| Tacoma Dome Boat Show | Tacoma WA | Late April | All types |
| Annapolis Used Boat Show | Annapolis MD | Late April | All types |
| Marina del Rey In-Water Boat Show | Marina del Rey CA | Early May | All types |
| Fort Lauderdale Spring Boat and Sport Show | Fort Lauderdale FL | Early May | All types |
| North American Small Boat Show | Newport RI | Mid May | All types to 30' |

*continued*

# THE SEVEN BASIC RULES OF THE BOAT BUYING GAME

FIGURE 5-3 *continued*

| NAME OF SHOW | LOCATION | APPROXIMATE DATE | TYPE OF SHOW |
|---|---|---|---|
| Chicago International Sailboat Show | Chicago IL | Mid August | Sail only |
| Seattle Boats Afloat Show | Seattle WA | Mid August | All types |
| Boston In-Water Boat Show | Boston MA | Late August | All types |
| Michigan City In-Water Boat Show | Michigan City IN | Late August | All types |
| Wooden Boat Show | Newport RI | Late August | All types of wood |
| Penn's Landing In-Water Boat Show | Philadelphia PA | Early September | All types |
| Port Huron Boat & Fishing Show | Port Huron MI | Early September | All types |
| Norwalk Boat Show | Norwalk CT | Early September | Power only |
| Newport Intnl. Sailboat Show | Newport RI | Mid September | Sail only |
| North Atlantic Sail Show | Stamford CT | Mid September | Sail only |
| North American Sail & Powerboat Show | Sandusky OH | Mid September | All types |
| Down East In-Water Boat Show | Portland ME | Mid September | All types |
| Southampton Intnl. Boat Show | Southampton England | Mid September | All types |
| Southern California Used Boat Show | Newport Beach CA | Mid September | All types |
| Bay Area Boat Show | San Leandro CA | Mid September | All types |
| Harrah's In-Water Boat Show | Atlantic City NJ | Late September | All types |
| Houston Intnl. In-Water Boat Show | Houston TX | Late September | All types |
| Norfolk Intnl. In-Water Boat Show | Norfolk VA | Late September | All types |
| Boat Show USA | Mt. Clemens MI | Late September | All types |
| San Diego Bay Boat Show | Chula Vista CA | Early October | All types |
| U.S. Sailboat Show | Annapolis MD | Early October | Sail only |
| U.S. Powerboat Show | Annapolis MD | Mid October | Power only |
| German Intnl. Boat Show | Hamburg, West Germany | Mid October | All types |
| Southern California Sail & Powerboat Show | Long Beach CA | Late October | All types |
| Miami Dinner Key Boat Show | Miami FL | Late October | All types |
| Fort Lauderdale Intnl Boat Show | Fort Lauderdale FL | Early November | All types |
| Tampa-St. Pete Boat Show | St. Petersburg FL | Early December | All types |
| San Diego Bay Used Boat Show | Chula Vista CA | Mid December | All types |

FIGURE 5-4
**"Repo" ads in *The New York Sunday Times.***

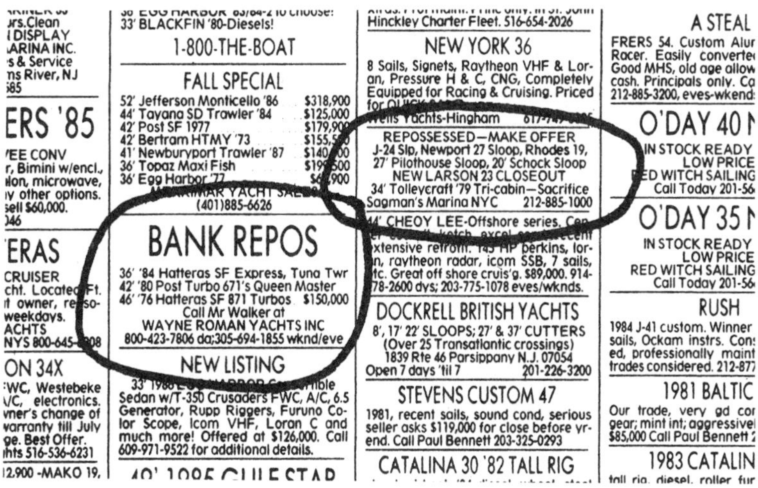
33' BLACKFIN '80-Diesels!
1-800-THE-BOAT

FALL SPECIAL
52' Jefferson Monticello '86 $318,900
44' Tayana SD Trawler '84 $125,000
42' Post SF 1977 $179,9
42' Bertram HTMY '73 $155,
41' Newburyport Trawler '87 $140,
36' Topaz Maxi Fish $19
36' Egg Harbor '77
(401)885-6626

BANK REPOS
36' '84 Hatteras SF Express, Tuna Twr
42' '80 Post Turbo 671's Queen Master
46' '76 Hatteras SF 871 Turbos $150,000
Call Mr Walker at
WAYNE ROMAN YACHTS INC
800-423-7806 da;305-694-1855 wknd/eve

NEW LISTING
Sedan w/T-350 Crusaders FWC, A/C, 6.5 Generator, Rupp Riggers, Furuno Color Scope, Icom VHF, Loran C and much more! Offered at $126,000. Call 609-971-9522 for additional details.

Hinckley Charter Fleet. 516-654-2026

NEW YORK 36
8 Sails, Signets, Raytheon VHF & Loran, Pressure H & C, CNG, Completely Equipped for Racing & Cruising. Priced

REPOSSESSED—MAKE OFFER
J-24 Slp, Newport 27 Sloop, Rhodes 19, 27' Pilothouse Sloop, 20' Schock Sloop
NEW LARSON 23 CLOSEOUT
34' Tolleycraft '79 Tri-cabin—Sacrifice
Sagman's Marina NYC 212-885-1000

CHEOY LEE-Offshore series.
xtensive refit. Perkins, loran, raytheon radar, icom SSB, 7 sails, etc. Great off shore cruis'g. $89,000. 914-78-2600 dys; 203-775-1078 eves/wknds.

DOCKRELL BRITISH YACHTS
8', 17' 22' SLOOPS; 27' & 37' CUTTERS
(Over 25 Transatlantic crossings)
1839 Rte 46 Parsippany N.J. 07054
Open 7 days 'til 7 201-226-3200

STEVENS CUSTOM 47
1981, recent sails, sound cond, serious seller asks $119,000 for close before yr-end. Call Paul Bennett 203-325-0293

CATALINA 30 '82 TALL RIG

A STEAL
FRERS 54. Custom Alu Racer. Easily convert Good MHS, old age allow cash. Principals only. Ca 212-885-3200, eves-wkend

O'DAY 40
IN STOCK READY
LOW PRICE
RED WITCH SAILING
Call Today 201-56

O'DAY 35
IN STOCK READY
LOW PRICE
RED WITCH SAILING
Call Today 201-56

RUSH
1984 J-41 custom. Winner sails, Ockam instrs. Con ed, professionally maint trades considered. 212-87

1981 BALTIC
Our trade, very gd co gear; mint int; aggressive $85,000 Call Paul Bennett

1983 CATALIN

ters in the Caribbean almost always have at least a moderate supply of such vessels.

The Caribbean (Tortola, for example) is also cluttered with worn but still serviceable charter boats. The supply is usually greater than the demand in the islands, and if you're adventurous enough to consider visiting such places to shop for your dreamboat, you may save thousands more than the expense of getting the boat back to wherever you'll be using her — presumably somewhere on the mainland.

***Shopping in different markets.*** The U.S. is divided geographically into two main boat markets — east and west of the Rocky Mountains. Within each of these two large areas, there are regional markets — seven in all, as shown in Figure 5-5. Each market has its own favorite types of boats, its own cult boats and dogs — and its own price structure. Consequently, if you're looking for a brand and model that's popular in your area but relatively expensive, see if there are boats of the same brand and model available in another market area where the same model may not be as popular. You might be surprised by what you find.

***Narrow the field.*** As soon as you can, and preferably one or two months before the end of the boating season in your area, pick the top two to four candidates among the brands and models you're considering for purchase, based on the exercises in the last chapter.

Then investigate these few finalists more intensively, including taking them out on sea trials if at all possible. The boats can be sisterships of the brands and models you're considering, rather than the actual vessel you'll end up buying; the idea is to see how the design performs at sea before the boating season ends and sea-trial opportunities vanish.

FIGURE 5-5
**The seven regional boat markets in the U.S.**

One good way to get the inside story on how a vessel performs is to ask a bunch of owners. Boat owners are often willing to share their opinions with potential new members of the fold, and usually have no reason to pull any punches on either the good or the bad news. Here's where you'll find them:

- **New boat dealers or manufacturers** are usually delighted to put you in touch with owners of boats they've sold; if you use this channel, ask to speak to an owner who's had his boat for at

FIGURE 5-6
***Cruising World's*** **monthly "Another Opinion" column puts boat shoppers in touch with boat owners willing to share their opinions. (Courtesy *Cruising World* magazine)**

## ANOTHER OPINION

For a firsthand opinion on any of the following boats, send a stamped self-addressed envelope to Another Opinion, *Cruising World*, 524 Thames St., Newport, RI 02840, or call (401) 847-1588. We will provide you with the names of owners willing to provide "Another Opinion" or we can add your name to the list of people to be contacted. (This is a *Cruising World* reader-to-reader service and the magazine is in no way connected with or responsible for the opinions provided by the owners.)

**A** A-16, A-21 • Able 20 • Achilles 24, 30 • Aegean Custom 38 • Alacrity 18, 19 • Alajuela 33, 38 • Alberg 22, 29, 30, 34, 35, 37, Sea Sprite 22 • Albin 25, Ballad 30, Cumulus 28, Singoalla 34, Vega 27 • Alden 36, 44, Barnacle, Casey 45, Challenger 38.6, Malabar 42, Priscilla • Allied Luders 33, Mistress 39, Princess 36, Seawind 30, 32, Seawind II, MK II, II 32, XL-42 • Allmand 31, 35 • Aloha 10.4, 28, 32, 34 • Amel 43, 46 • American 8.0, 23, 24, 25, 26, 30 Mariner 8.5, Mini toner • AMF Zuma • Amphibicon 25 • Anastasia 32 • Annapolis 25, 26, 35, 44 • Apollo, Alcort Force 5, Puffer 12'6" • Aquarius 21, 23 • Aries 32 • Atalanta 26 • Atkins Matthew Sailor 25'7" • Avon R 2.8, Redcrest **B** Baba 30, 35, Flying Dutchman 30 • Bahama Work Sloop 40 • Balboa, 8.2, 20, 23, 24, 26, Laguna 24 • Balsa 30 • Banjer 37 • Bayfield 25, 29, 32C, 36, 40 • Bay Hen 21 • Bay Island 30 • Beetlecat • Beneteau 345, First 26, 29, 345 • Block Island 40 • Blue Jay 13 '6" • Blue Nose 24, One Design • Bodega 30 • Bolger Black Skimmer, Otter II • Bombay Clipper 31, Express 26, Pilot • Boston Whaler Harpoon • Brewer 12.8, Sharpie Centennial 34 • Bristol 22, 24, 26, 27, 29, 29.9, 30, 32, 33, 35, 35.5, 40, 41.1, Caravel 22, Channel Cutter, Corinthian, Corsair 24 • Buccaneer 210, 220, 240, 270, 272, 275, 285, 295, 305, Bock 22 • Buchanan Albatross 42, Bonito 35 • Butterfly 12 **C** C&C 24, 25, 26, 27, 29, 30, 33, 34, 35, 38, 40, Competition 24, Corvette 31, Frigate 36, Landfall 38, 43, MK I 35, MK II, 27, 33, 34, 35, 36, 37, Redline 25, Redwing 30 • C&L 36 • Cabo Rico 38 • Cabot 36 • Cal 9.2, 20, 21, 24, 25, 27, 29, 31, 33, 34, 35, 36, 39, 40, 43, 48, 2/24, 2/27, 2/29, 2/30, 2/34, 2/46, 3/34, 3/46, Cal MK III 34, Cal T/227 • Caliber 28, 33 • Camper & Nicholson 345 • Canadian Northern 35, Sailcraft 22 • Cape Carib 33 • Cape Cod Cat Boat 17, Goldeneye 18, Marlin 23 • Cape Dory 14, 22, 22D, 25, 25D, 26, 26D, 27, 270, 28, 30, 36, Typhoon 19 • Cape George 31 • Cape Horn 21 • Capri 14.2, 25 • Carinita 20 • Carter 35 • Cartwright 40 • Cascade 29 • Casey Cutter 30 • Catalac 27, 9M • Catalina 22, 25, 27, 30, 34, 36, 38 • Catfisher 28, 32 • CC Chen 32 • Celestial 48 • Challenger 32, 35 • Chaser Custom 33 • Cheoy Lee 27, 30, 31, 32, 35, 38, 44, Bermuda 30, Clipper 33, 36, 42, Cruiseaire 30, Flyer III, Luders 30, 36, Newell Cadet 27, Offshore 26, 27, 28, 31, 33, 40, 41, Pedrick 41, 47, Rhodes Reliant 42.5, Robb 35 • Cherubini 44, 48 • Chinese Junk 30 • Chris Craft 26, 35, Capri 26, 30, Captain 26, Cherokee 32, Comenche 42, Powmmee 25 • Chrysler 20, 22, 26, Buccaneer 18, Mutineer 15, TMI 22 • Classic 31 • Clipper 26, CM21, CM23, CM26, CM30, Marine 21, 30, 32, MK23 • Columbia 7.6, 8.3, 8.7, 9.6, 10.7, 22, 23, T/23, 24, T/26, 28, 29, 30, 34, 36, 38, 39, 40, 43, 45, 50, 57, Contender 24, Defender 29, MK I 29, MK II 24, 26, 28, 29, 31, 34, Tripp 34, Design 32 • Colvin 35, 42 • Comfort 34 • Commodore 26 • Com-Pac 16, 19, 23, 23 MK II, 27 • Concordia 40 • Contessa 26, 32, 34 • Contest 25, 27, 29, 31, 33, 38, MK I 30 • Controversy 26, 27, • Corbin 39 • Coronado 23, 25, 27, 30, 32, 34, 35, 41, 45 • Corsair F 27 • Cortez 16 • Creala 40 • Crealock 34, 37 • Crescent 16 • Crocker cutter 31 • Crosby Osprey 23 • Cross 40 tri • Cruising 36 • CS 22, 27, 36 • CSY 33, 37B, 44 • CT 35, 38, 41 **D** Dawson 26 • Dehler 34 • Dickerson 35, 36, 41 • Dockrell 17, 22D, 27, 37 • Dolphin SR • Doughdish • Douglas 32 • Douglas & McLeod 22 • Dovekie • Down Easter 32, 38, 45 • Drascombe, Coaster 21, 22, Dabber, Drifter 22, Longboat 22, Lugger, Scaffie • DS 20 • Duet 24 • Dufour 27, 29, 31, 34 Arpege 30 • Durbeck 25, 46 **E** Eagle • Eastward Ho 24, 31 • Edel 540, 665, 820 • Elite 32 • Endeavour 32, 33, 35, 37, 40, 43 • Endurance 45 • Ensenada 20 • EO 36 • Ericson 23, 25, 25 + , 26, 27, 28, 28 + , 29, 31, 32, 35, 36, 39 , Cruising 31, 36, Independence (Liberty) 31 • Essex 26 • Evelyn 26 • Excalibur 26, 30 • Express 30, 35, 37 **F** Fairways Catfisher 28, Fisher 30 • Falmouth Cutter 22 • Fantasia 35 • Farallon 29 • Farr 37, Northstar 727 • Fast 40 • Fatty Knees 8 • FD-12 50 • Ferrocement 36 • Finmar 361 • Finnsailer 35 • Flamingo 21 • Fleur Blue 26 • Flying Dutchman 30 • Formosa 34, 51 • Freedom 25, 32, 33, 39, 40 • Fuji 32, 35, 45 **G** Galion 22 • Gauntlet 20 • Gemini 31 (cat) • Giles 38 • Gladiator 24 • Glen-L 15, 19, 21, 30, CB-21 • Glode 41 • Golden Hind 31 • Golif 21 • Grampian 23, 26, 28, 30, 31, 34, 2-34, Discovery 7.9, Eagle 27 • Grand Banks 32, 36, 42 • Great Dane 28 • Greenwich 24 • Gulf Coast 14, 20 T-4, 21, 23 • Gulf Pilothouse 27 • Gulfstar 37, 40, 41, 47, 36 M/S, 42 M/S, 53 M/S • Gulf Stream 42, 44 • Gulfweed 27 **H** H-28, H-36 • Haida 26 • Hallberg Rassy 31, 35, 49 • Halman Horizon 27 • Hans Christian 33, 36, 38, 43 • Harasty 29, 31 • Hardin 45 • Harpoon 5.2 • Hartley 50 (Tahitian) • Harmony 22 • Hartog 48 • Helms 25, 27, 32 • Helsen 20, 22 • Heritage 20, 38, West Indies 38 • Hermann 22, Catboat 17 • Herreshoff 27, 31, 38, America Cat 18, Eagle 22, Fish Class 21, Rozinante 28 • Hinckley 36, 38, Pilot 35 yawl • Hirondelle 24, HMS 18 • Hobie Cat 14, 16, 18 • Holder 20 • Holiday 30 • Horizon 34 • Hughes 29, 38, 49 • Hullmaster 27 • Hunter 22, 23, 25, 27, 28.5, 30, 31, 33, 34, 36, 37, 40, 54 • Hurley 17, 18, 20, 24, Alacrity 18 • Hylas 44 **I** Interlake 18 • International 210, 600, Daimyo, Folkboat • Iona 23, MK I 30 • Iroquois MK II 30 • Irwin 10/4, 23, 24, 25, 27, 28, 30, 31, 32, 32.5, 33, 34, 35, 37, 38, 46, Citation 30, 34, 37 MK III, 40, MK V 37 • Island Day Sailor 17 • Island Gypsy 36 • Island Packet 27, 31, MK II 26 • Island Trader 37, 38, 40, 41, 45 • Islander 23, 29, 30, 32, 33, 34, 36, 37, 40, Bahama 24, 26, 30, Freeport 36, 41, MK II 30, 32 **J** J 22, 24, 27, 28, 29, 30, 35, 36 • Jason-35 • Jeanneau Fantasia 27, Gin Fizz 37 • Johnson Y Boat **K** Karate 33 • Kaulua catamaran 31 • Keiser Galeforce • Kells 22, 23, 28 • Kelt 7.6M, 8.5M • Kenner Kittiwake 23, Privateer 26, Skipjack 22 • King-Choie 40' ketch • King's Cruiser 28, 29 • King's Legend 41 • Knarr (senior) • Kramer 24 • Krogen 38. **L** L-32 • Lafitte 44 • Lancer 25, 29, 30, 36, 44 • La Paz 25 • Laurin 28 • Lazer • Lazy Jack Schooner 32 • LeComte Fastnet 45, Medalist 33, Northeast 38 • Leigh 30 • Lentsch 29 (Tripp) • Liberty 458 • Lido 14 • Lightning 19 • Lindsey 38, Globemaster 39 • Lion • Lippincott 30 • Little Harbor 38 • Little King 18 • LM 27 • LOA 17 • Lockley Newport 17• Lubec 26 • Lucander 41 • Luders Design 45 • Luger 21, 26, Adventurer 30, Leeward 16, Seabreeze 16, Southwind 21, Tradewinds 26, Voyager 30, Windward 21 **M** MacGregor 21, 22, 25, 35, 36, Venture 21 • Mackinaw 35 • Macwester 26, 28 • McIntosh 47 • Marieholm MS-20, 32 • Marine 36 Ketch • Mariner 28, 31, 32, 40 • Marine Trader Pilot 34 • Mark 23• Marshall Sanderling • Mason 30, 43, Vaughn 48 • Matilda 20, 23 • Matthews Sailer 26 • Maxi 77, 7.7 • Maya 23 • Meadow Lark 37 • Mega 30 • Melges 20C, 28 "E" scow • Menger Catboat 17 • Mercer 44 • Merit 22, 25 • Mermaid 20 • Midship 25 • Mirage 24, 28 • Mistral 33 • Monk 36 • Monsun 31 • Montego 19, 20, 25 • Monteray 24 • Montgomery 7.11, 15, 17, 23 •Moody Robblion 35 • Morgan 22, 24, 27, 28, 30, 32, 33, 34, 36, 38, 40, 41, 45, 46, 382, 416, Classic 30, 330, 41, MK II 30, 37, OI 28, 33, 35, 36, 41, 415, 416, OI MK II 37, One Ton 36 • Morris 36 • Mower Snobird 11.5.5 • Mud Hen • Mull 27 • Murray 33 • Mustang 17 • Mystic 30 (Legnos) **N** Nacra Cat 5 • Nantai 37 • Nantucket Island 33 • Nash 26 • Nassau Dinghy • Nauticat M/S 33, 36 • Nautilus 36 • Newport 17, 20, 23, 27, 28, 40, Blue Crab 14, Holiday 19, II 28, MK II 30, Neptune 16, 24, Nomad 23, • Niagara 30, 31, 36, 42, 43 • Nicholson 31, 32, 345 • Nimble 30 • Nonsuch 26, 30 • Nordic Folkboat, Dinghy • Nordica 16, 20 • Nor'Sea 26, 27 • North American 23, Spirit 23 • Northeast 28 • Northern 25 • Northstar 22, 35, 500, 600, 727 • North Wind 47 • Norwest 33 • Nye 36, 40 **O** Oceanic 30 catamaran • O'Day 19, 20, 22, 23, 25, 27, 28, 30, 32, 33, 34, 37, 192, DSI, DSII 17, Javelin 14, Mariner 2&2, 19.2, Outlaw 26, Pop-Top 23, Tempest 23 • Olson 36, 38 • Olympic Adventure 47, Dolphin MK II 23, MK III 23, Princess 30 • Ontario 28, 32 • Opus 34 • Oxford 400 • Oysterman 23 Skipjack **P** Paceship 20, 26, Acadian 30, Eastwind 25, Mouette 20, Northwind 29, PY-23, Westwind 24 • Pacific Dolphin 24 • Pacific Seacraft 24, 27, 31, Crealock 34, Dana 24, Flicka, Mariah 31, MK II 25, Orion 27 • Palmer Johnson 41 • Panda 38, 40 • Pan Oceanic 38 • Parker-Dawson 26 • Passport 37, 40, 42 • Pearson 10M, 22, 23, 24, 26, 28, 30, 32, 33, 34, 35, 36, 39, 40, 303, 323, 365, 385, 390, 422, 424, 530, Ariel 26, Coaster 29.1, Commander, Electra 22.5, Ensign, Flyer, Invicta 38, Lark 24, Pilothouse 36, Renegade 27, Triton 28, Vanguard 32, 33, Wanderer 30, Weekender 26 • Permacraft 26 • Peterson 33, 43, 44 • Picnic 17 • Pilot Cutter 24 • Pioneer 30 • Piver Lodestar tri 35, Mariner tri 25, Nimble 30, Tri 25 • Pixie (Rabl design) • PJ 43 • Potter 25 • Prindle 16 Cat • Prout Snow Goose 34, 35, 37 • PT22 • Puffin 8 • Puma 23, 26 **Q** Quest 30 • Quoddy Pilot. **R** Rafiki 35, 37 • Ranger 20, 22, 23, 26, 28, 29, 32, 33, 37 • Rascal 14, Spindrift 14.5 • Rasmus 35 • Rawson 30 • Rebel 16 • Reinell 22, 23, 26, 2600 • Rhodes 19, 22, 27, 41, Bounty sloop, II, Centennial 22, Chesapeake 32, Continental 22, Idler 25, Meridian 25, 26, Ranger 29, Reliant 44, Swiftsure 33 • Robb Yawl 38 • Roberts 25, 36, 38, 44, Goodson 53, Mauritius 43, Offshore 33, 44, Spray 33, 36 • Rob Roy 23 • Rosborough Privateer ketch **S** S&S "Cruisailer" 41 • S2 6.7, 6.8, 6.9, 7.0, 7.3, 7.9, 8.0, 8.5, 9.1, 9.2, 11.0 • Sabre 28, 34, 38 • Sadler 34 • Sailbird 18 • Sailmaster 22, 22D, 26 • Sailstar 19, 26, Corinthian 20, Corsair 24, Orion 19 • Samson 36, Seabreeze, Sea Deuce 45, Sea Bird cutter, Sea Lord 53 • San Clemente 23 • Sanderling 18 • Sandpiper 32, 545, 565 • Sanibel 18 • San Juan 21, 23, 26, 28, 34 • Santana 21, 22, 23, 26, 27, 28, 30/30, 35 • Scampi 30 • Scanmar 35 • Sceptre 41 • Schneider Pennant 33 • Schucker 436 (motorsailer) • Seabird 26, Seabird II • Seaclipper 34 • Seafarer 22, 23, 24, 26, 29, 30, 31, 34, 36, 38 • Seamaid 45 • Searunner 31 tri, 37, 40 • Sea Sailor 30 • Sea Snark II • Sea Sprite 23, 27, 28 • Sea Wind 32 MK II • Sea Wings 36 tri • Seawolf 41 • Seidelmann 25, 299, 30, 34 • Shannon 28, 38, 50 • Shark 24 • Shipman 28 • Silhouette MK II • Siren 17, 30 • Sirrocco 15 • Skipper 20, Cuddy 20 • Slipper 17 • Slocum 43 • Snap Dragon 24, 26 • Sol Cat 18 • Soling • Somper Nicholson 35 • South Coast 21, 22, 23, 25.5, 26, 26A • Southerly 28, 115 • Southern Cross 28, 31 • Sovereign 7.0M, 24, 28 • Soverel 28, 30, 30 MK III, 36, 37, 48 • Sparrow 16 • Spencer 35, 44 • Spindrift 22 • Spirit 28, 6.5 • ST 37 • Starett 45 • Starwind 19, 22, 27, 223, Mutineer 15 • Stellar 30 • Stiletto • Stone Horse 23 • Stoutfellow 23 • Sturdee Cat 15 • Sumnercraft 12, 35 • Sunbird 16 • Sundance 20 • Sunfish • Sunstar 18 • Sun Yacht 27 • Swede 41, 55 • Sweden Yacht 36 • Sweet 16 • Swift 33 **T** Tahi Hiana 32 • Tahiti Ketch 30 • Tanzer 7.5, 8.5, 16, 22, 26, 28 • Targa 9.6 • Tartan 10.0, 27, 30, 33, 33R, 34, 37, 41, MK II 27 • Tatoosh 42 • Tayana 37, 42, V42, 52, 55, Surprise 45 • Telstar Tri • Terrapin 24 • Thomas 25'5" • Thunderbird 26 • Ticons T/27, T/30 • Tidewater 39 • TMI T 30 • Trac 14 • Tradewinds Tri 28 • Trailer Tri 680 • Traveller 32 • Tremolino 23 tri • Trintel 28 • Trintella 29, 42 • Trisbal 36 • Tristar Tri 31 • True North 34 • Tylercraft 24, 29 **U** Union 32, 36 • U.S. 25 • US Yacht 22, 25, 27, Eagle **V** Vagabond 42 • Valiant 32, 40, 47 • Vancouver 25, 36, 42 • Vandestadt & McGruer Siren 17, Sirius 21 • Vega 27 • Venture 15, 17, 21, 22, 23, 24, 25, 222, 224, Newport 23 • Victoria 18 • Vindo 30, 40, 50 • Vineyard Vixen 29, 34 • Vivacity 20, 21, 24 • Voyager 26 **W** Watkins 17, 25, 27, 29, 32, 36, 37, MK II 27, XL 23 • Wauquiez Centurion 42 • Wayfarer 16 • Westerly 30, Berwick 31, Centaur 26, Cirruss 22, Classic 25, Jouster, Longbow 31, Nomad 22, Pageant 23, Renown 33, Tiger 25, Windrush 25 • Westsail 32, 42, 43 • West Indies 38 • West Wight Potter 14, 15, 19 • Wharram 27, Tamgarpa 34 • Whitby 42, Alberg Yawl 37, System 30 • Wilderness 21, 30 • Wiley Mockingbird • Willard 8-Ton • Windmill 16 • Windrose 18, 20, 22, 24, 25 • Wings 25, 33 • Wright **Y** Yamaha MK II 33 • Yankee 28, 30, 38, Clipper 41 • Yankee 24 (Seahorse) • Yorktown 33, 39 • Young Sun 35, 43 **Z** Zap 26 • Zeeland • Zelandia.

least a couple of years if possible. If the bloom is going to fade from the rose, it's likely to be faded by then.

- **Annual rendezvous of owners** are a great place to get the real low-down on just how good a particular brand and model is. Both sail and powerboat manufacturers sponsor rendezvous, including Hatteras, Grand Banks, and Donzi among the power-boats and Hinckley, Tartan, and Sabre among the sailing group—plus many others. Some rendezvous are financed wholly by the manufacturers, others defray their costs by charging a tidy sum for a weekend bash with cocktail party, lobster dinner, etc. Since these rendezvous are usually "owners only," it may take some doing to get yourself invited to attend, or you could just plan to stroll along the dock and strike up conversations with owners to get the input you need.
- **Attending a one-design class sailboat regatta** is a great way to find out more about a particular one-design boat — and about the people you'd be racing with if you bought one. Inquire to the class secretaries of the classes you're interested in.
- **Try *Cruising World* magazine's "Another Opinion" service,** which will put you in touch with one or more owners of hundreds of sailboat classes and models. See Figure 5-6.

## Summary

Combing the market thoroughly is a matter of getting organized and being persistent. Set a schedule and live by it. Keep a notebook with lists of candidate boats, places to visit, and people to see or call. Systematically check out a range of brokers, dealers, manufacturers, and others that can help you. Remember, your objective is to eventually narrow the field down to a few finalists. This exercise, if done properly, will not only be entertaining and fun, but will leave you with a feeling of satisfaction that you've left no stone unturned in your quest for the best.

# CHAPTER 6

# Rule Three: Know What You're Buying

Different people can look at the same boat and have totally different reactions. One man's luxurious yacht is another man's garbage scow. Whether you end up loving or hating any specific boat is strictly a matter of your own individual tastes, preferences and desires.

Presumably, you've already defined the general type of boat you think you'd like best, using the techniques described in Chapter 4. And you want that boat to give you value, in terms of her overall size and space, her aesthetics, her performance, her comfort, her safety, reliability and operating ease, her physical condition, and, of course, her economy.

This chapter suggests some important things you can do to assure that you end up fully satisfying your tastes, preferences and desires when you buy.

## Systematize your approach

L. Francis Herreshoff, in his entertaining and informative book, *Sensible Cruising Designs* (International Marine Publishing, 1973), proposed an ingenious rating system for evaluating and comparing cruising sailboats. His system called for awarding a number of "plus points" for nine specific "plus" features and "minus points" for a list of nine "minus" features, for each vessel being considered. The number of points to be awarded for each specific feature is left up to each individual to decide. But by way of illustration, he noted his own preferences as follows:

Award "plus points" as follows:
  1. One point for each foot over 20 feet of waterline length

2. Ten points for each mast
3. Five points for ability to carry a dinghy on deck
4. One point for each berth
5. One point for each sail that can be set
6. Ten points if engine uses diesel fuel instead of gasoline
7. One point for each 50 nautical miles of "fuel cruising radius"
8. One point for each knot of speed under power
9. One point for each knot of speed under sail

Award "minus points" as follows:
1. One point for each $1,000 of initial cost
2. One point for each crewmember required to get underway quickly
3. One point for each foot of draft
4. One point for each foot less than 6 feet of headroom
5. One point for each running rope required
6. One point for each $100 of engine cost
7. One point for each 5 degrees heel angle when aground
8. One point for each cent per mile for fuel
9. One point for each foot of rating (according to a special cruising-boat rating rule)

Herreshoff's system works if you're willing to focus solely on the very narrow range of variables that he suggested produce "good" and "bad" cruising sailboats. Sure, those variables are important. But in today's complicated world, there are many other variables that are just as important. And of course, Herreshoff's system was meant only for cruising sailboats, not for powerboats or other types of watercraft.

## A new system for evaluating boats

A new system is called for, one that's more flexible, that covers all the bases anyone might want to cover in an evaluation of any boat, that can be as detailed or as broad-brush as desired, and that gives useful results, valuable in direct proportion to the amount of effort that goes into compiling the necessary data.

The system I evolved to meet those criteria is called the "Value Index System." It's a way of scoring all the good and bad features, grouped into eight categories, of any boat you inspect, using your own taste and judgment as a basis. The Value Index recognizes each individual boat shopper's relative priorities by asking him to give a score in each of the eight categories after carefully going over the boat, aided by a detailed checklist in the form of a Minisurvey. Figure 6-1 is a score sheet; Figure 6-2, a worksheet, supplies the score sheet data.

This scoresheet for the Value Index gives you a convenient way to compare the features of various boats you are trying to evaluate. Because it systematically combs through all the details that make up the eight categories, you can proceed without fear of becoming hopelessly confused in the process.

FIGURE 6-1
**A completed example of the value index score sheet.**

| FACTOR | BOAT #1 JONES 28 | | | BOAT #2 SMITH 27 | | |
|---|---|---|---|---|---|---|
| | SCORE* × | RELATIVE WEIGHT | = VALUE INDEX | SCORE* × | RELATIVE WEIGHT | = VALUE INDEX |
| 1. Size and dimensional analysis | 9 | 10% | .90 | 8 | 10% | .80 |
| 2. Construction | 4 | 10% | .40 | 7 | 10% | .70 |
| 3. Aesthetics | 7 | 8% | .56 | 6 | 8% | .48 |
| 4. Performance | 6 | 10% | .60 | 10 | 10% | 1.00 |
| 5. Comfort | 9 | 15% | 1.35 | 6 | 15% | .90 |
| 6. Safety, reliability and operating ease | 8 | 12% | .96 | 10 | 12% | 1.20 |
| 7. Physical condition | 9 | 20% | 1.80 | 6 | 20% | 1.20 |
| 8. Economy | 8 | 15% | 1.20 | 7 | 15% | 1.05 |
| Total score | 60 | 100% | 7.77 | 60 | 100% | 7.33 |

\* Note: the score for each of the eight factors is based on a scale of 0 to 10, with 0 being worst and 10 being best. Thus maximum total of the eight scores is 10 × 8 = 80; the minimum is 0 × 8 = 0.

## Do your own minisurvey

The Value Index System gives you a way to narrow down the field of candidates to a single boat. Once you've done that, you can hire a surveyor to check her out, if the $8- to $16-per-foot surveyor's fee is justified by the boat's relative size and condition. But in any case, before deciding whether a particular boat warrants hiring a surveyor, it's advisable to make a preliminary evaluation on your own, of the boats you might buy. The system for doing this is the Minisurvey Worksheet.

When you've narrowed down your search to just a few boats, you can make a comparative evaluation among them using the Minisurvey Worksheet as a guide. After you've had some practice checking over a couple of boats, you'll be able to perceive how one boat is stronger,

# THE SEVEN BASIC RULES OF THE BOAT BUYING GAME

FIGURE 6-2
**The minisurvey
worksheet.**

Name and type of
boat examined _____   Year built _____ New _____ Used __
Hull ident. # _____   Engine serial # _____
Date examined _____ Weather _____ Sea state _____
Person to contact _____   Telephone _____
Current owner name _____   Previous owner name _____
... and phone _____   ... and phone _____
Coast Guard Registration No. _____   Documentation No. _____

## 1. SIZE AND DIMENSIONAL ANALYSIS

LOA _____   Ballast/displacement ratio _____
LOD _____   Sail area/displacement ratio _____
LWL _____   Displacement/length ratio _____
Beam _____   Comfort Ratio _____
No-load displacement _____   Equipped price per pound of no-load
Half load displacement _____      displacement excluding any fixed
Ballast _____      ballast _____
Light displacement ex ballast _____   Ratio of HP/half-load displ _____
Sail area _____   Freeboard forward _____
Engine type, # of cyl, h.p. _____   Freeboard aft _____
Deadrise at transom in degrees _____   Least freeboard _____
Bridge clearance (WL to top of console
   or mast) _____

## 2. CONSTRUCTION

Materials of construction            Quality of construction

Hull _____   Hull _____
Deck _____   Deck _____
Cabintop _____   Cabintop _____
Cabin sides _____   Cabin sides _____
Transom _____   Transom _____
Keel _____   Keel _____
Outside ballast _____   Outside ballast _____
Inside ballast _____   Inside ballast _____
Exterior fittings _____   Exterior fittings _____
Interior fittings _____   Interior fittings _____
Spars _____   Spars _____
Sails _____   Sails _____
Other _____   Other _____

## 3. AESTHETICS

Overall design _____   Overall finish _____
Workmanship—on deck _____   Decorative touches _____
Workmanship—interior _____   Colors _____
Topside fairness/smoothness _____   Underwater fairness/smoothness _____
Ratio of wood/FG in finish _____   Amount of varnished wood _____

*continued*

76

FIGURE 6-2 *continued*

---

AESTHETICS *contiued*

FG finish inside lockers _____     FG finish under cabin sole _____
Fit of joints & seams _____     Fit of drawers & locker doors _____

---

## 4. PERFORMANCE

(For sailboats)                             (For powerboats)
Helm balance _____             Helm balance _____
Directional stability _____      Directional stability _____
Light air performance _____      Cruising range at crsg speed _____
   (upwind in 3–6 knots of air):     Max speed (smooth water)        _____
     working jib              _____ kn.     RPMs at max speed               _____
      genoa (_____%) jib _____ kn.     Fuel consumption at max speed   _____
      close-hauled angle _____     Cruising speed (smooth wtr)     _____
     (reaching/running):                RPMs at crsg speed              _____
     genoa (_____%) jib   _____ kn.     Fuel consumption . . .
      spinnaker (_____)   _____ kn.        at cruising speed          _____
Heavy air performance: _____         at 5 m.p.h.                _____
_____             at 10 m.p.h.               _____
_____             at 15 m.p.h.               _____
Cruising speed under power                     at 20 m.p.h.               _____
   in smooth water _____          at 25 m.p.h.               _____
   in rough water _____          at 30 m.p.h.               _____
Tendency of prop to emerge above               at 35 m.p.h.               _____
   surface in rough water? _____      at 40 m.p.h.               _____
Ratings: PHRF _____  IOR _____                 at 45 m.p.h.               _____
       CCA _____  Other _____            at 50 m.p.h.               _____

---

## 5. COMFORT

(Noise, vibration, temp, dampness)          (Space for living, ventilation)

Engine noise level in cabin _____      Headroom below (main cabin) _____
Engine noise level in cockpit _____     Headroom in head (at toilet) _____
Overall vibration from engine _____     General size of compartments _____
Insulation in hull _____        Height of port lights off sole _____
Signs of mildew _____         Ventilation below _____
Signs of rain/sea leaks _____       Chart table _____  Nav st'n seat _____
   (especially around ports;          Interior natural lighting _____
   fresh water in bilge?)             Interior artifcl lighting _____

(storage space & capacity)

Stg space—overall eval'tion _____       (Comfort in severe conditions)
Space for sails _____
Space for personal gear _____        Ease of going fwd at sea _____
Space for food _____            Tendency to roll at sea _____
Space for life raft _____         Tendency to pitch at sea _____

*continued*

# THE SEVEN BASIC RULES OF THE BOAT BUYING GAME

FIGURE 6-2 *continued*

## COMFORT *continued*

Fresh water capacity (gals.) _____
Fuel capacity (gals.) _____
Number of comfortable berths _____

Tendency to heel at sea _____
Tendency to broach at sea _____
Est. heel angle when aground _____

COMMENTS ON LAYOUT—PARTNER
#1
Things I like: _____

Things I don't like: _____

COMMENTS ON LAYOUT—PARTNER
#2
Things I like: _____

Things I don't like: _____

## 6. SAFETY, RELIABILITY, AND OPERATING EASE

. . . as relates to engine and
  appurtenances:
Engine accessiblity _____
Engine fire protection _____
Type of engine _____
Hrs on eng since o'haul _____
Date of major overhaul _____
Hrs on engine since new _____
Date when engine new _____
Engine clean or dirty _____
Engine FWC or SWC? _____
Engine oil test _____
Engine fuel test _____
Spark plug condition _____
Water pump condition _____
Plumbing (water and fuel hoses
  etc.) _____
Water flow from exhaust _____
Fuel shutoff on intake _____
Fuel filter _____
Engine water filter _____
Fuel tank material _____
Fuel tank placement _____
Fuel shutoff on intake _____
Fuel filter _____
Engine water filter _____
Shaft log condition _____
Propeller condition _____
Smoke in exhaust _____

. . . as relates to equipment:

General fire protection _____
Sea-cocks: type _____ access _____
Lifelines _____ Safety lines _____
Companionway ladder design _____
Swim ladder _____ Freeboard _____
Hull/deck laminate strength _____
Voids in laminate core _____
Bulkhead/hull attachment _____
Chainplate attachment strength _____
Main mast section size _____ × _____
Mast stepped cabin or below? _____
Number of spreaders _____
Shroud size: upper _____ lower _____
Type of reefing equipment _____
Ease of reefing _____
Type foam flotation if any _____
Keel mat'l _____ Keel attchmt _____
Number of toilets _____ Type _____
Holding tank material _____
Pumpout provisions _____ Y-valve __
Plumbing seacock type _____# _____
Electrical system voltages _____
Number × size of batts _____ × _____
Circuit brkers or fuses? _____
Transom strength (outbds) _____
Wiring neatness & type _____
Lightning protection _____

## 7. PHYSICAL CONDITION

Condition—hull (keelbolts, centerboard trunk & pin, centerboard, through-hulls, fair
  surface, hatch action, etc.) _____

*continued*

FIGURE 6-2 *continued*

---

PHYSICAL CONDITION *continued*

Condition—deck _____

Condition—steering gear (gudgeons, pintles, surface of rudder blade, etc.) _____

Condition—interior _____

Condition—sails _____

Condition—rigging (chainplates, turnbuckles, terminal ends of standing rigging, mast
    tangs, halyard sheaves, sail track, roller furling gear, etc.) _____
_____
_____

Condition—equipment (winches, electronics, etc.) _____

---

CONDITION—TRAILER (IF ANY) _____

Trailer type _____ Year _____ Mfr _____ Ident # _____

Capacity per tag _____ Licensed? _____ Bill of Sale okay? _____

Trailer rust check—On tongue _____ On cross beams _____
                   On springs _____ On axles _____

Condition of tires _____ Wheels _____ Bearings _____ Brg Buddies? _____

Hubs exposed to salt water? _____ Frame galvanized _____ . . . or painted _____

Condition of wiring _____ Brakes _____ Other _____

Loaded road clearance _____ Height of vehicle hitch required _____

---

### 8. ECONOMY

| | | Items of equipment included |
|---|---|---|
| Asking price | _____ | (note if personally tested to |
| Est. repair costs | _____ | check good working order): |
| Est. replacement costs | _____ | |
| Delivery costs | _____ | |
| Sales taxes etc. | _____ | ITEM       CONDITION |
| Other initial costs | _____ | |

Total of above     _____

Possible offer     _____

Probable annual operating costs for . . .

Items needing replacement/to add:

| | | |
|---|---|---|
| Dockage | _____ | |
| Maintenance | _____ | ITEM      EST. COST |
| Repairs/rplcmnts | _____ | |
| Insurance | _____ | |
| Taxes/fees | _____ | |
| Other | _____ | |

Total of above     _____

in better condition, better-made, nicer-looking, better-performing, more comfortable, or more economical than another similar boat, perhaps even one of the same brand and model.

To determine certain data for your minisurvey, you should take the boat for sea trials. In fact, you're well advised to insist on a sea trial. Only then will you know how the boat you may buy — this boat, and not her sistership — will perform. She may leak. She may vibrate. She may float lower in the water, due to water being absorbed into her hull over the years. You won't know these things unless you put her in the water and try her out.

When you go out for a spin, take a knowledgeable friend along, if possible, since two sets of eyes are better than one, especially for spotting subtle little things that a prospective buyer, in his excitement, might miss.

If possible, try the boat out in varying conditions: in waves as well as flat water, 5 knots of wind as well as 20 knots. This may be hard to arrange, and will almost certainly require two different days of trials, but is worthwhile if you (and the seller) are willing to spend the time.

Incidentally, only ask for a sea trial if you are genuinely interested in buying the boat. The seller or broker has better things to do than go joy riding with no possibility of a sale.

One final note on sea trials. If the harbor is frozen in when you home in on your dreamboat, as it may be if you're buying in prime buyer's market time (see Chapter 7), you can ask the seller to draft a sales contract that stipulates that purchase is subject to a survey and sea trials. You can offer to put a deposit into an escrow account, subject to full return if any problems show up at the trials. And you may try to see that the wording in the contract makes it clear that you're talking about *any* problems. But you should be prepared to accept some give-and-take on these points between yourself and the seller. Remember, the seller is likely to be reluctant to take his boat off the market simply because you put down a fully-returnable deposit. Such a deposit has no teeth, as the lawyers say; if the deposit is indeed fully returnable, the seller couldn't prevent you from walking away from the deal if, for example, you had found another better boat by the time the ice thawed.

## Some definitions

Most of the items in the minisurvey worksheet are more or less self-explanatory. But a few comments about the various categories listed on it may be helpful.

- **The hull identification number** or HIN (stamped on a tag or molded into the transom of boats built after November 1972) should be a series of 12 code numbers and letters prescribed by the Coast Guard, such as in Figure 6-3, which reads: ZTYSR384A787. Note: for various reasons, not all

FIGURE 6-3

**The vessel identification number on a Sonar: ZTY = Ontario Yachts; SR384 = model and production number; A = January; 7 = 1987; 87 = model year 1987.**

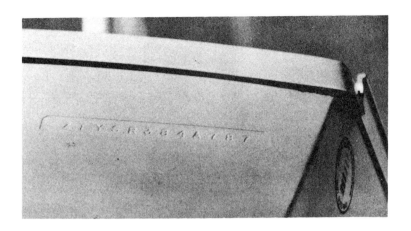

manufacturers follow the prescribed code exactly. If the number you read can't be translated by the following system, call the manufacturer for help. But here's what they normally mean:

ZTY     The first three letters are the code for name of manufacturer, such as BLB (Bayliner), CHL (Cheoy Lee), TSP (Tillotson Pearson), SSU (S2 Yachts), XDC (Zodiac) or ZTY (Ontario Yachts).

SR384    The next five characters (letters or numbers) denote model identification and the production number of the specific boat in the series; "SR384" stands for Sonar 384.

A7      The next two characters indicate the original month and year of Coast Guard certification for this particular model: The ninth character is a letter, A through L, designating the month (January through December); the tenth character is the last digit of the year of certification (e.g., 4 could be either year 1974 or 1984). In the example, the boat was certified in January 1987.

87      The last two characters indicate the last two digits of the model year, which normally (but not always) runs from August 1 through July 31. In the example, the model year runs from January through December.

    You may find this information useful, particularly if the seller claims the boat was built more recently than the HIN says it was. It happens.

- **The engine serial number** on an inboard engine is usually stamped on the block, and may also appear on a tag on top of the transmission or elsewhere. On outboards, the serial number is usually stamped on a plate riveted to the stern bracket. It's a good idea to try to match up the engine serial number with the vessel's official papers. If they don't match, find out why before buying. Who knows, you may find a 1977 engine in what the seller claims is a 1980 boat.
- **Dimensional data** is important for the person who is trying to observe the rule: "know what you're buying."

    Take for example the seemingly simple matter of LOA. The LOA (length overall) might be assumed to be the same as the LOD (length on deck) of the basic hull, from the stemhead (apex of the bow) to the stern rail. Bowsprits, boomkins, outboard rudders, outboard motors, pulpits, anchor brackets, dinghy davits, and other projecting paraphernalia, however, add inches and feet to the LOA measurement. Don't forget this when looking at boats of the "same" length. For example, the Flicka (Figure 6-4), a nice but very expensive small cruising sailboat with an LOD of 20 feet, is commonly listed in brokerage ads with the 24-footers. Sure, her LOA is almost 24 feet by the time you add the bowsprit and outboard rudder. Although she is a 24-footer when you're renting dock space by the foot, for all practical purposes she's a 20-footer. Let the buyer beware.

Sometimes there is confusion about the definition of displacement — the weight of the vessel, afloat at a dock. There are, it seems, different kinds of displacement.   There is the "dry" weight of the boat empty but otherwise ready to use, with no fuel, no water in the water tank, no supplies, and of course, no people. That's sometimes called the light or *no-load condition*, or *no-load displacement*. Then there is the weight with half of the maximum possible load of fuel, water, people etc. aboard, called the *half-load condition* or *half-load displacement*. Finally, there's the fully-loaded *full-load condition* or *full-load displacement*.

The half-load displacement could be hundreds or even thousands of pounds different from the no-load displacement of the same boat. That could be important to you, since knowing both figures for a cruising boat gives you an idea of how much gear the vessel is designed to carry. And on a trailerable boat, the weight can indicate how big a trailer you need. But the factory specifications you see seldom specify at which level the displacement is figured, let alone give both figures. Different designers use different conventions, so you'll have to guess, or call the designer to find out. Your safest guess if only one displacement figure is provided in the specs, is that a quarter, a third, or a half-load figure is the one given for cruising boats with living accommodations, and that the no-load figure is given for dinghies, daysailers, outboard runabouts and other small craft. And usually small outboard

FIGURE 6-4
**One important thing to remember about the 24-foot Flicka is that she is only 20 feet on deck.**

boat manufacturers give the bare hull weight excluding the engine weight, which can be considerable.

- **Engine type, size and horsepower** is important from the standpoint of performance and economy. Usually, a bigger and slower-running engine will last longer in your boat than a smaller high-speed engine of the same horsepower. (For an analogy, think of big truck engines, which often last for the better part of a million miles, versus car engines of similar horsepower, which don't.) Also, naturally, the more powerful the engine, the better performance you'll get in terms of speed. And usually (though not always), the more powerful the engine, the higher the fuel consumption. Not always, because engine fuel consumption and efficiency vary with many factors besides engine size, including load on the engine, engine speed (in r.p.m.), propeller pitch and size, air temperature, and other considerations. This means that to estimate the fuel consumption, you can refer to an engine efficiency curve such as the examples shown in Figure 6-5 — but to know the fuel consumption, you must climb onto the boat, go for a ride, and measure how much fuel is being used at different speeds. That's what the editors at *Boating* magazine do when they test-drive a powerboat. Typical fuel-speed curves from some of these tests are shown in Figure 6-6.

Incidentally, fuel costs for powerboats can be significant, but sailboat fuel costs tend to be negligible for obvious reasons. The 140 h.p. Evinrude on my Aquasport eats up about 8 gallons an hour at 4,500 r.p.m. (at which revs the boat is doing

FIGURE 6-5
**Typical engine fuel consumption curves.**

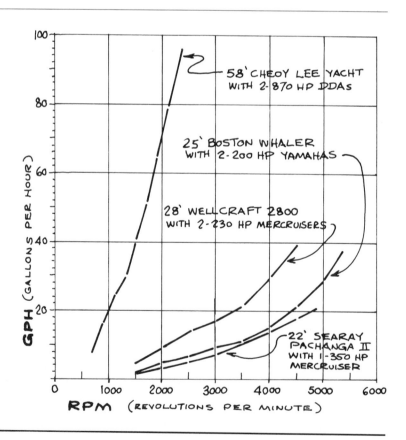

FIGURE 6-6
**Typical powerboat fuel-speed curves.**

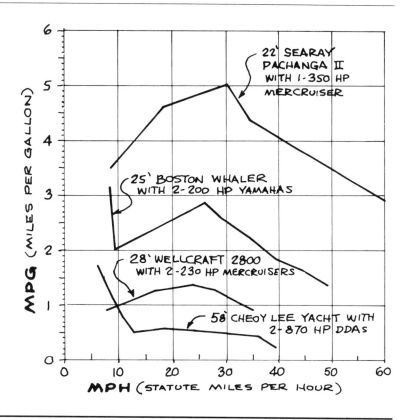

around 24 m.p.h.). That works out to about 3 miles per gallon. On the other hand, last summer I cruised my catboat roughly 500 miles, mostly under sail, and used 10 gallons of gas. That's 50 miles to the gallon.

- **Deadrise** is a term that has a complicated sounding definition but is really not so complicated once you understand it. Technically, it is the rise of the sides of a vessel's bottom above a baseline, measured at the intersection of the bottom with the molded breadth line. In simpler terms, it's the upward slope of a vessel's bottom. It can be measured in degrees as well as inches, and that's how powerboat people usually refer to it. See Figure 6-7, which also defines a few other terms you might not know.

A powerboat with a low deadrise at the transom of only a couple of degrees, like my old Aquasport 22, takes less power to get up on a plane and stay there than a high deadrise deep-V powerboat. The low deadrise also provides more stability when you're leaning over the side to reel in that big one. But in rough water, the ride is likely to be bumpier in the shallow deadrise boat. So you pay your money and take your choice.

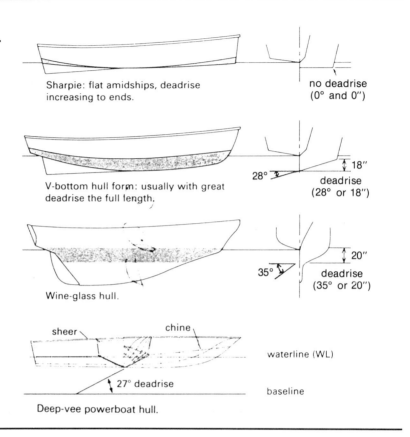

**FIGURE 6-7**
**Hull types and corresponding deadrise. (Deep-V hull drawing courtesy *Nautical Quarterly*)**

Sharpie: flat amidships, deadrise increasing to ends.

no deadrise (0° and 0")

V-bottom hull form: usually with great deadrise the full length.

28°  deadrise (28° or 18")  18"

Wine-glass hull.

35°  deadrise (35° or 20")  20"

sheer    chine

waterline (WL)

27° deadrise    baseline

Deep-vee powerboat hull.

- **The ballast/displacement ratio** (ballast in pounds divided by displacement in pounds) is specified for keel sailboats; the number for "ballast" is usually the weight of the portion of the keel projecting below the hull. That is, any inside trimming ballast located within the hull is excluded from this "ballast" statistic. The B/D ratio can give an idea of the sailboat's stability in heavy winds; the higher the ratio, the stiffer and more stable the boat — all other things being equal — since a weight lower down in the keel will provide more righting moment than the same weight located closer to the waterline.

  But more ballast means less weight-carrying capacity, and too much ballast will make a boat sluggish and slow. Good cruising sailboats may have a B/D ratio of around 30% to 40%. Racing sailboats, with ultralight hulls, decks, and rigging, may be higher, but rarely go beyond 50%.

- **The sail area/displacement ratio** also is a performance indicator. The SA/D ratio measures a boat's sailpower compared to her weight. Boats with high SA/D ratios tend to reach higher hull speeds more easily in light air and are more easily heeled, all other things being equal. Boats with low SA/

D ratios tend to travel more slowly in light air, and heel less in heavy air, again, all other things being equal. SA/D ratios above 21 are considered very high, 18 to 21 are high, 14 to 17 are moderate, and less than 14 are low.

The formula for SA/D is slightly complicated, but if you have a calculator that does exponents or a spreadsheet program on your home computer, you can figure these ratios easily. The formula is:

$$\text{SA/D} = \frac{\text{Sail area in square feet}}{(\text{Sailing displacement in pounds/64})^{0.667}}$$

A few examples are given in Figure 6-8 to illustrate the idea.

One feature of sailboats with high SA/D ratios is that even sizable boats are relatively easy to handle on land. The Laser 28, for example, weighs only 3,950 pounds, so it can be pulled with ease behind a full-size station wagon rated to pull 5,000 pounds, and out of the water using 2-ton or 3-ton electric hoists frequently available at yacht clubs with one-design

FIGURE 6-8
**The sail area/ displacement ratio for a variety of sailboat types.**

| TYPE OF BOAT | OVERALL LENGTH (IN FEET) | SAIL AREA (IN SQ. FT.) | DISPLACEMENT (IN LBS.) | SA/D |
|---|---|---|---|---|
| SA/D under 14 (low): | | | | |
| Flicka | 20'0" | 250 | 5,500 | 12.1 |
| Westsail 32 | 32'0" | 480 | 19,500 | 10.6 |
| SA/D 14–17 (moderate): | | | | |
| Dana 24 | 24'2" | 358 | 8,000 | 14.3 |
| ETAP 23 | 24'2" | 214 | 3,320 | 15.4 |
| Cape Dory 270 | 27'0" | 398 | 9,413 | 15.4 |
| Island Packet 27 | 27'0" | 405 | 8,000 | 17.0 |
| C&C Landfall 39 | 38'9" | 667 | 19,500 | 14.7 |
| Fast Passage 39 | 39'6" | 795 | 21,000 | 16.7 |
| SA/D 17–21 (high): | | | | |
| O'Day 272 | 26'11" | 306 | 4,870 | 17.0 |
| J/34 | 34'0" | 505 | 8,100 | 20.0 |
| Baltic 35 | 34'11" | 568 | 9,877 | 19.7 |
| SA/D over 21 (very high): | | | | |
| Laser 28 | 28'5" | 365 | 3,950 | 23.4 |
| Moore 30 | 30'0" | 465 | 2,000 | 46.9 |
| Diva 39 | 38'9" | 586 | 9,370 | 21.1 |

yet she is big enough to have many of the comforts of a full-size cruising boat.

Incidentally, sail area given on a boatbuilder's spec sheets is usually the area of the mainsail plus "100% foretriangle" (i.e., the "J" measurement, from the base of the mast forward to the jibstay, times the "I" measurement, from the base of the foretriangle to the intersection of jibstay and mast, times one-half). But once in a while, in order to ensure that his boat's statistics compare favorably with the competition, a marketer might claim the sail area is the total of the mainsail plus a big overlapping genoa. *Caveat emptor.*

- **The displacement/length ratio,** as explained in Chapter 4, is generally a reliable indicator of comfort and performance at sea.
- **The Comfort Ratio,** invented by naval architect Ted Brewer, is defined by the formula:

$$\text{Comfort Ratio} = \frac{\text{Displacement in pounds}}{0.65 \times (0.7 \text{ LWL} + 0.3 \text{ LOA}) \times \text{BD}^{1.33}}$$

$$\text{where LOA} = \text{length overall (on deck)}$$

$$\text{LWL} = \text{load waterline length}$$

$$\text{BD} = \text{maximum beam at deck.}$$

Brewer's Comfort Ratio, which he says was conceived "sort of tongue-in-cheek," but which I think (and he agrees) is nevertheless somewhat useful, gives us a measure of how much a particular hull will resist being moved by passing waves. The numerator in this formula is simply the boat's overall weight; the denominator is essentially an approximation of her sailing waterline plane. Values may range from beamy light boats like the J/24 (Comfort Ratio = 12.3) to narrow, heavy craft like the Dana 24 (CR = 31.6) and on up. Smaller boats tend to have lower CRs than larger ones; older boats — especially cruising sailboats — which tend to be heavier and narrower than modern types — have higher CRs.

A heavy boat with lots of inertia and a small waterline plane presenting relatively little surface area for waves to push against will have a high Comfort Ratio. She will move slowly and majestically in a seaway and have an easy motion, a mark of a comfortable cruising boat. But, as Brewer is the first to admit, the Comfort Ratio isn't perfect; a heavy, narrow boat may roll more, and is more likely to be swept by big seas than her lighter, fatter sisters.

A light boat with a big waterline plane will have a low Comfort Ratio. She will jump around in a seaway with a quick, lively motion, and her crew is more likely to have to hold onto something to avoid being slammed around in rough conditions.

Not as comfortable in these conditions as heavier, narrower boats — and thus the Comfort Ratio.

- **Price per pound** of a boat can be misleading if you aren't careful. Some reference guides to buying boats talk about cost per pound of boat as if boats were chopped liver. If you can't define whether the pounds are in terms of no-load displacement or half-load displacement or full-load displacement, and can't say whether or not they include or exclude ballast, the cost per pound becomes almost meaningless. But if you are careful always to define pounds as no-load displacement minus ballast, then a cost comparison between two boats with different ballast/displacement ratios can be somewhat meaningful — though by no means at the top of the list of crucial factors to think about when buying a boat. After all, a high price per pound may be an indicator of high quality and handcrafted elegance, or it may be a sign that you're looking at an inordinately heavy, overpriced tub. Still, if you're comparing two boats of roughly equal size and quality, the one with the lower price per pound may be the better buy. You might try asking the builder of the higher-priced boat why his price per pound is higher, and see if what he says makes sense. I've tried this approach; sometimes what he says makes sense, and sometimes it doesn't.

  Ballast is usually lead poured into a cavity mold; its raw price in recent years has varied between 15 cents and 60 cents a pound, so the lead contributes only a minimal value to the overall price of a typical cruising sailboat. (If ballast is in the form of steel punchings, the contribution is even less). Take, for example, the four boats shown with their stats in Figure 6-9. For these boats, the ballast might contribute only something like $1,000 to $3,000 to the overall prices. So excluding the ballast from the price-per-pound calculation eliminates a significant distortion in the results.

  Note that the Catalina 30's 92 cent per pound advantage over the Hunter ($3.92 versus $4.84) is increased to $1.31 if ballast is excluded. And note that the price of the Tashiba, at $128,000, is 220% higher than the Catalina, while her per-pound price excluding ballast is only 120% higher. The difference is that the Tashiba simply has a lot more wood and fiberglass packed into her, plus a lot more manhours of labor.

- **The ratio of horsepower to displacement** can give an indication of speed under power, particularly between two boats of roughly equal size. The higher the horsepower, the higher the speed. This is true of both displacement-type and planing-type hulls, and for both powerboats and sailboats. Refer to Chapter 4; Figure 4-2 shows the approximate relationships.

- **Aesthetics** are very much a personal matter. Either you like lots of varnished wood, or you don't. The same goes for fiberglass. The level of workmanship, on the other hand, can

FIGURE 6-9
**Price per pound for four
sailboats of similar length.**

| NAME OF BOAT | CATALINA 30 | HUNTER 30 | SABRE 30 | TASHIBA 31 |
|---|---|---|---|---|
| Sailaway price—1990 | $40,000 | $46,000 | $74,800 | $128,000 |
| Length overall | 29'-11" | 30'-1" | 30'-7" | 30'-9" |
| Load waterline length | 25'-0" | 25'-6" | 25'-6" | 25'-5" |
| Displacement (pounds) | 10,200 | 9,500 | 9,500 | 13,790 |
| less ballast (pounds) | 4,200 | 3,800 | 3,800 | 4,877 |
| Weight without ballast | 6,000 | 5,700 | 5,700 | 8,913 |
| Sailaway price per pound of displacement | $3.92 | $4.84 | $7.87 | $9.28 |
| Sailaway price per pound excluding ballast | $6.66 | $8.07 | $13.12 | $14.36 |

be objectively determined. You may not care if the joints and seams in paneling aren't perfect, but at least you'll know whether they are or aren't, by observing and noting what you see in the minisurvey worksheet. And remember, the person you'll later try to sell the boat to may care.

- **Performance** should be observed by you personally. Don't just ask the salesman, "How fast does she go?" and take his word for it. Practically all salesman, even honest ones, exaggerate a boat's estimated top speed.
- **Comfort** is another largely personal matter. If you're tall, you won't want a boat on which you'll be bumping your head on the cabin beams all the time. On the other hand, if you're short, you won't want a boat with a cabin so high that you can't see out the ports. A sailboat's tendency to heel in a breeze makes some people nervous while it thrills others. You need to decide what you like and what you don't like.
- **Safety, reliability and operational ease** can be hard for some buyers to judge. Of course, you can look at the engine nameplate to get its make and model and you can count the number of spreaders, but you may not be up on the different ways a keel can be attached and which are good and bad, or how to check for voids in a fiberglass laminate. Once you home in on your final choice, hiring a surveyor or using the services of a knowledgeable friend (depending on how much you're investing) to help you evaluate these matters might come in handy.
- **Physical condition** is an obviously important factor. But if you're viewing a poorly maintained boat, try to look beneath

the grime and dirt and imagine how she would look if she were cleaned up and polished. Check the topsides with a little cleaner to see if she *can* be polished; some faded topsides can't ever be brought back without painting. If you can clean her up and she's a good boat otherwise, you may have found a real bargain. Most people won't give a dirty boat a second glance, and the owner, in his ignorance, might end up letting her go for a song.

- **Economy** is what this book is all about, so this is really the heart of the worksheet. The objective is to tabulate the total costs of buying her and using her.

To help judge whether the asking price is fair, refer to the sample price array graph in Chapter 12. A price array graph such as Figure 12-13 can be done for any boat brand and model by plotting a series of asking prices obtained from broker listings and classified ads. You'll see that prices generally cluster along a "trend line." If a particular asking price is above this trend line, ask yourself if it is justified or simply overpriced. If a price falls below the trend line, try to think of reasons why it should be. If there are none, you may have found a bargain.

## When should you use a surveyor?

When you think you've picked the right boat for your needs, you can make an offer and put down a deposit, remembering to try to tie strings to it as I've suggested. The strings can be in the form of a suitably-worded sales contract, or a receipt signed by the seller stating that he agrees that your deposit is returnable if survey and inspection don't meet your expectations.

When you've picked a boat and put down a deposit, it's time to decide whether to hire a professional surveyor to make a complete inspection, which will reduce your risk of exposure to hidden problems (hidden, that is, from you but not from an astute pro), or to take a chance on doing your own survey and saving yourself a few hundred bucks.

Deciding whether to use a professional surveyor is like deciding whether to go to a doctor for a checkup. If you get a cold, you usually know you have a cold. Paying a doctor to confirm that fact would be a waste of money. If, however, your cold is accompanied by persistent itching and a mysterious green rash that has spread all over your body, you'd likely be concerned enough not to worry about the expense of a diagnosis; you'd ask a doctor to identify your illness and to tell you how to cure it. Deciding on whether to consult a doctor depends on the seriousness of the problem, and how much you know about curing it.

In the same way, whether or not you decide to use a surveyor to examine the health of your prospective purchase should depend on the boat's size and complexity, her age, her value relative to the cost of a survey and your honest assessment of your own abilities to ferret out and recognize problems (and potential solutions to those problems) without professional assistance. For example, you wouldn't be likely to pay a surveyor $500 (a typical fee) to survey an 8-year-old, 16-foot outboard runabout advertised for $2,000. But you'd almost certainly use a surveyor for a 15-year-old, $100,000 power yacht whose twin 400 h.p. engines have never been replaced. As the accountants say, it's a matter of materiality.

Hiring a pro is good insurance that you are buying exactly what you think you're buying. He'll inspect the hull, power up the motor to look and listen for problems, check the sails, even inspect the trailer if there is one. He'll look at the boat in the water and out. Then he'll give you a written report commenting on the details of her condition, and perhaps estimating how much expense would be involved in correcting any problems.

One advantage in using a surveyor is that if he comes up with some hidden defects that you, as a non-pro, couldn't be expected to find, you'll have a bargaining chip that you can use to lower the already agreed-to price by the cost of necessary repairs. It's not uncommon for a surveyor to find hidden defects (rot in the core of a fiberglass sandwich, for instance, or bad wiring in the ship's electrical circuitry) that would cost hundreds or even thousands of dollars to fix. And the documented judgment of an independent surveyor probably would carry more weight during a price negotiation than would the whining complaints of a prospective buyer.

What about arranging for a survey on a new boat? Again, it's a matter of materiality. Some big-boat buyers like to do this as an added precaution in the buying process; others don't bother. For new boats over 40 feet, particularly custom-built boats, a surveyor may inspect the hull not once but several times during construction. For huge boats there may even be a full-time resident owner's representative at the builder's plant to make sure all goes smoothly; he is, in effect, a surveyor.

Still, for brand-new boats under 40 feet or so, most people don't bother with a surveyor. They simply trust the builder, based on his reputation and the wording of his warranty. That's okay to do — but do check his reputation with knowledgeable friends or brokers not in the business of selling that particular boat. And ask the builder for examples of recent warranty work he's done, with names of references you can call.

For more on surveying and surveyors, see Chapter 13.

## Make a list of what equipment comes with the boat — and inspect every item

The minimum recommended list of equipment — for sailboats and for powerboats — is given in Appendix 6. Remember, it's the minimum recommendation, not everything you might want. If you're look-

ing at a used boat and find she's missing a working compass, life preservers, adequate-size fenders, or anything else on the Appendix 6 lists,
or if some items are there but are not in shape to use, be prepared to
add the purchase price of new ones to your budget if you decide to buy
that boat. Approximate prices are listed for each item in Appendix 6.

## Examine the seller's ownership papers

Be sure the boat (and trailer, if any) is really his to sell. There's
usually no problem if it's a new boat — assuming the manufacturer
or dealer isn't bankrupt and in receivership, or about to go there. If
you suspect a dealer or manufacturer might be on the weak side financially, don't give him any money or sign anything until you have
a chance to check up on him. That's sometimes easier said than done,
but consumers do get burned regularly, so be careful. Consider asking
for references (and checking them) or visiting the manufacturing plant.

If the boat is used and you're buying through a reputable broker,
you don't usually have to worry. After you sign a sales agreement —
which should have some clauses protecting you from losing your deposit — he'll put your deposit money in an escrow account until the
deal is completed and the seller passes title to you. At least he's supposed to put the money in escrow; be sure he does. That's usually a
matter of getting to know the broker well enough so that you feel you
can trust him. If you have doubts, you might check his bank references,
or ask to see the seller's registration or documentation. But if I were
that nervous, rather than insult the poor fellow, I'd find another broker
instead.

If you're buying a used boat from a private party, you can simply
ask to see his state registration papers or his Coast Guard documentation papers. And don't forget the trailer bill of sale and registration
papers. There are thousands of trailers on the highways with illegal or
non-existent registration. If you buy an unregistered used trailer, at
best you'll have a hassle getting it licensed. At worst you'll find out
it's a stolen trailer, and it will be confiscated from you.

## Summary

Buying a boat usually involves a major pile of cash changing
hands. That in itself is reason enough for a buyer to exercise prudence,
caution, and a systematic analysis to determine exactly what he's being
offered. A detailed survey of the boat conducted by the prospective
buyer, possibly with the help of a professional surveyor and/or knowledgeable friends, is the proper first step, once a favorite boat has been
picked from the many vessels available. The question of how the boat
looks, how she performs, how comfortable she is for those who will
be using her, her condition, how safe she is, and other details all should
command the full attention of the prospective buyer. A careful inquiry
on what goes with her, and a check to be sure all the necessary documents are in order, is also part of knowing what you're buying.

# CHAPTER 7

# Rule Four: Time Your Purchase Intelligently

If you were selling your used boat instead of buying it, you'd have a choice of two "windows" each year when you would aggressively try to sell: at the start of the boating season in your area, or at its end. The rest of the year, there are fewer potential buyers in the market, and gearing up to make an aggressive personal selling effort is less worthwhile. You could try to sell off-season, but unless you offered some special incentive — like cutting your price — you'd be less likely to attract many serious buyers.

When you're buying rather than selling, the seasonal concept is important to an understanding of why the numbers of boats being offered — and their prices — rise and fall and rise again as the year progresses.

So, although any time is a good time when it comes to buying a new or used boat, you may want to target your purchase at certain strategically favorable periods.

The selection of available used boats will be greatest when the most sellers are first putting their pride-and-joys up for sale: a month or two before the start, and a month or two before the end, of the season — but that's when asking prices will be highest, too. The last month or two of the season (e.g., October and November in the northeast) is a transition period; prices begin to drop as sellers start worrying that they won't sell before storage time.

To verify that a buyer's choice is greatest at certain seasons, you need only count the column inches of boat classified ads in your favorite newspaper. For example, the *New York Sunday Times* pages expand from ½ page in December to 1½ or 2 pages in January, to a peak of around 3 pages in April. Then the page count gradually tails off to about 2 in August, sweeps back up to 3 in September (local area boat show time), and then drops to 2 in October, 1 in November, and back to ½ page in December.

The pickings are fewer but the bargains are more numerous in the off-season or even in the middle of the on-season. Many of the best boats will have been snapped up shortly after they were offered in "prime time" — at the beginning or near the end of the boating season. Some leftovers will remain, either because they were overpriced and their owners stubbornly refused to reduce prices, or because demand was lower for that particular model and year of boat in that particular condition in that particular geographical area. Whatever the reason, if you start shopping in an off season you'll find fewer boats to choose from, but you'll enjoy a buyer's market for those boats, particularly if you're willing to pick from a new-boat dealer's leftover stock. He's likely to offer price concessions to clear his inventory for next year's models.

## When does the boat buying season begin and end?

The busy seasons for boat buying vary, depending on the geographical location of the big boating population centers — Maine, Massachusetts, the New York metro area, and Annapolis in the Northeast; Tampa/St. Pete and Miami/Fort Lauderdale in the Southeast; Buffalo/Niagara, Cleveland, Chicago, Port Huron, and Green Bay on the Great Lakes; Seattle and Vancouver B.C. in the Northwest; San Francisco, Los Angeles and San Diego in the Southwest, and Houston/Galveston, Gulfport, and New Orleans on the Gulf Coast. The timing of the customary boat buying seasons at any one of these locations is a function of the weather, mainly the average ambient daytime temperatures. Most boats are sold during periods when the temperature in the area is changing rapidly from cold to warm, or back to cold again. (Refer to Chapter 24 for a presentation of boat buying and selling seasons by region.)

## Market characteristics at the beginning of the season

A couple of months before the beginning of a new boating season, buyers are thinking hard about getting outdoors and out on the water for their vacations after a long hard winter (or, in the southeast, after a sweltering summer too hot to go out into). The buyer's psychology is right; pent-up demand explodes; sales are brisk, and inventories decline as dealers sell off boats stocked up in the pre-season. It's a seller's market, and prices are the highest of the year. Sellers are reluctant to bargain; they usually figure they'll test demand at the beginning of the season, and gradually reduce prices later if they have to.

## Market characteristics at the end of the season

As already mentioned, two months before the end of the boating season, prices are relatively high. But as the end approaches, prices tend to move lower, partly because boat dealers want to be sure to sell any inventory left over from the spring, and partly because all sellers want to avoid the nuisance and expense of haulout, off-season storage, and launching next season, to say nothing of having their money tied up in a nonproductive asset. It's usually a buyer's market, and deals can be made. But since the bargain hunters know this, there tend to be a lot of them out looking. That can mean that in a healthy economy, demand can outrun supply, keeping prices relatively high though still generally below start-of-season levels. But in a weak economy, prices at season's end may be extremely attractive to buyers.

## Other timing factors that can affect boat prices

The phase of the boating season affects both supply and demand and therefore prices, but aren't there other factors that affect prices as well? The answer is yes, there are many: the overall business cycle, foreign exchange rates, loan interest rates, stock market prices, the overall inflation rate, the outlook for availability and price of oil and gasoline, the state of the sailboat or powerboat industry, and the production backlog of specific manufacturers, to name a few of the most important ones.

## So what's the bottom line on timing your purchase intelligently?

If your goal is to buy a used boat at the lowest possible price, the absolutely best time to sign the papers making you the new boatowner is approximately 60 to 90 days before the start of the boating season in your area. That timing will allow you to sign up just before your potential competition comes in to start bidding up prices. For example, in the Northeast, where the boat-buying season starts at the beginning of March (60 days before the boating season begins around May 1), you should sign up in January or February.

That means (still using the example of the Northeast) starting a serious search for your boat in the fall (September or October), picking out some likely candidates, and even making offers (if you're serious). You need to make offers that you'll be willing to live with if any of the sellers surprise you and accept on the spot. If the sellers hold out (as they're likely to do if your price is low enough), you'll then keep in touch with them through the early winter, letting the pressure on them build. (Time will be on your side; see Chapter 8 for more on the importance of time to your negotiating strategy.)

By January or February, you will probably be the only buyer the seller is talking to. (A popular theory, shared by many boat brokers, is that nobody buys boats in January or February. That's one reason you see so many brokers at the SORC, or basking in the sun on Caribbean charter boats in those months). The psychology is right; the seller may think he'll never sell his boat if he doesn't do it now. You'll have a good basis for negotiating a final low price, maybe even lower than your original offer (which raises a point: you might justify a lower offer based on the idea that since his boat is a year older, its theoretical market price has been depreciated accordingly).

One problem with this approach is that someone else may come along and "steal" the boat for a slightly higher price than you have offered. Try to stay close enough to the seller to take timely action if competition appears. Again, see Chapter 8 for some suggestions on how to do this.

What if your goal is to buy the best boat, and money isn't so important?

If you want to make your selection from the widest possible choice of boats available, you'll need to sign on the dotted line 30 to 60 days after the boat *buying* season gets underway and about a month before the *actual* boating season begins. (Again, using the Northeast as an example, that would be in the period April 1 to May 1.) In this case, you'll have to forget any thoughts of buying at a bargain price, since you'll have heavy competition during this period from other buyers to whom price is not all that important. Furthermore, you'll have to move fast; good boats get snapped up quickly.

In any case, whether your objective is low price or best range of choices, keep in mind that you'll be most likely to reach your goal if you start many months before you expect to complete your purchase. That way you can become familiar with the market, spread the word that you're in a buying mood, and will be in a position to tune in on any great boat buying opportunities that happen to come along.

## Summary

There are two best windows of opportunity for a seller: at the start of a boating season, and at its end. The timing for start and end varies with geographical area, and is based largely on climatic seasonal temperature shifts.

For a buyer, the timing of his purchase depends on his goals. Two to three months before the local boating season opens is best if low price is the prime objective. If the widest possible choice of boats is paramount, he should wait until the month just before the boating season begins.

# CHAPTER 8

# Rule Five: Be a Strong Negotiator

Many people don't like to bargain. In fact, some of them cringe at the thought. They just don't care to negotiate prices — whether for their next boat or a used life preserver at a nautical tag sale. So what happens? They buy at list price, ending up on the short end of the negotiation every time. That's an example of a "win/lose" deal in negotiator's parlance. The practiced negotiator wins, the reluctant negotiator loses by leaving money on the table.

If you're buying or selling, you have no choice. You are negotiating whether you want to or not, and whether you know it or not. And if one of the parties to the purchase or sale isn't in the mood to negotiate, the party who is in the mood will have a strong advantage.

Consequently, timid, reluctant or inept negotiators are well advised to use the services of a go-between, such as a yacht broker, or perhaps a practiced friend to negotiate on their behalf. Or, alternatively, they can read this chapter and learn how to become comfortable with negotiatory procedure. Once they learn how, they'll wonder why they didn't start earlier.

When a reluctant negotiator who decides he needs a go-between is selling, use of a broker is almost always the best way to go. The broker gets his commission from the seller, and the amount of that commission is directly proportional to the final selling price of the boat. There's no potential conflict of interest, since (presumably) both the seller and the broker want the highest price they can get.

On the other hand, a yacht broker may or may not be the right go-between when it comes to buying. If a buyer who is a reluctant negotiator decides to use a go-between, he should search for a yacht broker who is not only smart, honest, and understands the buyer's true interests and sympathizes with them, but also one who is enlightened enough to value the potential for future client business more than the chance to make a quick incremental buck. There are plenty of such brokers around; no doubt many more than there are self-serving opportunists. Still, it pays to be careful; *caveat emptor*, as they say.

## The thing that makes negotiating worthwhile: money

Deciding not to negotiate is OK if you're buying a Sunday *Times* or a bar of soap. After all, everyone has limits on how much time he is willing to spend to save small amounts of money. But when you're about to spend thousands or tens of thousands of dollars on a boat, it should be obvious that you stand to lose hundreds or possibly thousands of dollars by deciding not to negotiate. For most of us, avoiding the loss of that much money is worth some significant expenditure of energy and time, particularly if we are comfortable — and in some cases even having fun — during the negotiation.

Being comfortable and having fun while negotiating is not difficult to arrange. Here's how.

## Avoid the "win/lose" trap

To be sure you end up negotiating in a win/win environment rather than a win/lose (or even a lose/lose one), follow these five suggestions:

- **Set the stage for joint cooperation to solve your mutual problems.** Convince the other party that you and he are problem-solving together. The seller's basic problem is obtaining fair value for his boat (either in cash, goods or services, or even in psychic benefits, such as when he decides to give his boat away to someone who he judges will "give it a good home"). The buyer's basic problem is to arrange to become the owner of a boat in exchange for something the seller desires to have. Thus the problem isn't necessarily just how much cash changes hands. In fact, the entire transaction could turn out to be cash-free.
- **Focus on identifying real interests, both yours and the other party's.** They may be different than you think.
- **If the interests of the parties diverge, look for ways to bring them together.** A win/win negotiation always satisfies the needs of both parties.
- **Verify all your assumptions.** What you see is not necessarily what you get. What you hear is not necessarily what the other party is trying to tell you. Read the fine print, and delve. Assume nothing; test everything.
- **Use time as a negotiating tool.** You frequently can apply the pressure of time to get the other party to accept your proposal

on your terms. So stay with it until your negotiation is either completed to your satisfaction or abandoned by mutual agreement.

These five principles are useful not just in boat buying, but in any negotiation. They form the basis for potentially huge savings when you buy or sell a boat, a car, or any other "big ticket" item. How do you go about following them? Here are some specific suggestions:

## 1. Make a sincere effort to negotiate cooperatively with the other party

*Try to establish a feeling of mutual trust between you and the other party.* Be sincere, friendly, relaxed; set an example for him to follow. Get him to see you as a human being with needs and desires, wants and vulnerability — not as a mere object to be manipulated like a chess piece. Get the other party to think of you as "his kind of guy" (or girl). In other words, get him to identify with you. How do you do this? Identify with him. Show concern for his needs, hopes and aspirations. Be friendly and reasonable. Cooperate with him, respect him, and he's almost sure to reciprocate. Avoid any indication that you're not his kind of guy; if it shows, it will hurt the negotiation badly, or in extreme cases, may even eliminate the possibility of negotiating.

*Avoid doing anything that will cause the other party to lose face.* Preserve his dignity. No insults, no accusations, no gratuitous or sarcastic remarks. And if you decide you can't say anything good about the other party's boat, don't say anything and don't continue negotiations to buy her. Simply explain that his vessel is just not the right one for you, and seek your dreamboat elsewhere.

*Try to get the commitment of others to your cause.* That means involvement. For example, if you're working with a yacht broker, make sure he gets to know your real needs and wants. Welcome his suggestions. People tend to support that which they help create.

*Show your expertise — but gently.* When people believe that you have more knowledge, skill, or experience than they do, they will accept what you say more readily. Therefore establish your expertise — and whatever other pertinent credentials you may have — early in the negotiation. That's not to say you should fake expertise you lack; it may be challenged, leaving you worse off than if you had remained silent. By the same token, don't pretentiously flaunt your knowledge; express it modestly and naturally, as opportunity allows. Along the same lines, don't hesitate to ask for clarification of remarks made by the other party, relating to his expertise. You're sure to learn something, and knowledge is power.

*Be ethical and true to your own standards of behavior, but deal with the other party based on his ethical frame of reference, not yours.* Don't lie, cheat, put him down or take any cheap shots. Think of what's fair and right from his point of view. If he slips up based on that point of view, let him know that you're on to him. Question him as to whether he thinks what he did was fair and right. Even if he's the worst kind of self-seeking opportunist, he's likely to be shaken up enough to give you an advantage in the rest of the negotiation.

*Don't get too emotionally involved.* Try to think of any negotiation as a game, to be played for fun and profit. Evaluate risks objectively, not emotionally. Stay alert, calm, cool and collected — and maintain a positive frame of mind.

## 2. Focus on identifying the real interests of both parties

First, try to identify the needs, interests and goals of the other party. That may not be easy, because his real needs may be totally different than his apparent or stated needs. For example:

| SELLER'S APPARENT OR STATED NEED | SELLER'S REAL NEED |
|---|---|
| "I paid $50,000 for my boat; I'm asking $40,000, but might take $35,000 under certain conditions." | "I must pay off gambling debts by next Tuesday or else! Therefore I'll accept $10,000 if it's in cash." |
| "I might decide to keep my boat if I can't get my price." | "My wife says if I don't sell the boat right away, she'll file for divorce." |
| "I want $5,000 for my boat." | "I might give my boat away free to someone who will give her a good home." |

Thus every negotiation has two components: (1) the demands and needs of each party that are stated openly, and (2) each party's real demands and needs, which are usually unstated and may or may not be purposely concealed. It behooves both sides to observe and ask questions of each other in order to determine their real needs — and then adjust their negotiating style to suit them.

Some negotiators are able to intuit the other party's spoken and unspoken needs. But if you're like most people, you will benefit by writing down a list of what you think the other side's needs are in order of priority. It'll help you to clarify the proper strategy to use in your negotiation, and you'll stand a better chance of coming out ahead in the end.

Be sure you understand your own priorities. That should be easy after having read the previous chapters, especially Chapter 3, on recognizing your motivations.

## 3. Look for ways to bring together divergent interests

What do you do if the other party's needs or requirements seem unrealistic? You can try using the evidence provided by the marketplace itself to show why your needs or requirements are more realistic than the other party's. For example, suppose you're interested in a boat for which the seller is asking an unrealistically high $30,000. You think the boat is worth no more than $15,000, and maybe less. You might offer him $10,000, and justify the amount by referring to ads for existing boats. For this purpose, save all ads for boats of the type you're seeking, and have them with you when negotiating time comes.

***Be persuasive.*** You may think using logic is the way to negotiate successfully. The truth is, maybe logic will matter, and maybe it won't. By using persuasion in buying (or selling), you can get the other party first to understand what it is you are proposing, and second, to believe that if he agrees to your proposal, he will be rewarded in some desirable way. This reward doesn't necessarily have to be anything he might have told you he wanted when negotiations started. By persuasion, you're trying to realign his interests with yours. To do this, you may need to try to sense what alternative rewards that you can offer will interest him.

***Stay flexible in your thinking — and be creative.*** If you come to an impasse with the other side, look for creative alternatives to circumvent the impasse. For starters, consider using one or more of your bargaining chips. Both you and the seller have as many possibilities for bargaining as your creative minds can dream up. For example, some possible bargaining chips are:

- Agreeing to buy at a boat show special price — while a show is in progress
- Agreeing to buy at a boat show special price — but after the show is over
- Agreeing to buy "as is"
- Agreeing to buy "where is" (e.g., on an "as is, where is" deal)
- Agreeing to provide a trade-in, or agreeing not to trade in
- Paying cash rather than taking a bank loan
- Offering to pay cash in advance, in return for reduced price
- Bartering something you have for something the other party has
- Eliminating certain equipment from the purchase price
- Upping your offer slightly
- Agreeing not to reduce your offer for a specified period of time

- Purchasing direct from the factory rather than through a dealer. This route is not recommended if your dealer has the impression he is operating in an exclusive territory. However, sometimes a dealer with an exclusive territory will be willing to take a smaller portion of the profit on the sale, if you agree to do all the work of getting the boat from the factory to her final home.
- Moving the F.O.B. point — e.g., combining pickup at a distant factory with your vacation
- Taking delivery by land (using over-the-road hauling) vs. by water — or vice versa
- Eliminating or reducing brokerage fees, either by negotiation or by dealing direct with principals — but only, of course, with the knowledge and concurrence of all parties involved. Avoid shady deals and secret alliances.
- Eliminating standard fees such as commissioning, make-ready, etc.
- Negotiating who pays yard storage, launching and spring fixup
- Negotiating after-the-deal seller's perks, such as free use of the boat for a limited period, allowing her occasional use as a demonstration unit, or offering to be a salesman for a boat show or two
- Negotiating after-the-deal buyer's perks, such as use of a slip, mooring, or marina space, discounts on future equipment purchases, etc.

## 4. Verify your assumptions

*If you're a seller, use the authority of the printed word to your advantage. If you're a buyer, be skeptical of all printed words.* Most people tend not to question signs, price tags, documents, and anything else that's in writing and official looking. The printed word often is taken at its face value, no questions asked. If the price says, "On sale, $9,999.99 Firm," most people assume that's what it is. Except you should understand that you may be able to negotiate purchase for $9,500. Or maybe $8,500. Or $7,500.

*Qualify the other party.* If he's a potential seller, find out if he's a serious seller. Ask him, for instance, what he'll do if he doesn't get his asking price. If he says he'll keep the boat, delve some more; look for his real motivation in announcing his boat is for sale. You should be concentrating your attention on boats that are really for sale.

Be aware that the seller may seek to qualify you too. Most sellers see little point in entertaining mere "hull thumpers" (the nautical equivalent of auto tire-kickers, who like to look but have no intention of buying). If you don't believe there are such folks, just imagine how many people spend several days a year at boat shows but never buy boats. Consequently, as a buyer, be prepared to be asked how long you've been looking, what boats you have seen, why they didn't measure up, when you expect to close on your final choice, and so on.

## 5. Use time as a negotiating tool

*Leave yourself plenty of time.*   Try to avoid getting yourself tied down to a deadline. Try to act nonchalant about time; if possible, appear to have no deadline at all, even if you actually do have one. You may be chafing at the bit to buy a particular boat, but control yourself. Let reason rule, not emotion.

*Try to limit the other party's time.*   It's worthwhile to assume that the other party has a deadline, and to attempt to find out what it is. Although the other party may appear to be cool, calm and collected, he may very well be under stress and pressure — and the pressure to settle on terms favorable to you could increase as his deadline approaches.

*Remember that deadlines are usually flexible.*   That's partly because they are almost always self-imposed by the negotiators themselves. Therefore do not blindly adhere to a deadline — especially one you have intentionally or unintentionally imposed on yourself, or that the other party attempts to impose on you. Be patient. Remain calm, but alert. When in doubt about what to do, doing nothing is often the best alternative.

If a deadline appears to be approaching, analyze it to determine if it is real; if it is real, evaluate the risk of extending it; if appropriate, negotiate it.

*Be persistent in your search.*   This point again relates to timing. Many boat buyers are too anxious. They want a boat when they want it, and that's usually right away, that very weekend. "Look at the sun shining! I'm missing it!" they'll say. But many an opportunity for buying the best boat available has been missed because the buyer decides to snap up the first half-decent vessel that comes along. He'd be better off taking the time to develop a number of possible options before making any offers.

Some sellers are too anxious, too, which is to the buyer's advantage. The best negotiating situations for buyers are those in which the seller has concluded that his boat has been on the market so long that he thinks he'll never sell her. He may take the next offer that comes along — even if it's ridiculously low. That's a good reason to ask the seller how long his boat has been on the market. It may start an interesting and profitable discussion on price.

*Be willing to take risks when negotiating; time is often in your favor.*   You may be wondering whether to offer a "lowball" price on some boat you're thinking about buying, say, within the next 30 days.

FIGURE 8-1

**The time/price function for used boat sales. As time marches on, sellers are willing to accept lower bids.**

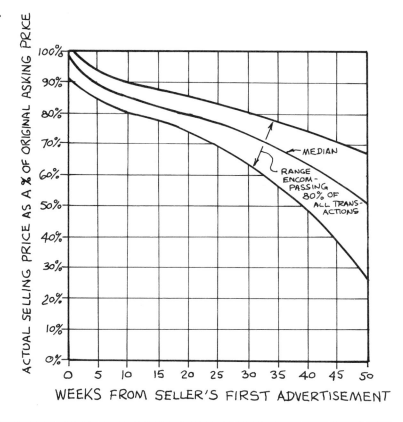

ACTUAL SELLING PRICE AS A % OF ORIGINAL ASKING PRICE

100%
90%
80%
70%
60%
50%
40%
30%
20%
10%
0%

MEDIAN

RANGE ENCOM-PASSING 80% OF ALL TRANS-ACTIONS

0  5  10  15  20  25  30  35  40  45  50

WEEKS FROM SELLER'S FIRST ADVERTISEMENT

Consider what will happen if your bid isn't accepted, and you have no immediate second choice, and therefore you don't buy a boat within the next 30 or 60 or 90 days. Will the world come to an end? No. Will the seller reconsider in 60 or 90 days, and accept your low offer? Quite possibly; it happens all the time. Will another opportunity come along? Most certainly. Will this new opportunity be as good as, or even better than, the one you may have missed by bidding too low? Maybe, but that's the risk you'll be taking. Don't take risks impulsively; figure the odds to determine whether the potential benefits are worth the possible cost of failure. Be calculating and rational, not emotional and impatient. Remember that one of your goals (probably) is to buy a boat you can happily live with for several years — so be willing to take the time to achieve that goal.

*Try to save the most critical issue — usually that's the price the boat will sell for — until the last possible moment in your negotiation.* If important concessions are to be made, they will typically occur at the "eleventh hour" relative to a deadline — whether the deadline is real or (as is more often the case) imagined — because one or both of the parties will feel pressure to conclude the negotiation before the deadline. That's when the other party, who by that time will have invested substantial amounts of time and effort in negotiations, will be most willing to see things your way. In fact, there's a direct relationship between the extent of a person's investment of time and energy in a negotiation and his willingness to compromise in order to reach a final agreement. Before a large investment in time and energy is made, it may be relatively easy for either a seller or a buyer to pull out; not so after substantial time and energy has been spent in negotiating.

*Be relaxed.* When it comes to dealing with money, people tend to get uptight. Don't. Remember, negotiating is a game. So, just like in Monopoly, be careful, but have fun. And take your time. It's on your side.

## Summary

The key ingredient of all successful negotiations is that each party should gain what he wants most. This usually means satisfying the psychological as well as the material needs of both parties. If you and the other party or parties can accomplish this, your negotiations will have a win/win outcome, the best possible eventuality.

And one more thing to remember: boating is supposed to be fun. Negotiating can be fun, too. So, when negotiating is inevitable, relax and enjoy it!

# CHAPTER 9

# Rule Six: Be Willing to Walk Away from a Deal

Be willing to walk away from a deal. This sounds like a simple rule, and it is. In fact, it's really just an extension of the advice on negotiating in the last chapter: Don't let yourself fall into an emotional trap, where you think you're in love with a boat, and end up buying her even though you know you shouldn't buy, either because she's beyond your budget, or she's too big for the dock space you have available, or for any number of other reasons. Remember, the boat *must be right* for your requirements. If she's not, walk away and don't turn back.

## Openers, closers, good guys and bad guys

Some people get trapped by fast-talking supersalesmanship, and find themselves owners of what yesterday they thought might be their dreamboat, but today they realize isn't. Only a few very foolish people would get themselves trapped like that, you say? Maybe — but there are enough of them so that some new boat dealers even employ "closers," supposedly professional super-salesmen who specialize in not taking no for an answer from any potential customer who walks through the door.

Sometimes the closers are also the openers. Beware the gold-chained salesman with his Hawaiian shirt unbuttoned almost to the waist who greets you with a flashy smile and a super-confident statement that he's "going to put you into one of our Supersport Zoomers today if it's the last thing I do," even before he's taken the time to learn anything about your real interests or budget. Chances are, he's a professional closer.

More often, though, these closers are preceded by other salesmen, sometimes called openers or qualifiers, who greet you as you walk into their show-sales area and question you in an attempt to find out if there's a possibility you'll buy one of their boats. The chance of you buying doesn't need to be a probability, just a possibility. To determine the odds, they may ask you what you now own (to help them judge what you might go for), and they may ask you if you're looking to buy a boat today. If you say you're not looking to buy right now (as the vast majority of boat-show visitors aren't), they ask whether you might buy a boat today if the price were right. If you say you wouldn't, they might make a graceful exit, they might send you to the closer for further working over, or they might continue questioning you to see whether they can bring you around.

If they introduce you to the closer, they might hang around to play the game of "good guy/bad guy," with one salesman acting as your knowledgeable new friend who won't let you make the mistake of buying the wrong boat, and the other posing as a pushy character trying to sell you something you don't want. The idea there, of course, is that your new friend protects you from buying the wrong boat from the pushy salesman, and therefore must have your best interests at heart. So you trust him, and end up buying from him. When you're gone, the good guy and the bad guy split the commission on the boat they sold you.

If you've never had the experience of being courted by a professional closer, I urge you to try it. It can be quite instructive, and entertaining as well. You can sometimes find these people at the larger boat shows, plying their trade at the lower priced, lower-quality-end of the boats on display — both power and sail. Just don't bring a checkbook, or any cash.

## Losing patience

Some people look for the right boat for a long time, and if they don't find her, they begin to lose patience. Sometimes something just snaps inside, their brain turns to Jello, and they end up buying the next boat that along, whether it's right or not — and it frequently isn't.

The danger here is in letting short-term desires ("I can't stand the thought of continuing to look for a boat for another month; I want action now") overshadow long-term objectives ("I'm looking for the right boat; I know she exists; it's a matter of finding her"). I suppose it's something like a bachelor beginning to panic about finding a mate. My advice: Develop criteria that you know will satisfy you, and keep looking. If you've done your homework on what boat will satisfy you (i.e., you've read and acted on the advice in the preceding chapters in this book), you'll eventually find the right boat to suit your needs. Don't settle for less.

# CHAPTER 10

# Rule Seven: Buy Low, Sell High

The punch line of the old joke about how to do well in the stock market is: "buy low, sell high." At first glance it sounds like good, reasonable advice, but at second glance you realize it's just a witty saying, with no clue as to how to go about buying low and selling high. It doesn't tell you anything about how to survey the marketplace. It doesn't tell you how to pick the right boats and avoid the wrong boats — the winners and the losers — once you find them, or how to time purchases so you don't get caught in a market downturn and end up losing, even with what normally would be a winner. Unless luck is always on your side, knowing how to do these things is the only way to successfully buy low and sell high.

That is, anybody can buy low, but if you buy losers, you won't be able to sell high. Losers stay low. And winners, if everybody knows they're winners, are already selling high, so if you want to buy a winner, you usually have to pay high.

Consequently, a principal key to financial success in the stock market — or in the boat market — is to be able to find winners that other people don't recognize as such. And, of course, to avoid losers.

To do this in the stock market, you can try looking for hot tips, listen to your broker's advice, or formulate your own securities investment strategy. Similarly, in the boat market you can take hot tips from friends, listen to advice from boat brokers and dealers, or formulate your own boat-buying strategy. The latter course of action is, of course, the one I recommend, and is why the preceding chapters of this book explore in great detail exactly how to formulate a boat-buying strategy.

As indicated in earlier chapters, good boat-buying strategy has several elements. First you decide that you really want to buy a boat, rather than a car or stocks and bonds or a vacation condo or any number of other fun alternatives, and you pick the type of boat you'd like to have. Then you attain a more or less intimate familiarity with the boat marketplace. While you're at it, you learn how to recognize the best times to buy. When you focus on specific buying opportunities, you carefully analyze them to see if they fit your particular criteria. If you pursue them, you use effective negotiating techniques. And, of course, you maintain a healthy objectivity and avoid making buying decisions based on emotion rather than facts.

But all this has been said in previous chapters. Is there anything else to the trick of buying low, selling high? Not really. It's a matter of being in the right place at the right time to find the right boat at the right price, buying her, enjoying her use, and then selling her again at a price favorable to you. In the next section, we'll explore the economics of boat ownership; and then, finally, review the economics of selling a boat.

# Saving on the Costs of Ownership

# CHAPTER 11

# The *Real* Costs of Boat Ownership

Sometimes boat buyers — particularly first-time boat buyers — don't think about how much their new boat is really going to cost in total. They tend to think only in terms of first cost, that is, the *initial capital* cost they pay to the seller to secure title to the boat. Initial capital cost may include:

- Purchase price for hull and attached equipment, as is and where is
- Extra cost for equipment not included in basic purchase price but deemed essential by buyer, such as cradle, sails, outboard, spinnaker gear, etc.
- Delivery costs paid to the seller
- Sales taxes paid to the seller
- Any import duties paid to the seller
- Cost of any repairs that must be made prior to the boat's use
- Any make-ready fees, launching or loading costs paid to the seller

## Ancillary costs

There is much more to the cost of owning a boat than just her purchase price. To start with, there are the *ancillary costs* of buying the boat, including any capital costs paid to a third party rather than to the seller. These include:

- The costs of your personal search for the boat (travel expenses and telephone plus the value of your own personal time)
- Costs of publications (including the cost of this book) that assist in your search

- Brokerage commissions, if paid to a third party by the buyer
- Make-ready costs and commissioning costs paid to a third party
- Surveyor's fees
- Attorney's fees
- Escrow account costs
- State sales taxes paid to a third party (or direct to the state)
- Service charges for preparing documentation papers
- Fees for documenting and/or registering the boat if not paid to the seller
- Fees for licensing the trailer, if any
- First year insurance costs
- Financing charges, fees, and interest on a boat loan, if any
- Possible broker's fee for bringing you, the customer, to a financial institution to get a boat loan
- Import duties if not paid to the seller
- Freight charges if not paid to the seller
- The cost of extra equipment and accessories you decide to add after taking delivery

Beyond the capital costs and ancillary costs of buying, there is another category of any boat's cost, namely, *operating expense*, which includes routine operating costs, maintenance, and gear repair and replacement. It also includes any financing costs, already mentioned above. This annual expense can run all the way from nothing at all to an average figure of around $40 or $50 per foot of overall length, or up to as much as $150 per foot or more. The continuing cost of a boat's routine operation and maintenance includes such items as:

- Fuel costs (especially significant for powerboats)
- Charges for the use of dockage or mooring equipment
- Cost of acquiring and dropping a mooring, if you are fortunate enough to live in an area where you can drop your own
- Annual personal property taxes
- Annual premiums for hull insurance
- Annual premiums for liability insurance
- Cost of preparation for winter storage (cleaning the bottom, winterizing the engine, building a cradle, etc.)
- Derigging and other decommissioning costs
- Seasonal haulout charges
- Cost of a winter cover and frame
- Winter storage costs for the boat
- Washing and winter storage of sails
- Cost of uncovering in spring
- Preparation for spring launching (painting bottom, waxing and polishing, cleaning the spars, etc.)
- Launching fee
- Post-launch chores, including rigging, tuning the engine, filling the water system, and other commissioning costs
- Periodic bottom-scrubbing charges during the boating season

- Annual dues and subscription fees for yacht clubs, class associations, marina associations, buyers' groups, and periodicals that help you keep up with how to get the most out of your boating activities

In addition to the costs of routine operation and maintenance, there will inevitably be non-routine repair and replacement costs for gear wear, failures or accidents. These might include costs for repairing or replacing such items as:

- Bent or broken propeller
- Ailing engine
- Dirty or water-contaminated fuel storage system
- Corroded fuel tank
- Corroded exhaust system
- Chips, cracks, crazing, or holes in a hull, deck, or cabin
- Electrical wiring problems
- Chafed running or standing rigging
- Worn or damaged sails
- Worn or damaged dodger, bimini, or other canvas work
- A "tired-looking" hull, deck, cabin, or interior
- Nonfunctioning electronic gear
- Worn or corroded trailer or trailer parts
- Upholstery
(Note: This list only scratches the surface. With a little imagination, many more items could be added.)

Finally, beyond the costs surrounding the initial purchase, annual maintenance costs, and repair costs, there is another category, called *opportunity cost*, that accountants do not usually recognize but which is nevertheless real. Opportunity cost is discussed in Chapter 18.

## Determining ownership costs

All these types of costs will be covered in detail in the chapters that follow. As you read, you may want to jot down some notes on how each type of cost applies to your boat and your situation. To help make this note-taking as convenient for you as possible, a structured multi-page worksheet for determining the real cost of boat ownership is presented at the end of this chapter.

You'll see from a quick inspection of the worksheet that you probably won't incur a cost for every one of the items listed, and that there are plenty of ways to save money by doing a portion of the work yourself rather than giving it to a yard or a mechanic to do. The difference between yard charges and do-it-yourself costs can be substantial — in the hundreds for a small boat or the thousands for a large one.

**SUMMARY (FROM WORKSHEET THAT FOLLOWS)**

|  | BOAT #1 | | BOAT #2 | | BOAT #3 | |
|---|---|---|---|---|---|---|
|  | INITIAL | ANNUAL | INITIAL | ANNUAL | INITIAL | ANNUAL |
| CAPITAL COST |  |  |  |  |  |  |
| ANCILLARY BUYING COSTS |  |  |  |  |  |  |
| ROUTINE OPERATION AND REPAIR COSTS |  |  |  |  |  |  |
| NON-ROUTINE REPAIR AND REPLACEMENT COSTS |  |  |  |  |  |  |
| TOTAL COSTS OF OWNERSHIP |  |  |  |  |  |  |
| LESS: ESTIMATED SALES PRICE WHEN RESOLD |  |  |  |  |  |  |
| PLUS: SALES COMMISSIONS AND OTHER SELLING EXPENSES |  |  |  |  |  |  |
| PLUS: OPPORTUNITY COSTS |  |  |  |  |  |  |
| NET COST OF OWNERSHIP |  |  |  |  |  |  |

Note: "Sales price when resold" is based on assumed sale in year _____ after total inflation rate increase of _____%. See Chapter 18 for method of handling calculations on inflation effects.

# SAVING ON THE COSTS OF OWNERSHIP

**Worksheet for
determining the real cost
of *your* boat ownership**

| SECTION ONE: INITIAL CAPITAL COSTS | BOAT #1 | BOAT #2 | BOAT #3 |
|---|---|---|---|
| Base price of boat FOB | ——— | ——— | ——— |
| Extras purchased with boat (list) | | | |
| | ——— | ——— | ——— |
| | ——— | ——— | ——— |
| | ——— | ——— | ——— |
| Extra equipment acquired at time of original purchase (list) | | | |
| | ——— | ——— | ——— |
| | ——— | ——— | ——— |
| | ——— | ——— | ——— |
| Cradle or trailer | ——— | ——— | ——— |
| Transportation charges | ——— | ——— | ——— |
| Make-ready and commissioning charges | ——— | ——— | ——— |
| State sales taxes | ——— | ——— | ——— |
| Other initial capital costs | ——— | ——— | ——— |
| TOTAL INITIAL CAPITAL COSTS | ——— | ——— | ——— |

| SECTION TWO: ANCILLARY BUYING COSTS | BOAT #1 | BOAT #2 | BOAT #3 |
|---|---|---|---|
| Searching costs: | | | |
|   Travel | ——— | ——— | ——— |
|   Telephone and postage | ——— | ——— | ——— |
|   Personal time value at ——— hours | ——— | ——— | ——— |
| Surveying | ——— | ——— | ——— |
| Escrow account costs | ——— | ——— | ——— |
| Gov't fees for documentation or registration | ——— | ——— | ——— |
| Service charges for professional help in preparing documentation papers | ——— | ——— | ——— |
| Initial season insurance—hull | ——— | ——— | ——— |
| Initial season insurance—liability | ——— | ——— | ——— |
| Financing costs: | | | |
|   Interest | ——— | ——— | ——— |
|   Broker's fees (i.e. dealer's reserve) | ——— | ——— | ——— |
|   Attorney's fees | ——— | ——— | ——— |
|   Closing fees | ——— | ——— | ——— |
|   Title search fees | ——— | ——— | ——— |
| Brokerage commissions (if not included in purchase price) | ——— | ——— | ——— |
| TOTAL ANCILLARY BUYING COSTS | ——— | ——— | ——— |

*continued*

| SECTION THREE: COSTS OF ROUTINE OPERATION AND MAINTENANCE | BOAT #1 | BOAT #2 | BOAT #3 |
|---|---|---|---|
| Fuel costs (at _____ gallons per mile) | | | |
| Slip rental cost | | | |
| Dockside power charges | | | |
| Dockside telephone charges | | | |
| Dockside water charges | | | |
| Mooring expense | | | |
| Annual docu. or registr. fees | | | |
| Annual insurance—hull | | | |
| Annual insurance—liability | | | |
| Derigging and other decommissioning | | | |
| Haulout costs | | | |
| Cost of a winter cover and frame | | | |
| Winterizing motor | | | |
| Other preparation for winter storage | | | |
| Winter storage costs | | | |
| Washing and storage of sails | | | |
| Regreasing trailer bearings | | | |
| Repainting trailer | | | |
| Cost of uncovering in spring | | | |
| Preparation for spring launching | | | |
| Launching costs | | | |
| Post-launch chores | | | |
| Periodic bottom scrubbing (_____ times at $_____ per time) | | | |
| Dues and subscriptions | | | |
| Other routine annual costs | | | |
| TOTAL ESTIMATED ANNUAL COSTS OF ROUTINE OPERATION AND MAINTENANCE | | | |

| SECTION FOUR: NON-ROUTINE REPAIR AND REPLACEMENT COSTS | BOAT #1 | BOAT #2 | BOAT #3 |
|---|---|---|---|
| Replacement of sails—annual fund | | | |
| Replacement or major overhaul of engines—annual fund | | | |
| Major hull refit—annual fund | | | |
| General unforeseen repairs—fund | | | |
| Other non-routine repair and replacement costs: | | | |
| | | | |
| | | | |
| | | | |
| TOTAL ANNUAL COSTS FOR NON-ROUTINE REPAIR AND REPLACEMENT | | | |

# CHAPTER 12

# Initial Capital Cost

In this chapter, we'll talk about *initial capital* costs — as opposed to the ancillary costs of buying, or operating costs, or maintenance costs, or repair and replacement costs, which are dealt with in succeeding chapters.

How much should your boat cost initially? Well, it depends.

It depends upon many variables, including how good a negotiator you are compared to the seller. But how much you logically should pay for a boat (your negotiating skills aside) depends to a very great extent on only eight factors:

- Her size in terms of overall length and relative weight
- Her age (since both inflation and depreciation due to changes in style and physical wear and tear affect market value)
- Her quality level and her builder's reputation (or her reputation as a dog or a cult boat)
- The kind of physical condition she's in
- The extent and condition of her equipment, including her engine or engines (especially important for a powerboat)
- The geographic area in which she is being sold
- When she is being sold (in terms of both season of the year and phase of the business cycle, which together determine market conditions)
- The marketing skills, needs, and attitudes of the seller (independent of your buying skills)

With all these factors affecting a boat's value, asking prices can vary all over the lot. Knowing how to determine the "fair" selling price (i.e. the amount that a reasonable seller is likely to be satisfied with, as opposed to what he's asking) can be a very useful skill. You can — and should — learn how to make this determination for both new and used boats.

# Which do you prefer: new or used?

Some people always buy new boats, often for the same reasons they always buy new cars. Some of these reasons include:

- The chance to own a new style or model — perhaps one not yet available on the used market
- The chance to get exactly what they want in terms of color, accessories, layout, etc.
- The security of knowing that they won't have to worry any time soon about major maintenance and component replacement
- Not having to deal with the results of the last owner's carelessness in terms of hidden damage to hull, engine, equipment, etc.
- Having a warranty that the dealer or builder will stand behind if any serious problems occur
- Being able to trade in the old boat, thus avoiding the hassle of selling her privately, and saving sales tax (figured on the net amount paid after trade-in allowance)
- Avoiding the hassle of a survey, documentation paperwork, title search, and other activities associated with buying used instead of new

On the other hand, good used boats also have their advantages, just as good used cars do. As with cars, the advantages are mainly financial, and include:

- Avoiding heavy first-year depreciation charges
- Not having the hassle and heavy expense of equipping the boat
- Eliminating most (but seldom all) of the nuisance of "debugging" a new boat
- Possibly getting the advantages of a trade-in (saving sales tax; no hassle getting rid of the old boat) if the circumstances are right

On balance, I'd recommend buying a used boat rather than a new one if you place a relatively high priority on saving money, and are therefore willing to forgo some if not all of the new-boat advantages listed above.

# Buying a new boat can be a lot like buying a new car

The market price for new boats is established pretty much like the market price for new cars. In both cases, there's a list price, established by the marketer. In both cases, this price is based in large part on the size, the general reputation of the product and its quality level as perceived by prospective buyers (a perception which may or may not be justifiable). And in both cases, there's usually some room to negotiate how much money actually changes hands. For example, a new-boat dealer's price spread generally runs between 15% and 20% of his wholesale cost (e.g., $1,500 to $2,000 on a $10,000 wholesale cost, for a retail price of $11,500 to $12,000; the spread is thus around 13% to 17% of retail.) Out of this spread, he must pay for overhead and any salesmen's commissions. The rest is pretax profit.

Furthermore, as with cars, the higher the list price for a boat of a given size, the more flexibility the dealer is apt to have in adjusting the selling price in order to make the sale.

Another similarity to the new-car market is in the area of options and accessories. Like a car dealer, a boat dealer may mark up his wholesale price of options and accessories (which are generally 40% to 50% under list prices) by 100% or even more. And as with cars, these extras may total 20%, 30%, or even 40% of the base price of the boat itself.

However, buying accessories for a boat is unlike buying accessories for a car, since with boats the buyer generally can choose to buy identical accessories from mail-order discount houses at significantly lower than list prices, and install them himself.

Because many boat accessories are owner-installable, sometimes an alert dealer will reduce the price of these accessories to a point where he can cover his installation costs and still make some extra profit on the sale, while satisfying the customer that he's getting a fair deal and the benefit of dealer installation and guarantees as well. But more often, if the dealer doesn't think it will jinx the sale, he may attempt to charge full list price for accessories. The moral of this story is that, to get a discount on accessories, you'll probably have to ask for it.

## New boats: what's a "fair" price to pay?

So what is a fair price for a new boat? If you ask a new boat dealer, typically he'll say it's his list price, which in turn is based on what he and the manufacturer have agreed the market will bear. The eight factors mentioned at the beginning of this chapter all go into the development of new boat list prices. But as with the car market, when all the dickering is over, the lowest price a dealer will accept in the end depends on how badly he wants to unload his inventory, and the highest price a buyer will pay in the end depends upon how badly he wants what the dealer has. There are few, if any, specific rules of thumb that apply to determine this end price, given the breadth and depth of the boat market, and the range of attitudes among sellers and buyers. However, one benchmark for the potential discount available on any new boat might be its reported "boat show special" price at any of the many boat shows constantly being staged around the country. This price often is 5% to 20% below list.

Boat-show special prices are usually billed as this-show-only offers. However, don't assume that the dealers who discount boats at shows usually lose money on them, or even just break even. Indeed, some dealers boast that a major part of their annual sales are made at boat shows. Millions of dollars are claimed to change hands at the big Annapolis, Miami and New York boat shows alone. Most assuredly, some of it is profit to dealers.

One of the characteristics of the boat market that makes it difficult to apply generalizations is its breadth and depth. The number of new-boat choices is mind-boggling. Refer to Figures 1-2 and 1-3, which graphically depict the scatter of prices for powerboats and sailboats of various sizes. As you can see, the range of prices for any given boat size is very wide. There are Chevrolets among boats, and there are Mercedes and BMWs.

For example, in 1990 you could buy a brand-new Catalina 30 (29'11" length overall) for $40,000 sailaway. ("Sailaway" is a standard term used in the marketing of sailboats and sometimes powerboats, which means, roughly, that the boat is in the water and adequately equipped to leave the dock on a trip without jeopardizing the safety of her passengers.) Another sailboat, the Tashiba 31, weighing about 35% more but otherwise of practically the same dimensions as the Catalina 30, sold at the same time and place for $128,000 sailaway.

The Catalina, mass-produced in a large, modern factory using materials and manufacturing methods carefully chosen for their cost-effectiveness, is a good example of how clever design can produce a desirable product at a very competitive price.

On the other hand, the hand-crafted Tashiba, meticulously built one at a time in a Far Eastern yard to absolutely first-rate standards, is a good example of what is available to the sailor who is looking for a floating work of art, handmade to his personal specifications, and who is willing to pay a pretty penny to get what he wants.

## Used boat prices are a lot like used car prices, too

As I've already mentioned, there are lots of similarities between the market for new boats and the market for new cars. That also goes for used versions of each.

But there are also a few differences between used cars and used boats in the marketplace. One significant difference is that boats have much lower annual depreciation rates (the gradual reduction or loss of value due to wear and obsolescence).

For boats, just as for cars, the rate of market price depreciation is greatest at the instant the boat is removed from the dealer's premises. And just as for cars, a boat's annual depreciation then diminishes year by year. For sailboats, depreciation continues until the hull is about twenty years old; then additional annual depreciation levels off. That is, in 1990, a boat built in 1965 or 1966 (now 24 or 25 years old) may command practically the same price as a boat built in 1969 or 1970 (20 or 21 years old), if it is otherwise identical in brand, model, condition, equipment, etc. Most cars depreciate considerably faster, mainly due to more frequent styling changes and the automobile's comparatively lower durability.

## FIGURE 12-1
**Boat prices depreciate more slowly than automobile prices.**

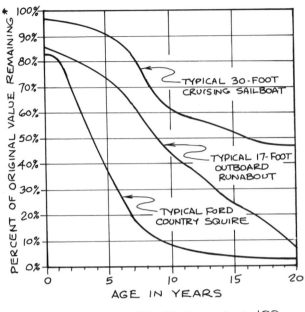

$$\ast \quad \text{PERCENTAGE} = \frac{\text{USED PRICE NOW} \times 100}{\text{PRICE WHEN NEW} \times \text{"PPAF"}}$$

WHERE "PPAF" = PURCHASING POWER ADJUSTMENT FACTOR = $\frac{\text{CPI-U WHEN NEW}}{\text{CPI-U NOW}}$

## FIGURE 12-2
**Some calculated depreciation rates.**

| BRAND AND MODEL | PRICE OF 1980 BOAT WHEN NEW, IN 1980 DOLLARS | 1980 PRICE ADJUSTED TO 1990 DOLLARS | AVERAGE USED PRICE FOR THE 1980 BOAT IN 1990 | APPARENT DEPRECIATION | RESIDUAL VALUE AS % OF ORIG. $ |
|---|---|---|---|---|---|
| **Powerboats** | | | | | |
| Bertram 33 dsl | $104,600 | $166,300 | $83,800 | 49.7% | 50.3% |
| Carver 28 gas | 34,800 | 55,300 | 17,500 | 68.4 | 31.6 |
| Mako 17 | 4,600 | 7,300 | 1,850 | 74.7 | 25.3 |
| Boston Whaler 13 | 2,100 | 3,300 | 850 | 74.2 | 25.8 |
| **Sailboats** | | | | | |
| Tartan 37 | $ 66,700 | $106,000 | $60,000 | 43.4% | 56.6% |
| Sabre 30 | 37,800 | 60,100 | 26,600 | 55.7 | 44.3 |
| Catalina 30 | 26,700 | 42,500 | 27,700 | 34.8 | 65.2 |
| Catalina 22 | 5,000 | 8,000 | 3,400 | 57.5 | 42.5 |

Source: Data in Figure 18-2, adjusted using Consumer Price Index.

Powerboats, with engines that wear out, constant vibration and pounding that take their toll, and constantly changing styles, have depreciation rates closer to automobiles than sailboats, especially small runabouts, as indicated in Figure 12-1.

Still, there's considerable variability in depreciation (see Figure 12-2) with the amount depending on size, type of boat, and condition, as well as age. For a further discussion of depreciation, see Chapter 18.

## Figuring what a used boat should cost

Used boats are somewhat easier to pigeonhole as to fair market value than are new boats. For one thing, asking prices for literally thousands of brand/model combinations are widely publicized in the boating mags, *Soundings* and other newspaper classifieds, used-boat specialty publications, brokerage listings, and other places. (See list of various boat price sources in Appendix 2.)

Hence, someone getting ready to buy or sell a boat can refer to these published asking prices to get an idea of what price tag to target. A seller usually starts by advertising at a price he thinks is fair — maybe a price above what he thinks he'll actually get, but a bit below the published prices, to stir up some interest within the marketplace. Then, if the boat doesn't sell at that price, he can either hold out for a while and wait for a buyer, or lower his advertised price to encourage more potential buyers to inquire. Either way, his decision is reflected in the boat-ad press (assuming he advertises), and the price he asks becomes part of the body of prices that influence other sellers looking at published prices to establish initial asking prices for their own similar boats.

It's an eternal chain reaction, the end result of which, in theory, brings boat asking prices down close to levels at which they are eventually sold and bought. I say "close to" because used boats seldom sell at the asking price; there's almost always a negotiation, and the published price ends up somewhat above the actual sales price. And I say "in theory" because, for the last six years or so, sailboat sellers haven't been reducing their prices to the point where they're particularly attractive to buyers. As a result, the sailboat market has been stagnant. Until recently, this problem hasn't impacted on the powerboat market to the same extent as the sailboat market. Generally speaking, advertised prices for powerboats appropriately reduced by, say, 5% to 15% for negotiation, tended to reflect actual selling prices. But in 1990 the powerboat market started to stagnate too.

Another thing that makes it reasonably easy to figure out the right price for a used boat — although more so for sailboats than powerboats — is the identification of the eight variables listed at the beginning of this chapter. Each has an effect on the price of any used boat, and all but one of the eight variables are readily quantifiable, at least most of the time. The only variable that's not is the one pertaining to the marketing skills, needs, and attitudes of the seller, which usually can be judged only in a face-to-face bargaining session.

## Making a used-boat price calculation

If you've been thinking that by quantifying the eight variables listed above you should be able to establish a fair market price for practically any boat, you're right — at least partially. I've devised Henkel's Eight Universal Rules of Used Boat Pricing, which work for sailboats, but not for powerboats. I'll explain how to handle powerboat pricing later; let's look at the rules for sailboats now. Here they are.

*Rule #1: A sailboat's base market price at any specific point in time varies with her age and her overall length on deck.* Just how this so-called base market price varies is shown in Figure 12-3. The data in the table (in thousands of dollars) establish a base figure, which is then adjusted according to rules #2 through #8. The base figure assumes that:

FIGURE 12-3
**Sailboat prices (expressed here in thousands of dollars) vary with age and length.**

AGE OF A SAILBOAT IN YEARS

| L.O.D. | NEW | 1 | 2 | 3 | 4 | 5 | 6 | 7 | 8 | 9 | 10 | 11 | 12 | 13 | 14 | 15 | 16 | 18 | 20 | 21 OR MORE |
|---|---|---|---|---|---|---|---|---|---|---|---|---|---|---|---|---|---|---|---|---|
| 7 | .34 | .33 | .31 | .30 | .29 | .27 | .25 | .24 | .22 | .21 | .21 | .24 | .24 | .22 | .20 | .19 | .18 | .16 | .15 | .15 |
| 8 | .69 | .65 | .63 | .60 | .57 | .55 | .52 | .49 | .47 | .45 | .43 | .45 | .44 | .42 | .39 | .38 | .36 | .33 | .31 | .30 |
| 9 | 1.03 | .98 | .94 | .90 | .86 | .82 | .79 | .75 | .72 | .68 | .64 | .65 | .64 | .61 | .58 | .56 | .54 | .50 | .46 | .45 |
| 10 | 1.37 | 1.30 | 1.25 | 1.20 | 1.15 | 1.10 | 1.06 | 1.01 | .97 | .92 | .86 | .85 | .84 | .80 | .77 | .74 | .72 | .67 | .62 | .60 |
| 11 | 1.71 | 1.62 | 1.56 | 1.50 | 1.44 | 1.38 | 1.32 | 1.27 | 1.21 | 1.16 | 1.08 | 1.05 | 1.03 | .99 | .95 | .92 | .89 | .83 | .78 | .75 |
| 12 | 2.05 | 1.95 | 1.87 | 1.80 | 1.73 | 1.65 | 1.59 | 1.53 | 1.46 | 1.39 | 1.29 | 1.25 | 1.23 | 1.18 | 1.14 | 1.10 | 1.07 | 1.00 | .93 | .90 |
| 13 | 2.40 | 2.27 | 2.19 | 2.10 | 2.01 | 1.93 | 1.86 | 1.78 | 1.71 | 1.63 | 1.51 | 1.46 | 1.43 | 1.38 | 1.33 | 1.29 | 1.25 | 1.17 | 1.09 | 1.05 |
| 14 | 2.74 | 2.60 | 2.50 | 2.40 | 2.30 | 2.20 | 2.12 | 2.04 | 1.96 | 1.86 | 1.72 | 1.66 | 1.62 | 1.57 | 1.51 | 1.47 | 1.42 | 1.33 | 1.24 | 1.20 |
| 15 | 3.08 | 2.92 | 2.81 | 2.70 | 2.59 | 2.48 | 2.39 | 2.30 | 2.21 | 2.10 | 1.94 | 1.86 | 1.82 | 1.76 | 1.70 | 1.65 | 1.60 | 1.50 | 1.40 | 1.35 |
| 16 | 3.42 | 3.24 | 3.12 | 3.00 | 2.88 | 2.76 | 2.66 | 2.56 | 2.46 | 2.34 | 2.16 | 2.06 | 2.02 | 1.95 | 1.89 | 1.83 | 1.78 | 1.67 | 1.56 | 1.50 |
| 17 | 4.11 | 3.89 | 3.75 | 3.60 | 3.45 | 3.31 | 3.19 | 3.07 | 2.96 | 2.81 | 2.59 | 2.47 | 2.41 | 2.34 | 2.26 | 2.20 | 2.13 | 2.00 | 1.87 | 1.80 |
| 18 | 5.13 | 4.86 | 4.68 | 4.50 | 4.32 | 4.14 | 3.99 | 3.85 | 3.70 | 3.52 | 3.24 | 3.07 | 3.00 | 2.91 | 2.82 | 2.74 | 2.66 | 2.50 | 2.34 | 2.25 |
| 19 | 6.50 | 6.16 | 5.93 | 5.70 | 5.47 | 5.24 | 5.06 | 4.88 | 4.70 | 4.46 | 4.10 | 3.88 | 3.79 | 3.68 | 3.57 | 3.47 | 3.37 | 3.17 | 2.96 | 2.85 |
| 20 | 8.21 | 7.78 | 7.49 | 7.20 | 6.91 | 6.62 | 6.40 | 6.17 | 5.95 | 5.64 | 5.18 | 4.89 | 4.78 | 4.64 | 4.51 | 4.38 | 4.26 | 4.01 | 3.74 | 3.60 |
| 21 | 10.26 | 9.72 | 9.36 | 9.00 | 8.64 | 8.28 | 8.00 | 7.72 | 7.44 | 7.06 | 6.48 | 6.10 | 5.96 | 5.79 | 5.63 | 5.47 | 5.32 | 5.01 | 4.68 | 4.50 |
| 22 | 12.66 | 11.99 | 11.55 | 11.10 | 10.65 | 10.21 | 9.87 | 9.52 | 9.18 | 8.71 | 7.99 | 7.52 | 7.34 | 7.14 | 6.94 | 6.75 | 6.56 | 6.18 | 5.77 | 5.55 |
| 23 | 15.39 | 14.58 | 14.04 | 13.50 | 12.96 | 12.42 | 12.00 | 11.59 | 11.17 | 10.60 | 9.72 | 9.13 | 8.91 | 8.67 | 8.43 | 8.20 | 7.97 | 7.51 | 7.02 | 6.75 |
| 24 | 18.47 | 17.50 | 16.85 | 16.20 | 15.55 | 14.90 | 14.41 | 13.91 | 13.42 | 12.72 | 11.66 | 10.95 | 10.69 | 10.40 | 10.12 | 9.84 | 9.57 | 9.02 | 8.42 | 8.10 |
| 25 | 21.89 | 20.74 | 19.97 | 19.20 | 18.43 | 17.66 | 17.08 | 16.49 | 15.91 | 15.08 | 13.82 | 12.97 | 12.66 | 12.32 | 11.99 | 11.66 | 11.34 | 10.69 | 9.98 | 9.60 |
| 26 | 25.65 | 24.30 | 23.40 | 22.50 | 21.60 | 20.70 | 20.01 | 19.33 | 18.64 | 17.68 | 16.20 | 15.19 | 14.82 | 14.43 | 14.04 | 13.66 | 13.28 | 12.52 | 11.70 | 11.25 |
| 27 | 29.76 | 28.19 | 27.15 | 26.10 | 25.05 | 24.01 | 23.22 | 22.42 | 21.63 | 20.51 | 18.79 | 17.62 | 17.19 | 16.74 | 16.29 | 15.85 | 15.41 | 14.53 | 13.57 | 13.05 |
| 28 | 34.20 | 32.40 | 31.20 | 30.00 | 28.80 | 27.60 | 26.69 | 25.78 | 24.87 | 23.58 | 21.60 | 20.24 | 19.75 | 19.23 | 18.72 | 18.21 | 17.71 | 16.70 | 15.60 | 15.00 |
| 29 | 38.99 | 36.94 | 35.57 | 34.20 | 32.83 | 31.46 | 30.43 | 29.39 | 28.36 | 26.88 | 24.62 | 23.07 | 22.51 | 21.92 | 21.34 | 20.76 | 20.19 | 19.04 | 17.78 | 17.10 |
| 30 | 44.12 | 41.80 | 40.25 | 38.70 | 37.15 | 35.60 | 34.43 | 33.26 | 32.09 | 30.42 | 27.86 | 26.10 | 25.46 | 24.80 | 24.14 | 23.49 | 22.84 | 21.54 | 20.12 | 19.35 |
| 31 | 49.59 | 46.98 | 45.24 | 43.50 | 41.76 | 40.02 | 38.70 | 37.39 | 36.07 | 34.20 | 31.32 | 29.33 | 28.61 | 27.87 | 27.13 | 26.40 | 25.67 | 24.21 | 22.62 | 21.75 |
| 32 | 55.41 | 52.49 | 50.55 | 48.60 | 46.65 | 44.71 | 43.24 | 41.77 | 40.31 | 38.21 | 34.99 | 32.77 | 31.96 | 31.14 | 30.31 | 29.50 | 28.68 | 27.05 | 25.27 | 24.30 |
| 33 | 61.56 | 58.32 | 56.16 | 54.00 | 51.84 | 49.68 | 48.05 | 46.42 | 44.79 | 42.46 | 38.88 | 36.40 | 35.51 | 34.59 | 33.68 | 32.77 | 31.87 | 30.06 | 28.08 | 27.00 |
| 34 | 68.06 | 64.48 | 62.09 | 59.70 | 57.31 | 54.92 | 53.12 | 51.32 | 49.52 | 46.94 | 42.98 | 40.24 | 39.25 | 38.24 | 37.23 | 36.23 | 35.23 | 33.23 | 31.04 | 29.85 |
| 35 | 74.90 | 70.96 | 68.33 | 65.70 | 63.07 | 60.44 | 58.46 | 56.48 | 54.50 | 51.66 | 47.30 | 44.28 | 43.19 | 42.08 | 40.97 | 39.87 | 38.77 | 36.57 | 34.16 | 32.85 |
| 36 | 82.08 | 77.76 | 74.88 | 72.00 | 69.12 | 66.24 | 64.07 | 61.90 | 59.73 | 56.62 | 51.84 | 48.52 | 47.33 | 46.11 | 44.90 | 43.69 | 42.49 | 40.08 | 37.44 | 36.00 |
| 37 | 89.61 | 84.89 | 81.75 | 78.60 | 75.45 | 72.31 | 69.94 | 67.57 | 65.21 | 61.81 | 56.59 | 52.97 | 51.66 | 50.34 | 49.01 | 47.70 | 46.38 | 43.75 | 40.87 | 39.30 |
| 38 | 97.47 | 92.34 | 88.92 | 85.50 | 82.08 | 78.66 | 76.08 | 73.51 | 70.93 | 67.24 | 61.56 | 57.61 | 56.19 | 54.75 | 53.31 | 51.88 | 50.45 | 47.59 | 44.46 | 42.75 |
| 39 | 105.68 | 100.12 | 96.41 | 92.70 | 88.99 | 85.28 | 82.49 | 79.70 | 76.91 | 72.90 | 66.74 | 62.46 | 60.92 | 59.36 | 57.80 | 56.25 | 54.70 | 51.60 | 48.20 | 46.35 |
| 40 | 114.23 | 108.22 | 104.21 | 100.20 | 96.19 | 92.18 | 89.17 | 86.15 | 83.14 | 78.80 | 72.14 | 67.51 | 65.85 | 64.16 | 62.48 | 60.80 | 59.13 | 55.78 | 52.10 | 50.10 |
| 41 | 123.12 | 116.64 | 112.32 | 108.00 | 103.68 | 99.36 | 96.11 | 92.86 | 89.61 | 84.94 | 77.76 | 72.76 | 70.97 | 69.15 | 67.34 | 65.53 | 63.73 | 60.12 | 56.16 | 54.00 |
| 42 | 132.36 | 125.39 | 120.75 | 116.10 | 111.45 | 106.81 | 103.32 | 99.82 | 96.33 | 91.31 | 83.59 | 78.22 | 76.29 | 74.34 | 72.39 | 70.45 | 68.51 | 64.63 | 60.37 | 58.05 |
| 43 | 141.93 | 134.46 | 129.48 | 124.50 | 119.52 | 114.54 | 110.79 | 107.05 | 103.30 | 97.92 | 89.64 | 83.87 | 81.80 | 79.71 | 77.62 | 75.54 | 73.46 | 69.30 | 64.74 | 62.25 |
| 44 | 151.85 | 143.86 | 138.53 | 133.20 | 127.87 | 122.54 | 118.54 | 114.53 | 110.53 | 104.76 | 95.90 | 89.73 | 87.52 | 85.28 | 83.05 | 80.82 | 78.60 | 74.15 | 69.26 | 66.60 |

- Condition is "average"
- Equipment status is "average" in terms of quantity, quality, and age
- The brand and model have no special status as either a cult boat that commands a premium or a dog that must settle for a below-average price
- The design is in the middle of the medium displacement range (i.e., D/L ratio between 240 and 249)
- No geographical or seasonal adjustments apply
- Seller's personal effectiveness in reaching and selling to his target market is middle-of-the-road

***Rule #2: Price is proportional to relative displacement*** per Figure 12-4 (which refers to displacement/length ratio) and Figure 12-5 (which provides a close approximation of the D/L Ratio without the need for a calculator, if waterline length and displacement are known).

***Rule #3: The boat's physical condition affects price*** according to the data in Figure 12-6.

***Rule #4: Equipment quality, quantity, and age affect the boat's price*** according to the data in Figure 12-7.

---

FIGURE 12-4
**Price is proportional to the displacement/length ratio; approximate price adjustments are shown.**

| DISPLACEMENT/ LENGTH RATIO (D/L) | ADJUSTMENT FACTOR |
|---|---|
| Below 80 (ultralight) | −18% |
| 80 to 99 " | −16% |
| 100 to 119 (light) | −14% |
| 120 to 139 " | −12% |
| 140 to 159 " | −10% |
| 160 to 179 " | −8% |
| 180 to 199 " | −6% |
| 200 to 219 (medium) | −4% |
| 220 to 239 " | −2% |
| 240 to 249 " | None |
| 250 to 259 " | +2% |
| 260 to 279 " | +4% |
| 280 to 299 " | +6% |
| 300 to 319 (heavy) | +8% |
| 320 to 339 " | +10% |
| 340 to 349 " | +12% |
| Over 349 " | +14% |

---

# FIGURE 12-5
## Approximations of displacement/length ratios by displacement in pounds and waterline length in feet.

WATERLINE LENGTH IN FEET

| DISPLACEMENT (POUNDS) | 8 | 10 | 12 | 14 | 15 | 16 | 17 | 18 | 19 | 20 | 21 | 22 | 23 | 24 | 25 | 26 | 27 | 28 | 29 | 30 | 31 | 32 | 33 | 34 | 35 | 36 | 37 | 38 | 39 | 40 | 41 | 42 | 43 | 44 | 45 |
|---|---|---|---|---|---|---|---|---|---|---|---|---|---|---|---|---|---|---|---|---|---|---|---|---|---|---|---|---|---|---|---|---|---|---|---|
| 50 | | | | | | | | | | | | | | | | | | | | | | | | | | | | | | | | | | | |
| 100 | 87 | | | | | | | | | | | | | | | | | | | | | | | | | | | | | | | | | | |
| 200 | 174 | 89 | | | | | | | | | | | | | | | | | | | | | | | | | | | | | | | | | |
| 400 | 349 | 179 | 103 | 65 | 53 | | | | | | | | | | | | | | | | | | | | | | | | | | | | | | |
| 600 | | 268 | 155 | 98 | 79 | 65 | 55 | | | | | | | | | | | | | | | | | | | | | | | | | | | | |
| 800 | | 357 | 207 | 130 | 106 | 87 | 73 | 61 | 52 | | | | | | | | | | | | | | | | | | | | | | | | | | |
| 1000 | | | 258 | 163 | 132 | 109 | 91 | 77 | 65 | 56 | | | | | | | | | | | | | | | | | | | | | | | | | |
| 2000 | | | 517 | 325 | 265 | 218 | 182 | 153 | 130 | 112 | 96 | 84 | 73 | 65 | 57 | | | | | | | | | | | | | | | | | | | | |
| 3000 | | | | | 397 | 327 | 273 | 230 | 195 | 167 | 145 | 126 | 110 | 97 | 86 | 76 | 68 | 61 | | | | | | | | | | | | | | | | | |
| 4000 | | | | | | 436 | 363 | 306 | 260 | 223 | 193 | 168 | 147 | 129 | 114 | 102 | 91 | 81 | 73 | 66 | 60 | | | | | | | | | | | | | | |
| 5000 | | | | | | | 454 | 383 | 325 | 279 | 241 | 210 | 183 | 161 | 143 | 127 | 113 | 102 | 91 | 83 | 75 | 68 | | | | | | | | | | | | | |
| 6000 | | | | | | | | | 391 | 335 | 289 | 252 | 220 | 194 | 171 | 152 | 136 | 122 | 110 | 99 | 90 | 82 | 75 | 68 | | | | | | | | | | | |
| 7000 | | | | | | | | | | 391 | 337 | 293 | 257 | 226 | 200 | 178 | 159 | 142 | 128 | 116 | 105 | 95 | 87 | 80 | 73 | 67 | | | | | | | | | |
| 8000 | | | | | | | | | | | 386 | 335 | 294 | 258 | 229 | 203 | 181 | 163 | 146 | 132 | 120 | 109 | 99 | 91 | 83 | 77 | | | | | | | | | |
| 9000 | | | | | | | | | | | | 377 | 330 | 291 | 257 | 229 | 204 | 183 | 165 | 149 | 135 | 123 | 112 | 102 | 94 | 86 | 79 | 73 | | | | | | | |
| 10000 | | | | | | | | | | | | | 367 | 323 | 286 | 254 | 227 | 203 | 183 | 165 | 150 | 136 | 124 | 114 | 104 | 96 | 88 | 81 | 75 | | | | | | |
| 11000 | | | | | | | | | | | | | | 355 | 314 | 279 | 249 | 224 | 201 | 182 | 165 | 150 | 137 | 125 | 115 | 105 | 97 | 89 | 83 | | | | | | |
| 12000 | | | | | | | | | | | | | | | 343 | 305 | 272 | 244 | 220 | 198 | 180 | 163 | 149 | 136 | 125 | 115 | 106 | 98 | 90 | | | | | | |
| 13000 | | | | | | | | | | | | | | | 371 | 330 | 295 | 264 | 238 | 215 | 195 | 177 | 161 | 148 | 135 | 124 | 115 | 106 | 98 | 91 | | | | | |
| 14000 | | | | | | | | | | | | | | | | 356 | 318 | 285 | 256 | 231 | 210 | 191 | 174 | 159 | 146 | 134 | 124 | 114 | 105 | 98 | 91 | | | | |
| 15000 | | | | | | | | | | | | | | | | 381 | 340 | 305 | 275 | 248 | 225 | 204 | 186 | 170 | 156 | 144 | 132 | 122 | 113 | 105 | 97 | 90 | | | |
| 16000 | | | | | | | | | | | | | | | | | 363 | 325 | 293 | 265 | 240 | 218 | 199 | 182 | 167 | 153 | 141 | 130 | 120 | 112 | 104 | 96 | 90 | | |
| 17000 | | | | | | | | | | | | | | | | | | 346 | 311 | 281 | 255 | 232 | 211 | 193 | 177 | 163 | 150 | 138 | 128 | 119 | 110 | 102 | 95 | 89 | |
| 18000 | | | | | | | | | | | | | | | | | | 366 | 329 | 298 | 270 | 245 | 224 | 204 | 187 | 172 | 159 | 147 | 135 | 126 | 117 | 108 | 101 | 94 | 88 |
| 19000 | | | | | | | | | | | | | | | | | | | 348 | 314 | 285 | 259 | 236 | 216 | 198 | 182 | 168 | 155 | 143 | 133 | 123 | 114 | 107 | 100 | 93 |
| 20000 | | | | | | | | | | | | | | | | | | | 366 | 331 | 300 | 272 | 248 | 227 | 208 | 191 | 176 | 163 | 151 | 140 | 130 | 121 | 112 | 105 | 98 |
| 25000 | | | | | | | | | | | | | | | | | | | | 413 | 375 | 341 | 311 | 284 | 260 | 239 | 220 | 203 | 188 | 174 | 162 | 151 | 140 | 131 | 122 |
| 26000 | | | | | | | | | | | | | | | | | | | | | | 354 | 323 | 295 | 271 | 249 | 229 | 212 | 196 | 181 | 168 | 157 | 146 | 136 | 127 |
| 27000 | | | | | | | | | | | | | | | | | | | | | | | 335 | 307 | 281 | 258 | 238 | 220 | 203 | 188 | 175 | 163 | 152 | 142 | 132 |
| 28000 | | | | | | | | | | | | | | | | | | | | | | | 348 | 318 | 292 | 268 | 247 | 228 | 211 | 195 | 182 | 169 | 157 | 147 | 137 |
| 29000 | | | | | | | | | | | | | | | | | | | | | | | 360 | 329 | 302 | 277 | 256 | 236 | 218 | 202 | 188 | 175 | 163 | 152 | 142 |
| 30000 | | | | | | | | | | | | | | | | | | | | | | | | 341 | 312 | 287 | 264 | 244 | 226 | 209 | 194 | 181 | 168 | 157 | 147 |
| 31000 | | | | | | | | | | | | | | | | | | | | | | | | 352 | 323 | 297 | 273 | 252 | 233 | 216 | 201 | 187 | 174 | 162 | 152 |
| 32000 | | | | | | | | | | | | | | | | | | | | | | | | | 333 | 306 | 282 | 260 | 241 | 223 | 207 | 193 | 180 | 168 | 157 |
| 33000 | | | | | | | | | | | | | | | | | | | | | | | | | 344 | 316 | 291 | 268 | 248 | 230 | 214 | 199 | 185 | 173 | 162 |
| 34000 | | | | | | | | | | | | | | | | | | | | | | | | | 354 | 325 | 300 | 277 | 256 | 237 | 220 | 205 | 191 | 178 | 167 |
| 35000 | | | | | | | | | | | | | | | | | | | | | | | | | | 335 | 308 | 285 | 263 | 244 | 227 | 211 | 196 | 183 | 172 |
| 36000 | | | | | | | | | | | | | | | | | | | | | | | | | | 344 | 317 | 293 | 271 | 251 | 233 | 217 | 202 | 189 | 176 |
| 37000 | | | | | | | | | | | | | | | | | | | | | | | | | | 354 | 326 | 301 | 278 | 258 | 240 | 223 | 208 | 194 | 181 |
| 38000 | | | | | | | | | | | | | | | | | | | | | | | | | | | 335 | 309 | 286 | 265 | 246 | 229 | 213 | 199 | 186 |
| 39000 | | | | | | | | | | | | | | | | | | | | | | | | | | | 344 | 317 | 293 | 272 | 253 | 235 | 219 | 204 | 191 |
| 40000 | | | | | | | | | | | | | | | | | | | | | | | | | | | 353 | 325 | 301 | 279 | 259 | 241 | 224 | 209 | 196 |
| 41000 | | | | | | | | | | | | | | | | | | | | | | | | | | | | 334 | 309 | 286 | 266 | 247 | 230 | 215 | 201 |
| 42000 | | | | | | | | | | | | | | | | | | | | | | | | | | | | 342 | 316 | 293 | 272 | 253 | 236 | 220 | 206 |
| 43000 | | | | | | | | | | | | | | | | | | | | | | | | | | | | | 324 | 300 | 279 | 259 | 241 | 225 | 211 |
| 44000 | | | | | | | | | | | | | | | | | | | | | | | | | | | | | | 307 | 285 | 265 | 247 | 230 | 216 |
| 45000 | | | | | | | | | | | | | | | | | | | | | | | | | | | | | | | 292 | 271 | 253 | 236 | 221 |
| 46000 | | | | | | | | | | | | | | | | | | | | | | | | | | | | | | | 298 | 277 | 258 | 241 | 225 |
| 47000 | | | | | | | | | | | | | | | | | | | | | | | | | | | | | | | 304 | 283 | 264 | 246 | 230 |
| 48000 | | | | | | | | | | | | | | | | | | | | | | | | | | | | | | | | 289 | 269 | 251 | 235 |
| 49000 | | | | | | | | | | | | | | | | | | | | | | | | | | | | | | | | | 275 | 256 | 240 |
| 50000 | | | | | | | | | | | | | | | | | | | | | | | | | | | | | | | | | | 262 | 245 |
| 51000 | | | | | | | | | | | | | | | | | | | | | | | | | | | | | | | | | | 267 | 250 |
| 52000 | | | | | | | | | | | | | | | | | | | | | | | | | | | | | | | | | | | 255 |

**Example:** To figure D/L ratio for a Catalina 30:

LWL = 25'0"

Displacement = 10,200 lbs. (20% of way between 10,000 and 11,000 lbs.)

Interpolation:

At 11,000 lbs., D/L = 314

At 10,000 lbs., D/L = 286

Tabular difference = 28    $\dfrac{28 \times 20\% = 5.6;\ \text{round to } 6.}{}$

Therefore D/L Ratio = 286 + 6 = 292.

126

FIGURE 12-6
**A boat's physical
condition affects the
price.**

| PHYSICAL CONDITION | EXPLANATION | PRICE ADJUSTMENT |
|---|---|---|
| Handyman special | Fix before using | −40% |
| Pretty bad | Rough but usable | −30% |
| Not too bad | Below average by a little | −10% |
| Average | Average physical condition for her age | 0% |
| Pretty good | Above average by a little | +5% |
| Very good | Everything works | +10% |
| Excellent | Like new | +15% |
| Gold Plater | Maintained professionally, stored indoors, never in salt water, never raced, used lightly by perfectionist. | +20% |

*Rule #5: Brand and model can affect price under certain conditions.* There are cult models and dog models, definitions of which were given in the Introduction. Figure 12-8 gives adjustment factors.

Cult boats often prompt owners to organize class associations or clubs. For example, cruising catboats in general are cult models. The Catboat Association (address in Appendix 2), a national organization

FIGURE 12-7
**The quantity, quality and
age of equipment affect
the price of the boat.**

For all "extra" equipment (other than basic sails, basic winches, etc.) such as VHF, DS, Speedo, WD, WS, etc., and excepting major items such as trailer, new engine, etc.:

1. If there are at least six "extra" items of equipment and everything works, but most of the equipment is the same age as the boat: 0% adjustment.

2. If at least two items of equipment don't work *perfectly*, or have been removed permanently from boat leaving "scars", or there are fewer than six extras, but otherwise equipment is as per (1) above: −5% adjustment.

3. If there are many extras, beyond six items, everything works, and many or most items are newer than the boat: +5% adjustment.

Note: for intermediate situations, you can interpolate between −5% and +5%. For special items such as trailer, new engine, etc., add 50% of the amount originally spent on these items. If a diesel engine is more than 15 years old or a gas engine is more than 12 years old, subtract an amount appropriate for rebuilding or replacement (see Figure 17-1 for specifics).

# SAVING ON THE COSTS OF OWNERSHIP

FIGURE 12-8
**Price adjustment for
"cult" and "dog" models.**

| | |
|---|---|
| Heavy cult following | +5% |
| Fading cult status | +2½% |
| Neither cult nor dog status | 0% |
| Somewhat doggy | −2½% |
| A real bow-wow | −5% |

with over 1,000 members, issues a newsletter three times a year, sponsors a well-attended annual meeting, and promotes regional catboat rendezvous each weekend during the sailing season. Cruising catboats, which have the advantages of extremely shallow draft plus lots of interior space for their length, generally command higher than average prices for their length. For example, the Marshall catboat in Figure 12-9, though only 18 feet long, sells for around $18,000 new, while a 20-year old version commands a price of approximately $9,000.

On the other hand, designs that seek to be all things to all people (such as a combination sailboat/planing powerboat) generally end up

FIGURE 12-9
**Catboats are "cult boats" that command a high market price. A 20-year-old Marshall 18 sells for around $9,000. (Courtesy Marshall Marine)**

being dogs on the used boat market. In certain areas, fleets of certain boat brands and models are especially popular; different cult boats are found in different parts of the country. Talk to the old salts along the waterfront to identify the cult models and dog models in your area.

*Rule #6: Geographic selling location affects a sailboat's price* as indicated in Figure 12-10. The percentage factors shown are approximations; the relationships are very complex and hard to put into mathematical form. Consider them to be rough rules of thumb.

*Rule #7: Timing — in terms of both the season of the year and the phase of the business cycle — affects price.* These effects are quantified in Figure 12-10, which incorporates factors indicating seasonal fluctuations by geographic area. I have not included factors for phases of the business cycle, since the economic interrelationships involved are too complex to describe here in any useful, quantitative way.

*Rule #8: A seller's personal effectiveness in reaching and communicating with his target marketplace can affect the actual price obtained by approximately ± 5%.* Effectiveness in turn depends on the seller's individual marketing skills and objectives, how much effort he expends, etc. Little things count. For example, a poor telephone speaking voice or a thick foreign accent might be an impediment to selling. Or a boat that is basically sound but whose owner has left her messy and dirty can affect price out of proportion to the work needed to clean her up. And these are just two examples. There are so many variables that determine a seller's effectiveness that no attempt is made here to quantify the effect of each. The overall quantification

FIGURE 12-10
**Geography and season
both affect sailboat price.**

| LOCATION | SPRING | SUMMER | FALL | WINTER |
|---|---|---|---|---|
| ME, NH, VT | −2% | 0% | −4% | −6% |
| MA, CT, RI | 0% | −2% | −2% | −4% |
| NY, NJ, PA | +2% | 0% | 0% | −2% |
| Annapolis area | +6% | +4% | +4% | +2% |
| VA to GA | +2% | 0% | 0% | −2% |
| Florida | 0% | −2% | 0% | 0% |
| Gulf Coast to TX | +2% | 0% | 0% | −2% |
| Southern CA | +6% | +4% | +4% | +2% |
| Northern CA | +2% | 0% | 0% | −2% |
| Pacific Northwest | +2% | 0% | 0% | −2% |
| Great Lakes | +4% | +6% | 0% | −2% |
| Other | +2% | +4% | 0% | 0% |

of plus or minus 5% as a possible range of effect is probably the most arbitrary number in the whole concept of Henkel's Rules.

## A sailboat example

To illustrate how to use these Eight Universal Rules, we'll use an example of a 1984 Catalina 30 (see Figure 12-11 for basic statistics), bought new for $35,000, and now, in the spring of 1991, for sale in the state of Connecticut. Put yourself in the seller's place so, as a potential buyer, you can begin to see how he thinks.

---

FIGURE 12-11
**Basic statistics for a
Catalina 30 sailboat.**

Length overall and length on deck = 29'11"
Length waterline = 25'0"
Beam = 10'10"
Draft = standard = 5'3"
Draft = shoal = 4'4"
Sail area = 444 square feet
Displacement = 10,200 pounds
Ballast = 4,200 pounds (lead)
Designer: Frank Butler

---

The first step in establishing a sailboat's market price is to apply Rule #1. To do this, consult Figure 12-3, which indicates that the base price for an 11-year-old, 30-foot average boat priced in May, 1991 is $26,100.

Rule #2 states that price is proportional to displacement (if all other variables are held constant). The Catalina 30's waterline length is 25'0" and her displacement is around 10,200 pounds. Having referred to Figure 12-4 and Figure 12-5, and having thus determined that the Catalina 30's length/displacement ratio is in the neighborhood of 292 (which is considered medium displacement), we can determine an adjustment factor of +6%:

$$\$26,100 \times 1.06 = \$27,666$$

Next we make an adjustment for relative physical condition. Here we get subjective. We're allowed to pick from a variety of verbal descriptions in Figure 12-6. Say we decide that she's "pretty good." Then:

$$\$27,666 \times 1.05 = \$29,049$$

Equipment is treated similarly, per Figure 12-7. Let's say that the boat's equipment is 20% of the way between the "0% adjustment case" and the "+5% adjustment case." This yields an adjustment factor of +1%. There's no trailer or other big-ticket special equipment and the engine has never been replaced, so no other equipment adjustments are necessary.

$$\$29,049 \times 1.01 = \$29,339$$

Next is the consideration of brand and model. The Catalina 30 is among the world's most popular cruising sailboat models, with over 6,000 built since her introduction in 1975. Owners may be found all over the U.S., with heavy concentrations in California and along the Eastern Seaboard. Check Figure 12-8: She probably rates +5% as a cult boat.

$$\$29,339 \times 1.05 = \$30,806$$

Geographic location (Connecticut), bordering on Long Island Sound, is a plus, since the Catalina 30 is a particularly popular brand and model there. And you're selling her in the spring when demand is usually at its strongest in New England. Referring to Figure 12-10, no adjustment is required.

$$\$30,806 \times 1.00 = \$30,806$$

Rule #8, that the seller's personal effectiveness can affect the actual price obtained by approximately ±5%, is impossible to evaluate without knowing something about the selling skills of the person involved. For this example, let's say they are "average," so no adjustment to calculated selling price is needed. The "real" current market price, then, is $30,806; you might want to round off to $30,800.

## Testing the rules

How accurate is this method of calculating value? To test it, you can use the same tables to calculate values for any sailboat, compare calculated prices with advertised prices for similar vessels, and see for yourself. For example, take the Catalina 30 (chosen here because it has been in production for more than 15 years, an unusually long time, and because there is an active market for the boat, providing us with an extensive array of statistics). The tabulation in Figure 12-12, and the same data plotted in Figure 12-13, show the results.

Note that the advertised prices ($31,000 to $37,900 for the 1984 Catalina) are above what our calculations tell us is the "real" selling price for this boat. The main reason for the gap is that sellers usually add something—to pay the 10% commission if a broker is used, and for negotiating room. And since most sellers know the usual practice is for buyers to offer less than the asking price, they typically raise the asking price to a point about 10% to 25% above what they really expect to get. So you can safely assume that if you made an offer on any of the above boats, based on the "Henkel Universal Rules," the seller would be very likely to accept it. The system really works.

## Calculating powerboat prices

If you try to calculate powerboat prices using the same set of tables, you'll run into trouble for several reasons.

# SAVING ON THE COSTS OF OWNERSHIP

FIGURE 12-12

**A sampling of Catalina 30s
for sale during the spring
of 1991**

| EXAMPLE # | BUILT (YEAR) | AGE IN 1991 (YRS) | DESCRIPTION | LOCATION | ASKING PRICE |
|---|---|---|---|---|---|
| 1 | 1977 | 14 | Atomic four, broker | CT | 28,000 |
| 2 | 1977 | 14 | Atomic 4, dlr, whl, rf | CT | 24,500 |
| 3 | 1978 | 13 | Tall rig, well maint | CT | 24,000 |
| 4 | 1978 | 13 | Broker | MA | 22,000 |
| 5 | 1978 | 13 | Excellnt, sale urgent | NJ | 19,000 |
| 6 | 1979 | 12 | Broker | RI | 23,000 |
| 7 | 1980 | 11 | Wheel, tall rig, instr | RI | 29,000 |
| 8 | 1980 | 11 | Dk blue, dsl, rf, dlr | RI | 30,000 |
| 9 | 1982 | 9 | Tall rig, dsl, dlr | NY | 26,000 |
| 10 | 1982 | 9 | Broker | CT | 32,500 |
| 11 | 1982 | 9 | Broker | MA | 32,000 |
| 12 | 1982 | 9 | Tall rig, 86 dsl, good | CT | 30,000 |
| 13 | 1982 | 9 | 2 sls, dsl, electrncs | GA | 30,000 |
| 14 | 1983 | 8 | Many extras, can deliv | CAN | 33,500 |
| 15 | 1983 | 8 | Very clean, dsl, wheel | NH | 32,000 |
| 16 | 1983 | 8 | Broker | MA | 33,500 |
| 17 | 1984 | 7 | Broker | VT | 31,000 |
| 18 | 1984 | 7 | Broker | CT | 34,900 |
| 19 | 1984 | 7 | Broker | MA | 36,000 |
| 20 | 1984 | 7 | 3 cyl dsl, st winches | CT | 36,000 |
| 21 | 1984 | 7 | Brkr, upgraded inter'r | CT | 37,900 |
| 22 | 1984 | 7 | Broker | MA | 34,900 |
| 23 | 1984 | 7 | Broker | MA | 36,000 |
| 24 | 1984 | 7 | Broker | MD | 36,500 |
| 25 | 1985 | 6 | Broker | ME | 35,000 |
| 26 | 1985 | 6 | Tall rig, little use | NH | 35,000 |
| 27 | 1985 | 6 | Shoal drft, tall rig | NC | 37,900 |
| 28 | 1985 | 6 | Tall rig, dsl, wheel | NC | 39,800 |
| 29 | 1985 | 6 | Tall rig, shoal, mint | CT | 34,000 |
| 30 | 1985 | 6 | Tall rig, loaded, brkr | NC | 34,800 |
| 31 | 1985 | 6 | Broker listing | NC | 34,900 |
| 32 | 1985 | 6 | Diesel, 2 sls, electr | MI | 39,000 |
| 33 | 1986 | 5 | Broker | ME | 42,500 |
| 34 | 1986 | 5 | Broker | MD | 37,750 |
| 35 | 1986 | 5 | Diesel, AP, bimini | NJ | 37,500 |
| 36 | 1986 | 5 | Tall rig, bimini, RF | MD | 37,500 |
| 37 | 1986 | 5 | Broker | MA | 44,500 |
| 38 | 1987 | 4 | Broker | MD | 40,000 |
| 39 | 1987 | 4 | Broker | CT | 37,900 |
| 40 | 1987 | 4 | Broker | FL | 39,900 |
| 41 | 1988 | 3 | Broker | CT | 42,900 |
| 42 | 1988 | 3 | Broker | MA | 55,000 |
| 43 | 1988 | 3 | Tall rig, dsl, oven | CT | 42,000 |
| 44 | 1988 | 3 | Wing keel, brkr | MA | 57,000 |
| 45 | 1991 | 0 | Wing kl, full batt | NY | 57,576 |

For one thing the market, even in these difficult economic times, is just stronger for powerboats than for sailboats: there's more demand, and high demand tends to increase prices, sometimes erratically. For another thing, the type and condition of a powerboat's engine (or engines) can contribute to or detract from the boat's value to a much greater extent than a sailboat's engine generally does. It's a matter of size and complexity: a sailboat's sails and rigging are the main source of power for a sailboat; hence her engine is likely to be smaller, simpler and less costly than that of a powerboat of a similar size. In fact, a used powerboat's engines may account for half her value, or even more.

Consequently, her engines have a big influence on any powerboat's value. Size, type, age, general condition, freqency and extent of major overhauls, hours of use and type of use are all important.

For all these reasons, if a powerboat and a sailboat of the same size, weight, age and general condition are put on the market, the

FIGURE 12-13
**Price array graphs are useful in analyzing prices for both powerboats and sailboats. The examples shown are for a Bertram 28FB (left) and a Tartan 27 (right).**

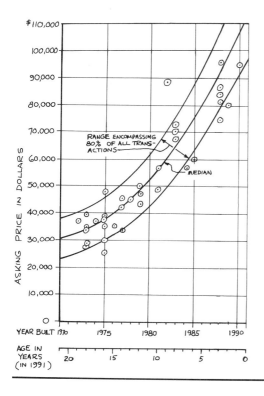

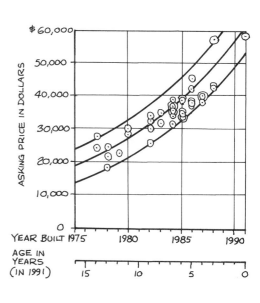

powerboat will almost always command a significantly higher price, at least until she's 20 years old or so, at which time prices may be roughly equal.

Conclusion: It's virtually impossible to find a sufficiently tight correlation of powerboat selling prices to size, weight or even engine horsepower.

The best guide to used powerboat prices anybody has come up with so far is one constructed from plotting asking prices against age for specific brands and models. I call the resulting chart a price array graph. Figure 12-13 illustrates the technique. It's only a rough guide, only a little better than the commercially available boating price guide books, which tend to err on the high side. Even so, I find a price array graph useful whenever I'm analyzing the market for a particular make and model of boat—power or sail.

Caution: when doing a price array graph for a powerboat, be sure to concentrate on boats with a common size, number and type of engines, to prevent too wide a scatter of data points.

To help you estimate the effect on powerboat value of a change in engine size, typical engine prices up through the top of the outboard engine power range are graphed in Figure 12-14. As you can see, the bigger the engine, the wider the range between lowest and highest cost.

## Other sources of information on boat prices

Besides the information given here, there are a number of reference tools you can use to get a line on boat prices:

- **The NADA Official Boat Guide, the ABOS/Intertec Blue Book, the BUC New Boat Price Guide and the BUC Used Boat Price Guide** all gather information on powerboat and sailboat prices, computerize it, and print it out in book form each year. New boat prices are at "suggested retail, F.O.B. manufacturer's plant" levels, reportedly obtained directly from manufacturers. Used boat prices are said to be gathered from brokers and dealers. Be aware that there are few if any pictures and very little in the way of verbal descriptions; the books are virtually wall-to-wall numbers printed in tiny computer typeface. Also keep in mind that, as Figure 12-13 shows, used boat prices can and do vary widely, depending on some factors which are beyond measurement by any centralized clearinghouse, including the NADA, ABOS, and BUC people. Still, the data in these books may be useful as a rough guide. Check your local library or ask to see your broker's copies; the cover prices ($50-plus for the used-boat edition) are probably not worth the investment for individuals on a one-time buying spree. Anyway, they're strictly a guide. The real price of a boat is whatever the owner is willing to sell it for; you won't find that price in any book.
- **Dealer price lists** are easily obtainable from individual dealers. Actual selling prices may be somewhat higher after you add

FIGURE 12-14
**1990 engine prices by
horsepower.**

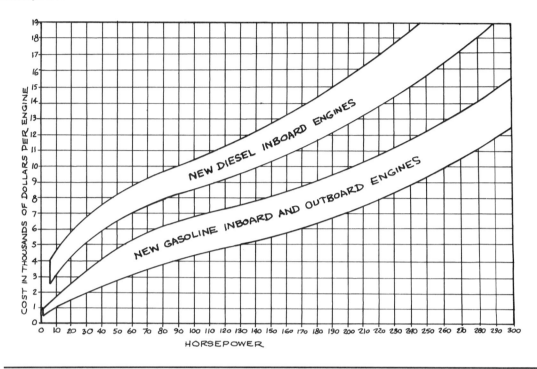

make-ready costs, freight, taxes, and other charges — or
somewhat lower, after you apply your negotiating skills.

- **Ads in periodicals and brokers' listings** can give a fairly good
  picture of relative boat prices, if you can get enough of them
  for a given make and model year. But remember: they're asking
  prices, not selling prices, which could be 5%, 10% (or 50%)
  lower.

- **Listing services,** such as **Boat Owners Multiple Listing Service**
  (see Appendix 2 for a more complete list) charge sellers a fee to
  list boats, then charge buyers for the privilege of reviewing
  listings. Fees for buyers are nominal and may be worth
  investigating if you are looking for a specific make and model
  and are having trouble finding enough listings.

## Summary

How much you initially pay for your next boat depends on a
variety of factors. Some of these factors you can measure and control

and some you can't. One big factor is whether you buy new or used. With new boats, you start with a "manufacturer's list" price and bargain with the dealer or manufacturer on price discounts on a package that usually includes a long list of items besides base price, such as accessories, extra equipment, special services such as make-ready, and perhaps others. With used boats, you start with a fair market price for a boat-plus-equipment package using Henkel's Universal Rules for sailboats, or an estimate based on a price array graph for powerboats, and negotiate from there, with a broker or directly with the owner. In either case, the key to paying the "right" price is in knowing what the market will bear.

# CHAPTER 13

# The Ancillary Costs of Buying

The ancillary costs of buying a boat can add up to a significant amount and mustn't be ignored when you plan your budget. Generally, these costs fall into three categories: (1) searching and inspection costs incurred prior to actually buying a boat; (2) costs associated with insuring and financing your boat, and (3) other front-end costs such as brokerage commissions, documentation fees, etc.

Insurance and financing each warrant detailed discussion, and you'll find complete information on these important matters in Chapters 14 and 15. In this chapter we'll examine the other elements of ancillary cost to see how much each cost category might cut into your budget, and to check out whatever cost-saving possibilities might exist. Then we'll give you some guideline estimating factors for each cost category, to help you to prepare your boating budget.

## Search and inspection costs

*Telephone and travel costs.* Some of these costs — for example, your telephone bills for calls to brokers and owners with boats for sale, are usually inconsequential compared to other boat-buying costs, and you might choose to ignore these minor items when developing a budget or looking for cost savings. But if you travel to distant locations several times in pursuit of boats for sale, perhaps spending a weekend or two at motels and taking your family out to dinner while you're at it, the costs can add up.

There's no way to avoid going to see a prospective dream boat if the broker or owner has convinced you she's a potential buy. But you may save some money by restraining yourself from taking off every time you get another invitation to "come see some boats" at far distant locations. You can save both money and time by accumulating candidates on a list over a period of weeks, and making a half dozen or a dozen appointments all at once. That's very efficient, and gives you a good chance to compare the features of one candidate with those of the others while all are fresh in your mind.

*Your personal time.* Your personal time has value, and you may want to ration it during the search and inspection phase. Otherwise you may find yourself spending so much time looking for the right boat that you begin to experience "boat buying burnout." Then your interest in the search may fade, and you may become impatient to take some action, any action. If that happens, there's a good chance you'll end up buying something that doesn't really suit your purposes.

The solution to that problem is to not let it get started. Stay cool and unemotional and pace yourself in your boat-searching activities.

If you're a doctor, lawyer, plumber, consultant, or perform other services that you charge for on an hourly basis, you may want to include your theoretically lost fees during your time away from work (if any) in your boat-buying budget as a legitimate out-of-pocket cost. But most of us would probably ignore the value of our own time for budgeting purposes, figuring it's recreational.

*Surveying costs.* When the search narrows to one or two finalist boats, you may decide to have a surveyor check her, or them, out for you. Generally a surveyor charges a flat fee (plus expenses). This may run in the range of between $7 and $7.50 per foot of boat length for a bank or insurance survey (not complete enough for a buyer), to somewhere between $8 and $12 a foot for a complete buyer's survey. (Note, though, that some surveyors charge as much for an insurance survey as for a buyer's survey—and presumably make it just as complete, but with greater emphasis on the boat's hazardous features.) Exact cost will depend on:

- **The size of the boat.** Larger boats sometimes command more per foot; for example, a 25-foot boat might cost about $8 to $10 per foot (for a fee of around $200 to $250), whereas a 50-foot boat might cost about $11 to $14 a foot (for a fee of around $550 to $700). But many surveyors just charge $10 or $11 a foot regardless of length, up to 40 feet or so. From 40 to 65 feet, prices rise with the complexities involved; over 65 feet, typically charges are made by the hour.
- **The type of boat.** Some surveyors specialize in wood, others in fiberglass, still others do all types. Commercial boats would cost more than the pleasure boat you're no doubt interested in. Powerboats with twin engines may require a higher charge than sailboats with a single engine. Some surveyors won't do odd types such as ferrocement boats. A surveyor may charge less for a type (or even a certain brand and model) of boat he

knows well, and more for one with which he's unfamiliar. His basic charge is usually mostly a function of how much time it will take him to do the job.

- **The difficulty of surveying a particular boat.** Again, it's a matter of time, and maybe of effort. If a surveyor has to empty lockers to examine the inside surfaces of the hull skin, or pry away ceiling and crawl into tiny spaces or wait while the crane operator takes a long lunch break before hauling the boat for inspection, he'll charge more.
- **The age of the boat.** Older boats tend to have more things wrong with them, which means more work for the surveyor and thus more cost to you. This tends to be especially true of wood boats, which require close scrutiny for the presence of rot.

A *buyer's survey*, or *prepurchase survey*, is as complete as possible, designed to eliminate surprises for the buyer. On a used boat, the surveyor almost always turns up a list of defects of some nature, however minor. These can be used as a negotiating tool when buying (or when selling, if the list turns out to be small or non-existent).

Occasionally an engine survey is performed separately and charged for separately, by a mechanic rather than a boat surveyor. This survey might include a compression check, exhaust gas analysis, oil analysis, etc.

A *bank survey* or *insurance survey* is usually less extensive and therefore less expensive, and is sometimes required for bank financing or insurance purposes. You can find more information on surveys for insurance purposes in Chapter 14.

Least expensive is an *appraisal survey*, or *value survey*, which costs around $100 to $150 (usually a flat fee) plus expenses, and doesn't say much about condition. A bank might ask for one of these, but otherwise you probably wouldn't need it.

One way to save money on a survey is to help save the surveyor time. That means preparing the vessel for him before he arrives, being there when he shows up (or even driving him in your car, which could save his out-of-pocket travel charges), and doing whatever you can do to make his job easier. Have the sails spread out so he can examine them. Remove any impediments to his inspection of the hull (e.g., empty all lockers). If equipment is to be surveyed along with the boat, be sure it's there. If you're a buyer, secure a checklist of what comes with the boat, and make sure the seller has made all gear available for inspection.

You may be able to save the entire cost of a survey if one has been performed within the last few months, and you can get a look at the report. But be careful to distinguish between a condition or value survey made for the seller's purposes, and the more extensive inspection you need.

You can also save money if you arrange for a survey when the seller is hauling the boat anyway, either for maintenance or storage.

Then there's at least a chance that he'll pay for the haul. Or you might agree to split hauling costs, perhaps in return for some other concession.

Be sure everything is in place when the yard is ready to start up the crane and hoist away. Otherwise you'll get charged waiting time—at the full $70 to $90 an hour cost for a crane operator and helper.

One more thought on surveyors: there are good ones, and there are bad ones. To avoid wasting your money by hiring a bad one (and consequently having to have a second survey done to give you the reliable information you're paying good money to get), use care in choosing a surveyor in the first place. Here are some suggestions on how to find a good one:

1. First, decide if you want to use a surveyor located near where the boat is now, or near where she'll be if you buy her. You may save money on the surveyor's travel expenses if you pick one close to where the boat is now — though this would be false economy if you can find a better surveyor elsewhere.

2. In the area you pick, ask boatbuilders, yards, marine insurance agents (particularly your agent if you've picked one), and brokers (and of course your broker if you're using one) for suggested recommendations. Explain what type of boat you're contemplating, and what she's made of; certain surveyors tend to specialize in certain types and materials. If you're thinking about a powerboat, of course, an expert survey of her engines is crucial. And not all surveyors are equally at home with engines.

3. If you ask around but draw a blank, contact the NAMS (National Association of Marine Surveyors, address and phone in Appendix 2). They'll give you some names and phone numbers to try.

4. Armed with several recommendations, check the bank you'll use for financing and the agent you'll use for insurance to be sure everyone on your list is acceptable to them for any survey reports they might require.

5. Call each of the surveyors on your list and discuss your needs. Ask about his breadth and depth of experience, and any specialties he might have. Has he surveyed similar boats before? How many? How long ago? Ask for a blank copy of the survey form or checklist he uses. Ask about his fees — but mainly for the record, since you'll probably find everyone's fees are in the same ballpark; other considerations are more important in deciding who to use. Finally, ask for names of clients you may contact as references. See if he'll offer names of people whose boats are similar to yours, and who live near you.

6. Call the references and chat about their surveys.

7. Based on the impressions you've gained from all of the above, make your choice.

# Other front-end costs

You might face other kinds of front-end costs from registering your boat trailer with your state's department of motor vehicles to paying import duty and lighterage fees for a vessel you purchase abroad. But the following are the cost items most likely to appear in your budget.

***Brokerage commissions.*** Technically, these are almost always paid by the seller, so it would seem such costs have no place in a list of buying costs. Still, I advise you to think of it as a cost to you, since if you somehow can save the seller the brokerage fee (by buying from him directly, for instance), you're very likely to save money yourself. Of course, even if you negotiate with the owner and buy direct from him, he will still be obligated to pay a brokerage commission if you originally found out about the boat through the broker; fair is fair.

Still, there are some situations where the seller may be relieved of his obligations to pay a brokerage commission. For example, say a friend mentions to you that a mutual acquaintance has a boat for sale. You call the acquaintance, see the boat, and want to strike a deal. If the boat happens to be on an open brokerage listing, the seller isn't normally obligated to pay a commission if he sells direct to you. He just notifies all listing brokers that the boat is no longer available, and that's that.

If, however, the boat is currently listed on an exclusive or central listing basis (see Chapter 5 for definitions), the seller must pay a commission — usually 3% for a central listing and the full 10% for an exclusive listing — even if he sells the boat to someone the broker has never heard of.

Even in these cases, though, there's an escape hatch for the seller. Most brokers adhere to the custom by which, through giving 30 days' written notice to his central listing (or exclusive) broker, a seller can escape payment of any commissions. During the 30 days, the broker has the opportunity to come forward with other potential buyers. But if no prospects acceptable to the seller are turned up, at the end of the 30-day period the seller is no longer obligated to pay a commission.

Caution: it's wise to be aboveboard with brokers; mention the name of the buyer when delisting, so they'll harbor no suspicions that you're going around them to one of their existing customers to save the commission.

Another case: you walk into a broker's office and announce you're in the market for a Widget 36. The broker doesn't have a Widget 36 on his active list at the moment — but wait! He picks up the phone, calls old Charlie Smith who has a Widget 36, and asks if it's for sale. Charlie says to the broker: "Sure, didn't you see my classified ad last week? She's for sale right now for $40,000." The broker says to you, "I think I can arrange for you to see a Widget 36 early next week, for sale at $44,000." Unless you had already seen the ad in the classified section, you're honor-bound to deal with the broker, and doing so is almost sure to cost you more.

The moral of the story is that you may avoid paying brokerage fees if you comb the for-sale-by-owner market first, before contacting any broker.

*Documentation and/or registration fees.* U.S. Coast Guard documentation is a procedure originally designed for registration with the federal government of large commercial vessels in international trade, to show proof of ownership. Today, the main purpose of private yacht documentation is to verify ownership by officially naming the owner and listing any mortgages or liens on the boat. That information is helpful to banks and other financing institutions who want to be sure you'll have clear title in case they have to repossess your vessel. It's also handy for you, the purchaser, to know you really own what you think you own. And there used to be some other advantages, too.

At one time, if you documented your yacht, you could escape state personal property tax, and possibly state sales tax as well, if you — illegally — failed to report your ownership to the state. Now, however, that loophole and similar ones, such as registering in Delaware to avoid state taxes, are closed or being closed. The best course of action is to pay your taxes and be done with it.

Another advantage used to be that the Coast Guard took care of documentation for free, which was a real bargain because you could avoid not only state taxes but also state boat registration expenses altogether in many states by having your vessel documented. Many states have closed that loophole, too. And documentation is no longer free: the Coast Guard now charges a basic fee of $100 for documenting a new boat or redocumenting a used boat with a name change. The charge is $50 if redocumentation involves no name change.

So why document? If your boat is to be financed and will be used as collateral for a loan, you'll probably have to have her documented to satisfy the finance people.

The only other advantage is that documented vessels aren't required to have those tacky little three-inch-high numbers on the bow, so the hull may look a little more streamlined. Some states, however, still require an annual renewal sticker plastered to the bow to show you've paid for registration, even though you aren't displaying numbers.

*Professional documentation services vs. do-it-yourself.* When you apply for a boat loan at a bank or finance company, you'll almost surely be told you'll need to document your new boat if she's big enough. Ask if their rules will allow you to do the documentation work yourself, to save the $200 to $500 service fees (over and above the Coast Guard's fees) that are typical for boats up to 40 feet. (Bigger boats can be even more expensive.) Some banks will agree, others won't. Naturally, you save a bundle by doing the job yourself. It isn't that hard to do, and will probably take you a couple of hours all told, if you have a simple boat with no weird history of ownership. If you decide to do the job yourself, write or call your nearest Coast Guard office and ask them for the necessary forms, which come with all the necessary instructions you'll need to do the job. If you can't find the number for your area, you can telephone the Coast Guard information office in Washington D.C., at (202) 267-2992. They're open from 7 a.m. to 4 p.m. weekdays. Or you could try any of the numbers in Appendix 2 listed under "Sources of boat industry and goverment information on boating.

Not just any yacht is eligible for documentation. For one thing, a system of mathematical formulae prevents documentation of vessels less than 5 net tons (boats of around 25 to 27 feet LOA). If your vessel is borderline on size, you may be able to save yourself needless effort by figuring whether your boat is above or below the 5 net ton limit, before contacting the Coast Guard and wading into the red tape.

To calculate your boat's net tons in Coast Guard terms — which have nothing to do with 2,000-pound tons — you proceed as follows:

1. Find your boat's "overall length L," defined by the USCG as "the horizontal distance between the foremost part of the stem and the aftermost part of the stern, excluding bowsprits, boomkins, rudders, outboard motor brackets, and similar fittings or attachments."
2. Find the "overall breadth B," defined as "the horizontal distance, excluding rubrails, from the outside of the skin (outside planking or plating) on one side to the outside of the skin on the other, taken at the widest part of the hull."
3. Determine the "overall depth D," defined as "the vertical taken at or near midships from a line drawn horizontally through the uppermost edges of the skin at the sides of the hull (excluding the cap rail and trunks, cabins, or deckhouses) to the outboard face of the bottom skin of the hull. This excludes the keel unless the keel is covered by the skin."
4. Multiply length times breadth times depth. The answer is called "LBD."
5. Determine the "gross tonnage" or GT. This varies:

   - For most powerboats, GT = 2/3 (LBD/100)
   - For most sailboats, GT = 1/2 (LBD/100)
   - For multihulls, GT = the sum of the tonnages of the hulls
   - For houseboats or other vessels where the "volume of a deckhouse is disproportionate to the volume of the hull," the volume of the deck is calculated (with the answer in cubic feet), the answer is divided by 100 to get the GT of the deckhouse, and the GT of the deckhouse is then added to the GT of the hull

6. Determine the "net tonnage" or NT:

   - For inboard-powered sailboats, NT = 0.9 x GT
   - For powered vessels not designed for sailing, NT = 0.8 x GT
   - For vessels with no propelling machinery in the hull, NT = GT

FIGURE 13-1
**Guidelines for estimating
ancillary buying costs.**

| | UNIT OF MEASURE | BOTTOM OF RANGE | AVERAGE VALUE | TOP OF RANGE |
|---|---|---|---|---|
| **Searching and inspection costs:** | | | | |
| Travel to inspect boats: Mileage | $/mi | $0.25 | $0.50 | $1.20 |
| Travel to inspect boats: Meals | $/day | 5.00 | 30.00 | 140.00 |
| Travel to inspect boats: Lodging | $/night | 30.00 | 80.00 | 200.00 |
| Telephone and postage | total | 5.00 | 20.00 | 100.00 |
| Personal time value at _____ hours | $/hr | varies by individual | | |
| | | | | |
| **Surveyor's fees:** | | | | |
| For buyer's survey except engine | $/ft | $8.00 | $12.00 | $18.00 |
| Extra for full engine survey | Engine | 175.00 | 375.00 | 550.00 |
| "Condition" or "value" survey only | $/ft | 4.00 | 7.00 | 10.00 |
| Avg. charge per hour, exc travel | $/hr | 35.00 | 50.00 | 70.00 |
| Fee for travel | fee | varies with conditions | | |
| | | | | |
| Yard fees for haulout survey, to 40' | $/ft | 3.00 | 5.00 | 7.00 |
| Yard fee extra for layday in slings | $/ft | 3.50 | 5.00 | 6.00 |
| **Costs associated with financing:** | | | | |
| Interest costs, no points: | | | | |
| | | | | |
| $10,000 to $15,000 loan, 5 yrs | prime rate + | 2.5% | 3.5% | 4.5% |
| $15,000 to $25,000 loan, 10 yrs | prime rate + | 2.0% | 2.5% | 3.5% |
| $25,000 to $250,000 loan, 15 yrs | prime rate + | 1.0% | 2.0% | 3.0% |
| | | | | |
| Broker's fees (i.e. dealer's reserve) | % of value | none | 0.5% | 1.0% |
| Attorney's fees | $ fee | none | vary widely | |
| Closing fees | $ fee | none | vary widely | |
| Title search fees | $ fee | none | vary widely | |
| | | | | |
| **Other front-end costs:** | | | | |
| Brokerage commissions (if not included in purchase price) | —— | as agreed by broker (see Chapter 6 for fee structure and conventions) | | |
| Gov't fees for documentation | flat fee | $100.00 | $125.00 | $150.00 |
| Gov't fees for registration | $/ft | none | vary widely | |
| Service charges for professional help in preparing documentation papers | flat fee | 200.00 | 500.00 | 2,000.00 |
| Initial season insurance—new hull | % of mkt value | 0.4% | 0.8% | 1.2% |
| Initial season insurance—5 yr old hull | % of mkt value | 0.9% | 1.3% | 1.6% |
| Initial season insurance—older hull | % of mkt value | 1.4% | 2.2% | 3.0% |
| Initial season insurance—liability for private boat, $300,000 limit | Total premium | 10.00 | vary widely | |

144

For example, to calculate the net tonnage for a Catalina 30 sailboat:

L = 29'11" = 29.92'

B = 10'10" = 10.83'

D = 5'3" = 5.25'

LBD = 29.92 × 10.83 × 5.25 = 1,701

$$GT = \tfrac{1}{2} \, \frac{1{,}701}{100} = 8.50$$

NT = 0.9 × GT = 7.7 net tons

(Note: The shoal draft version would have a lower NT)

This method is called the "simplified method" by the Coast Guard. There is also a "formal method," but we needn't get into that here.

*State registration.* If your boat is too small to document or if you decide not to bother, you'll almost certainly have to register her in the state where you keep her.

Nationwide, only about 70,000 vessels are documented. Around 9 million are state-registered, out of a 15-million boating population. The other 6 million or so unregistered, undocumented boats are exempt from registration laws by virtue of either being small — 14 feet or less in many states — or having little or no engine power. In many states, boats with less than 10 horsepower are exempt, which explains the popularity of 9.9 h.p. engines.

Virtually all states require some form of boat and/or outboard motor registration, and 7 states title outboard engines separately from boats, but only 21 states have titling laws, which require a certificate of title similar to that of an automobile. The certificate is originated when the boat is manufactured, and is passed along from owner to owner, with appropriate notations on any liens on the vessel. The remaining states ask only for a bill of sale, plus details on previous registration if it existed.

## Guideline estimating factors for ancillary buying costs

If you like working against a written, organized budget, you may want to take advantage of the guideline estimating factors in Figure 13-1, for use in figuring potential costs. They'll give you a representative range for estimating purposes, although for accurate figures you'll need to make your own survey of local costs. Even then, costs can vary widely; two marinas a mile apart may have fees wildly different from each other.

## Summary

When planning your boat-buying budget, don't forget the ancillary costs of buying: Search and inspection costs, financing and insurance costs, and fees for brokerage, documentation and registration. If you plan ahead and spend a little extra effort, your savings in these areas can be quite worthwhile.

# CHAPTER 14

# Buying and Saving on Insurance

Some people are insurance-conscious. Others are either "unconscious" or would prefer to self-insure.

A self-insured person accepts the risk of having to pay claims out of his own pocket, instead of assigning that risk to an insurance company and paying annual premiums for the privilege of doing so. Most self-insured people either can't find suitable coverage and so are forced to self-insure, or figure that "disaster may strike somebody near me, but it'll never strike me." And some blue-water voyagers are forced to self-insure because of the prohibitive cost of a no-navigational-limits policy.

In these days of drop-of-a-hat litigation, an "I'm immune" attitude is just not a reasonable approach for the average citizen. The possibility of losing huge amounts in a major lawsuit is real. In fact, unless a boat owner is rich — really rich — he can't afford not to have boat insurance, at least to cover the risk of being personally liable for injuries to others in an accident.

If you decide to borrow money to buy your boat and to use the boat as collateral (which is the usual practice on boat loans), the question of whether to buy coverage or self-insure will be answered for you. That's because practically all banks and finance companies insist on both hull and personal liability insurance if the boat is to be used as collateral for a loan.

These two main types of coverage, *hull insurance* and *personal liability insurance*, are usually wrapped up in a single policy, with the hull component typically accounting for roughly 85% or 90% of the premium and the liability component accounting for the rest. More than 100 different insurance companies write both hull and liability insurance, so there is plenty of variety, not only in what coverage is included and what is excluded, but also in terms of the premium charged for the coverage provided. So it definitely pays to shop among several potential insurers before deciding which one to go with.

If you have a regular insurance agent, start with him, provided he's a boater himself. Marine insurance is a specialized business, and you're better off choosing someone who knows a bent prop or a broken mast when he sees one. If you don't have a nautically-minded insurance advisor, try your local Yellow Pages. Call one of the agents who carries insurance underwritten by the companies listed in Appendix 2; that should save you time eliminating agents who don't handle boat insurance.

## Hull insurance

Hull insurance protects your investment in your dreamboat, while she is in the water as well as while she's on land, against all legitimate loss unless specified otherwise on the policy. If your boat is stolen, or burns up in a fire while stored in a boatyard, she's covered. If a tree falls on her in your backyard or a truck smashes her and her trailer on the highway, you're covered — again, subject to any limits given in your policy.

Policy limits may specify navigation year-round, or navigation for only part of the year (for example, from April to November in the Northeast), and layup ashore for the remainder of the year. The longer you keep your boat laid up ashore, the lower the risk to the insurance carrier, and therefore the lower the premium cost to you. Policies vary from carrier to carrier of course, but typically you can figure on saving somewhere around 2% or 3% of your policy cost for each month you add to the layup period. So think hard about when you'll be using your boat, and specify as long a layup period as you can without sacrificing any significant boating time.

Other variables on hull insurance can affect your cost, too:

- **Navigational limits.** Some policies offer reduced rates if you confine your navigation to a narrowly defined area (or, conversely, increased rates for wide-area coverage).
- **Chartering.** Premiums may be higher — or your policy may be cancelled — if you charter your boat to others. If you have visions of making a little money on the side by chartering, check with your agent first.
- **Size of deductible.** You can reduce your premiums by agreeing to accept a higher deductible, that is, the amount which can be incurred in claims without any payments to you by the insurer.
- **Payment for survey.** You can choose an underwriter who will pay for a condition and value survey, if he requires one. Most insurers will insist that you pay for a survey, but I've come across a few that are willing to pay themselves, or that will

waive a survey. Either way, be sure to factor any surveying costs into the overall picture when shopping for insurance.

- **High marks on survey.** One other variable that can save (or cost) you money is the condition of your boat as judged by an insurance surveyor. If the boat is in fine physical shape and has no safety problems, you'll get high marks on the condition survey and may find that the insurer will offer a lower premium as a result. Moral: if you're going to have a condition survey, make a rigorous check beforehand to be sure she'll pass with flying colors. Here are some suggestions:

1. Make sure all safety equipment is in good working order, from life-lines and stanchions to running lights and foghorn. Check lifelines for chafe; wiggle the stanchions to be sure they're not loose; turn on the lights; blow the horn. Check fire extinguisher pressure, and be sure all extinguishers are readily accessible, not buried under a pile of sails in the cockpit locker. The same goes for life preservers and emergency flares. Check dates printed on flares to be sure they're not obsolete.

2. Check all through-hull valves, hoses and clamps for leaks, corrosion or other signs of deterioration. Wiggle the valves and the hose connections to them. Why? Let me tell you a story.

   Once I was cruising under power on my Tartan 27 and the engine began to heat up. I noticed that some water was coming out of the exhaust, but not as much as usual. I dismantled the entire cooling system piece by piece, from the water pump next to the inlet hose at one end to the exhaust riser at the other end, looking for what I supposed must be an obstruction. After finding only a few stray pieces of seaweed, I reassembled the system and started up the engine. Again I found overheating and half the normal amount of water being pumped out the exhaust. Finally, after scratching my head for a while, I decided to check to see if the inlet seacock valve had somehow worked its way partially closed. As I reached in to try to turn the handle on the valve, my wrist accidentally pushed against the hose connected to it. Suddenly the hose was dangling in mid-air, and water was spurting in through what turned out to be a fully open valve. I closed the valve in a hurry, and found the problem: someone had installed a brass rather than a bronze pipe nipple on the valve, over which the inlet hose to the engine had been slid. The brass had corroded to the point that air was being pumped into the engine right along with the cooling water.

   So don't forget to try to wiggle your valves, and the hose connections to them.

3. Finally, tidy up the entire boat so that the surveyor receives an overall good impression. That alone could affect his report to the underwriter, and thus your premium.

There are other ways you can save money on insurance premiums, too:

- **No-loss history.** Usually you can deduct about 4% for each full year of no losses experienced while you are insured with a given carrier. If you have a loss, the no-loss deductible disappears and you have to start over. And if you change companies, you usually have to start over, too. The moral of this story may be: don't change carriers without thoroughly investigating what your premium structure will look like with the new carrier.

- **Deduction for safe boating practices.** You may qualify for a small savings (5% or so) if you have taken Power Squadron courses (worthwhile in any case for anyone new to boating). If your whole family has taken courses, you may receive further credits. Also, some states have a required boating safety course for teenagers; that may qualify you for still further credits against your premium.

- **Deduction for other circumstances.** In some cases with some companies, you might get a small credit for a number of years of no-loss experience, even if it has been with other insurers. I know of one case where extra years of experience enabled an owner to insure a 20-year-old boat that otherwise might have been uninsurable, at least at a reasonable premium cost. You might also receive discounts for automatic fire extinguishing systems, diesel power instead of gasoline, American Red Cross safety education courses, and possibly other items as well. Check with your agent.

The cost of premiums — and indeed, the risk of not being insurable at all — goes up with the age of your boat. Each year in the life of your boat adds something like 0.1% of her insured value to your hull insurance premium cost. So one way of saving on insurance is to buy a newish boat rather than an oldish one.

## Liability insurance

Liability insurance, which protects you against financial loss arising out of injuries to others or damage to the property of others, is relatively inexpensive as liability insurance goes — at least compared to, say, a liability policy for a car. Rates vary from company to company and from one boat to another, and from one owner to another. If you're an expert sailor with a 14-foot daysailer on a trailer and have a no-loss history, you may be able to buy $300,000 worth of liability coverage for a paltry $10 a year or so. On the other hand, the same liability coverage may cost you several hundred dollars if you zoom around in a large, powerful, high-speed motorboat.

Above $300,000, you can usually add coverage up to around $1,000,000 for a surprisingly small extra cost. You can save by opting for the lower liability limits, but I wouldn't recommend it, especially for powerboaters. These are litigious times, and the coverage is cheap at the price.

Sometimes both liability and property coverage for smaller boats, especially the trailerable kind, can be carried on your homeowner's policy. That's a cost-effective way to buy protection, if you're lucky enough to have the right type of homeowner's policy. But you should keep in mind that a basic homeowner's policy usually provides only $500 or $1,000 in coverage for theft or physical damage to the boat, its equipment, accessories, outboard, trailer, etc. That's not much. Also, sometimes the policy won't pay for a boat or trailer that's stolen any place away from your home. And theft of personal articles may only be covered if there are signs of forced entry into a secured space. There may be other exclusions: ice and freezing damage, chartering, live-aboard use, protection of sails while racing, navigation in certain locations, etc. Check your homeowner's policy, and discuss it with your agent before deciding on what type of insurance you think you need — or you think you can get away with.

## What to do when you just can't find insurance

Different insurance companies have different views on coverage, loss claims and premium rates. For example, during your shopping tour you may find that coverage is denied to you because your boat is too old, too small, too large, is home-built or co-owned, because you're planning to use the boat in dangerous waters (such as on an ocean voyage, or where a hurricane has recently done damage, or where frequency of burglaries is unusually high), or because you lack experience in operating boats. Different companies have different ideas about risk; if one company won't handle your boat, try another. If you keep drawing a blank, what's your next step? Your options boil down to four:

1. **Self-insure.** For low-value craft (market value under $2,000 or so), self-insuring your hull (i.e., accepting the risk of possible damage or loss without compensation) may be your best choice. Another alternative is to get coverage under a rider on your homeowner's policy (see below). But for boats with higher market values, most homeowner's policies cease to apply, and with the greater potential for disastrous loss, many owners would prefer to share the risks with an underwriter rather than to self-insure.

2. **Look for a solution through your regular agent.** Try contacting the agent who insures your home, your cars and other property. If you've had few or no claims on those policies, your agent may be able to find an underwriter to accept your boat as

an additional risk. Or you may find that he offers to provide liability insurance as a rider on your homeowner's policy, but can't provide hull insurance. Many people end up on this basis, with liability covered but self-insured on their hulls.

3. **Find a standard market marine insurer who underwrites your type of boat.** A few companies such as Allstate will write policies for "difficult" craft (e.g., wooden boats) if they comply with simple guidelines. Allstate stipulates no home-builts, nothing under $2,000, nothing over $100,000 (with a few exceptions), and nothing over 10 years old. A quick phone call to Allstate yielded a surprisingly low quote for an imaginary 9-year old, 24-foot plywood outboard (120 h.p.) cabin cruiser used in salt water and worth $10,000: $161 premium, including $111 for $10,000 hull insurance, $45 for $300,000 of liability coverage, and $5 for $5,000 medical payments.

These figures apply for a $250 deductible. If you think, as I do, that that's a very reasonable price, consider this: you can reduce the premium by an additional 5% to 30% by having:

- an electric bilge pump (5% savings on the hull insurance)
- a VHF radio, compass, depth finder, and fume detector (another 5%)
- no operator under 25 and all operators with experience of 3 years or more (another 5%)
- passed a boating education course (another 10% on the hull, 20% on the liability)
- no losses in the first year ( 5% discount on the second year's premium)

One catch: the great majority of difficult-to-insure boats are more than 10 years old and so wouldn't qualify.

In any case, regardless of which companies you obtain quotes from, beware of extra-low rates. They may be set based on loss experience by very hard-nosed claims adjusters, or contractual fine print may impose limitations and exclusions you don't want to live with. Moral: check the fine print before buying coverage.

4. **Seek out an agency that specializes in the risks associated with your type of boat.** Some of the companies listed in Appendix 2 may be helpful to you. For example, Hagerty Marine specializes in insuring wooden boats of all types, if they are in excellent condition and otherwise meet the strict requirements of the underwriter. Another source of hard-to-find insurance is the C. L. McCabe Insurance Agency in Annapolis, which, as McCabe agent Barb Mellon says, is "willing to take the garbage, whereas most insurance agencies aren't. Insuring older wooden boats, for example, is a very time-consuming business, and also very expensive. But there's not a boat that I can't insure. If you have the time, and the patience, and the understanding, I can

do something for you." McCabe is a "surplus lines" agency that is set up to handle high-risk boats — but at a price. Typical annual costs for hull and liability insurance range from 4% to 11% of the hull value, after a deductible, so your old $10,000 Pacemaker might carry a premium of $1,000 a year. But if you want it, you want it.

When you make a claim for a loss, some insurers will raise premiums, others won't. If an insurer gives discounts for customers with a no-claim history, the discount almost always disappears when a claim is made, sometimes for several years. And if you make a succession of claims, when the number of claims or magnitude of the combined claims reaches a certain point, it's very likely that your policy will be cancelled.

Watch the small print, especially if you're shopping for price. For a policy with a lower premium, you may be getting less coverage. This may take the form of lower limits on maximum payment per claim or per year. Or contracts may specify claims will be paid based on "actual cash value" (i.e., depreciated value) instead of "replacement cost agreed value." Or types of coverage may have narrow limits, such as "bodily injury and property damage only" instead of the "broad-form protection and indemnity" contract.

When it comes to hull insurance premium rates, insurance companies are agreed on at least one thing: owners of older boats will have to pay premiums comparable to those for newer boats of the same size and type, even though the newer boats may be worth much more. Why? For one thing, insurance carriers say that repairs on an old 30-footer will likely cost as much as, or possibly more than, the same repairs on a new boat. They also say used boats tend to be a bit riskier in general. Remember my brass valve nipple?

## Summary

Insurance is more complicated than many people realize. There are many choices to be made, and much money to be saved or squandered. But all my advice on marine insurance boils down to three guidelines:

1. Since your boat may be the largest investment you'll ever make other than your home, you should protect her and yourself adequately; go for as much insurance as you need to be protected financially in the event of a disaster.
2. You should plan on spending the necessary time shopping for the right combination of company, benefits, exclusions and premium requirements to satisfy your own unique needs at minimum cost.
3. After you and your boat are insured, you should use her as carefully as if neither you nor she had any insurance at all.

# CHAPTER 15

# Financing Your Dreamboat

You've picked out your dreamboat, a 40-foot yawl, and decided life is too short to wait until you can buy her outright with your savings. If you wait to accumulate enough cash for that, you might never buy her, or any other dreamboat for that matter. While you have $10,000 saved up, the yawl is selling for $50,000 — firm — so you're going to need to take out a $40,000 loan.

When you go to a bank or finance company to ask for a loan to buy the yawl of your dreams, what kind of reception will you get?

The answer is that it depends on a number of things, which we'll examine in this chapter.

The extent of your banker's enthusiasm for granting you a boat loan depends for one thing on the material from which your boat is made. Although fiberglass is by far by most common boatbuilding material these days, and most of the remarks in this chapter will apply to "glass" boats, there are other materials used to make boats, including wood, steel, aluminum, and ferrocement, to name the most common.

## Loans on non-fiberglass boats

Whether you get the cold shoulder if your boat happens to be made of one of these other materials depends, among other things, on which loan officer you pick and how enlightened he is. For example, most bankers think of wooden boats in pretty much the same way that most insurance underwriters do. To them, wooden boats, new or used, are just like fiberglass, except for one thing: there's more reason to be worried about future maintenance and durability. They know that without the proper preventive maintenance, there can be a significant risk of any boat sinking or rotting away to a state requiring major, expensive repair. But they may make a loan on a wooden boat anyway, if the owner shows good evidence of being the type of person who will take proper care of it.

On the other hand, many bankers and insurers believe, rightly or wrongly, that the risk with wood is always significantly greater than with fiberglass, even with proper maintenance. And since bankers and insurers make a business of trying to minimize, and if possible eliminate, the risk they perceive, these credit sources tend to be unexcited about offering their services to wood boat buyers.

Consequently, when you are shopping for a loan for a wood boat (or one made of any other non-fiberglass material) and wish to use the boat herself as collateral for the loan, you should expect to find that many banks and finance companies won't be interested in even briefly discussing your needs. Some will be quick to inform you that they simply have a policy against making loans on boats made of wood (or steel or ferrocement, etc.) regardless of condition, age, or value. In such cases, pleading will do no good; don't waste time trying.

However, don't be discouraged, either. If your dreamboat will pass a rigid professional survey, is in good enough shape to command a reasonable market value, and will be used by you for "normal" pleasure boating (i.e., no circumnavigations or extensive chartering), in all likelihood you'll be able to find a suitable source of financing using the boat as collateral. And even if she doesn't measure up as collateral, you may get financing by other means, described in more detail below.

In researching the material for this chapter, about half the banks and finance companies interviewed about a possible wooden boat loan gave me a flat no. In some cases it seemed as if the companies hadn't ever really given the issue much thought, and didn't plan to. In one case, when I asked a banker if his answer would still be no even if the boat were brand-new, he laughed and said everyone knew no one made wood boats any more; consequently, he asserted, there was no such thing as a new wood boat.

He's wrong, of course. To verify that, just take a look at the builder ads in *WoodenBoat* magazine, a bimonthly with a 100,000-plus circulation.

Despite such pockets of ignorance, we did find a positive response from some banks and finance companies. For example, a senior vice president in charge of retail lending for a major Connecticut bank told me unhesitatingly that his bank does indeed grant wooden boat loans. "The risks aren't too bad," he said, "but boats are fairly large ticket items, so we've got to be very careful."

## Other bank restrictions

Besides being choosy about your boat's construction material, quite a few banks have other restrictions as well. For example, some have lower limits on the amount they're willing to loan. The typical lower limit is $10,000, though some banks won't do business for less than $25,000 or even $50,000.

Some lenders only make loans on new boats. Some won't deal with live-aboards. And some may not want your boat-loan business unless you're already a regular customer.

Naturally, it pays to ask the lender what his restrictions are before getting too involved.

## Bargain rates

Some banks give preferential rates — maybe 1/4% to 1/2% off — to customers who maintain checking or savings accounts. And if you've successfully negotiated loans in the past, the bank you deal with may be willing to talk about reduced rates, assuming you've had a good payback history.

Lenders who set up sales booths at boat shows sometimes offer discounts on the base rate during the show only. But watch out for extra points or fees charged up front, which can more than compensate the banker for his lower rate in some cases.

At a recent boat show, I stopped at one of the yacht financing services booths and asked a representative behind the counter to tell me how I could get the cheapest possible financing deal. Her response was clear and to the point: "The cheapest way to buy a boat is to pay cash," she said. "The next cheapest way is to arrange for a short-term loan at a low simple interest rate with no points and no prepayment penalties. One of the major problems with having to pay points is that on a 15-year loan, for example, you may see an attractive deal where most of the market is asking for a 14½% APR [annual percentage rate] and someone says, 'We've got 13¾% at 3 points.' That looks real nice, and the Truth-in-Lending laws require that the quote of APR include—but that 13¾% is based on 15-year amortization. If you pay that loan off early, or if you go to trade your boat two years down the road, you're going to find that what those points have actually cost you is an equivalent interest rate of around 15%, and it's become very expensive. If you don't pay it off, and you hold it the full 15 years, then you pay the 13¾% and come out ahead." Moral: beware the "bargains," and watch the penalties for early repayment of the loan. Few of us keep one boat for 15 years.

## Banker's priorities

A number of other receptive bankers and finance company executives interviewed stated that when considering a boat-loan application, whether for wood, fiberglass, or any other material, the number one priority item is the applicant's credit quality, and his ability to pay. Consequently, the bank or finance company will conduct a very thorough investigation of the applicant's creditworthiness. They will request a personal financial statement (income statement and personal balance sheet listing all assets and liabilities, such as the sample form in Figure 15-1), plus a copy of the applicant's most recent federal tax

FIGURE 15-1

**Sample balance sheet form application for a boat loan. (Courtesy First Federal Bank of Connecticut)**

LIST ALL CREDITORS, OPEN OR CLOSED, FOR BANKS, CREDIT CARDS, DEPT. STORES, ETC.

| NAME AND ADDRESS OF CREDITOR | ACCOUNT NO. | BALANCE | MO. PAYMENT |
|---|---|---|---|
| | | | |
| | | | |
| | | | |
| | | | |
| | | | |
| | | | |
| | | | |
| | | | |
| | | | |
| | | | |

| DESCRIPTION AND COMPANY | REGISTERED IN NAME OF | QUANTITY | CURRENT MARKET VALUE | PLEDGED |
|---|---|---|---|---|
| | | | | |
| | | | | |
| | | SUB-TOTAL | | |

| DESCRIPTION OF PROPERTY | TITLE IN NAME OF | DATE PURCHASED | COST | MARKET VALUE | NAME OF MTG. HOLDER | BALANCE OWING | MONTHLY PAYMENT |
|---|---|---|---|---|---|---|---|
| | | | | | | | |
| | | | | | | | |
| | | | | | | | |
| | | | | SUB-TOTAL | | | |

| POLICY AMOUNT | NAME OF COMPANY | OWNER OF POLICY | BENEFICIARY | CASH SURRENDER VALUE | LOANS |
|---|---|---|---|---|---|
| | | | | | |
| | | | | | |

**CONTINGENT LIABILITIES**

ARE YOU LIABLE FOR ALIMONY, CHILD SUPPORT OR MAINTENANCE PAYMENTS?    IF YOU HAVE ANY LEASE OBLIGATIONS?
☐ YES   ☐ NO   If Yes, $ _____ PER _____ FOR _____ MONTHS   ☐ YES   ☐ NO   If Yes, $ _____ PER _____ FOR _____ MONTHS
ARE YOU AN ENDORSER, GUARANTOR, CO-MAKER?
☐ YES   ☐ NO   DESCRIBE:
HAVE YOU EVER BEEN A SUBJECT OF BANKRUPTCY PROCEEDINGS OR ARE THERE ANY UNSATISFIED JUDGEMENTS AGAINST YOU?
☐ YES   ☐ NO   If yes, where _____ and when _____ . Describe circumstances _____

**HOW DID YOU HEAR ABOUT US?**

☐ NEWSPAPER   ☐ TV   ☐ REFERRAL   ☐ DIRECT MAIL   ☐ OTHER _____

I(We) warrant the truth of the above information that will be relied upon by First Federal in the furnishing of credit to me(us) and hereby authorize First Federal, any credit bureau or other investigative agency employed by such person, to investigate the references herein listed or statements or other data obtained from me(us) pertaining to my(our) credit and financial responsibility.
I certify that the statements and representations on this Financial Statement constitute a true and accurate account of my financial condition as of the date below.

SIGNATURE(S) _____ DATE _____     _____ DATE _____

First Federal Bank of Connecticut, A Federal Savings Bank       3101 (11/85)

*continued*

FIGURE 15-1 *continued*

## FIRST FEDERAL BANK
OF CONNECTICUT

## CONSUMER LOAN APPLICATION
80 ELM STREET, NEW HAVEN, CONNECTICUT 06510

| OFFICE | | | | | AMOUNT OF LOAN | | TERM | |

☐ **YES** I would like to discuss the peace of mind available through your low cost insurance plans.     PURPOSE

THIS APPLICATION IS FOR
☐ Individual Account  ☐ Joint Account with Co-Applicant

FOR COMMUNITY PROPERTY STATES THIS APPLICATION IS BASED UPON
☐ My (Our) Marital Community     ☐ My Sole and Separate Property and Income

**APPLICANT**

| NAME (LAST) | (FIRST) | (INITIAL) | SOCIAL SECURITY NUMBER | DATE OF BIRTH |
| ADDRESS | | | DRIVER'S LICENSE NUMBER | HOME PHONE NO. ( ) |
| CITY, STATE, ZIP CODE | ☐ OWN ☐ RENT | HOW LONG Yrs. Mos. | ANY OTHER NAME USED FOR CREDIT PURPOSES | NO. DEPENDENTS |

PREVIOUS ADDRESS *(If less than 5 years at present address)*

| FIRM NAME OR EMPLOYER | ADDRESS | | BUS. PHONE NO. ( ) |
| POSITION | HOW LONG Yrs. Mos. | ANNUAL SALARY $ | TYPE OF BUSINESS |
| PREVIOUS FIRM NAME OR EMPLOYER | ADDRESS | | HOW LONG Yrs. Mos. |
| BANK ACCOUNTS  BANK NAME AND LOCATION | | CHECKING ACCOUNT NO. | SAVINGS ACCOUNT NO. |
| BANK ACCOUNTS  BANK NAME AND LOCATION | | CHECKING ACCOUNT NO. | SAVINGS ACCOUNT NO. |
| NAME AND ADDRESS OF MORTGAGE HOLDER OR LANDLORD | | | MONTHLY MORTGAGE PAYMENT OR RENT $ |
| NAME OF NEAREST RELATIVE NOT LIVING WITH YOU | ADDRESS | RELATIONSHIP | HOME PHONE NO. ( ) |
| NAME OF PERSONAL REFERENCE | ADDRESS | | HOME PHONE NO. ( ) |

YOU ARE NOT REQUIRED TO DISCLOSE INCOME FROM ALIMONY, CHILD SUPPORT OR MAINTENANCE UNLESS YOU WANT US TO CONSIDER IT IN CONNECTION WITH THIS APPLICATION.

YEARLY BONUSES/COMMISSIONS: $     YEARLY DIVIDENDS: $     NET INCOME FROM REAL ESTATE: $

OTHER $     SOURCE AND ADDRESS

**CO-APPLICANT**

| NAME (LAST) | (FIRST) | (INITIAL) | SOCIAL SECURITY NUMBER | DATE OF BIRTH |
| ADDRESS | | | DRIVER'S LICENSE NUMBER | HOME PHONE NO. ( ) |
| CITY, STATE, ZIP CODE | ☐ OWN ☐ RENT | HOW LONG Yrs. Mos. | RELATIONSHIP TO APPLICANT | |

PREVIOUS ADDRESS *(If less than 5 years at present address)*

| FIRM NAME OR EMPLOYER | ADDRESS | | BUS. PHONE NO. ( ) |
| POSITION | HOW LONG Yrs. Mos. | ANNUAL SALARY $ | TYPE OF BUSINESS |
| PREVIOUS FIRM NAME OR EMPLOYER | ADDRESS | | HOW LONG Yrs. Mos. |
| BANK ACCOUNTS  BANK NAME AND LOCATION | | CHECKING ACCOUNT NO. | SAVINGS ACCOUNT NO. |
| BANK ACCOUNTS  BANK NAME AND LOCATION | | CHECKING ACCOUNT NO. | SAVINGS ACCOUNT NO. |

YOU ARE NOT REQUIRED TO DISCLOSE INCOME FROM ALIMONY, CHILD SUPPORT OR MAINTENANCE UNLESS YOU WANT US TO CONSIDER IT IN CONNECTION WITH THIS APPLICATION.

YEARLY BONUSES/COMMISSIONS: $     YEARLY DIVIDENDS: $     NET INCOME FROM REAL ESTATE: $

OTHER     SOURCE AND ADDRESS

**INPUT COLLATERAL**

| REAL ESTATE  ADDRESS | | | |
| BOAT/RECREATIONAL VEHICLE MAKE | MODEL | YEAR | PURCHASE PRICE (Attach Sales Agreement if Applicable) |
| SERIAL NUMBER (if available) | ENGINE TYPE | | $ |
| IF USED, LIENS OUTSTANDING | | | |

PLEASE SUPPLY SEPARATE FINANCIAL STATEMENT FOR CO-APPLICANTS WHO DO NOT HAVE A SPOUSAL RELATIONSHIP TO APPLICANT

| ASSETS | AMOUNT | LIABILITIES | AMOUNT OWED | MO. PAYMENTS |
|---|---|---|---|---|
| TOTAL CHECKING ACCT. BALANCES | | NOTES PAYABLE TO BANK: *SEE SCHEDULE A* | | |
| TOTAL SAVINGS ACCT. BALANCES | | NOTES PAYABLE TO FIRST FEDERAL BANK OF CT | | |
| NOTES RECEIVABLE | | 1. | | |
| STOCKS AND BONDS: *SEE SCHEDULE B* | | 2. | | |
| REAL ESTATE: *SEE SCHEDULE C* | | 3. | | |
| CASH VALUE IN LIFE INSURANCE: *SEE SCHEDULE D* | | CHARGE ACCTS: *SEE SCHEDULE A* | | |
| AUTOMOBILES *(YEAR AND MAKE)* | | REAL ESTATE INDEBTEDNESS: *SEE SCHEDULE C* | | |
| 1. | | TAXES PAYABLE | | |
| 2. | | MEDICAL BILLS DUE | | |
| 3. | | OTHER LIABILITIES: *ITEMIZE* | | |
| OTHER ASSETS: *ITEMIZE* | | 1. | | |
| 1. | | 2. | | |
| 2. | | 3. | | |
| 3. | | 4. | | |
| **TOTAL ASSETS** | | **TOTAL LIABILITIES** | | |

return (form 1040). A check with credit agencies also will be made; and the applicant's personal qualifications as a skipper may be questioned. For example, says a senior loan officer from Connecticut, "We want to make sure that we don't have a guy going from a 22-foot speedboat to a 44-foot Bertram in one jump without any experience. We'd like to see any credentials the guy might have."

Since bankers place great value on knowing the loan applicant, you should be sure to consider your regular banker — the one who handles your checking and savings accounts, and possibly your home mortgage — as a potential lender. Several lending officers said that once a loan is successfully negotiated, other future loans made to the same person are much easier to say yes to.

If you pass the test on credit and ability to pay, the loan officer's number two priority will be activated: he'll want to determine the suitability of your dreamboat as collateral. The usual routine is as follows:

***Documentation.*** To insure that the boat is not stolen property or encumbered by prior liens, many credit institutions require Coast Guard documentation on all vessels over 25 feet. Chances are good that if your dreamboat has been financed by a previous owner it is already documented. Then there's little for you to do except present the Coast Guard with the documentation papers for updating when you buy the boat. If the boat has never been documented, you can do it yourself or pay a documentation agency to do it for you. The lender can help you locate a reliable agency if you need help — and in some cases the lender may insist that an agency, either his or one of your choice, be involved. That's so he can assure himself that there's no hanky-panky in the documentation paperwork, such as forgery, false statements, etc. Keep in mind that not all lenders are so cautious, and if you find one that'll let you do your own documentation, you can save several hundred dollars for very little effort on your part.

***Survey.*** Practically all used boat loan sources require a surveyor's report, including an appraisal. (Note: sometimes this is in the form of an appraisal survey, which is not as rigorous — or as expensive — as a buyer's or prepurchase survey. More often, the banker accepts the condition and value survey usually required anyway for insurance purposes.) The better shape a used boat is in, and the lower her age, the more marketable she becomes. That in turn will make her more likely to be acceptable to the loan officer as collateral.

If the boat is new, usually a surveyor's report isn't necessary, and the bank can verify her value through other sources.

***Insurance.*** You won't be able to use the boat as collateral unless she's fully insured, since if she sinks or burns and sustains a total or major loss, the bank will want to close out any collateralized loan immediately, using insurance proceeds to do so. As explained earlier, finding someone who is willing to insure fiberglass boats more than

15 or 20 years old (or in some cases only 10) can be a tricky business. So can finding insurance for any wood or other non-fiberglass boat, especially older models. You may have less trouble provided that a condition and value survey, approved by both the insurance company and the lender, indicates the boat is in tip-top condition, and your own record of insurance claims, if any, doesn't indicate undue risk to the insurance underwriter. But for an older boat you plan to finance, better not sign any papers unless you stipulate that purchase as well as any deposits you put down are subject to availability of financing.

*Marketability.* If you default on your loan, the bank will repossess your boat and try to sell her; thus the bank will want to be sure she is reasonably marketable.

Finding a credit source that will accept your boat as collateral may be problematic if she's not fiberglass or is getting old. However, if the applicant's credit and ability to pay are good, all is not lost even if the boat doesn't meet the loan company's typically rigorous standards, provided the applicant is lucky enough to own equity in a house. In that case, says one bank officer, "We don't pay any attention to the boat; we don't even care about it." Under those circumstances, his bank and many others will offer a choice of a second mortgage, an equity credit line, or a home equity loan, for up to 80% of the owner's equity in the house and property.

The advantages of using your house rather than your boat as collateral are that the interest rate will be lower than for a straight boat loan and that it is much easier to find willing lenders. In fact, it may be the only way to finance your boat if she can't be insured. The fact that home loans are offered at lower cost than boat loans should not be surprising, since there is less perceived risk to a lender for a house and the land it's on as collateral, than for a boat. Real estate generally appreciates in value, while these days boats rarely do. And after all, most houses don't sink or get stolen.

The main disadvantage to using home equity to obtain credit is that you are using up a valuable potential source of future credit on a discretionary item — your boat. Many people prefer to pay the extra cost inherent in financing their boat through other channels, specifically in order to preserve the unused credit available on their residence. They reason that, while most borrowers do not get into such trouble, an overzealous spender can lose his home if he fails to make the required monthly payments. And it's not uncommon for people to overestimate the amount of debt they can handle, which eventually lands them in financial trouble.

## Gathering facts on the deals available

You're a good credit risk. You've obtained a high quality survey that gives your dreamboat a glowing report, and have lined up appropriate insurance coverage. You've also shopped around for credit and narrowed the field down to three lenders that you like, and that apparently like you and your dreamboat. Now it's time for you to compare what kinds of loans each of the three offers, and pick one you want to work with. In making your choice, remember that differences in cost should be the main determinant, but other factors — such as giving special consideration to the friendly banker who has your current checking and savings accounts and your home mortgage — should not be overlooked. Remember, you never know when you might need a friend.

Bankers and finance companies have a language all their own, and making accurate apples-to-apples comparisons between the deals of several lenders can get very complicated. However, all the details of their deals boil down to five factors:

- **Size.** How big a loan is being offered as a percentage of the value of the boat? If the boat is being used as collateral, you'll probably get no more than 80% of the amount you spend to buy a new boat, or 75% on a used boat. The amount may possibly be much less, down to around 50%, depending on what the lender thinks about your creditworthiness and what he thinks about lending against boats in general and your boat in particular.
- **Term.** How many monthly payments will be made? The more creditworthy you are, the longer will be the term offered by the lender. You'll be paying a lower monthly rate on a long-term loan, since the total principal is divided up into more pieces. But remember, you're paying more for total interest on the longer-term loan. Fixed-rate loans generally don't go beyond 12 years, and the maximum may be considerably less for older boats. However, with adjustable rates, boat loan terms may go as high as 15 or even 20 years.
- **Interest rate.** Each lender's interest rate will be expressed as a percentage. Typical advertised rates these days are based on the prime rate (a base rate used by bankers, which rises and falls with general economic conditions), plus between 2.5% and 4%. But the calculation of how often the rate is compounded is not usually announced; instead, an annual percentage rate (APR) will be given, which is intended to permit easier comparisons between lenders. However, what you need to make a good apples-to-apples comparison is not the percentage interest rate, but the actual dollar amounts of interest and principal you'll be paying each month. Be sure you ask each lender to provide this information. Also, most lenders will give you a choice between *variable rate* (also called *adjustable rate*) interest and *fixed rate* interest. Variable rate is cheaper than fixed rate when a loan first goes into effect, but can escalate later if the economy starts to heat up and the prime rate starts climbing. (Most variable interest rates are tied into the prime rate, which in May, 1991 was 8.5% nationally, cut by the Feds from higher levels in an attempt to stimulate the U.S. out of an economic

recession. If and when the economy stabilizes and you think it will stay that way, so the prime rate will remain low during the period you'll be paying off your loan, choose variable rate. If you think the economy will head back toward the double-digit inflation and high interest rates of a few years ago, pick the fixed rate. It's your gamble; either way, the bankers have figured things so they'll come out ahead.

- **Up-front charges.** Lenders have ways of reducing the advertised interest rate on a loan. One way is to chop the interest you'll pay during the period of paying back the money you owe, and adding an equivalent amount up front in *points* (one point is one percent of the loan) and fees (legal fees, application fees, origination fees, title search fees, and others). Be sure you understand each deal in terms of all the up-front costs before you pick a lender.
- **Back-end penalties.** Check to see if there is a prepayment penalty. Most boat buyers sell the boat before the loan matures, so they prepay. Usually that's just a matter of giving the bank the principal amount still due on the loan, and that's that. Any future interest charges are forgiven. Occasionally there is a penalty in points or other terms; usually there isn't. And in some cases where a loan agreement calls for a prepayment penalty, the lender will waive it if you are moving up to a bigger boat and he finances her.

## Effects of the new tax law

The Tax Reform Act of 1986 affected boat buyers in two main ways.

*Interest deductibility.* Interest deductions on consumer loans for such big-ticket items as cars and most boats have been repealed, effective January 1, 1987. (To ease taxpayers' pain slightly, there was a gradual phaseout on interest deductibility: 100% of consumer interest was deductible in 1986, 65% in 1987, 40% in 1988, 20% in 1989, 10% in 1990, and 0% in 1991.) But the law still permits an interest deduction for boat owners, provided the boat can be lived aboard, and provided the boat owner doesn't have a second home he's already deducting interest on.

The way it works is this: The 1986 law continues to allow interest deductions on debt secured by the taxpayer's principal residence or dwelling unit, and a second residence or dwelling unit, up to the original purchase price of the residences plus actual cost of improvements. Note that debt must be secured by the residences and not just by the personal credit of the owner to qualify for an interest deduction. Since the definition of "dwelling unit" (in Section 280A of the Tax Code) includes "boat" (as well as "house, apartment, mobile home" and other similar property), a boat, provided it is large enough to live aboard and thus be a dwelling unit, can qualify under the new law as a second residence. Of course, the boat should have appropriate basic living necessities: a head, a galley, and at least one berth.

Since the new law permits interest deductions for no more than two residences, a boat can't qualify if the owner already has first and second home mortgages and is deducting interest on both. However, the new law stipulates, "In the case of a taxpayer who owns more than two residences, the taxpayer may designate each year which residence (other than the taxpayer's principal residence) the taxpayer wishes to have treated as the second residence." If a boat can be a residence, then it seems clear that the taxpayer may deduct the interest on the boat instead of the second home, if he so chooses.

## The luxury tax

The federal government recently instituted a 10% excise tax on all new cars and recreational boats and airplanes sold for more than $100,000. This new luxury tax begins to take effect at a hundred grand. That is, if your new toy, for example, costs $150,000, you pay 10% of the $50,000 in excess of the hundred, which amounts to a $5,000 tax. At $200,000, you'd pay a $10,000 tax; at $300,000 the tax would be $20,000. At this writing the tax is still in effect, but the buying public and the boating industry have not taken kindly to it, and there are signs that repeal may be in the offing in late 1991.

## Figuring your best deal

What is the best deal for you on a loan, given the complications of variable vs. fixed interest rates, different payout times, up-front and back-end penalty costs, and the options created by the the new tax law?

The key to comparing the numbers in different loan proposals is to find the deal with the lowest *present value*. For those who haven't heard about the basic concept of present value, a little explanation is in order.

The idea of present value is simple. Money has a time value. For example, you'd rather have $1,000 right now than that same $1,000 a year from now. That's because money in hand today is worth more than the same amount received later. How much more? That depends on your rate of return — how much you could get if you invested the money in, say, a savings account or a mutual fund.

Here's a hypothetical example. Say that whenever you have any extra cash, you put it into a bond fund that's paying interest of 12.5% a year. If you start with $1,000 in the bond fund, at the end of a year you'll have $1,125. You'll have to pay tax on the amount earned; let's say that today and in future years that amounts to 28% of the $125 (at 12.5%) that you've gained, or roughly $35, leaving you $1,080. That means that your after-tax rate of return ("ROR") on extra cash is 8.0%, which is the $80 you've added to the original $1,000.

Armed with this 8.0% rate, you can figure the present value of $1,000 received at various times. If you receive the money right now — in the present — it's worth $1,000. But what if you can't get at the $1,000 until a year from now? Intuitively, you know it's worth less, but how much less? The answer is that $1,000 received a year from now is worth $925.90 received today — since that's the amount which, if invested at your rate of return of 8.0%, will equal $1,000 in a year.

By writing out the equation above, it's easier to see how the $925.90 was calculated; by transposing terms, we get:

$$\frac{\$1,000.00}{1.080} = \$925.90$$

However, if you're looking at a schedule of payments throughout a year (such as the monthly payments on a boat loan), the present value of the stream (to an accuracy close enough for our purposes) is the *average* of the table values at the *beginning* and the *end* of the year. Thus, for example, the present value of a stream of payments of $83.33 a month (totalling $83.33 × 12 = $1,000 for a year) would be greater than the $925.90 above, since the money is available not in a lump sum at the end of a year, but instead, in 6 months (on the average). Thus, the present value would be half way between $925.90 and $1,000, or $962.30.

You can find the $962.30 in the "8%" column of the present value tables reproduced in Appendix 4. From those same tables, you can get the present value of $1,000 not available until various future times for a wide range of possible interest rates available to you and other consumers.

What does all this have to do with evaluating alternative loan proposals? The answer is that you can use the above present value factors to get an apples-to-apples comparison of various loan deals. First you need to determine in each case how much money you'd be paying out up front, plus how much you'd pay out in principal and interest each year until the loan is paid off, plus how much tax savings you'd get each year for interest deductions. You can then multiply the amount you'd pay in each time period by the appropriate factor in the table to get the present value of each of these payments and savings. Then add up all the present values and you have the after-tax cost of each loan proposal to you in current dollars. And, naturally, the deal with the lowest present-value total is the most economical choice for you.

If you're thoroughly confused by all of the above, don't despair; you're not alone. I have seen strong businessmen close to tears, unable to grasp the principle behind the present value concept, that *a buck in the hand today is worth more than a buck you don't get until next year*. Once you understand why that's so, the rest is easy.

## An example

To simplify this matter, consider an example using two five-year loan proposals, one from Bank A and one from Bank B. To avoid unnecessary confusion, we won't go through all the calculations the two competing banks had to make to give you the payment schedule you asked for. We'll assume that your after-tax rate of return is 8%. We'll also assume that both banks gave you the amounts of the interest payments included in the total payments due, and you figured the tax savings you'd make on interest and included it as part of the numbers in the payments due column. We'll simply present the resulting amounts representing the stream of payments each bank is asking you to make, adjusted for what you'll get back from Uncle Sam in tax savings (see Figure 15-2).

This calculation shows that your best deal from Bank B is better than from Bank A, even though total payments to Bank B at $33,300 are greater by $300 than they would be to Bank A. That is because the present value of the total cash you will have to pay to the bank is only $27,687, $210 less than with Bank A's deal, where the present value is $27,897.

## Other uses of the present value concept

Figuring out which financing deal is best isn't the only use of the present value concept when you're checking out boat-buying opportunities. It also gives you what you need to evaluate any offers that involve the time value of money. Take, for example, the advertisement in Figure 15-3 that begins: "Take stock in America." A boat dealer is offering "free bonds" to which he assigns a value of $10,000. Is this

FIGURE 15-2
**Comparison of bank loan proposals. Despite the fact that you'd pay $300 more to Bank B than you would to Bank A, Bank B's deal is better. The text tells you why.**

| TIME | BANK A'S LOAN PROPOSAL | | | BANK B'S LOAN PROPOSAL | | |
|---|---|---|---|---|---|---|
| | PAYMENT DUE | PRESENT VALUE FACTOR | PRESENT VALUE OF PAYMENT | PAYMENT DUE | PRESENT VALUE FACTOR | PRESENT VALUE OF PAYMENT |
| Now (up front) | $3,000 | 1.00 | $3,000 | $300 | 1.00 | $300 |
| During first year | 6,000 | 0.9623 | 5,774 | 6,600 | 0.9623 | 6,351 |
| During second year | 6,000 | 0.8910 | 5,346 | 6,600 | 0.8910 | 5,881 |
| During third year | 6,000 | 0.8250 | 4,950 | 6,600 | 0.8250 | 5,445 |
| During fourth year | 6,000 | 0.7639 | 4,583 | 6,600 | 0.7639 | 5,042 |
| During fifth year | 6,000 | 0.7073 | 4,244 | 6,600 | 0.7073 | 4,668 |
| Total payments | $33,000 | | $27,897 | $33,300 | | $27,687 |

FIGURE 15-3

**Is a $10,000 savings bond worth $10,000? See text for answers. (Source Sunday *New York Times*)**

their present value? No, it's their value at maturity, which is 11 years down the road. You could go out today and buy a $10,000 Series EE U.S. Savings Bond for $5,000 — and that is what such a bond is worth to you or to the boat dealer now, *not* $10,000 as intimated in the ad.

## Summary

The daily business of life seems to be getting more and more complicated, and bankers and finance companies, to say nothing of federal and state tax authorities, don't seem to be helping to make it any simpler. Still, if you want to finance your dreamboat you'll probably be able to do it, assuming you can meet a lender's credit requirements. Just keep in mind that taking out a boat loan has costs associated with it that you can avoid if you pay cash. And the cost of financing will vary depending on which lender you choose. How to figure your loan cost is a matter of finding the lowest *present value* among your loan options.

# CHAPTER 16

# Routine Maintenance and Operating Costs

Some small boats may be used for years without incurring a single penny of cost for operation or maintenance. But such craft are the exception. Even a Sunfish needs a good cleaning and a coat of wax once in a while, and even the smallest outboard boat requires buying fuel to make it run, and once a year needs a little maintenance to keep it running at peak performance.

On a few operating and maintenance costs — such as fuel — you have no choice; you must buy fuel in order to operate your boat. But for many other items, you have an opportunity to save money by shopping around or by doing certain things yourself. For example, you can rent a slip in a marina, or you may be able to drop your own mooring into the adjacent harbor mud and enjoy large savings. You can have a boatyard erect a frame and drape a rented winter cover over your boat for you at a cost likely to run into three figures, or you can build your own frame out of scrap wood, dig out an old tarp from your basement, do your own draping, and end up with zero to pay.

## Cost estimating factors

The information in Figure 16-1 identifies a range of specific operating and maintenance costs for typical pleasure boats, from 6-foot dinghies to 50-foot cruisers and the possible range of cost for each item, including labor if a boatyard were to do the work. You can use this information to help you decide what maintenance and operating you want to do yourself, and what you want to farm out to others.

FIGURE 16-1
**Estimating routine
operation and
maintenance costs.**

| TYPE OF COST | | UNITS OF MEASURE | TYPICAL COSTS | | |
|---|---|---|---|---|---|
| | | | BOTTOM OF RANGE | AVERAGE | TOP OF RANGE |
| Fuel costs: | diesel oil | $/gal | $1.00 | $1.60 | $2.00 |
| | gasoline | $/gal | 0.90 | 1.50 | 2.00 |
| | at consumption rate of | gal/mile | see boat spec sheet | | |
| | miles travelled per yr | miles | see boat spec sheet | | |
| Slip rental cost | | $/ft/mo | 3.50 | 7.50 | 12.00 |
| Dockside electricity charges | | $/mo | 25.00 | 50.00 | 80.00 |
| Dockside telephone charges | | $/mo | 5.00 | 20.00 | 50.00 |
| Dockside water charges | | $/mo | free | 10.00 | 20.00 |
| Mooring expense for rental | | $/ft/yr | 15.00 | 25.00 | 38.00 |
| Mooring expense if owner-supplied | | $/ft/yr | 1.00 | 6.00 | 10.00 |
| Annual insurance: new hull | | value | 0.4% | 0.8% | 1.2% |
| Annual season insurance: 5-yr-old hull | | % of mkt value | 0.9% | 1.3% | 1.6% |
| Annual season insurance: older hull | | % of mkt value | 1.4% | 2.2% | 3.0% |
| Annual season insurance: liability $300,000 limit | | Total premium | 10.00 | varies widely | |
| Derigging and decommissioning | | $/ft | 2.00 | 4.00 | 6.00 |
| Haulout costs | | $/ft | 4.00 | 5.50 | 9.00 |
| Wash bottom at haulout | | $/ft | 0.50 | 1.50 | 3.00 |
| Wash sails | | $/sq ft | 0.15 | 0.28 | 0.50 |
| Cost of a winter cover and frame: | | | | | |
| Frame | | $/ft | 1.00 | 6.00 | 12.00 |
| Cover | | $/sq ft | 0.20 | 0.30 | 0.40 |
| Labor to erect and tie down | | $/ft | 3.00 | 6.00 | 10.00 |
| Winterizing engine(s) | | Per engine | 10.00 | 100.00 | 200.00 |
| Other misc. prep for winter storage | | Total | 50.00 | 600.00 | 1,000.00 |
| Winter storage costs: on land | | $/ft | 6.00 | 16.00 | 30.00 |
| Winter storage costs: in water | | $/ft | 8.00 | 18.00 | 32.00 |
| Cost of uncovering in spring | | $/ft | 3.00 | 6.00 | 10.00 |
| Paint bottom prior to launch | | $/ft | 1.00 | 8.00 | 20.00 |
| Launching costs | | $/ft | 4.00 | 5.50 | 9.00 |
| Post-launch chores | | $/ft | 0.50 | 2.00 | 10.00 |
| Periodic bottom scrubbing | | $/ft | 1.00 | 1.50 | 2.00 |
| Yacht club dues | | Total | varies widely | | |
| Boating magazine subscriptions | | Each | 8.00 | 20.00 | 75.00 |
| Other routine annual costs | | Total | varies widely | | |

If you peruse the cost data in Figure 16-1, you'll be able to see
that on almost any boat, if you do the work yourself, the savings can
be significant.

To get an idea of just how much money you might save by using
your own materials and labor to minimize operating costs and by doing

# SAVING ON THE COSTS OF OWNERSHIP

a good portion of maintenance work yourself, we'll take a look at an example. Figure 16-2 lists a typical 30-foot powerboat's annual operating and maintenance costs. The first column assumes the owner feels money is no object, and the second one assumes the owner takes an aggressive do-it-yourself approach.

As you can see, the do-it-yourselfer in this example saves over $2,000 per year by applying a little elbow grease. If he puts that savings in the bank each year and lets it compound at 6% interest (after income tax), in 10 years he'll have over $28,000 saved, enough to buy lots of new toys for his boat.

## A closer look at specific costs

*Fuel costs* depend on a variety of factors, including the number and size of the engines being run, the weight of the hull being propelled, the speed of the hull, the efficiency of the propeller or propellers, and even how clean the immersed portion of the hull is.

Fuel costs per mile of running time tend to be higher for powerboats than for sailboats, since powerboats generally run at consid-

FIGURE 16-2
**Saving money on operating and maintenance costs. (Example: 30-foot power cruiser.)**

| ITEM OF COST | OWNER HAS YARD DO EVERYTHING | OWNER ATTEMPTS TO DO AS MUCH AS POSSIBLE HIMSELF | DO-IT-YOURSELF SAVINGS |
|---|---|---|---|
| Fuel cost at 2 m.p.g. and 500 miles/season at $1.50/gal | $375 | $375 | $0 |
| Slip space rental (4 months) | 900 | 0 | 900 |
| . . . or use own mooring | 0 | 50 | (50) |
| Insurance | 500 | 500 | 0 |
| Prep for decommissioning | 120 | 30 | 90 |
| Build frame and cover | 300 | 0 | 300 |
| Haulout cost | 150 | 150 | 0 |
| Wash bottom at haulout | 45 | 0 | 45 |
| Winter storage charge | 480 | 240 | 240 |
| Uncover in spring | 150 | 0 | 150 |
| Paint bottom | 500 | 200 | 300 |
| Launch | 150 | 150 | 0 |
| Two bottom scrubs during season | 45 | 0 | 45 |
| Dues and subscriptions | 80 | 80 | 0 |
| TOTAL | $3,795 | $1,775 | $2,020 |

FIGURE 16-3
**Typical powerboat fuel
usage.**

| | SIZE (LOA) | DIESEL POWERED BOATS | | | GASOLINE POWERED BOATS | | |
| --- | --- | --- | --- | --- | --- | --- | --- |
| | | CRSG SPEED (M.P.H.) | FUEL USAGE (G.P.H.) | (M.P.G.) | CRSG SPEED (M.P.H.) | FUEL USAGE (G.P.H.) | (M.P.G.) |
| Sunrunner | 20 | – | – | – | 23.0 | 5.5 | 4.18 |
| Sisu | 22 | 18.4 | 2.5 | 7.36 | – | – | – |
| Crosby | 24 | – | – | – | 23.0 | 3.0 | 7.67 |
| Sleekcraft | 26 | – | – | – | 32.0 | 9.0 | 3.55 |
| Cruisers Inc. | 28 | – | – | – | 26.0 | 12.0 | 2.16 |
| Tollycraft | 30 | 27.6 | 17.0 | 1.65 | – | – | – |
| Scout | 30 | – | – | | 10.4 | 1.0 | 10.40 |
| Chris-Craft | 32 | – | – | – | 31.5 | 32.0 | 0.98 |
| Grand Banks | 32 | 9.2 | 3.0 | 3.07 | – | – | – |
| Tollycraft | 34 | 21.9 | 18.0 | 1.22 | – | – | – |
| Trojan | 36 | – | – | – | 26.0 | 37.0 | 0.70 |
| Ocean Yachts | 38 | 27.0 | 34.3 | 0.79 | – | – | – |
| Tollycraft | 40 | 20.7 | 18.0 | 1.17 | – | – | – |
| Cruisers Inc. | 42 | 26.1 | 29.8 | 0.88 | – | – | – |
| Viking | 45 | 32.0 | 47.0 | 0.68 | – | – | – |
| Californian | 48 | 23.8 | 33.4 | 0.71 | – | – | – |

Note: m.p.h. = knots × 1.15

erably higher cruising speeds. Sailboat fuel usage typically runs in the range of 3 to 5 miles per gallon, whereas powerboats can get anywhere from 7 or 8 miles per gallon or more all the way down to 3 gallons per mile (1/3 mile per gallon) or worse. Figure 16-3 shows typical fuel usage for a random assortment of powerboats in different size ranges, while Figure 16-4 plots fuel usage vs. length in graph form. Use the graph to estimate probable fuel consumption for whatever size boat you're considering.

Whether you're in a powerboat or a sailboat, you can save money on fuel costs as follows:

- **Maintain your bottom.** Keep your bottom slick, clean and smooth. Use antifouling paint to prevent slime and barnacles; apply paint carefully to avoid speed robbing ridges and rough spots.
- **Watch your prop.** Make sure the diameter and pitch of your prop is correctly matched to your engine's r.p.m. and power and to your preferred cruising speed. And don't let it become chipped, pitted, worn or rough. Have it checked periodically, and paint it at least once a year with a hard-finish gloss paint.

FIGURE 16-4
**Powerboat fuel usage vs. length.**

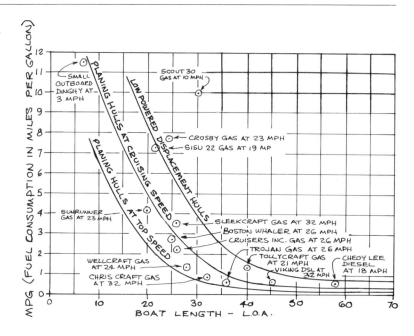

- **Keep boat weight low.** Don't overload with useless gear.
- **Balance weight in the boat.** Keep weight out of the ends. Seat passengers to help achieve a plane quickly without plowing. Use power trim if available to minimize hull surface in the water, once on a plane.
- **Shut down when stopped.** Excessive idling eats fuel.
- **Stay tuned up.** Set the timing right; keep plugs, carburetor, and injectors clean.
- **Cruise at economical speeds.** Check your m.p.g. at various speeds, construct a fuel usage curve, and then try to maintain the optimum cruising speed needed to give the best mileage. Typically, best compromise between speed and economy is to cruise throttled back one-third from wide open. For example, if you owned the Wellcraft 28 footer whose fuel consumption is plotted on Figure 16-5, you'd want to cruise at a speed of around 23 miles an hour to optimize fuel consumption. If you can't stand going that slowly, fine, but you should know it'll cost you money.

    The same is true at harbor speeds. As Figure 16-5 shows, 7 m.p.h. would be a lot more economical than 9 m.p.h.
- **Run courses in a straight line** when under power. Wandering from a direct point-to-point course adds distance and increases fuel consumption needlessly.

    ***Slips and moorings*** are getting more and more expensive,

FIGURE 16-5
**Fuel consumption at different speeds for a Wellcraft 2800. (Courtesy *Boating* magazine)**

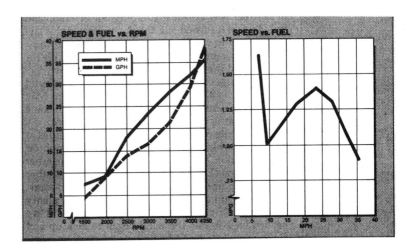

as condos take over more and more of the waterfront and cause the supply of suitable boat space to shrink while demand for space increases. So if you can find a spot in a protected harbor to drop your own mushroom mooring and chain, you should do so.

Some waterfront towns still permit anyone to drop a mooring in the local harbor without charge, wherever there is appropriate swinging room and adequate protection from wind and waves. Restrictions vary widely from town to town; often the town will want to approve the position of the mooring, specify its size for a given boat, and inspect it at regular intervals.

If you're lucky enough to locate a town that allows it, you can plop a 300-pound mushroom shackled to a ½-inch galvanized chain into the mud for a one-time inital cost of around $350, plus annual maintenance costs that might run about $50 to $100. That's just about as low-cost a place to put your boat as you're likely to find.

*A few words on dockominiums.* A recent phenomenon resulting from the conversion of waterfront property to non-marina use (mainly to condominiums) is the advent of "dockominiums," wherein a boatowner buys rights to keep his boat at a given slip more or less as long as he wants. Prices vary widely, from around $1,200 per foot of boat length to $6,000 per foot or so (i.e., for a 30-foot boat, $36,000 to $180,000). In addition there are maintenance and management fees that may run upwards of $5 a foot per month or about $2,000 a year for a 30-footer. That doesn't include charges for metered outlets for telephone, power, or cable TV, or initiation fees or dues if it's a "club" arrangement.

"Docko" deals come in many varieties and forms, but generally they all boil down to four types:

# SAVING ON THE COSTS OF OWNERSHIP

FIGURE 16-6
**Moorings ready to be set in the mud for the season. The big one on the left weighs 500 pounds, and is suitable for mooring a 50-foot sailboat or 55-foot powerboat.**

1. **Fee simple.** The boatowner owns outright a piece of land adjoining a slip, and the right to use the slip plus a specific part of a common area (parking lot, access way, etc.) owned jointly with other dockominium buyers. An annual fee is charged for maintenance and management. This arrangement is similar to a traditional condo. The owner clearly has the right to sell his dockominium if he chooses, although there may be restrictions in his deed or other sales document.

2. **Long term lease.** Here the state or local government owns water rights, and leases their use, typically for 99 years. Usually the lease is to a management corporation, which then buys or constructs slips and a common area which it subleases to individuals.

FIGURE 16-7
**Sizes, prices, and use limits of mushroom moorings and chain for boats 15 to 35 feet in length.**

LENGTH OF BOAT ON MOORING

| OPEN POWERBOATS | CABIN POWER AND SAILBOATS —ALL TYPES | MINIMUM SIZE OF MUSHROOM (POUNDS) | TYPICAL COST | CHAIN LINK DIA. | TYPICAL DISCOUNT COST PER FT. |
|---|---|---|---|---|---|
| Under 15' | — | 75 | $90 | 3/8" | $1.60 |
| 15' | Under 18' | 100 | 120 | 3/8" | 1.60 |
| 20' | 18 to 20' | 150 | 150 | 1/2" | 2.70 |
| 22' | 20 to 24' | 200 | 190 | 1/2" | 2.70 |
| 25' | 25 to 29' | 250 | 220 | 5/8" | 4.20 |
| 35' | 30 to 35' | 300 | 270 | 5/8" | 4.20 |
| – | 35 to 40' | 400 | 350 | 3/4" | 7.50 |
| – | Over 40' | 500 or more* | varies | 3/4" or more | varies |

Note: The above table indicates typical sizes only. Exact size depends on specific harbor conditions, windage on boat, weight of boat, etc. Consult your local harbormaster for recommendations.
* For boats over 40 feet in length, one rule of thumb for mooring anchor weight is 10 pounds for each foot of LOA—and always round *up*, to be on the safe side.

3. **Co-op.** A boat owner buys a share in a corporation which in turn buys or leases a marina. The share gives its owner rights to use a specific slip. Again, there may be restrictions on sale of those rights.
4. **Private club.** Members of a private club arrange to lease or buy a marina, with each member entitled to use club facilities plus a particular slip. Usually the member cannot sell his rights, at least not to an outsider and not at a capital gain.

Needless to say, if you're investigating buying or leasing a docko, read all the contractual fine print. Especially note these questions to ask:

- Are you permitted to sell your rights if your circumstances change later? If so, how and with what stipulations? If not, what happens if you want out?
- What are the expected total annual charges for management, maintenance, balloon payments in later years, expected escalation in charges, and anything else?
- Is there a ceiling on annual charges that may be assessed?

What rights do you have if charges escalate to the point you think they're unfair?

Today docko prices appear to be escalating in value to the point where in some locations, investors have been enticed to buy and resell, presumably at healthy capital gains after a few years of ownership. There are all kinds of deals; any specific deal may or may not be a good one.

How can you tell a good deal from a bad one?

First of all, look for a docko that's conveniently located, is re-saleable, and is located in an area where the population can afford the sizable investment involved. After all, when you decide to sell your stake, you don't want to have to strain to find a buyer.

Second, try to find a deal that specifically limits potential year-to-year increases in monthly charges, or at least gives you some control over fees you'll be charged. You don't want to get locked into monthly fees beyond your future ability to pay.

Third, compare buying a resaleable dockominium to the alternative of renting a conventional marina slip. You can use the present value concept (Chapter 15) to do this. Figure 16-8 compares docko costs to slip rental fees.

An owner with a 30-foot boat has a choice: he can buy a resaleable docko for $100,000 plus annual maintenance charges of $2,000 escalating at 5% a year, or he can rent a slip in a conventional marina at $3,000 annually, escalating at 10% a year. He figures he'll leave boating in 10 years, at which point he thinks — conservatively — that he can sell his docko for at least twice what he paid for it (i.e., a growth in value of 7.2% per year). He has $100,000 in cash to buy the docko outright. If he decides to rent instead, he'll put his $100,000 in a bank, where he figures — again, conservatively — that he'll earn 4% a year after tax, which he can use to help pay the slip rent. Which alternative is more economical? See Figure 16-8 for the answer.

*Annual insurance costs.* Refer to Chapter 14 for more information on this subject.

*Fall haulout, winter maintenance, spring launching, and similar costs.* These costs vary widely from region to region. In the north, boats are hauled in the winter to protect them from ice damage. In the south, they're hauled to clean off the barnacles, scum and other marine life that eventually collects despite application of antifouling bottom paint.

*Periodic bottom scrubbing.* This is something you can do yourself — thus saving some money — or have someone else do. Kids sometimes rent themselves out during the summer for pocket money; check local bulletin boards to find them. Or you can always have your local marina do the work if you're willing to pay top dollar in exchange for no-hassle convenience.

FIGURE 16-8
**A comparison calculation
using the present value
concept.**

| YR. | P.V. FACTOR AT 8% R.O.R. | CHOICE A: BUY A RESALEABLE "DOCKO" | | CHOICE B: RENT A SLIP FROM YEAR TO YEAR | | | |
|---|---|---|---|---|---|---|---|
| | | ANNUAL NET CASH (OUTFLOW) OR INFLOW | NET CASH FLOW PRESENT VALUE | NET CASH (OUTFLOW) OR INFLOW FROM SLIP RENTAL | ANNUITY ON CASH IN BANK (4% AFTER TAX) | COMBINED CASH FLOW OF RENT AND INCOME | NET CASH FLOW PRESENT VALUE |
| 0 | 1.000 | (100,000) | (100,000) | — | + (100,000) = | (100,000) | (100,000) |
| 1 | .962 | (2,000) | (1,924) | (3,000) | + 4,000 = | 1,000 | 962 |
| 2 | .891 | (2,100) | (1,871) | (3,300) | + 4,000 = | 700 | 624 |
| 3 | .825 | (2,205) | (1,819) | (3,630) | + 4,000 = | 370 | 305 |
| 4 | .764 | (2,315) | (1,769) | (3,993) | + 4,000 = | 7 | 5 |
| 5 | .707 | (2,431) | (1,719) | (4,392) | + 4,000 = | (392) | (277) |
| 6 | .655 | (2,553) | (1,672) | (4,832) | + 4,000 = | (832) | (545) |
| 7 | .606 | (2,680) | (1,624) | (5,315) | + 4,000 = | (1,315) | (797) |
| 8 | .561 | (2,814) | (1,579) | (5,846) | + 4,000 = | (1,846) | (1,036) |
| 9 | .522 | (2,955) | (1,543) | (6,431) | + 4,000 = | (2,431) | (1,269) |
| 10 | .481 | (3,102) | (1,492) | (7,074) | + 4,000 = | (3,074) | (1,479) |
| 11 | .446 | 200,000 | 89,200 | 0 | + 100,000 = | 100,000 | 44,600 |
| Tax on gain | | (25,000) | (11,150) | | | 0 | 0 |
| | | TOTAL | (38,962) | | | TOTAL | (58,907) |

Conclusion: Based on the above conservative assumptions, in this case the boat owner would be better off buying the docko. But what if he made 20% on his $100,000 in the stock market instead of 4% at the bank? What if his docko couldn't be sold for double the purchase price? What if docko fees escalated faster than 5% a year? For these and other "what ifs," you can figure your own answers using the above format.

*Yacht club and boat club dues.* These costs vary from little or nothing to thousands per year. For example, the 1976 *Lloyd's Register* (which isn't published anymore, but which once listed most of the nation's hundreds of yacht clubs) shows a Quanset Yacht Club, organized in 1936, that charged annual dues of $1 a year. Maybe by now it has doubled to $2. The same book lists the Royal Palm Yacht and Country Club in Boca Raton, Florida, with a $12,500 initial fee plus $1,350 annual dues. That's probably doubled, too.

Still, joining a club and keeping your boat there can be considerably less expensive than staying at a marina, and is likely to be more fun, too, if you like to socialize.

If you're new to boating and are thinking of joining a club, find a club member (by walking around the club parking lot until one comes along, if you can't think of a better way) and introduce yourself. Explain what you're looking for (sailboat racing, a swinging bar on Saturday nights, predicted log contests) and ask what his club offers. If there's no match with your particular interests, perhaps he'll be able to suggest another club nearby. If you find what seems like a match, check the dues and other costs. If the price is in your range, contact one or more flag officers (commodore, vice commodore, rear commodore) to see how you can apply.

*Magazine subscriptions.* At subscription prices of $10 to $50 a year, boating magazines represent some of boating's best buys. Get a variety (lots to choose from — see Appendix 2) and keep up with what's going on — including trends in prices of boats and equipment.

# CHAPTER 17

# Repair Costs

Tabulating the costs of every type of boat repair work is virtually impossible. There are just too many variables. Some repairs may be owner-performed, and others may be done by professionals. In some cases, even a pro may find it difficult or impossible to do certain repairs, particularly on sophisticated electronic equipment which, though only four or five years old, may already be obsolete and for which circuit boards or other special components may no longer be available. In other cases, repair costs may be so high that replacement makes more sense. And there are so many varieties of repair, from laying up a new section of a fiberglass hull to replacing old spark plugs in an outboard, that the mind boggles.

It wouldn't be very useful to try to tabulate a listing of repair costs — it would be hundreds of pages long and still wouldn't cover every possible type of repair by every type of repairman. Instead, suggestions are offered below on how to save money when it comes to maintenance, replacement and repairs.

## Practice repair avoidance

You can practice "repair avoidance" by buying a sturdy, well-built boat in the first place. Avoid boats with flimsy, thin-skinned hulls that use non-corrosion-proof materials in their construction.

## Stick to fiberglass for lowest repair costs

If you buy a wood boat, you'll pay a premium for a passable professional carpentry job, unless you're in Maine or the state of Washington, where you can still find good craftsmanship at reasonable prices. These days, wooden boat owners tend to buy them because they love wood's look, smell and feel, and they love to work with it, too. For them it makes sense. But wood isn't for the non-craftsman, unless he's a rich non-craftsman.

Steel and aluminum yachts aren't quite as craft-intensive as wooden ones, but they still need a lot more tender loving care than fiberglass. If you are conservative, put your money into fiberglass.

## Go easy on wood trim

In general, avoid buying a boat with a lot of wood in the interior. For many years the most popular style for most sailboats and for many traditional-style power boats was the "wood cave" effect, in which the boat's interior was sheathed from top to bottom in stained and varnished mahogany or teak. Wood-free boats were sneezed at as "floating bathrooms" or "Clorox bottles." But in recent years, European builders have introduced tasteful, pastel-colored, brightly-lit, vinyl-padded interiors which have enjoyed wide appeal among boat buyers. These designs have changed the character of boating interiors from an old-time "private men's club" environment to one more modern and sophisticated. If your boat has such a European-inspired interior, it may find a broader market when you sell it.

That's not to say you shouldn't buy a "wood cave" if you like it, or that you'll be stuck with it forever if you do. If you like her looks, chances are others will, too. Maybe not too many others, but some. And as the man says, if you're only selling one boat, all you need is one buyer.

Some boats, such as Hinckleys, Aldens and Little Harbors, feature interiors loaded with beautifully hand-crafted wood. They're more like palaces than caves. These builders have always commanded a premium price in the marketplace and probably always will, partially because of their elegant wood interiors rather than in spite of them. But such yachts are not for do-it-yourselfers or budget-conscious folk. To keep their wood pristine takes a lot of labor or a lot of money.

In any case, if you opt for lots of wood, remember that eventually it will need extensive maintenance to keep it in tip-top condition. How much work? A lot more than a few swipes of a damp cloth on fiberglass.

## Organize your maintenance

Keep usage logs, maintenance schedules and equipment replacement tables to help plan your non-routine repairs and replacements. By knowing when to take action on these items, you'll keep your boat and her equipment in good condition. Moreover, you won't be subject to as many surprises as you will be if you practice a policy of "If it ain't broke, don't fix it." With this in mind, the following cycle periods for maintenance, repair and replacement of some of the more costly items of equipment might come in handy.

- **Inboard engines,** even if they're well-cared for, typically need an overhaul after about 1,000 to 3,000 hours of use if gasoline, big diesels (over 100 h.p.) that are run very regularly (e.g. power for commercial craft). For these engines, figure on removing cylinder heads for cleaning and inspection every 12,000 hours, and doing a major overhaul at around 20,000 hours. Keep track of running time in your log, and add it up at the end of each season. And if your engine has been misused (overloaded, over-revved, overheated or underlubricated for any significant period of time), count on a major overhaul sooner.

- **Outboards** need overhaul more often than do inboards, after 1,000 hours or so of use.
- **Sails** used in heavy winds wear out much faster than those used only in light air, but on the average a headsail or spinnaker lasts one season in grand prix racing, two seasons in regional and club racing, three seasons if one season is only for practicing and casual racing, and longer if it's a soft-cloth cruising sail that's not abused. Mainsails usually last about twice as long as headsails, though serious racers often replace a whole suit at once rather than piecemeal. When my kids, as teenagers, raced Blue Jays seriously, I replaced all three sails every two years. But my Tartan 27 mainsail, which by itself cost more than a full suit of Blue Jay sails, was still going strong after 15 years of steady but gentle use.
- **Gasoline tanks** made of galvanized steel, black iron, or aluminum, even if well-maintained, may only last about 10 years, or longer under certain conditions — but don't count on it. Replacement can be very tricky and therefore expensive, but some builders persist in using such materials anyway, rather than more expensive monel (the very best material for the job), copper, stainless steel, or other more corrosion-resistant materials.
- **Diesel fuel tanks** should be of aluminum, monel, stainless steel, plain (ungalvanized) steel, or "black iron" sheet (with the steel or iron painted on the outside to protect against atmospheric corrosion; the fuel oil will protect the inside). If the tank material is stainless steel, watch out for pitting where non-corrosion-resistant steel has occluded the surface (so-called "crevice corrosion").

Galvanized steel tanks are acceptable for gasoline, but not for diesel fuel. Watch out for boats that were originally gasoline-fueled but have been repowered to diesel. Be sure they don't have galvanized tanks. The galvanizing flakes off and can clog the injectors.

Fiberglass fuel tanks are sometimes used, but are generally not recommended. For one thing, if there is a fire on board, the tank will burn and add fuel to the fire. For another thing, if the lamination layup is at all flawed, there may be some wicking of glass through the skin of the tank, causing seepage over a period of time.

Incidentally, good yacht design practice calls for tanks

that are removable if necessary for repair or replacement. Nevertheless, lots of tanks aren't.

- **Winches** eventually wear out if they're not regularly cleaned and lubed according to manufacturer's specs. Usually a light oil is required to lube the pawls, and a special waterproof grease that coats the surfaces well and is not too thick is used on other interior surfaces. If you're faithful to a maintenance program, the winches may never wear out.
- **Running rigging and docklines** will begin to show wear after four or five years of average use. You can double the life of sheets and docklines by reversing the ends or shortening the line or wire a bit so the chafe points at blocks, cleats, or chocks move to fresh locations. Nevertheless, plan on replacement every 10 years or so.
- **Standing rigging** on sailboats can be made to last the life of the boat if material is stainless steel, if swaged terminal ends are kept from corroding (apply a little WD-40 followed by a light coat of grease at each juncture of wire and fitting at the beginning of boating season and again at the end) and if the rigging isn't abused.
- **Compasses** are subject to deterioration from sunlight (which darkens and spalls the clear plastic sphere containing the card) and from freezing, unless protected by a compass fluid reservoir. You should also shield your compasses from the sun when not in use (you can buy covers for this purpose for most brands) and if your boat is stored for the winter in sub-freezing temperatures, detach all compasses and take them home for inside storage in the off-season. Then they'll last forever. Otherwise, figure 10 years.
- **Electronic equipment in general** should be treated like the delicate equipment it is. Keep away from moisture and sudden shock loads, and store at home in the winter. Then you can figure on replacement due to technological obsolescence rather than wear or breakage. Figure 5 years to 20 years for a replacement cycle, depending on the type of equipment.

## Do the maintenance and repair yourself if you can

Maintenance and repair work in any of the above categories can be done by a boat owner if he has the necessary skills and tools, although it often is farmed out to a professional sailmaker, mechanic, etc. If the boat owner is a do-it-yourselfer, his cost will be his material cost plus nothing for his labor, assuming he values his labor at zero. On the other hand, if the boat owner gives a repair job to a pro, the cost will be the total of materials, often valued at list price rather than discount on the bill, plus labor at an average yard billing rate of something like $25 to $45 per man-hour, or, at the "carriage trade" yards, up to $50 or even $60 an hour.

FIGURE 17-1
**Replacement fund
contributions and
replacement costs for a
typical 30-foot sailboat.**

|  | ANNUAL FUND CONTRIBUTION | REPLACEMENT COST |
|---|---|---|
| Replacement of sails every 6 years: |  |  |
| Mainsail | $300 | $1,800 |
| 150% genoa | 250 | 1,500 |
| 100% jib | 200 | 1,200 |
| Spinnaker | 225 | 1,350 |
| Major rebuild of engine, every 10 years: |  |  |
| For one 30 h.p. 4-cyl. Atomic 4 (gas) | 350 | 3,500 |
| For one 15 h.p. 1-cyl. Yanmar (diesel) | 300 | 3,000 |
| Replacement of engine (alternative to rebuild): |  |  |
| For one 30 h.p. Atomic 4 | 500 | 5,000 |
| For one 15 h.p. Yanmar | 450 | 4,500 |
| Major hull refit: |  |  |
| Fair, sand, and paint hull | 500 | 5,000 |
| Miscellaneous accumulated items (electronics, rigging, winches, compasses, etc.) | 400 | —— |
| Total annual fund contribution | $3,475 |  |

Whichever route you choose, you might want to establish a replacement fund to which you contribute each year. Then when major work is necessary, you'll have the cash to do the work without strain, pain, or the extra cost of bank loan interest. For a typical 30-foot sailboat, the numbers might look like those in Figure 17-1.

# CHAPTER 18

# Inflation, Depreciation, and Opportunity Cost

If you want to know how much money you've *really* made (or lost) on the purchase and sale of your last boat, you must understand how inflation, depreciation, and opportunity cost affect boat prices, and take these factors into account in your calculations. This chapter explains how to do this.

## Inflation effects

To a consumer (such as a boat buyer), inflation is measured by the Consumer Price Index For All Urban Consumers (CPI-U), published monthly by the U.S. government. The Index gives us a handy way of figuring the current purchasing power of the dollar, as measured by what a "market basket of goods and services" costs at any given time. Figure 18-1 shows the fluctuations of the CPI-U for a 30-year period ending in 1990.

To examine the relationship between inflation and boat prices, let's first look at new-boat prices. For convenience, we'll start with some sample new-boat prices for two points in time, 1980 and 1990 (Figure 18-2).

The data in Figure 18-2 show that, in general, new boat prices rose much more rapidly than inflation during the 10-year period, at least if the particular models in this sample are any indication, and that the

FIGURE 18-1
**The inflation rate has
been creeping up at the
rate of about 4% to 5%
in recent years, after
much bigger increases in
the late 1970s and early
1980s.**

| YEAR | CONSUMER PRICE INDEX* | YEAR-TO-YEAR PERCENTAGE INCREASE | YEAR | CONSUMER PRICE INDEX* | YEAR-TO-YEAR PERCENTAGE INCREASE |
|---|---|---|---|---|---|
| 1959 | 29.1 | 0.7% | 1975 | 53.8 | 9.1 |
| 1960 | 29.6 | 1.7 | 1976 | 56.9 | 5.8 |
| 1961 | 29.9 | 1.0 | 1977 | 60.6 | 6.5 |
| 1962 | 30.2 | 1.0 | 1978 | 65.2 | 7.6 |
| 1963 | 30.6 | 1.3 | 1979 | 72.6 | 11.3 |
| 1964 | 31.0 | 1.3 | 1980 | 82.4 | 13.5 |
| 1965 | 31.5 | 1.6 | 1981 | 90.9 | 10.3 |
| 1966 | 32.4 | 2.9 | 1982 | 96.5 | 6.2 |
| 1967 | 33.4 | 3.1 | 1983 | 99.6 | 3.2 |
| 1968 | 34.8 | 4.2 | 1984 | 103.9 | 4.3 |
| 1969 | 36.7 | 5.5 | 1985 | 107.6 | 3.6 |
| 1970 | 38.8 | 5.7 | 1986 | 109.6 | 1.9 |
| 1971 | 40.5 | 4.4 | 1987 | 113.6 | 3.6 |
| 1972 | 41.8 | 3.2 | 1988 | 118.3 | 4.1 |
| 1973 | 44.4 | 6.2 | 1989 | 124.0 | 4.8 |
| 1974 | 49.3 | 11.0 | 1990 | 130.7 | 5.4 |

*Based on the Consumer Price Index for All Urban Consumers, U.S. City Average, All Items. CPI-U for 1982–84 = 100.0.

relationship of new-boat prices to overall inflation is not well defined. In fact, with variances from the CPI-U running all the way from 91% to 198% more, any uniform correlation appears to border on being non-existent.

Figure 18-2 also indicates that price behavior in the powerboat market today appears to be very different from that in the sailboat market, with most of the powerboat price boosts considerably greater than most of the sailboat increases over the last 10 years.

I've already noted (in Chapter 12) that used powerboat prices behave more like new and used car prices—partly because powerboats wear out faster, like cars, and partly because the powerboat market is more active. New powerboats are sold to a crowd that likes to trade in and buy new every two, three, or four years. In contrast, most sailboats stay with their owners five years or more.

# SAVING ON THE COSTS OF OWNERSHIP

FIGURE 18-2
**Tabulation of sample
new-boat price changes,
1980 to 1990**

| | NEW BOAT PRICES | | PRICE INCREASE IN PERCENT | PERCENT INCREASE VS. CPI-U (UP 59%) |
|---|---|---|---|---|
| | 1980 | 1990 | | |
| **Powerboats** | | | | |
| Bertram 33 dsl | $104,600 | $216,000 | 207% | 148% more. |
| Carver 28 gas | 34,800 | 70,100 | 201 | 142 more. |
| Mako 17 | 4,600 | 9,600 | 209 | 150 more. |
| Boston Whaler 13 | 2,100 | 5,400 | 257 | 198 more. |
| | | | | |
| **Sailboats** | | | | |
| Tartan 37 | $ 66,700 | $137,000 | 205% | 146% more. |
| Sabre 30 | 37,800 | 74,800 | 198 | 139 more. |
| Catalina 30 | 26,700 | 40,000 | 150 | 91 more. |
| Catalina 22 | 5,000 | 9,500 | 190 | 131 more. |

Notes: Mako and Whaler prices do not include engine; all others do. The 1990 models are comparable in size to their 1980 counterparts, but in some cases include a greater variety of standard features and equipment, and more up-to-date styling. During the same period, 1980 to 1990, the CPI-U increased by 59%.

These differences have resulted in healthy powerboat sales in recent years, while sailboat sales have persistently lagged behind.

One other factor impacts on the weakness in new sailboat prices. For the last several years, there have been large quantities of used but basically durable fiberglass sailboats for sale in what some observers see as a saturated market. This trend seems destined to continue until some new equilibrium point is reached between supply and demand for used sailboats.

Until the owners of these used sailboats sell them, they aren't likely to move into new boats. And they're not selling them at current asking prices.

That situation may mean that there will have to be a significant drop in used sailboat prices before the new sailboat market gets going again. In effect, the U.S. will have to have a used sailboat "crash" in prices to clean out a severe case of overhanging inventory.

It may already have begun. Recently I heard of a used C&C 35 Mark I (a prized cult boat) selling for $27,000, and a C&C 33 going for $18,000. In a market where new boats in that size range can easily cost $100,000, those prices sound eminently reasonable.

# Depreciation effects

How does inflation affect *used* boat prices? This is an even tougher question than how inflation affects *new* boat prices. That's because when it comes to used boats, it's hard to separate inflationary effects from the effects of depreciation. That is, at the same time that *inflation* is trying to push prices *up*, *depreciation* is pushing them *down*. Depreciation, the loss in value of an object as time passes, is normally associated with ordinary wear and tear, gradual technological obsolescence, and inevitable shifts in design styling.

We've already made one calculation for depreciation (in Chapter 12). Now let's look at it from another angle.

If we assume that inflation and depreciation are the two main determinants of used boat prices, we can set up a table using hard data to separate the two and see if we can spot any trends. Figure 18-3 takes the same boats in Figure 18-2 and compares today's used-boat prices with the original new-boat sticker prices.

Let's analyze the figures. First of all, the Bertram 33, a relatively

FIGURE 18-3
**Tabulation of boat price
changes for 1980 model
boats**

| | NEW PRICE IN 1980 | AVG. USED PRICE OF 1980 BOAT IN 1990 | OVERALL PRICE CHANGE IN PERCENT | PERCENT CHANGE | |
|---|---|---|---|---|---|
| | | | | ASSUMED DUE TO INFLATION | DUE TO DEPREC'N BY DIFFERENCE |
| **Powerboats** | | | | | |
| Bertram 33 dsl | $104,600 | $83,700 | −20% | +59% | −79% |
| Carver 28 gas | 34,800 | 17,500 | −60 | +59 | −109 |
| Mako 17 | 4,600 | 1,850 | −60 | +59 | −119 |
| Boston Whaler 13 | 2,100 | 850 | −60 | +59 | −119 |
| **Sailboats** | | | | | |
| Tartan 37 | $ 66,700 | $60,000 | −1% | +59% | −69% |
| Sabre 30 | 37,800 | 26,600 | −30 | +59 | −89 |
| Catalina 30 | 26,700 | 27,700 | +4 | +59 | −55 |
| Catalina 22 | 5,000 | 3,400 | −32 | +59 | −91 |

Notes: Mako and Whaler prices do not include engine; all others do. The 1990 models are comparable in size to their 1980 counterparts, but in some cases include a greater variety of standard features and equipment, and more up-to-date styling. During the same period, 1980 to 1990, the CPI-U increased by 59%.

high-priced powerboat for her size, and the Catalina 30, a relatively low-priced sailboat for her size (at least in terms of cost to buy new), seem to hold their value best in their respective categories, having the lowest net loss in value due to depreciation.

Why do these two boats retain their value in the used market so well compared to the others in this sample? My theory is that the reasons are different for the Catalina than for the Bertram.

The Catalina, a simple, easy to sail, mass-produced, low-first-cost vessel that includes lots of extras in her original price, appeals to new sailors, particularly those looking for a big bang for their bucks. (Note that among 30-foot sailboats, Catalina traditionally has been the low-price leader in both new and used categories.) After they buy, owners are bombarded with friendly overtures from fellow members of the Catalina owners' association, a manufacturer-supported group. The association publishes a quarterly newsletter called the *Mainsheet* which reports on the doings of all 14 of the Catalina classes, and makes Catalina owners feel they are part of a big, happy family. It's no wonder that many Catalina owners move up to bigger Catalinas; they're presold by the owners' association. The net result of this combination of price advantage and preconditioning to buy is that the demand for used Catalinas is heavy. This in turn supports a 10-year-old used-boat price that for the Catalina 30 is around 69% of the new boat price. That's the highest ratio of used to new price in our sample (see Figure 18-4).

FIGURE 18-4
**Used prices as a percentage of new prices, for 1980 boats vs. 1990 boats**

| | PRICE IN 1990 | | USED PRICE AS A PERCENTAGE OF NEW PRICE |
|---|---|---|---|
| | NEW 1990 BOAT | USED 1980 BOAT | |
| **Powerboats** | | | |
| Bertram 33 dsl | $216,000 | $83,700 | 39% |
| Carver 28 gas | 70,100 | 17,500 | 25 |
| Mako 17 Angler | 9,600 | 1,850 | 19 |
| Boston Whaler Sport | 5,400 | 850 | 16 |
| **Sailboats** | | | |
| Tartan 37 | $137,000 | $60,000 | 44% |
| Sabre 30 | 74,800 | 26,600 | 36 |
| Catalina 30 | 40,000 | 27,700 | 69 |
| Catalina 22 | 9,500 | 3,400 | 36 |

Notes: Mako and Whaler prices do not include engine; all others do. The 1990 models are comparable in size to their 1980 counterparts, but in some cases include a greater variety of standard features and equipment, and more up-to-date styling. During the same period, 1980 to 1990, the CPI-U increased by 59%.

While the Bertram is at the top end of the scale for powerboats in terms of used-boat-to-new-boat-price-ratio, her ratio is lower than two of the four sailboats in our sample, and in the same ballpark as the other two. Again, that's because powerboats wear out faster. Their engines turn many hundreds of thousands more revs per season. So their used-boat values tend to be less in proportion to new boat values.

## What's the bottom line on inflation and depreciation effects?

What does all this tell us?

From the charts, we can see that boats don't necessarily appreciate at the CPI-U rate. Some might rise much faster than CPI-U, some more slowly, depending on all kinds of factors. Unfortunately, quantification of these factors is very difficult. Not necessarily impossible, just difficult. And beyond the scope of this book.

On the whole and generally speaking, powerboats don't seem to follow any single pattern relative to inflation or depreciation. However, sailboats of a given size and weight seem to be affected in a predictible way by the combined effects of inflation and depreciation. That phenomenon permitted us to construct a base market price for sailboats of various ages (Figure 12-3).

To sum up: for someone who is shopping for a boat and wants to know how much a particular brand or model has appreciated or depreciated in value before deciding on a purchase, the above methods can be used to compare alternatives.

## Opportunity cost

The opportunity cost of any action is *the value of what one has given up for it*. When you buy a boat, your opportunity cost is the value of the most valuable alternative that has been foregone in order to buy her. Thus, if the cash used to buy the boat might also have been used to invest in a rising stock market, the opportunity cost of your transaction is the money you failed to make on the stock market, assuming you would have invested your initial investment in your boat, plus the ancillary costs of buying, plus the maintenance and repair costs incurred while you owned the boat, less the proceeds of the sale of the boat when you sold her.

For example, let's say you bought a 35-foot powerboat, using $100,000 from your cash savings account in late 1984, when the Dow Jones Industrial Average was at 1,200. In early October 1987, when the Dow reached 2,600 points just before the "crash of '87," you sold the boat for $90,000 cash, which you put back into your savings account. In the three years you owned her, you spent an average of about $17,000 a year or a total of $51,000 for upkeep and other boat-related expenses, so that your total out-of-pocket cost for the boat was $151,000. After pocketing the $90,000 you got for her, your net out-of-pocket cost was $61,000. Let's assume there were no tax consequences, so the $61,000 is your net cost before tax *and* after tax.

If you had invested your original $100,000 in Dow stocks (assuming that, in your eyes, that was your most valuable alternative) instead of buying and maintaining a boat, your money would have risen to a value of $217,000 by early October, and assuming you were smart enough to have cashed in before the market tumbled, you would have made $117,000 gross profit, or about $80,000 net profit after brokerage fees and income taxes.

Your opportunity cost, therefore, is the sum of your out-of-pocket cost for the privilege of owning the boat, $61,000, plus the profit after tax on the foregone alternative, $80,000. So one could say that your three-year dalliance with boat ownership cost you $61,000 + $80,000 = $141,000, which is your opportunity cost.

What good is knowing your opportunity cost? For one thing, it helps you to get an idea of how much value, in terms of personal satisfaction, you need to get out of boating in order to justify the money you're putting into it.

The way you calculate value will vary depending on your personality and how you feel about boating. If you are an avid boater, you'll be more likely to keep spending money on your pastime even if the opportunity cost numbers are substantial.

Here's one way of looking at it. In the example, you received three years of the fun of boating — say 180 days if you went out an average of 60 days a year — for a cost of $141,000, or a cost of about $780 a day. You may also have received value out of not having to worry about whether the stock market was going up or down, since you had no money in it. If you had plenty of income — let's say $200,000 a year, or about $1,000 per working day — and didn't need the savings-account money to pay for ordinary living expenses, you might think you had received very adequate value from the $780 a day cost.

If you liked to putter around the boat after work each night, even when you didn't take her out, you might want to take credit for, say, 300 days a year instead of 60 days a year of fun, so your cost per day might be $156, an even better value.

On the other hand, if you were the worrying kind, you might have wanted to *subtract* value for the three years you agonized as the market kept rising and you weren't participating.

## Now you can go to work

This chapter completes the discussion on the costs of ownership. Now you can go back to the worksheets for figuring *your* ownership economics at the end of Chapter 11, and see how much your boat is *really* costing you.

# PART FOUR

# The Seven Basic Rules of the Boat-Selling Game

*Rule One: Market Your Boat Professionally*
*Rule Two: Know What You're Selling*
*Rule Three: Establish Rapport With Potential Buyers*
*Rule Four: Sell Special Features and Benefits*
*Rule Five: Location Counts*
*Rule Six: Time the Sale Right*
*Rule Seven: Buy Low, Sell High*

# CHAPTER 19

# Rule One: Market Your Boat Professionally

Marketing any product professionally involves a series of structured action steps. Marketing your boat is no different. To produce a speedy sale at a satisfactory price, whether your boat is a creampuff or a dog, the best approach is to vigorously pursue a series of smart marketing moves:

1. Plan out your sales program.
2. Prepare your boat for sale with loving care.
3. Place advertising tuned to your target buyers.
4. Be available to inquirers, with a cheery greeting and a sales pitch ready.
5. Keep records of prospect calls.
6. Follow up on all inquiries.
7. When a prospect says, "I'll buy her," be ready to close.

Let's look at each one of these steps in more detail.

## Plan out your sales program

Decide what's to be done, on what schedule, and by whom. Research the market if necessary, to determine the identity of your target buyers, what they read, their preferences and buying habits. And decide early whether to use a broker or to try selling your boat on your own.

It's important to decide up front whether to use a broker, since your sales program will be vastly different if your broker is doing most of the work for you. Figure 19-1 reviews the pros and cons of using a broker vs. the do-it-yourself approach.

There are other reasons for choosing one way or the other. You have had hands-on experience with your own boat, so are best equipped to emphasize her good features and smooth over whatever faults she may have. Also, buyers tend to think they'll get more of a bargain if no broker is involved. That buyer's philosophy can work very much to your advantage.

If you give the selling job to one or more brokers, you should set up a system for monitoring the job they're supposed to be doing.

Before you choose a broker, interview each candidate. Ask each one to explain his system, including where and when he'll advertise your boat, how else he plans to develop prospects, and what procedures he uses to keep you and other owners informed as to his activities.

I would favor the brokers who promise to call you at frequent intervals (maybe even every week or so) with progress reports, compared to those who say they'll call you if and when they have an offer. If he has a lot of boats to sell, it may be a case of the squeaky wheel getting the grease — but you shouldn't have to call him; he should call you, to let you know how things are going.

Of course, the proof of the pudding is in the eating. If prospects are seeing the boat and making offers, that's good. It's evidence that your broker is doing his job and you have only to reduce the price or bide your time or both to sell the boat.

If buyers are looking but not making offers, there's something wrong. An astute broker should be able to suggest action that will improve the situation.

If no one is responding to the broker's ads, calls, For Sale signs and other bait, investigate the situation closely. It may be time to change brokers.

Make a written schedule for your sales program, being sure to leave enough time for cleaning up the boat and placing ads. Remember, the lead time is a *couple of months or more* from ad placement to publication in most monthly magazines.

FIGURE 19-1
**Should you use a broker
or sell on your own?**

| USE A BROKER IF . . . | SELL ON YOUR OWN IF . . . |
| --- | --- |
| You don't have the time or the skills to do a good selling job. | You have the time and skills to do it right. |
| You dislike negotiating. | You feel comfortable as a negotiator. |
| You feel the services for which you'll pay a 10% commission are worth the cost to you. | You prefer to do the marketing yourself and pocket the 10% commission money. |

## Prepare your boat for sale with loving care

Clean her up and fix her up so she sparkles like a jewel; in other words, "package" her. Here are some suggestions:

- **Unload excess equipment.** Decide which items you don't want to sell (such as your favorite docklines, a special fat fender, or a swimming ladder) and remove them from the boat and from any inventory lists before showing the boat.
- **Remove all loose clutter.** Try to get everything that's movable off the boat, including sails. If you insist on leaving sails on board, be sure they're clean, dry, neatly folded, and stowed in their bags.   It's better to take your sails home if possible, since doing so will give an impression to prospective buyers that you follow careful maintenance procedures, the on-board space available for storage will seem greater to anyone inspecting the boat, and there's less risk of someone messing up your neat stowage arrangement during a viewing.
- **Clean up on deck.** Be especially careful to note any gelcoat crazing, loose stanchions, worn lifelines, frayed lines, tarnished spars, or other signs of wear, tear and lack of maintenance.
- **Buff and polish fiberglass topsides.** If your boat has been painted, do it again if there's the slightest question of needing to. If the topside finish is faded, you can try rubbing compound (on a small test patch first) but be prepared to accept failure. After 5 to 10 years or so, depending on the pigment in the gelcoat, colored pigments may fade to a blotchy condition. Then your choice is to paint (which may reduce the value of the boat rather than improve it if it's not a first-class job), to rub baby oil into the surface (which sometimes helps, but only temporarily), or to sell the boat "as is" and accept a substantially reduced price.
- **Oil or varnish any wood trim.** Since some buyers like bare teak (oiled or not) and others like wood trim bright (varnished), I'd avoid using varnish unless it's already in place. The new owner can varnish bare teak more easily than he can strip off the seven to nine coats you'd apply if you were doing a first-class job.
- **Clean up below.** Pay special attention to scrubbing the head and the galley areas until they gleam. Those are first stops for some shoppers. Again, note any signs of wear and tear or need for maintenance.
- **Deodorize** the cabin, all lockers, the engine room, and any other nooks and crannies. The objective is to make the boat appear as new. This is difficult, but worth an aggressive effort.

  To remove mildew and stains, use a chlorine cleanser. Warning: be sure that the area you're working in is well ventilated; if not, chlorine cleansers may severely irritate your nose and eyes.

  The icebox deserves special attention, since it can get

pretty grungy and develop odors. After scrubbing until spotless (and using one of the special fiberglass stain removers to take out rust rings in the bottom), leave a dish of baking soda inside for a few days to absorb any remaining odors.

Drain and flush the holding tank if it's ever been used. If it hasn't, add that fact to your list of selling points.

When the mildew and other odor-producing sources are gone, you'll still have the odor of the chlorine cleanser. Try forced ventilation to dry everything out, and maybe spray a little air freshener if you think it will help.

- **Make any necessary repairs and do any maintenance that can help make the boat seem more desirable.** Change the engine oil, replace the spark plugs, change engine filters, clean, polish and possibly spray-paint the engine, clean and regrease all winches, lube all turnbuckles, etc. When in doubt, fix it.
- **Empty and refill the water tanks.** If the water in the system is at all questionable after refilling, throw a handful of baking soda into the tank, swish it around if you can, pump it out, and check for odor and color again. Sometimes organic growth gets going in the tank or the plumbing between tank and faucets. You may have to remove the feed lines (usually vinyl hoses) and pull a detergent-soaked cloth through on a string to remove the growth. If growth in the tank is the culprit, look for an inspection plate in the top surface. Usually there is one that covers a hole big enough for your arm.
- **If your boat has a cabin, decorate the interior with "boat show props."** It may sound corny, but it looks great. Aim for spots of bright color, and a clean look. Wicker baskets, fruit, dried flower arrangements, wineglasses and a wine bottle, a boating magazine with a colorful cover and a handsome book or two might top off the impression nicely.

## Place advertising tuned to your target buyers

Decide on where to place ads, when to place them, what they should say. Here's a checklist of things to do that will help make your ad campaign successful:

- **If you use a broker to help you sell, discuss advertising with him** before you plan your campaign. He probably has his own methods and approaches. Ask him to tell you about them. What he says will probably influence your decision to use him instead of one of his competitors.

    The remaining suggestions assume you're selling the boat yourself, rather than through a broker.
- **Compose an ad that's designed to sell.** Most experts agree that an effective boat sales piece will show an asking price. It will also indicate the brand, model, and year, and if possible will describe some unique feature possessed by the boat. Keep the

message short, use eye-catching color if possible, and include clear, appealing graphics.

- **Place a For Sale sign on the boat with the price and your name and telephone number.** Some yards, marinas, and even yacht clubs don't like the idea of signs, and don't permit them; naturally, you should check with the appropriate folks first. If you do show a sign, be sure it's big and colorful enough to be noticed. Many people use orange and black "For Sale" signs available in most hardware stores. Try to place the sign at the eye level of a person strolling by, angled to catch the attention of people coming from any direction. And if traffic passes your boat on two or three sides, put up two or three signs.

- **Run an ad once in your local weekly paper or three times (Friday, Saturday, Sunday) in a daily.** See what happens. If you get no response, it could be due to any number of things. Perhaps it's the wrong season, you haven't supplied enough information in the ad, your price is too high, or your boat isn't popular enough. But most likely, it's because you aren't reaching enough potential buyers through a local paper.

  If you get at least one or two replies to your ad, consider running the same ad for a second week. Otherwise, switch to a medium that gives your boat greater exposure to people in the market for a boat like yours.

- **Place ads where buyers of your type of boat are looking.** The very best place to advertise is in a class association newsletter or magazine. If you have access to this type of publication, place an ad and run it until your boat is sold. Many class groups let you run your ad free or at nominal cost, so it's an opportunity you can't afford to pass up.

- **Use bulletin boards.** The bulletin boards at yacht clubs, marinas, and marine stores are good places to advertise. Bulletin boards host a wide variety of ad sizes, from torn scraps of paper to file cards with messages hand-lettered in fine script to photo-copied sheets that include lengthy text and maybe photos or drawings. Whatever form you pick, be sure it's neat, legible, short enough to read in 30 seconds or less, and not so big that it crowds out the other messages on the board. A diagram of your boat showing a side view is a good idea if you can draw one or copy one from a magazine or catalog.

  When you visit bulletin boards, don't forget to take pushpins, thumb tacks, or a staple gun with you.

- **Try running your ad in *Soundings*, the boating newspaper.** The *Soundings* audience is large, comprised of both sailors and powerboaters, and if your message is sufficiently appealing, you should get some response.

- **Consider placing an ad in a nationally distributed publication.** Besides the classifieds in the major boating mags (Appendix 2), there are the newsletter put out by Boat/US, newsstand-distributed boats-for-sale publications, and the listing services (also in Appendix 2). Placing an ad in a national publication is a fairly expensive proposition—$35 to $60 or more per ad for anything longer than a couple of lines—so you should pick and choose if you decide to experiment. Try to pick one that has major circulation in your area. Try it once and see what happens. If a publication doesn't pull buyers for you the first time, forget it and hunt for a publication that does.

---

FIGURE 19-2

**A sampling of boat-selling terms you can use in your ad.**

| HER CONDITION IS SO GREAT AND HER EQUIPMENT IS SO COMPLETE . . . | AND HER COMFORT, BEAUTY AND PERFORMANCE IS SO GREAT . . . |
|---|---|
| Nice. | Strong/fast. |
| Really nice. | Rocket! |
| Like new. | Fast. |
| Well equipped. | Very fast. |
| Super equipped. | Very competitive. |
| Good shape. | Super fast. |
| Unused. | Fastest in this size. |
| Perfect! | Winner |
| New paint. | Wow! |
| Recent Awlgrip. | Super setup. |
| New rig. | Roomy. |
| New sails. | Two heads. |
| Furler. | Large cockpit. |
| Dinghy. | Huge interior. |
| Loran. | Aft cabin. |
| Full electronics. | Simple. |
| Three sprder rig. | Open layout. |
| Wheel. | Old world charm. |
| Spin gear. | Graceful. |
| Loaded! | Sparkling. |
| Mint. | Cruise in style. |
| Showboat. | Beauty. |
| Wow! | |
| In exceptional condition. | |
| Clean. | |
| Creampuff. | |
| Handyman special. | |
| Needs work. | |
| Needs minor work. | |
| Needs restoration. | |
| Partially restored. | |
| Simple. | |
| Good. | |
| Excellent. | |
| Used one season. | |
| Full warranty. | |

*continued*

195

# THE SEVEN BASIC RULES OF THE BOAT-SELLING GAME

FIGURE 19-2 *continued*

| THE PRICE IS . . . | REASON FOR SALE IS . . . |
|---|---|
| A steal! | Demo. |
| Bargain! | Trade. |
| A good buy. | Must be sold . . . must sell. |
| Try $10k. | Must sell this week. |
| Priced to sell. | End of season clearance. |
| Below replacement value. | Repossessed—make offer. |
| Excellent value. | Owner anxious. |
| End of season clearance. | Owner moving. |
| Sacrifice! | Moving down . . . willing to swap. |
| Reduced. | Moving inland. |
| Rock bottom. | Moving up. |
| Practically free. | Getting divorced. |
| Free. | Retiring from boating. |
| | No time for boating. |
| | Boat needs work—no time to fix. |
| | Need money. |

| SO I'LL TAKE . . . | . . . AND YOU SHOULD . . . |
|---|---|
| Top bid. | Take your best shot. |
| Any reasonable offer. | See the difference. |
| Make offer. | Call now. |
| Will consider trade. | Act fast! This one won't last. |
| Best offer. | |
| $10k or best offer. | |
| $10k or near offer. | |
| Practically any offer. | |

FIGURE 19-3
**A glossary of boat-selling terms.**

### WORDS & PHRASES REFERRING TO THE CONDITION OF THE BOAT

**Creampuff.** Interpretation: My boat is in better-than-new condition. You won't believe your eyes. Must see to appreciate. Comment: It better be true, or you'll never sell her, even if your price is well below creampuff price, since the ad will attract an audience that is not likely to be interested in second-best, regardless of price.

**Excellent condition.** Interpretation: It is difficult for the casual observer to distinguish my boat from new. Her engine has been overhauled, her sails replaced recently, everything works perfectly, and she sparkles and shines like the crown jewels. Comment: Exaggeration not recommended.

**Good condition.** Interpretation: I'm proud of my boat, and spend considerable time maintaining her. But she's not perfect; above average, perhaps. Comment: This has my blessing as a good, honest assessment.

*continued*

FIGURE 19-3 *continued*

## WORDS & PHRASES REFERRING TO THE CONDITION OF THE BOAT *continued*

**Needs work (or "Needs minor work").** Interpretation: My boat is in pretty bad shape, but nowhere as bad as a handyman special. If you ask, I'll enumerate her problems for you. Comment: If the work needed is obvious, this approach is recommended. You don't want to give prospects the idea that the boat is in better shape than she is.

**Handyman special.** Interpretation: My boat is in such bad shape that her repair is beyond my abilities. She has so many problems that I won't be able to tell you about all of them; indeed, I don't even *know* about all of them. Please take her off my hands. Comment: Not recommended unless your plans are to take her to the dump if you don't sell her.

**Needs restoration.** Interpretation: My boat is a Handyman Special that was once a fine yacht. Comment: This approach will draw only the specialists from the antique and classic boat crowd. If that is your intent, fine.

## WORDS & PHRASES REFERRING TO THE PRICE BEING ASKED

**Best offer (with no price listed).** Interpretation: Make me an offer, and I'll tell you if it's a good one. Comment: Not recommended; only the most aggressive prospects will reply. The approach is similar to a restaurant that asks its patrons to pick items from the menu without seeing their prices. I consider the words "best offer" to be an impediment to communication between negotiating parties.

**. . . or near offer (or) ONO (after listing price).** Interpretation: If you offer me less than 90% of the price I'm asking, I'll begin to feel insulted. Comment: This approach is not recommended; better to get as many offers as you can with OBO.

**. . . or best offer (or) OBO (after listing price).** Interpretation: Offer whatever you think is fair. I don't promise to accept it, but I won't be insulted by whatever you say. I encourage *all* offers. Comment: A similar phrase is "offers encouraged". This is a good approach.

**Sacrifice.** Interpretation: You have my permission to make an offer lower than you think I might accept. I probably *will* accept it, and you'll have the bargain of the week. Comment: I consider this less dynamic than "Bargain," which is more forthright. However, it's a matter of personal taste more than anything else.

**Bargain.** Interpretation: Same as "sacrifice," more or less. Comment: "Bargain" is clear, to the point, and tuned to any buyer's wavelength.

**Act fast! This one won't last.** Interpretation: My price is so low that if I had told anybody before you, the boat would already have been sold. Comment: Smart buyers will wait two weeks after the ad appears, then call and offer a fraction of the asking price, since obviously the boat *did* last. Hence this wording may backfire.

**Owner anxious.** Interpretation: My boat's been on the market for months and I'm beginning to wonder if I'll ever sell her. I'll come down 10% in price without batting an eye, and maybe a lot more if you press me. Comment: This approach is recommended if you want to sell fast; state the lowest price you're willing to part with her for, and say you're anxious in the same ad. It's a one-two punch that smacks of believability. But be prepared for some hounding by buyers looking for an even lower price.

**Priced to sell.** Interpretation: My boat is priced below the other boats advertised, which generally are *not* priced to sell. Comment: This phrase is a meaningless waste of printer's ink.

**Must sell.** Interpretation and comment: Same as "Sacrifice," more or less.

**Must sell this week.** Interpretation: Wait until Sunday and I'll accept any reasonable offer. Before Sunday, I'm going to hold out for a little more. Comment: More or less the same ad and therefore the same comment as "This one won't last."

**Any reasonable offer accepted.** Interpretation: I'll think about an offer 10% to 20% below where I think the market is. Below that, forget it; any offer wouldn't be reasonable. Comment: The word "reasonable" confuses the issue, since it's such a subjective word. I'd prefer to say . . .

*continued*

FIGURE 19-3 *continued*

## WORDS & PHRASES REFERRING TO THE PRICE BEING ASKED *continued*

**All offers considered.** Interpretation: Everybody come and look. I may have what you want, and at a good price too! Comment: This will draw bigger crowds, but be prepared for some insulting offers.

**Reduced.** Interpretation: My boat was ridiculously overpriced before, and I didn't get any "reasonable offers"; now she's just a little overpriced. Comment: Better to just name your new price and don't make the buyer aware you've had trouble marketing the boat.

## EXPLANATIONS FOR WHY THE BOAT'S FOR SALE

**Owner moving.** Interpretation: I wish to eliminate any buyer's suspicion that I'm selling because there is something wrong with the boat. Comment: This statement is not recommended, since the question remains: Why doesn't the owner take his boat with him? Sellers, however, *should* have a reason for selling. But it should be more specific. For example, consider these ten popular reasons to sell . . .

**Moving inland.** Interpretation: I can't use my boat where there's no water. And there's no water inland, right? Comment: Right.

**Moving up.** Interpretation: I'm so rich I can afford to buy something bigger, and you'll benefit from all the money I've lavished on the boat I'm selling. Comment: This is a good phrase, since it combines *two* reasons to buy: (1) the boat probably has been well treated since the owner is well off, and (2) the owner isn't selling her because she's defective.

**Moving down—willing to swap.** Interpretation: Let's talk trade. Comment: This is a relatively rare but interesting approach. I suggest proceeding with caution. Most people *don't* move down, but some do if they can no longer commit the time and money to a larger boat.

**Getting divorced.** Interpretation: Well . . . it depends. Comment: The owner may want a high price or a low one, depending on conditions of the settlement. Buyers should ask about price early on.

**Retiring from boating.** Interpretation: If you buy from me, you'll get everything: extra cushions, extra docklines . . . all the things that people "moving up" take off the boat they're selling. Comment: This is a good ad line; it should draw new boaters who haven't accumulated all the gear yet.

**No time for boating.** Interpretation: I'm too busy and have changed priorities. I may even be leaving boating permanently. Comment: This is a plausible reason for selling, but it has negative connotations (boating is a lot of work, takes a lot of time, etc.) Use the space to push features and benefits instead.

**Boat needs work.** Interpretation and Comment: This is a poor reason for selling. As such, don't use it.

**Need money.** Interpretation: I can't afford to maintain my boat properly, so she's pretty beat up. Comment: This is the nautical equivalent of "Lost our lease" and is not recommended as a sales line.

## MISCELLANEOUS PHRASES

**Brokers protected:** If a broker has a ready buyer for my boat, let him step forward; I'm willing to negotiate a commission with him. (This phrase will encourage brokers to call you.)

**No brokers:** The boat is being sold privately, and I will not accept offers of sales help from brokers—nor bills for services rendered after the fact. (This phrase is not usually necessary; it goes without saying.)

- **Don't forget word-of-mouth advertising.** Tell your friends you're selling — especially those with similar boats, who may be tied into the informal network of enthusiasts for certain boat styles and models. Tell your friends your price.

To help you in composing your ad, Figure 19-2 shows a list of typical selling phrases. Figure 19-3 is an accompanying glossary.

## Be available when calls start to come in

Be confident, be positive, be pleasant, be accomodating, and most important, *be there*. How many times have you read an ad in the paper, called the number in the ad, and been put off by an answering machine asking you to leave a message, or worse, a no-answer?

Be sure the boat is accessible to prospects, preferably with you or a broker there to answer any questions and to give each prospect a promotional brochure.

## Present an image of success

The sales pros do it; so should you. Try to look neat and mildly prosperous. If possible, avoid wearing paint-spattered, worn-out work clothes. At minimum, it will leave the impression that you probably have cared for your boat well. And at best it may be just the subtlety that sells the boat.

## Compose an effective brochure

The leave-behind piece deserves special mention. This should be a photocopied capsule description of your boat, one to three pages in length. It should inform prospects about four things:

1. **The characteristics of the boat.** Physical dimensions and statistics, engine size and type, age, listed extras, builder name and address, etc. *Include line drawings of the boat,* preferably from at least two angles: the outboard profile and the accomodations plan. A photo is optional; line drawings are better since they show more information and are usually more flattering to the boat than snapshots.

   The original manufacturer's brochure will provide you with a rich source of material for your own sales piece. So will boating magazine write-ups, usually published within a year or so of the time a new design appears on the market.

2. **Special features and benefits of the boat that make her unique and desirable.** Primary features such as colors, condition (if spectacular), trailerability, seaworthiness (if provable), etc. Secondary features are important too: interior lining that makes cleaning easier, large tankage capacity, anti-blistering gelcoat, any guarantees by the builder that can be transferred to the new owner, etc.

3. **Your asking price.** How much, what does it cover, what doesn't it cover, what might be negotiable, etc. Can the buyer use your slip or mooring for the rest of the year? Will you deliver the boat free? All should be summarized in the brochure.

4. **Who you are and how you can be contacted.** This usually includes name, address (optional), and day and evening telephone numbers. Some folks who post their brochures on bulletin boards include a strip of pre-slit, tear-off telephone numbers across the bottom for the prospects' convenience.

The leave-behind is an important selling tool. Primarily, of course, it provides the prospect with all the essential information. But it also gives buyers a chance to compare details of your boat with others he is looking at. And it will help him remember your boat weeks after his visit.

If you have a video camera or can borrow one, consider making a short promotional video film of your boat. If you make the film in the summer, it may help you sell the boat when winter comes. You'll need a separate chase boat for a first-class film. Take some action shots of the boat moving at hull speed, and others showing how easy it is to get underway, pick up a mooring, back into a dock, etc. Shoot some onboard closeups and demos showing off the boat's finer points: her sparkling new engine, the roller-furling genoa, jiffy reefing, the Loran and RDF, and so on.

An extensive, detailed leave-behind has the advantage of reminding a semi-interested shopper that your boat does have advantages he won't find elsewhere. But sometimes a one-pager that doesn't delve into a lot of detail is OK, too, and can be used as a bulletin board poster

FIGURE 19-4
**Leave-behind/bulletin board poster for a Bertram 28 FB.**

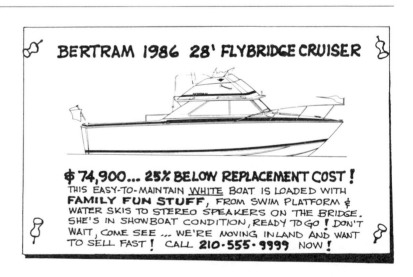

as well as a leave-behind. Ideally, make both for use in different situations.

One caution: When you put together your brochure, don't stretch the truth. A misrepresentation (such as calling your 1981 boat a 1982 model) could result in a lawsuit against you. So check and recheck the accuracy of any claims you make.

## Organize your sales pitch

A word about your sales pitch is in order. The key element is to hammer at the features and benefits of your boat, tactfully and at the prospect's pace. Don't rush it. If you know what you're selling (Chapter 20), you'll know what features and benefits you can push. You should be selective on which features and benefits to emphasize, depending on what the buyer wants. That means you must know the customer. Establish a rapport with him (Chapter 21) and find out what he's looking for before making your pitch.

Once you make your pitch, be sure he understands all the benefits you are offering. Help him to weigh each point and decide on his feelings about it. Give him plenty of proof. Stress the benefits to him, giving examples he can relate to. Anticipate and meet his objections.

For example, be ready to answer these and other commonly asked questions:

- Why are you selling?
- Is your price firm?
- If not, what is the lowest price you'll sell for?
- Are you willing to bargain?
- Will you demonstrate the boat for me?

Provide the prospect with solutions to any problems he comes up with. Prevent misunderstandings or lack of knowledge on the part of the prospect. Any uncertainties will represent a source of fear for him and will prevent him from proceeding toward a decision to buy. *Fear* is the basis of all real buyer objections.

## Try for a quick close

For any prospect who visits the boat, listens to your pitch, and appears interested in buying, try to close the sale there and then if you can do so without seeming to use "hard-sell" tactics. A pushy sales approach can turn off even the most enthusiastic prospects.

Remember, your objective is to get a prospect to say "I'll buy her." And what's the simplest way to get anyone to do anything? Ask him! If you've done a good job of "pitching," the sale often takes care of itself. But not always. It's amazing how many potential sales are lost simply because the person selling doesn't ask for the "order."

Of course, you have to do the pitching first, to break down the buyer's resistance, to understand his objections, if any, and to meet them decisively. You have to convince him that he needs what you've got, that your boat is the best one available to him, that you are the best person to deal with, that the price is right, and that now is the right time to buy.

## Keep records of prospect calls

Make a note of each caller's apparent interest level so you can follow up periodically to remind the prospect that your boat is still for sale. If a prospect decides he's not interested, it may be because of price. If you can determine this by asking, offer to call him back if you don't sell the boat and later decide to lower the price.

A corollary is to keep records of who is interested even after you sell the boat. You never know when a sale might fall through at the last minute or even way past the last minute. I've actually sold a boat and received the money in full, and two weeks later had the buyer come back asking if I would buy back the boat. It wasn't the boat; she was fine, better than he had anticipated. It was just that he had found an even better boat he wanted to buy instead. Luckily, I still had the records I had kept of inquiries, including names and phone numbers of people who had called after the sale, which I had obtained "just in case." I gladly gave the new owner these names, and have no doubt he was able to sell my boat quickly and easily.

## Follow up on all inquiries

Write a brief letter of thanks to every prospect who looks at your boat and include an invitation to call again after they've shopped a while. Even if someone has told you he's not interested, write a follow-up note. People sometimes do change their minds. And if after a month or two has gone by and you decide to lower your price, write or call previous prospects to see if they can be turned around.

## When a prospect says, "I'll buy," be ready to close

When you finish showing a prospect the boat and he has asked all the questions he wants to ask, and you have supplied all the answers, the moment of truth has arrived. Will he buy the boat, or won't he?

Sometimes a buyer will simply say, "I'll take her," and the deal is closed. But often the prospect finds it hard to say yes, even though he thinks he wants the boat. He'll make some semi-affirmative statement such as, "I like her, but maybe I should look at some other boats before I decide," or, "Let me think it over for a few days." That's your signal to explain to him — apologetically — that you can't hold the boat for him. Tell him that your policy has to be "first come, first served." Try to help him to want to close the deal by encouraging him to reason with you aloud. For example, ask him what features are missing on your boat that he might expect to find elsewhere. He may have some minor points he's concerned about; be prepared to make minor concessions. You may think they're minor and he may think they're major. See if you can find out if he's hesitating because of price. If so, encourage open discussion. You may get him to make an offer.

If you feel that price is the only problem, you may have the urge to offer to negotiate. It's a ticklish subject, since you don't want to appear too eager to cut your asking price, which presumably is already on the table. First, see if you can elicit an offer. No point in caving in unnecessarily.

Simply ask the prospect for an offer. If he makes one and it's within a reasonable range, offer to split the difference (a very common situation), or to come down a third or a quarter of the way. Strive to keep your bargaining position open while drawing the prospect's offer higher and higher.

In any event, try not to press the prospect so hard that he becomes uncomfortable. If he really wants to give the matter a few days' thought, let him go gracefully. *Resist the temptation to use hard-sell techniques.* Volunteer to call him if someone else comes along with an offer below your asking price. If he responds to this approach, view it as a sign he may be hooked. If he indicates you shouldn't bother, it's more likely that he's no longer a prospect.

If you're successful in closing a sale, take immediate action. Here's what to do:

- **If he's paying cash, draw up and sign a bill of sale** when you get the money, not before. The buyer may need this proof of ownership for various reasons, including state registration. A sample bill of sale is shown in Figure 19-5.
- **If he's paying by check, insist on a certified check or cashier's check.** Stories are rife about people who buy a boat, sail it away, and can't be found when the check later bounces.
- **If a trailer is involved, make out a separate bill of sale for it.** It's usually required for state registration. (See Figure 19-6)
- **If your boat is officially documented,** plan ahead to make it easy for the purchaser to continue the chain of documentation. Special Coast Guard forms are required, including a special bill of sale. You should arrange to have these forms in your possession when a buyer arrives.

   Whatever its form, a bill of sale is simply a document describing the boat (type, model, builder, serial number, color, etc.) and preferably stating that: the boat is the seller's to sell; there are no liens or other claims against the boat (or the claims are detailed); and the boat is being sold "as is, where is" with any warranties it may carry against specific problems. The document is intended to record transfer of title from the seller to the buyer. Some states also require that the price of the sale be specified.
- **If liens currently exist on the boat,** proceed slowly, methodically, and very carefully. Contact the bank or finance

# THE SEVEN BASIC RULES OF THE BOAT-SELLING GAME

FIGURE 19-5
**Bill of sale for a boat.**

## VESSEL BILL OF SALE

This is to certifiy that, on (month and day) _____ , (year) ____ ,

I (name of seller) _____

of (address) _____

sold, transferred and assigned the right, title and interest in the

vessel described below to (name of buyer) _____

of (address) _____

in consideration of (selling price and/or other consideration) _____

_____ ,

receipt of which is hereby acknowledged.  The vessel is a (length in

feet) _____ (make and model) _____ , with the

following identifying numbers and characteristics:

(hull ident. #) _____ , (other ident. #) _____ ,

(former names if known) _____ ,

obtained by the seller from (name and address of previous seller)

_____ ,

(built in year) _____ by (mfr. name) _____ ,

having a color scheme as follows: (topsides) _____ , (deck) _____ ,

(cabin) _____ , (bottom) _____ .  Included with the purchase are:

Trailer (make, model, year, ident. #) _____ ,

Engines (make, model, year, ident. #) _____ ,

Other (equipment, electronics, sails, etc.)_____

_____ .

I certify that this sale is being made under the following
warranties, conditions, and encumbrances: (if none, so state) _____

_____

_____ .

I declare under penalty of false statement that the information
furnished above is true and complete to the best of my knowledge and
belief.

     Signed: (seller) _____ .

     Date (of transfer) _____ .

FIGURE 19-6
**Bill of sale for a trailer.**

| BILL OF SALE H-31 Rev. 8-86 | INSTRUCTIONS | STATE OF CONNECTICUT Department of Motor Vehicles |
|---|---|---|
| | 1. Seller of motor vehicle or vessel must complete, sign and give this form to the purchaser. 2. Purchaser must present the completed form to the Motor Vehicle Department with other forms required for proper registration. | |

| SALE OF (Check one) | ☐ MOTOR VEHICLE ☐ VESSEL | |
|---|---|---|

| SELLER | NAME | |
| | ADDRESS | |

| SELLING PRICE | $ | The owner (seller) of this motor vehicle or vessel described below hereby transfers to the purchaser the described motor vehicle or vessel in consideration of the amount (selling price) entered at left, receipt hereby acknowledged. |
|---|---|---|

| PURCHASER | NAME | |
| | ADDRESS | |

| DESCRIPTION OF MOTOR VEHICLE | MAKE | YEAR | COLOR(S) | MODEL NAME OR NO. | BODY STYLE(4-Dr. Sedan, etc.) |
|---|---|---|---|---|---|
| | ODOMETER READING | VEHICLE IDENTIFICATION NO. (Not engine no.) | | | |

| DESCRIPTION OF VESSEL | YEAR BUILT | HULL I.D. NO. (Required if built 1973 or later) | | MAKE | |
|---|---|---|---|---|---|
| | COLOR - PRIMARY - SECONDARY | MODEL | LENGTH | STATE WHERE LAST NUMBERED | PREVIOUS NUMBER |

| CERTIFICATION AND SIGNATURE | I declare under penalty of false statement that the information furnished above is true and complete to the best of my knowledge and belief. | SIGNATURE OF SELLER X | DATE |
|---|---|---|---|

company when you first decide to sell the boat. Ask about proper procedures and follow them to the letter. The worst thing you can be is uninformed in this situation, and have a buyer change his mind and back out of the deal because of it.

- **When the buyer puts down a deposit,** he'll ask you how much you want. Ask for 10% for boats selling for less than $10,000, and $1,000 for boats of higher value. Ask for cash, certified check, or cashier's check.
- **If buyer financing is involved,** try to determine whether the buyer might have a problem obtaining the necessary credit. Discuss the matter up front and determine how the deposit will be handled. Sometimes it's better to ask the buyer to either give you a substantial nonrefundable deposit ($1,000 or even more) or take his chances on the boat's selling before he arranges financing. Try to avoid agreeing to a sale subject to financing, particularly if you are in the middle of an active, seasonal market. You may be stuck with your boat for a whole year or longer if the buyer can't get credit.
- **Give the buyer a receipt for his deposit, signed by both parties.** The receipt, which you should type up in advance and sign when you get the deposit, should specify that the deposit is not refundable if the buyer changes his mind or can't arrange financing. If you agree to return the deposit under certain conditions, name the conditions (such as "subject to survey"). Make two copies; you keep one signed by the prospect, and he keeps one signed by you.
- **Specify which costs associated with the sale are to be borne by which party.** This is appropriate for complicated deals involving

surveying, arranging and executing sea trials, yard handling and launching to accommodate a prospect, possible damage suffered while the boat is under control of a prospect, etc.

All these costs are normally for the account of the prospect, whether he buys or not. Still, it is wise to state as much on both the deposit receipt and the bill of sale.

- **Tell your insurance agent** that the boat has been sold after the money and the papers change hands, not before. When the policy is cancelled, it's cancelled.

- **Consider running the sale through your new-boat dealer** if you're selling your old boat and moving up to a new one. The buyer shouldn't care; he might even prefer to be buying from a dealer (even though, because of disclaimers the dealer will write into the deal, he's really no better off legally). The advantage is strictly to the seller, if he lives in a state that charges sales tax on new boats, because *he can reduce the basis for tax on the transaction* by the amount he obtains for his boat. State laws vary, but the following scenario is typical.

  You buy a new Widget 30 for $40,000 from a dealer. If your sales tax rate is 8%, you'd pay $3,200 to the state on the purchase, assuming you sold your old boat privately. The sale price on your old boat was $30,000, so the new owner pays $2,400 when he gets his state registration for the boat. (That $2,400, of course, is in addition to the $30,000 he paid to you.)

  But say you go to your dealer, tell him you've already found a buyer, but you'd like him to pass your old boat through his books to save on tax. It's possible that he'll tell you he's too busy for Mickey Mouse transactions like this, but if he's a nice guy, he'll charge you a small fee ($100 to $500) for doing the paperwork, and will bill you a net $10,000 for your new boat less the trade-in. Now you're paying $800 in tax, plus up to $500 to the dealer, or a total of $1,300 instead of $3,200, which amounts to a $1,900 net tax savings.

  Caution: before you try this approach, check with your dealer to be sure that the laws of your particular state permit such transactions.

- **If he asks, tell the buyer about your insurance coverage.** If you carry insurance on the boat, don't hesitate to tell the prospect what amount and what company, if he asks. If you can't get insurance because the boat is too old or in bad shape, let prospects know that, too. Chances are, if he really wants the boat, he won't care if he has to self-insure the hull and buy separate liability. And if he does care, he may tie you up in litigation if you aren't up-front about the matter.

- **Notify your state's registration or titling agency** when title passes, in accordance with laws specific to your state.

- **Keep all paperwork for at least a year,** or longer if special circumstances warrant, in case questions arise. For example, I heard of a case in which local tax officials came after a man for collection of personal property taxes during a period when he no longer owned his boat. Nevertheless, he had to produce a copy of his bill of sale to prove it and escape payment.

## Consider donating your boat

Maybe you're impatient to sell, but you can't find a buyer right away, even at a genuine bargain price. Or maybe you really want to contribute something of significant value to a worthwhile charity, but don't have the cash to do it. That's when to think about donating your boat to a worthy cause.

Government-operated on-the-water schools (for example, Maine Maritime Academy at Castine, the Naval Academy at Annapolis, the Merchant Marine Academy at King's Point) all have donation programs. However, none of these places will accept just any boat, and yours may or may not qualify under their guidelines. Other possible outlets are colleges, religious groups, and waterfront community organizations that solicit and use donated boats for worthwhile purposes. You'll find lots of these organizations in boating classified ads in the national magazines, the *New York Sunday Times*, and other large-circulation newspapers. The ads seem to proliferate around Christmas time and become sparse in the summer.

Caution: You may or may not receive a full tax deduction for donating your boat, depending on several factors. These include: how the boat valuation was arranged, the tax-deductible status of the par-

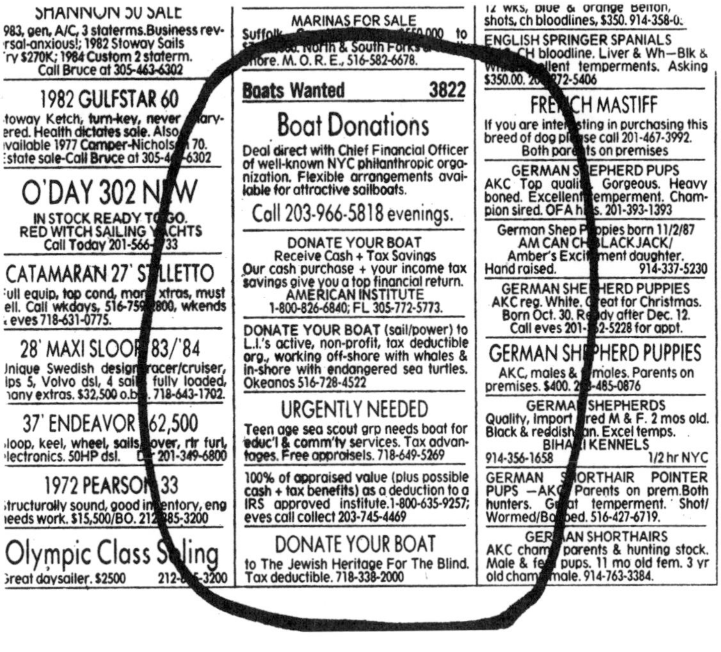
SHANNON 50 SALE
983, gen, A/C, 3 staterms. Business rev-rsal-anxious!; 1982 Stoway Sails ry $270K; 1984 Custom 2 staterm. Call Bruce at 305-463-6302

1982 GULFSTAR 60
toway Ketch, turn-key, never ...ary-ered. Health dictates sale. Also vailable 1977 Camper-Nichols... 70. state sale-Call Bruce at 305-4...6302

O'DAY 302 N...W
IN STOCK READY T...GO.
RED WITCH SAILING ...CHTS
Call Today 201-566-...33

CATAMARAN 27' S...LETTO
ull equip, top cond, man... xtras, must ell. Call wkdays, 516-75...800, wkends eves 718-631-0775.

28' MAXI SLOO... 83/'84
Inique Swedish design racer/cruiser, lps 5, Volvo dsl, 4 sail... fully loaded, nany extras. $32,500 o.b... 718-643-1702.

37' ENDEAVOR ...62,500
loop, keel, wheel, sails, ...over, rlr furl, lectronics. 50HP dsl. D... 201-349-6800

1972 PEARSO... 33
tructurally sound, good in...entory, eng needs work. $15,500/BO. 212-...85-3200

Olympic Class S...ling
Great daysailer. $2500 212-...-3200

MARINAS FOR SALE
Suffolk ... $550,000 to ... North & South Forks ... hore. M. O. R. E., 516-582-6678.

**Boats Wanted 3822**

Boat Donations
Deal direct with Chief Financial Officer of well-known NYC philanthropic organization. Flexible arrangements available for attractive sailboats.
Call 203-966-5818 evenings.

DONATE YOUR BOAT
Receive Cash + Tax Savings
Our cash purchase + your income tax savings give you a top financial return.
AMERICAN INSTITUTE
1-800-826-6840; FL 305-772-5773.

DONATE YOUR BOAT (sail/power) to L.I.'s active, non-profit, tax deductible org., working off-shore with whales & in-shore with endangered sea turtles. Okeanos 516-728-4522

URGENTLY NEEDED
Teen age sea scout grp needs boat for educ'l & comm'ty services. Tax advantages. Free appraisels. 718-649-5269

100% of appraised value (plus possible cash + tax benefits) as a deduction to a IRS approved institute. 1-800-635-9257; eves call collect 203-745-4469

DONATE YOUR BOAT
to The Jewish Heritage For The Blind. Tax deductible. 718-338-2000

12 wks, blue & orange Belton, shots, ch bloodlines, $350. 914-358-0...

ENGLISH SPRINGER SPANIALS
...CH bloodline. Liver & Wh—Blk & Wh... ...llent temperments. Asking $350.00. 20...-...72-5406

FRE...CH MASTIFF
If you are inte...sting in purchasing this breed of dog pl...se call 201-467-3992. Both par...ts on premises

GERMAN S...EPHERD PUPS
AKC Top quali... Gorgeous. Heavy boned. Excellent ...emperment. Champion sired. OFA h...s. 201-393-1393

German Shep P...ppies born 11/2/87
AM CAN CH ...LACKJACK/
Amber's Exci...ment daughter.
Hand raised. 914-337-5230

GERMAN SHE...HERD PUPPIES
AKC reg. White. ...reat for Christmas. Born Oct. 30. Re...dy after Dec. 12. Call eves 201-...52-5228 for appt.

GERMAN SH...PHERD PUPPIES
AKC, males & ...males. Parents on premises. $400. 2...-485-0876

GERMA... SHEPHERDS
Quality, Import ...red M & F. 2 mos old. Black & reddish ...an. Excel temps.
BIHA...I KENNELS
914-356-1658 1/2 hr NYC

GERMAN S...ORTHAIR POINTER PUPS —AK... Parents on prem. Both hunters. G...at temperment. Shot/Wormed/Bo...bed. 516-427-6719.

GER...AN SHORTHAIRS
AKC cham... parents & hunting stock. Male & fe... pups. 11 mo old fem. 3 yr old cham... male. 914-763-3384.

FIGURE 19-7
**Ads soliciting boat donations. (*The New York Sunday Times*)**

ticular organization, whether you have a capital gain on the transaction at the valuation assigned, whether you are subject to AMT (alternative minimum tax) and other considerations. Check with your accountant or refer to one of the do-it-yourself tax guides, such as J.K.Lasser's *Your Income Tax*, available in discount stores. Or just ask the IRS for advice. It's free.

## Summary

Marketing your boat professionally consists of planning your program in advance, doing a good job getting your boat ready to show, focusing your advertising efforts, being available and putting your best foot forward when prospects call, having an organized sales pitch, keeping good records, following up, and being ready to close the deal the instant the prospect says yes. That may seem like a lot of activity, but if you organize your efforts, it'll be a breeze.

# CHAPTER 20

# Rule Two: Know What You're Selling

Full familiarity with the product you're trying to sell is absolutely fundamental to good salesmanship in any business. And when you're selling your boat, you should think in businesslike terms. The keys to success in applying Rule Two are to know your boat's market value so you can price her right, and to know her good points and bad points, so you can accentuate the positive and eliminate the negative in your sales pitch.

## Picking the right asking price is crucial

If it's too low, you'll sell your boat quickly, possibly without a bit of haggling, but you'll "leave money on the table" for the buyer to walk away with. If your price is too high, you'll be lucky to get any offers, let alone sell the boat.

How do you price your boat properly? Study the market; know how much similar boats are selling for. Calculate your boat's market price using the methods in Chapter 12. Physically check the marketplace; visit and inspect a few boats like yours currently on the market to see how your boat stacks up against the competition. It's all part of knowing your product, the better to sell it.

Then study the hints in Figure 20-1. Finally, set your price and try it out.

The price you end up selling for should be competitive. That is, it should be equal to or lower than prices for similar boats recently on the market that have already been sold. Don't make the mistake of looking at brokerage listings and assuming that boats are moving at those prices. Almost certainly, they aren't. Instead, try calling adver-

# THE SEVEN BASIC RULES OF THE BOAT-SELLING GAME

FIGURE 20-1
**Checklist for pricing your boat properly.**

☑     **Determine your pricing structure.** Decide on your asking price, terms of sale (cash, cashier's check or certified check, owner financing), policy on discounts and allowances (how much you'll reduce the asking price for various circumstances), price for any extras, etc. Be sure to check market conditions before setting your pricing structure. Remember, *your selling price has nothing whatsoever to do with the price you paid when you bought the boat.* The price of a boat or any other product is set by whatever price the market will bear.

    Lack of understanding of this law of economics over a wide cross-section of sellers is one cause for the long slump in the sailboat market.

☑     **Set your asking price slightly below the advertised market.** If your boat is priced at the same level as similar boats currently on the market, she's one of many. If she's slightly below (3% to 5%) and all other things are equal, the buyers will come to see her first and you're likely to sell her more quickly.

    Remember, your *asking* price usually turns out to be 5% to 15% above your *selling* price, after you get through bargaining with the ultimate buyer. If you were to use a broker, the percentage difference might be even more. Take these factors into account when setting your *asking* price.

☑     **Try making some equipment optional to keep your base price low.** Everyone who has ever bought a new car knows the deal: there's the discounted base price quoted to you and there's the actual final price you pay, which is the quoted price plus extras you decide you want, plus taxes, plus other items not included in the base price. New boats are sometimes (but not always) sold the same way: a base price, plus extras such as trailer, outboard engine, safety equipment, sails, docklines, fenders, yacht ensign, sunshade, etc.

    If you plan to include extras when you sell your boat, make sure prospects see the value you're offering. One way to do that is to reduce the base price by an amount equal to the current used-market value (not the original price) of loose equipment you might either keep or sell with the boat. Then you can bargain up from a relatively low base price, using the extra equipment as a bargaining chip.

---

tisers of boats like yours a few weeks after their ads have appeared to ask about actual selling prices; if you're lucky, some sellers may be willing to tell the truth about how much they collected on the sale.

To help you in figuring the right price, Figure 20-2 reviews the pricing factors mentioned in Chapter 12.

---

FIGURE 20-2
**Selling price depends on . . .**

- A boat's size in terms of length and weight
- Her age
- Her quality level and builder's reputation
- Her physical condition
- The extent and condition of her equipment, especially engines
- The geographic area where she's being sold
- When she is being sold
- The seller's marketing skills, needs, and attitudes

---

I should mention that a boat's price depends on some other less important factors as well:

- **How clean your particular boat is — literally.** Some experts say you can make 10% or more extra ($2,000 on a $20,000 boat) by spending a full day with scrub brush, polish cloth and vacuum cleaner just before you show her. Or, looked at the other way around, you might stand to lose 10% if you don't make a serious clean-up effort.
- **Whether the builder is still in business.** Owners of "orphan" boats with questions about problems they're experiencing have no one to ask except owners of other similar orphan boats. As a result, orphan boat owners' groups have been organized to give "support services" of the type supplied by the builders before they disappeared. An active orphan boat owners' group mitigates the inconvenience of owning a boat no longer in production.
- **Overall construction quality.** Cheaply made boats sell for cheaper prices. "Yacht quality" vessels — such as Hinckley, Little Harbor, and Alden sailboats and powerboat names like Rybovich, Grand Banks, and some of the smaller builders such as Lee Wilbur and Falmouth Marine — command premium prices.
- **Designer's reputation.** The known designers with active offices who have been in business for a number of years are often a safer bet than new kids on the block. But not always. Venerable and respected firms like Sparkman & Stephens and William Garden have designed many winners — but a few losers, too. And the new kids on the block may have some great designs which shouldn't be ignored just because their creators aren't yet well known.
- **Whether there's an active class or owners' association.** Boats are more fun if there are other owners you can meet and compare notes with — to say nothing of racing or having predicted log contests. And fun is the reason most people buy boats.
- **Trends in style, design, public taste.** Few people want to own an ugly boat. Thus ugly boats are a drag on the market, and warrant lower prices. If a boat is really ugly, the owner may be unable to sell it at any price, in which case he may have to give it away.
- **The urgency of your need to sell.** "Must sell this week" ads announce to the buying public that the seller is desperate, and is willing to reduce price below market to make a sale. If you're really desperate, by all means say so if you're willing to accept the consequences in terms of price received.
- **Popularity of the boat in your immediate area.** If almost everybody in your neighborhood has got a similar boat, there are likely to be some trades going on at premium prices. That's

because people are willing — even anxious — to pay a premium to buy from someone who will be accessible if something goes wrong with their boat after they buy it. And, usually, the people you know (because they're in your neighborhood) are the people you find easiest to trust.

- **Possible special or unique features.** This boat may have gone around the world, or belonged to a deposed monarch, or have won the Bermuda Race. Such features may or may not add value to the boat, depending on the buyer. Certainly advertising that the boat had a famous former owner wouldn't hurt. Whether to advertise that the boat went around the world is another question; it might invite suspicion that the hull structure has been weakened during the long strain of such a voyage. I'd only mention it if the boat is in top condition, with any damage incurred during the trip fully repaired.

If the price you finally set is too high, you'll know because no one will call. If it's too low, you'll know because your phone will ring off the hook. The best price you can set is the one that attracts a single buyer who pays cash and doesn't haggle. I personally have never experienced that situation, but it could happen!

## Know her good points and bad points

To be sure you haven't overlooked any features or benefits you can use to help sell your boat, or problems you'll need to fix, check out your boat by filling out the minisurvey worksheet in Chapter 6 as if you were a prospective buyer who had read this book. Then step back, put on your buyer's hat, and decide why you, as an imaginary buyer, would or wouldn't buy this boat. Then simply figure out how to emphasize the positives and eliminate — or at least minimize — the negatives you've listed.

# CHAPTER 21

# Rule Three: Establish Rapport With Potential Buyers

How do you establish rapport? Start by putting yourself in the prospect's shoes. Listen to his needs. Try to gauge his enthusiasm as you describe or show him your boat. Focus on his interests. Then find a way to fit your boat to those interests. Try this step-by-step process:

***Be cordial.*** When prospects telephone, be enthusiastic but not pushy. Sound pleased; say, "I'm glad you answered my ad," or words to that effect. Ask him to repeat his name, write it down and use it occasionally during the conversation.

If the buyer seems at a loss for words at the start of his call (a common situation), ask, "Would you like me to tell you something about the boat?" Proceed with a brief description, covering the material in the ad the prospect has already seen, and enlarging on it a bit. Pause frequently for possible questions. Answer courteously but briefly; your objective at this point is simply to get him interested enough to come see the boat.

If the prospect seems slightly interested but short on time at the moment, offer to send him a copy of your brochure. And don't forget to get his address as well as his phone number, which you should enter in your logbook of sales prospects.

If and when the prospect actually shows up to see your boat, use your first name when introducing yourself and shake hands. You may even want to offer your guests a beverage if it seems appropriate (though if you don't feel comfortable about it, don't do it). Try to put the prospect in a relaxed frame of mind.

Above all, be positive and enthusiastic about your boat. Talk about the good times you've had aboard, and how much you'll miss her after she's sold. Remember that for most people, shopping for a boat is an exciting adventure. It is an exhilarating experience and you can nourish their excitement with your enthusiasm.

***Tune in on the prospect's wavelength.*** Look for the advantages he seeks to gain by buying a boat, and play to that tune. Does he want speed? Your boat is the fastest in the harbor and you can prove it. Does he want seaworthiness? A sistership of your boat has gone around the world. He wants economy? You're selling $30,000 worth of boat and equipment for a mere $15,000. How can he beat that?

Listen more than you talk. Look for signals of what turns him on. When you do talk, concentrate on you and your, not I, me and mine.

When you're talking to a prospect, use his language. Determine his experience level early in the conversation. If he's new to boating, use layman's terms. Don't use language that could confuse or intimidate him. But be sure you know what you're talking about. If your prospect is an old salt, you don't want to appear uninformed.

***Be sure you are seeing things as the prospect does.*** Keep your thoughts on his objective (to buy a boat), not yours (to sell one). Ask what boats he's seen, and what he liked and didn't like about them. Don't start too early to explain how yours compares favorably with those he's seen. Wait for him to finish his story.

***Stay tuned in.*** Don't forget your objective (to sell your boat to the prospect before the day is out). If you start talking about something completely unconnected with the boat or the prospect's desires, you're tuning out. Stick to the subject at hand. Answer questions fully but briefly. Don't babble on; listen.

Be sure the prospect has enough information. Give him a brochure. Be sure to mention that you have maintenance records and all your old yard bills, which will give the impression that you are a systematic, caring owner, and have them ready in case he wants to see them.

Don't reveal any defensiveness or hurt feelings when fielding complaints from prospects; develop a thick skin. And if the prospects' complaints are justified, think positively: see what you can do about fixing the boat to prevent future complaints.

Rapport is a two-way street, so while you're getting into the prospect's mind, you should permit him to get into yours. You'll build trust by doing so. Of course, many prospects could care less about unlocking your subconscious; you can assume most are interested in buying a boat, not psychoanalyzing you. Still, make a strong effort to be friendly. If the prospect likes what he sees, it could mean the difference between selling your boat and not selling it.

# CHAPTER 22

# Rule Four: Sell Special Features and Benefits

Everyone is unique, especially when it comes to needs and wants. But by establishing rapport with your prospects, you'll know what special features and benefits they're looking for (or would like, even if they don't yet realize it), and you can focus on emphasizing and offering those features and benefits.

## Typical features and benefits buyers look for

Since everyone is different, you'll want to have in mind all the possibilities your prospects might go for. Find out early in your discussions what specific items each specific prospect feels he must have. Below is a starter list that covers a representative sample of "must haves." As you can see, the categories are straight from the worksheet in Chapter 6, with a few items added. You can expand the list with your own ideas and use it to help in selling to your target buyers.

## Typical "must haves" that buyers look for — desired features and benefits

- ☑ must have shallow draft as required at home slip or in anticipated cruising grounds
- ☑ must have enough berths for whole family
- ☑ must have short enough mast or superstructure to navigate under a certain bridge

# THE SEVEN BASIC RULES OF THE BOAT-SELLING GAME

- ☑ must have freeboard low enough for convenient swimming
- ☑ must have cockpit big enough to fish from
- ☑ must have flying bridge
- ☑ must have two-cabin, or three-cabin, or four-cabin layout
- ☑ galley must be L-shaped, U-shaped, or I-shaped
- ☑ must have a separate nav station
- ☑ must have an enclosed head
- ☑ must have (or must not have) a dinette

### Aesthetics
- ☑ must look modern, traditional, futuristic, classical, contemporary, etc
- ☑ hull must be made of a specific material (usually fiberglass but sometimes wood, aluminum, steel, etc.)
- ☑ must have a glossy "yacht finish," or a plain "workboat finish"
- ☑ must be white, blue, green, black, pink, red, yellow, etc.
- ☑ must have extensive wood in trim, or little or no wood in trim
- ☑ must have joinerwork of cabinetmaker quality
- ☑ wood must be teak, mahogany, oak, ash, pine, etc.

### Performance
- ☑ must attain a certain cruising speed or racing speed
- ☑ must have a well-balanced helm
- ☑ must have good directional stability
- ☑ must have good light-air performance
- ☑ must have good heavy-air performance
- ☑ must have good performance in all conditions
- ☑ must have a certain cruising range at a certain speed
- ☑ must have a certain rating under racing rules
- ☑ must sail at a certain close angle to the wind

### Comfort
- ☑ must have a low vibration or noise level
- ☑ must be dry below
- ☑ must be dry on deck in a sea
- ☑ must be warm below in cold weather
- ☑ must be cool below in warm weather
- ☑ must have large stowage capacity
- ☑ must have berths of a certain size or softness
- ☑ must be comfortable in heavy or rolling seas
- ☑ must have enough headroom for tall owner
- ☑ must have low windows for short owner
- ☑ must have enough elbow room for obese owner
- ☑ must not heel excessively

### Safety and reliability
- ☑ engine must use diesel fuel
- ☑ stove must use certain kind of fuel

- ☑ must have engine fire protection, or general fire protection
- ☑ engine must be fresh-water-cooled
- ☑ must have seacocks of a certain type
- ☑ must have a companionway ladder of a certain slope, or a certain width, or a certain depth
- ☑ fiberglass layup schedule must be of a certain quality, or wood scantlings must be of a certain prescribed standard
- ☑ stanchions must be a certain diameter and wall thickness, with lifelines of a certain diameter
- ☑ bulkhead/hull attachment or hull/deck attachment must be of a certain type or meet certain standards
- ☑ lightning protection must be of a certain design
- ☑ electrical wiring must be of a certain standard

### Convenience and ease of operation
- ☑ must have a wheel, or must have a tiller
- ☑ must have jiffy reefing or roller reefing of a certain type
- ☑ must have special furling gear
- ☑ must have certain special equipment, to be specified

### Physical condition
- ☑ must be spotlessly clean
- ☑ must have no gelcoat stress cracks
- ☑ must recently have been painted or varnished
- ☑ must be in excellent, or good, or average, or poor condition
- ☑ engines must have no more than X hours on them
- ☑ must be a handyman special

### Economy
- ☑ must have an asking price no higher than X
- ☑ must use diesel, or must use gasoline
- ☑ must use no more than a certain quantity of fuel per hour or per mile
- ☑ must have a certain size engine
- ☑ must not have annual maintenance expenses greater than a certain amount
- ☑ must not have annual operating expenses greater than a certain amount

### Equipment, extras and freebies thrown in
- ☑ must have certain types or brands of equipment
- ☑ must have equipment of a certain quality level
- ☑ must include free lessons on how to operate the boat
- ☑ must throw in help with launching, haulout, maintenance, etc.
- ☑ must throw in help with moving the boat from seller's harbor to buyer's
- ☑ must throw in free delivery to the buyer's location

&#9745; must get free use of a marina slip for the time left on the seller's rental contract

&#9745; must offer help in finding an appropriate boating or sailing school for the buyer

Some of these musts are relatively easy to accommodate. Others cannot be accommodated unless your boat happens to have the required items already built in. Others perhaps could be added if the buyer is adamant.

## The other side of the coin: dealing with objections

If a prospect has a list of must haves that your particular boat doesn't possess, that's an objection you must deal with.

Every prospect is different, and one man's objection ("I insist on steering with a tiller; I hate wheels") is another man's top priority ("I hate tillers"). Consequently, you probably won't be able to anticipate objections in advance, and will just have to deal with them as they occur. Almost every buyer will have at least one; since most prospects don't want to be seen as an easy mark, they look for a reason to resist a bit.

If an objection seems vague, gently ask the prospect to clarify it for you. A sincere prospect will listen carefully to your arguments, while a frivolous tire-kicker will soon abandon his game. Ask questions; draw him out. Concentrate on understanding and interpreting the answers you receive.

Once an objection is spelled out specifically, you can often dispell it. If a prospect doesn't see enough storage space, you can point to the cavernous cockpit lockers and the hidden space under the berths. If the boat is too far from his home to move it conveniently, you can offer to move it at your expense. If the price is too high, you can ask him how much he's prepared to pay. And so on.

Try to replace objections about which you can do nothing with equivalent positive features. If the engine is too small to suit a prospect's taste, point to the fuel savings, or to the good performance under sail that makes the engine practically superfluous.

## How you can sell special features and benefits

Once you've figured out what the prospect wants, homing in and concentrating on selling the features he most desires is your next task. If you've established the necessary rapport (Chapter 21), this shouldn't be too hard. Tune in. Listen hard for signals. Ask questions. Emphasize the positive. That's really what selling is all about.

# CHAPTER 23

# Rule Five: Location Counts

Be sure you're selling at the right place — which is where the buyers are.

The old saw among realtors that the three most important factors in selling a parcel of real estate are location, location, and location also applies — in a way — to selling boats. I wouldn't say that a boat's location is the most important factor in attracting buyers (make and model probably is) but it is, without a question, important.

Advertising in the right places is important too, but we've already covered that in Chapter 19. Here we're talking about the location of the boat. There are three questions to be concerned about:

1. Is the boat a popular type in the geographical region in which she's being displayed?
2. Is she being continuously displayed in a high-traffic area?
3. Are there any special opportunities for display?

Let's look at each of these questions in turn.

## Is the boat a popular type where she's being displayed?

I once bought an old wooden Beetle Cat on Cape Cod, fixed her up, and trailered her down to Connecticut to use her on Long Island Sound. She was fun to sail on light and medium-air days on the Sound, but wet and uncomfortable in the short, steep chop that can come with windy weather on the Sound, due to her low freeboard and convex hull sections. She just was not a good boat for local conditions.

When I decided to sell her, I put an ad in the Darien paper (usually a good place to advertise boats) but received not a single call.

Eventually I took her back to the Cape — where Beetle Cats are extremely popular, particularly in relatively protected Pleasant Bay, near Chatham. I advertised her in the Chatham paper, was besieged by calls, and sold her for my asking price the first day to a local who was willing to buy her sight unseen. (I insisted he look at her before making a final decision.)

This story illustrates a rule: boats designed for certain conditions won't sell well where conditions don't suit. An aluminum car-topper won't sell well in a saltwater area, where the corrosive salt can attack and etch aluminum surfaces. A varnished-mahogany speedboat won't sell well in open estuaries. It's hard to sell an iceboat in Florida.

All these craft can be sold with relative ease in their home markets. So when you decide to sell your boat, be sure she's in the right place, a place where conditions are suited to bring out the best in her.

## Is she located in an accessible, high-traffic area?

If lots of people can see the boat as they drive along a street or stroll along a sidewalk or pier, and the boat has a For Sale sign displayed, you'll attract more prospects. People who weren't even thinking about buying a boat, searching the classifieds or calling brokers, might decide to buy your boat just because they see the sign, and like her looks. It can and does happen. So...

- If you can move her from a mooring to a finger pier, do so.
- If you can move her from water to land (and can relaunch her for a demo and without undue time or expense), do so.
- If you can move her from your backyard to your front yard, do so.
- If you can move her from your front yard to a boatyard or other high-traffic spot, do so.
- If your boat is trailerable, and you can move her to a gas station on a main drag, do so.

If you find a gas station where used cars are displayed and sold, try making a deal with the station manager to park your boat there for the same purpose. Start by offering him a fixed amount for his trouble — maybe in the range of $50 to $200, depending on the size and value of the boat. Explain to him that he doesn't have to take any of his own time to sell the boat, and if a prospect asks, he can just point out that the owner can be reached at the phone number on the sign.

If he balks because you're not offering him a big enough commission to do this easy job, you could try giving him a better deal if you think it'll sell your boat. For example, you could try offering to pay him, say, 5% to 8% of the actual selling price to display the boat, for a trial period only — say for one or two weeks at the most. During that period, you can raise the asking price of the boat by the same 5% to 8%, so you don't net less. Of course, if you bring someone in on your own to look at the boat and he buys it, you'll have to pay the gas station manager as you promised, unless you agree in advance to some other compensation base if you find a buyer independently. One way or another (unless you and he agree differently), the manager should be paid for the display services he's provided, even if the display doesn't result in a sale.

Note: In some communities, selling cars and boats from gasoline service stations is illegal. It's also illegal in some communities to display signs in certain locations, even in a residential yard. Check local authorities for specifics.

Boatyards sometimes have similar regulations, unless the boat is listed with a resident broker. Always check first, to avoid embarrassment — if not a claim for a commission!

## Can you find special opportunities for display?

Examples of high-traffic areas where boats can be taken for short periods for peak exposure include:

- used boat shows
- sailing regattas in which other boats in that class are racing
- rendezvous and raft-ups
- crowded beaches on sunny Saturdays and Sundays
- popular anchorages on Saturday nights in mid-season
- trailer-parking spaces near public launching ramps

Putting your boat in a place where lots of prospects are looking should make your selling job significantly easier. Just be sure the place you put it is legal, safe, and won't cost you any sales commissions beyond what is reasonable. And don't forget to hang a For Sale sign on her. A big one.

# CHAPTER 24

# Rule Six: Time the Sale Right

You may recall that Rule Four of the Seven Basic Rules Of The Boat-Buying Game is: Time your purchase intelligently." The same principle applies to selling.

## The two windows for selling

As explained in Chapter 7, when you're selling a used boat, you have a choice of two high-demand "windows" each year. One window is at the start of the boating season in your area, and the other is at the end. At those two time periods, each of which lasts two to four months depending on location, there are a peak number of prospects looking to buy, demand tends to exceed supply, and asking prices tend to be the highest of the year.

At all other times of year, you may have to reduce your boat's price significantly to have a chance of selling, and in fact you may still find no buyers; supply may simply exceed demand.

**Seller's market timing.** Figure 24-1 gives sellers an idea of how market timing goes by geographical region.

**Buyer's market timing.** When sellers' markets end, *buyer's* markets begin. Thus we can show the schedule for buyer's markets by elimination, as in Figure 24-2.

Armed with both these charts, a seller can develop a better sense of whether he's in a seller's market (advantageous for him) or a buyer's market (disadvantageous for him).

FIGURE 24-1
**Timing of the seller's
market by geographical
area.**

| GEOGRAPHICAL REGION | START-OF-SEASON SELLER'S MARKET | | END-OF-SEASON SELLER'S MARKET | |
|---|---|---|---|---|
| | *begins in—* | *ends in—* | *begins in—* | *ends in—* |
| Northeast & Mid-Atlantic | March | June | September | October |
| Southeast | October | December | April | June |
| Great Lakes & Central states | April | June | September | October |
| Northwest | February | May | October | December |
| Southwest | —Continuous all year— | | —Continuous all year— | |
| Gulf Coast | September | November | March | May |

The other comments in Chapter 6, directed toward boat buyers, apply equally to boat sellers. How the timing of your sales program matches various economic factors — the phase of the overall business cycle, foreign exchange rates, loan interest rates, stock market prices, the overall inflation rate, fuel prices and outlook for availability, the

FIGURE 24-2
**Timing of the buyer's
market by geographical
area.**

| GEOGRAPHICAL REGION | IN-SEASON BUYER'S MARKET (BETWEEN START AND END OF BOATING SEASON) | | OFF-SEASON BUYER'S MARKET (BETWEEN START AND END OF THE OFF-SEASON) | |
|---|---|---|---|---|
| | *begins in—* | *ends in—* | *begins in—* | *ends in—* |
| Northeast & Mid-Atlantic | July | August | November | February |
| Southeast | July | September | January | March |
| Great Lakes & Central states | July | August | November | March |
| Northwest | June | September | January | January |
| Southwest | —Continuous all year— | | —Continuous all year— | |
| Gulf Coast | June | August | December | February |

state of the boating manufacturing industry — may crucially affect how well you will do on a sale.

## Summing up: the best time to sell

Don't start too early. If you price high (as you should when you start to advertise), you won't sell in the off-season. Your boat will then have been on the market for a while, which, right or wrong, gives it the wrong cachet. After all, your boat is so desirable, it should be swept up by enthusiastic buyers as soon as it's offered up for sale.

What's the right timing? If you have completed your advertising arrangements and have your boat solidly on the market and listed in ads that appear 30 to 60 days before the boating season begins in your area, you're set up to take full advantage of whatever market opportunities may exist.

If you procrastinate and fail to advertise in that time frame, try to correct your error as soon as possible. The longer you wait, the less chance you have of selling before the season turns to the buyers' advantage.

And that's all there is to selling at the right time.

# CHAPTER 25

# Rule Seven: Buy Low, Sell High

If you've read this book from front to back, you may have a feeling of déjà vu, since "buy low, sell high," appears to be exactly the same as the rule for buyers explained in Chapter 10. It *is* the same rule, but from the seller's standpoint rather than the buyer's. And therein lies a big difference.

When you're a buyer, *buying low* is mainly a matter of being in the right place at the right time to find the right boat at the right price. As detailed in Part 2, this can be accomplished by:

1. Deciding what you want
2. Studying the market for what you want until you're intimately familiar with the price structure of what's available
3. Learning to recognize the best times to buy
4. Analyzing buying opportunities to see if they fit your criteria
5. Using effective negotiating techniques
6. Staying objective and avoiding emotional decisions

*Selling high* is a matter of positioning your boat in the right place at the right time, and at the right price. Again, to review:

1. Sell your boat using the same tricks and techniques used by the pros, from advertising in the right places to following up with prospects who have seen your boat
2. Price her to the market
3. Know your boat's good and bad points, and capitalize on that knowledge by emphasizing the positive and eliminating the negative in your sales pitch
4. Establish rapport with each of your prospects. Tune your pitch to his real (though not necessarily stated) needs

## THE SEVEN BASIC RULES OF THE BOAT-SELLING GAME

5. Concentrate on selling the unique features and benefits that every boat, including yours, possesses
6. Arrange to put the boat up for sale at the "right" location
7. To get the highest offers, be sure to pick the right time to sell

That's it. You now know everything you need to buy, own, and sell your boat without losing your shirt. And best of all, you now know that buying and selling can be a blast instead of a hassle. So.... good luck on moving in, up, and out — and have fun!

# *Three Dozen of My Favorite Boats*

Everybody has his and her favorite boats. For whatever it's worth, the following pages list three dozen of mine—outstanding examples of their specific types, from tiny yacht tenders to world cruisers.

## Three good tenders
The Dyer Midget 8
The Dyer Dhow 9
The Trinka 10

## Three good boats for kids— and their parents
Concordia's Beetle Cat
Hobie Power Skiff 13
The 13½' Blue Jay

## Six minimum cruisers
A Trio of Cruising Catboats
The Aquasport 22-2
The South Coast 23
The Grady-White 232-G Gulfstream

## A woody loaded with nostalgia
The Grand-Craft Luxury Sport

## A pair of racing sloops
Rod Johnstone's J/24
Charlie Morgan's Morgan 24

### A good maxi-trailerable power cruiser
Chris-Craft's new 252 Crowne

### Two sailboats you can build
The 25' Black Skimmer
The 26' Norwalk Islands Sharpie

### My all-time favorite sailboat (at the moment)
The Remarkable F/27 Trimaran

### A comfortable shoal-draft yawl
Sparkman & Stephens' Tartan 27 Yawl

### Three good 28-footers
L. Francis Herreshoff's 28' Rozinante
The Cape Dory 28 Fly Bridge Cruiser
Commodore Munroe's 28' *Egret*

### Seven in the mid-range
Bill Garden's 30' *Mist of Lemolo*
Clive Dent's Cape Dory
  300 Motorsailer
Frank Butler's Catalina 30
Thomas Gillmer's Seawind 31 Ketch
McLear & Harris' Allied Sea Breeze 35 Yawl
The Grand Banks 36 Trawler Yacht
Murray Peterson's 36' Coasting Schooner

### Six big cruisers—40 feet and above
Bill Tripp's Hinckley Bermuda 40
Ray Hunt's 40' Concordia Yawl
Phil Rhodes' 41' Reliant Yawl
Ted Brewer's Whitby 42
Jay Benford's 50' Florida Bay Coaster
Sparkman & Stephens' 51' Yankee, a World Cruiser

## Three good tenders
A yacht tender (also known as a dinghy, dink, punt, skiff, or pram) needs to satisfy most if not all of the following requirements to meet my definition of "good."

- She should be light enough for two people to lift and carry up a beach;
- She be able to be converted to a sailboat;
- She should have a transom capable of receiving a small (2- or 3-h.p.) outboard motor, if the owner desires;
- She should have soft gunwale padding to keep from scarring the topsides of the mother boat;
- She should behave herself when under tow behind a mother boat; and finally,
- She should row easily and well.

The above criteria automatically rule out inflatables, which generally make both poor rowers and poor sailers.

For a boat to row well, the main rules of thumb are:

- The longer she is, the better; short boats don't have as much "carry" (i.e. a tendency to keep moving through the water when rowing is temporarily ceased).
- The narrower she is in relation to length, the better, all other things being equal. Some purists prefer a tender with a beam no less than one third her length. But this results in a longish boat, and some compromise is usually necessary if a relatively small tender is desired. Luckily, purists notwithstanding, there are plenty of 4 × 8 dinghies, and even a few 4 × 7 dinghies, that row quite satisfactorily.
- She should have a keel or skeg to provide directional stability. Without directional stability, the boat will run off course between strokes, requiring constant correction—a very tiring pursuit.
- Her waterline should sweep aft at or below the bottom of the transom. A dragging transom causes a vast amount of drag, slowing the boat and tiring the rower.
- She should be arranged so that her load can be distributed fore and aft to avoid submerging the transom. This usually means double pairs of oarlocks to vary the rowing position as the number of occupants changes. It also means seats arranged so the rower can sit comfortably at either rowing position. A longitudinal thwart along the spine of the boat solves this problem, but is not as comfortable as transverse thwarts, and usually limits the boat's capacity to some extent.

To be a good sailer, a tender should have sufficient sail area—at least 35 square feet for an 8-footer, 45 square feet for a 9-footer, and 60 square feet for a 10-footer. She'll be too sluggish in light air with less. Her spars should be strong and stiff, at least 2-inch-diameter anodized aluminum tubing with a reasonably heavy wall thickness; preferably an extruded section—but a lightweight, springy wood such as Sitka spruce is also acceptable. Pine is too brittle; mahogany is too heavy.

Her hull should be proportioned as for rowing to allow good carry. And her interior should not be cluttered to the point where it's impossible to be comfortable when sailing and shifting weight from side to side while tacking (which ordinarily rules out longitudinal thwarts).

To manage an outboard engine, her transom must be well reinforced to handle both the thrust and the dead weight of the engine—and her stern must be buoyant enough to prevent severe "squatting" when running at top speed under power. Unfortunately, boats that have wide sterns that don't squat much also tend to have poor rowing and sailing characteristics.

Most tenders are a compromise, and are apt to do well under one or two out of the three sources of power, but are not so good at the other. My favorites do all three well, and thus have my ardent admiration.

**Spec check on my favorite three tenders**

| BRAND AND MODEL | SOLD BY | LENGTH | BEAM | WEIGHT (LBS., EXCL. SAILING GEAR) | SAIL AREA (SQ. FT.) |
|---|---|---|---|---|---|
| Dyer Midget | The Anchorage | 7'11" | 4'1" | 90 | 35 |
| Dyer Dhow | The Anchorage | 9'0" | 4'6" | 106 | 45 |
| Trinka Ten | Johannsen Boatworks | 10'0" | 4'2" | 130 | 60 |

The 9' **Dyer Dhow** was designed during World War II by the late Phil Rhodes, in collaboration with Bill Dyer, for use as a lifeboat on minesweepers and PT boats, which had limited deck space. Originally Dhows were built in wood, but by 1949 they were among the first boats ever to be produced in fiberglass. Thousands have been built, and both the Dhow and the 8' **Dyer Midget** are still in production. They enjoy continued popularity because they do what they are supposed to do: Row well, sail well, power well, and tow well.

The Dhow has three stays as well as a thwart to support the mast, whereas the Midget uses a modified gunter rig, as shown in the accompanying drawing of an early wood model. Otherwise the Midget and the Dhow are very similar in appearance. Until you try to lift one and find that the 9-footer is considerably heavier and more awkward to carry than the 8-footer, you can hardly tell which is which except for the interior details, such as the enclosed centerboard trunk in the Dhow versus the daggerboard case in the Midget, and the keel-stepped mast in the Midget versus the thwart-stepped version in the Dhow.

Both the Midget and the Dhow are high-quality boats, with a price to match. But sailors with upper-end budgets who are shopping for a traditional 8- or 9-footer with first-class construction and a top pedigree would be smart to check out a Dyer.

**The Dyer Midget.**

In a test of eight 10-footers for *Boat Journal* a few years ago, the **Trinka Ten** won my heart on both sailing and rowing. She felt light and sensitive, but at the same time seemed well-mannered and easy to control. And for sheer beauty, her traditional wineglass transom is hard to beat.

Like the Dyers, the Trinka people pay attention to all the little details that, when handled properly, distinguish a great boat from just a good one. The Trinka comes with a bright white hull, canvas-covered, closed-cell urethane foam gunwale fender, double rowing stations, mahogany daggerboard, rudder and tiller, and a hiking stick. (The hiking stick is a particularly good idea that all builders would do well to include as standard.) Options cover virtually everything a dinghy enthusiast might want, including teak floorboards, self bailer, lifting eyes, kickup rudder, and choice of hull colors, among other things.

One unusual feature: the Trinka's bow eye position is very close to the waterline (though, interestingly, designer Bruce Bingham's original

**The Trinka 10.**

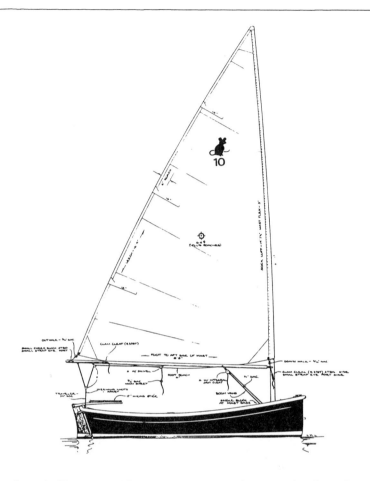

drawings indicate a mid-stem eye position). Most dinghies have their bow eyes either at mid-stem or close to the stemhead. The idea on the Trinka is that a low bow eye position tends to improve a dinghy's stability under tow in rough water or at high speed. So why don't all the builders put their bow eyes at the waterline? Probably because the low position makes it more awkward to tie in a line.

In summary, you'd almost certainly be happy with any of the three boats I've described here. They are all beautifully designed and lovingly executed. New, they're on the expensive side but will last a lifetime if properly cared for. Used, they are more affordable and can still give almost as much pleasure. The choice is yours.

For further information, contact:

Dyer Boats, The Anchorage
57 Miller Street
Warren, RI 02885
(401) 245-3300

Trinka Boats
Johannsen Boatworks
P.O. Box 570097
Miami, FL 33257-0097
(305) 445-7534

# Three good boats for kids—and their parents

***Concordia's 12' Beetle Cat.*** A great many folks who spent summers near New England waters learned to sail in Beetle Cats (photo on page 7). These same people as adults sing praises to the little Beetle for her ability to point high, foot fast, and go like a bird off the wind. They also like her other outstanding features, such as the comfortable and spacious cockpit that's big enough to accommodate four adults. It's rimmed with high oak coamings that give good back support, yet is low enough to the water so you really feel the magic of being afloat *in* it rather than *on* it.

Moreover, the Beetle Cat draws a mere 5 inches with her board up, allowing explorations into all kinds of gunkholes, and permitting her to be kept at a mooring in a mere puddle of a cove.

With a high peaked gaff-rigged single sail of 100 square feet, she will move in just a bare suggestion of a breeze, and is easy to handle and quite forgiving to new hands at sailing. Her great beam (6') and relatively heavy displacement (450 pounds), are a lot for a boat with a waterline of only 11'8", and make her unusually stable for her size.

She's small enough to be carried on a lightweight trailer pulled by most ordinary cars, so it's easy to take her along on your vacation and store her in your garage.

The Beetle Cat was designed in 1920 by one John Beetle. The first one, constructed of cedar planking on an oak frame, touched water in 1921, and 70 years later they are still being produced in wood to the original patterns, under the auspices of the Concordia Company in South Dartmouth, Massachusetts. Well over 4,000 have been built, with fleets flourishing on Cape Cod and vicinity. Their owners—mostly, but not always, kids—race avidly in the summers. Why not join them?

**Spec check:**
LOA ................ 12'4"
LWL ................ 11'8"
Beam .............. 6'0"
Draft, board down .... 2'0"
Sail area ........... 100 sq.ft.
Weight, approx. ....... 450 lbs.

For further information contact:
The Concordia Company
P.O. Box P-203
South Dartmouth, MA 02748
(508) 999-1381 (Main yard)
or (508) 996-9971 (Beetle Cat
Division)

***The Hobie Power Skiff 13.*** The Hobie 13 is a shiny little bundle of compressed fun. She's designed to satisfy everybody from neophytes with a personal watercraft who'd like to take a step up from wake-jumping to experienced mariners who seek a sensibly designed, high-quality, virtually bulletproof small outboard to fish, use as a yacht tender, or take a group across the bay to the beach. In short, this is one of those rare boats that will appeal to both serious and casual users.

As soon as I stepped into a Hobie 13 for a test for *Boat Journal* a couple of years ago, I knew she was no "typical" boat. Though only 13'2" long, 5'9" wide, and weighing a mere 548 pounds without engine or fuel tank, she feels much bigger and heavier. Moreover, she's not only unusually stable for her size, but handles extremely well at all speeds, and exudes an unmistakable aura of stability and safety.

At all speeds she is quiet, sure-footed, and dry as a bone. With one aboard (she'll hold four) and a Yamaha CV40 powerplant, she'll do 40 m.p.h. In fact, lightly loaded, the 13 will go about the same speed as the horsepower on the stern: 40 m.p.h. with a 40 h.p engine, 30 with a 30, 25 with a 25—and will get on up a plane with a 9.9-h.p. mill (which will drive her at around 15 tops). For me, and I suspect for most people, a 25- or 30-h.p. engine probably would provide all the juice this little rocket needs.

Besides performance and handling, the Hobie 13 has many unusual features that set her apart from other boats in her category. Most impressive to me is the brute strength of her hull and fittings. You can literally lift the whole boat—including her motor and trailer—vertically into the air from any single fitting on deck: cleat, rail, or bow eye. That's impressive evidence of toughness and solid construction, and not something that Hobie's competitors are likely to be able to duplicate.

With a boat-motor-trailer package (with a Yamaha CV-30 and an EZ Loader trailer) costing over $9,000, the Hobie 13 is not your typically priced 13-footer. But then, her extremely impressive construction and performance aren't typical either. In summary: If you admire competence and quality, this boat is worth a close look.

**Spec check:**
Length (LOA) ......... 13'2"
Beam ................ 5'9"
Dry trailering weight
   (boat plus motor and
   trailer) ............. 985 lbs.
Rated power .......... 45 h.p. maximum
Top speed ........... Approximately 40 m.p.h.
   with a 40 h.p. motor

For further information contact:
Hobie Power, A Division of
   The Hobie Cat Company
P.O. Box 1008
Oceanside, CA 92054
(619) 758-9100

***The 13½′ Blue Jay.*** Sparkman & Stephens designed the Blue Jay way back in 1948, mainly as a "junior Lightning" for teaching kids around 10 to 14 years old how to handle a sailboat with a jib and spinnaker. The more recent International Optimist Dinghy, a single-hander, is also a junior trainer and currently one of the most popular boats around, but kids can't learn crew teamwork and foresail handling in a boat that has only one sail and holds only one person. The Blue Jay, which has gained long-term popularity in the Northeast but nowhere else (other similar boats having covered the market in other regions of the country), does what she was designed to do and does it extremely well. Consequently, the class is still going strong, and sail numbers are now up in the 7,000s.

This pretty little boat weighs only 275 pounds, yet is big enough for three 12-year-olds or two 14-year-olds—but not so big that a lot of strength is required to sail her. Best of all from the point of view of a family on a budget, used fiberglass boats can be had for $1,500 or less (though new they're upwards of $4,000 equipped for racing). They are trailerable so you can easily store one in your backyard, and once you get the hang of it can be set up in less than half an hour from arrival at the

**The 13½ Blue Jay.**

launching ramp (or beach) to sailing away. Annual maintenance is simple, fast, and inexpensive. How about buying one for your kids for Christmas?

**Spec check:**
```
LOA .................. 13'6"
LWL .................. 11'5"
Beam ................  5'2"
Draft, board up .......   6"
        board down  ....  3'9"
Weight  .............. 275 lbs.
Sail area  ............ 90 sq.ft.
```

For further information contact:

Blue Jay Class Association
Julie Dunbar, Secretary
P.O. Box 651
Pearl St.
Mantoloking, NJ 08738
(908) 295-0238

Blue Jay Builder:
Formula Yachts
P.O. Box 9176, 145
Noank, CT 06340
(203) 572-1110

## Six minimum cruisers

***A trio of Cape Cod Catboats.*** For the type of small-boat sailing most of us do—knocking about in relatively sheltered waters, daysailing and weekend sailing along shore—a traditional gaff-rigged cruising catboat is an absolutely splendid choice. She's pretty, full of character, and easy and fun to sail. Her deck is free of expensive winches and complicated rigging, and she can be singlehanded with ease. She can be made ready to sail, tacked, reefed, and put to bed in no time flat. She floats in water not much deeper than the morning dew and has more room for her length than any other sailing design.

All these great features are perhaps unsurprising in a design that's been perfected over 140 years. But maybe the best thing about catboats is the people who own them. They're a salty lot with a love for tradition, and many are highly experienced mariners who have commanded bigger, more imposing boats. John Garfield, owner-president of Marshall Marine, a firm that specializes in building catboats, notes that many of his boats are sold to owners who simply lack the time to enjoy larger craft. "The smaller the boat, the more it's used," says Garfield. "We've sold a lot of boats to a lot of muckymucks: bank presidents and heads of big companies, heavies who want to sail but just can't take the time for a bigger boat." Whatever their motivation, between the muckymucks and the just plain folks, U.S. catboaters are over 1,300 strong, according to the U.S. Catboat Association.

The Cape Cod Shipbuilding version of the catboat, a 17' fiberglass model designed by Charlie Wittholz, is one I like—and happen to have owned for the last few years. Our family boat, *Pipcat*, resembles two other

**The Cape Cod Cat.**

popular, well-found models, the Marshall 18 and the Menger 19, in a number of ways worth mentioning. For example, all three are good-looking variations on the basic traditional Cape Cod catboat design theme, with gaff rigs and generous cockpit coamings faired into cabin trunks rounded at the forward end, punctuated by traditional bronze oval cabin portlights.

All three boats have big, roomy cockpits that could comfortably accommodate six average-size people for a quiet daysail, though with all that weight in a 17- to 19-foot boat, you couldn't expect to sail very fast. And the cockpit seats, from 6′4″ in the Marshall 18 to almost 8′ in the Menger, can be slept on—though none of the boats has cockpit seats wider than 18″, a bit narrow for sleeping comfort, especially if you toss and turn a lot.

All three also have a deep skeg aft, so they need a relatively steep ramp to launch and retrieve easily. Still, none is too deep or too heavy to be trailerable and ramp-launchable. All have provisions for a galley and head, and all can accommodate an optional inboard engine. A 4- or 6-h.p. outboard is adequate for most needs, but if you *really* want sufficient power for any occasion, all three of the little cats are available with 9-h.p., one-lung Yanmar 1GM diesels installed under the cockpit.

These little gems are priced new from around $14,000 to upwards of $20,000, and used from around $6,000 to $12,000 for one 15 or 20 years old. That, for a 17-foot to 19-foot sailboat, may seem like a lot of money. But with the extra beam, you get more boat for each foot of length. And in terms of mobility, ease of use, and dollars per hour of fun, catboats in general are an outstanding choice. The three vessels described here are no exception.

**The Menger Cat 19.**

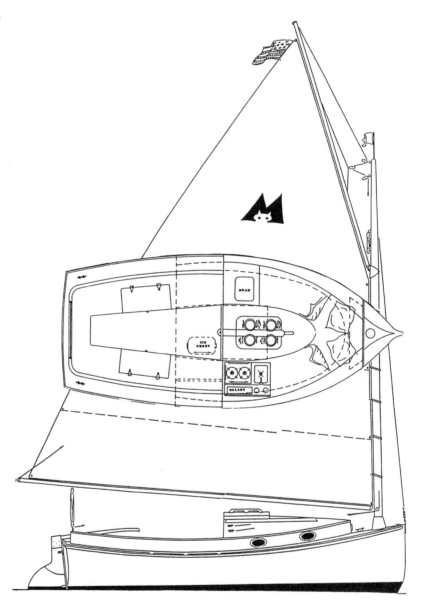

| Spec check: | CAPE COD 17' CAT | MARSHALL 18' | MENGER 19' |
|---|---|---|---|
| LOA (without rudder) .... | 17'0" | 18'2" | 19'0" |
| LWL .................... | 16'5" | NA | 18'5" |
| Beam .................. | 7'11" | 8'6" | 8'0" |
| Draft, board up .......... | 20" | 19" | 22" |
| board down ....... | 5'0" | 4'4" | 4'6" |
| Sail area ............... | 250 sq.ft. | 253 sq.ft. | 270 sq.ft. |
| Displacement .......... | 2,200 lbs. | 2,200 lbs. | 2,900 lbs. |

For further information contact:

Cape Cod Shipbuilding
P.O. Box 152
Wareham, MA 02571
(508) 295-3550

Marshall Marine
P.O. Box P-266
South Dartmouth, MA 02748
(508) 994-0414

Menger Boatworks
121 Maple Avenue
Bay Shore, NY 11706
(516) 968-0300

*The Aquasport 22-2.*  My first big (if 22 feet LOA can be termed big) powerboat was an Aquasport, a golden oldie made in the 1960s. We bought her in the mid-1980s to use primarily as a spectator boat for watching sailboat regattas and to buzz around our part of Long Island Sound. Later I discovered we could cruise comfortably on her overnight by utilizing her 6-foot-long raised fishing platform forward. This was equipped with 3-inch-thick cushions for sleeping, and sheltered by a folding spray dodger, to the back end of which a modesty curtain could be zipped. We added a portable ice chest and a large-mouth bucket to provide all the comforts of home. Well, almost.

Driven by a single 140-h.p. Evinrude outboard, she can cruise along at 25 to 30 knots, and will get close to 5 miles to a gallon of gas if you don't jam the throttle forward too often. Her modified-V hull with very low deadrise at the transom provides a soft ride and good planing performance without soaking up excessive horsepower.

With the dodger folded down, visibility from anywhere in the boat is excellent, and with her great beam and hard chine aft, she is as stable a platform as you could wish for. As a result, she is outstanding not only as a spectator boat at regattas but also as a photo boat—for both still and video.

I bought her for $5,000 and sold her five years later for $3,500, for a basic ownership cost of $300 a year, excluding maintenance. Today you could probably buy her for $3,000, and if you kept her for a few years and then resold her, your ownership costs would probably be even lower than mine.

**The Aquasport 22-2.**

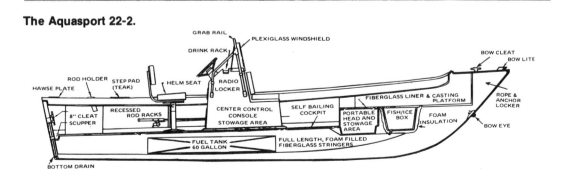

The Aquasport group that built my golden oldie has long since left the scene, and the original company has been bought and sold several times in the last few years. Hardly anyone there remembers the old low deadrise hull; the current line of Aquasports all sport a much deeper V aft. Consequently, for information on where to buy the model I'm talking about, the new Aquasport company can't help you. You'll have to consult the classifieds in *Soundings, Offshore,* or other regional publications.

**Spec check:**
LOA ................. 22'2"
Beam ............... 7'11"
Draft, motor up ....... 9"
Weight, with outboard,
     approx. ........... 1800 lbs.
Maximum h.p. ........ 230 h.p.

---

**The South Coast 23.**

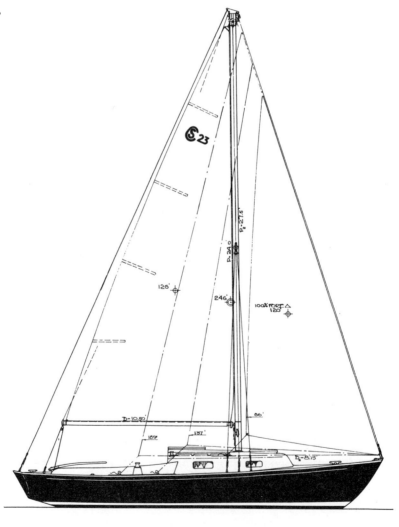

*South Coast 23.*   South Coast Seacraft, the company that molded the fiberglass South Coast 23 back in the early 1960s, is no longer around, but no doubt some of its product is. My wife and I bought a kit boat from them in the fall of 1964 and finished it out together over the winter and spring of 1965. (See pages 20 and 21 for details on this.) Designer Carl Alberg gave her what I think are especially pretty lines, and I finished her off to look as much as possible like a miniature Hinckley Pilot yawl, complete with triple port lights in the low cabin trunk and a tiny mizzen mast over the counter. The extra sail never bothered her balance, and came in handy in heavy air when we'd strike the main and sail under jib and jigger.

The mizzen sail was also useful to control the position of the boat when approaching or leaving a mooring. And the mizzen mast gave us a place to fly our private signal.

With either her sloop or her yawl rig, she sailed well enough to suit me, though her shallow keel with no centerboard gave her a tendency to make a bit of leeway when hard on the wind. The keel cavity was wide enough to house a centerboard under the floor, and I think she would have done better with one installed. An ambitious do-it-yourselfer with the urge to point high might consider acquiring one of these beauties and retrofitting a board.

We sold her in 1974 to buy a bigger, roomier boat when the family grew from two to four. I often wonder what's become of her since. She sported "SC 18" on her sail; if you come across her, let me know where I can find her for a little fond reminiscing.

If you want to buy one of these cute little ships, you'll have to search her out, like the Aquasport, in the classifieds. You ought to be able to pick one up for somewhere in the range of $2,000 to $4,000.

## Spec check:

LOA ................. 23'0"
LWL ................. 17'6"
Beam ............... 7'3"
Draft .............. 2'10"
Displacement ........ 3,750 lbs.
Ballast ............. 1,475 lbs.
Sail area ........... 246 sq. ft.

*Grady-White 232-G Gulfstream: Sibilant Sea Boat.*   Spacious. Safe. Solid. Seaworthy. Simply splendid.

These are some of the sibilant-sounding adjectives that came to mind when I tested a new Grady-White Gulfstream 232-G for *Motor-Boat* magazine in 1989.

Michael Clymin, the proud new owner of my test boat, kindly consented to come along on the test run and tell me about his decision to buy this particular boat. "My wife and I are both retired," explained Clymin by way of introduction. "We were looking for a boat that would have plenty of comfort and at the same time be very seaworthy. We plan to do some fishing, and also some touring and exploring, maybe as far as the Bahamas. So we wanted a boat that would really ride rough water well.

"We have three daughters, two married, and three grandchildren," continued Clymin. "When everybody comes down, we wanted to have enough space to take the entire family, and a boat where we wouldn't worry about taking the little grandchildren—one with a big enclosed cockpit and a cuddy cabin with a place to change. We're not going to use it for sleeping very much, but the sleeping capabilities if we need them are a nice extra."

The G-W 232-G cabin, we noted, fits Clymin's needs to a T. It features an unusual double-decker two berth layout, plus a sink, icebox, head (optional), and storage. And the cockpit has an especially high coaming, good for keeping the tots from going adrift.

Clymin went on. "My wife," he said, "was particularly interested in a very protected walkaround space, where you could grab the rail as you start to walk. On this boat, with the hardtop, as you go forward you've got a secure post to hold onto, a good rail on the outboard side of the boat, and a deep walkway." I went forward, noting that there's 9 inches of width on the side decks, enough to get both feet side by side, so you can walk without tripping yourself, and a stainless rail 16 inches off the deck, on the low side but adequate.

By this time it was obvious to me that Mr. Clymin had done considerable research, and I asked how he had gone about it. "Among other things," he responded, "we went to the February boat show in Miami, and looked at other brands. But we just couldn't find a hull configuration or a layout that we found pleasing. We looked at and tested several other boats, and they were nice, but had less beam than the Grady-Whites. And I just felt much better off with a wider beam. We figured that a wide-beam boat would ride the rougher water better and be more seaworthy. And since we're going to keep the boat in the water continuously, the narrower beam you'd need for trailering was not something that concerned us.

"This boat has a 9'3" beam that gives us a lot more square footage and, I think, a much better ride.

"I also think that, in comparison with competitive boats, the appointments on this boat are outstanding. And I like the idea of the Grady-White double hull, with the good finish and nice gelcoat on both the inside and the outside. The construction seems to be very, very good to me.

"Many manufacturers cover up a lot of things with carpet—in the cabin and sometimes the cockpit. But that's only a maintenance problem: you get mildew and dampness, and wet carpet is easier to slip on than a non-skid gelcoat. I didn't want carpet; I wanted a maintenance-free boat, and one that would be as slip-proof as possible. The non-slip molded fiberglass finish on the sole of this boat is just what I wanted.

"Another very important reason for me to choose this boat is that I wanted twin engines. Some of my friends said: 'Don't get two big engines, get one big one and maybe a kicker engine, because any mechanical problems you have probably won't be because of the motor, but because of possible water in the fuel.' To help overcome fuel problems, this boat has two fuel tanks, both completely independent, so if you have a problem with water in the fuel, you can switch from one tank to the other. I didn't find that feature on many of the other boats I looked at. But it's a standard feature on this model.

"The standard tankage capacity is over 140 gallons of fuel—one 93-gallon and one 55-gallon tank. I went to two tanks with nominal capacity of 90 gallons each. So we have roughly 180 gallons of fuel, and if we want to run to the Bahamas, for example, we can do it with a certain amount of security."

Everything Mr. Clymin said made good sense to me, and as I continued looking around, I was more and more impressed. For instance, besides improving stability and increasing space, the 232-G's wide beam provides a solid base for the "Grady Drive," G-W's name for its cast aluminum outboard mounting system. The foam-filled bracket keeps the motors out of the cockpit, which in turn provides even *more* cockpit space, and quieter operation to boot. In fact, in our noise tests, the G-W was close to the best, with a whisper-quiet 61 dB at idling speed and 86 dB at top r.p.m.

Performance? Excellent for this type of craft. With three aboard the test boat, the 232-G maxed out at 46 m.p.h., with a nice smooth ride in a one-foot chop. Easy turning, easy control. Although you can choose from a variety of engines (OMC, Yamaha, Suzuki etc.), I really liked the Yamaha counter-rotation package on Mr. Clymin's boat.

The price of all this splendor? Equipped as our test boat, the 232-G in 1989 listed in the neighborhood of $48,000 to $50,000. Base boat was around $30,000. Not cheap; but, as they say, quite a bit for the money.

**Spec check:**

Length (LOA) ......... 23'5" (ex. outboard bracket & engines)
Beam ................ 9'3"
Weight (with twin .... 5,000 lbs. (approx.)
   outboards)
Fuel capacity (two .... 148 gallons std., 183 gallons optional
   tanks)
Cruising range ........ 230 miles w/std. tanks, 290 miles with
   (approx.)             larger second tank option.
Power ............... Various options, outboards and I/Os to
                    350 h.p. On test boat: twin counter-
                    rotating six-liter Yamaha V-6 150s.
Fuel economy, ........ 1.6 m.p.g. at 33 m.p.h.
   maximum
Fuel economy, at ..... 1.3 m.p.g. at 45 m.p.h.
   top speed
Noise range in ........ 61 to 86 dB
   operation

For further information contact:
Grady-White Boats, Inc.
P.O. Box 1527
Greenville, NC 27835-1527
(919) 752-2111

## A woody loaded with nostalgia

**The Grand-Craft Luxury Sport.** How'd you like a speedboat that's a near-replica of something your great-grandparents might have ridden around in? A boat made of wood—not just any wood, but hand-selected mahogany gleaming with 10 or 12 coats of varnish? A boat that looks like a 1930s runabout but uses modern glues and equipment for a stronger, more durable hull and significantly better performance than her forebears? Would you go for a boat that takes six months to build, and is put together in a small Midwestern town by craftsmen who really care about the product? A boat sold by a company that cares so much about tradition that they even employ the grandson of the man who founded Chris-Craft to help them translate their concepts into reality?

If you'd like such a boat, consider the following.

The Grand-Craft 24 is beautifully constructed of select mahogany, shaped to relatively traditional lines with an eight-degree deadrise, flat bottom at the transom, a narrow entry, and chine spray rails, a combination that achieves a notably dry, smooth, and swift ride. The WEST System, in which epoxy resin is used to encapsulate the wood, is

**The Grand-Craft
Luxury Sport.**

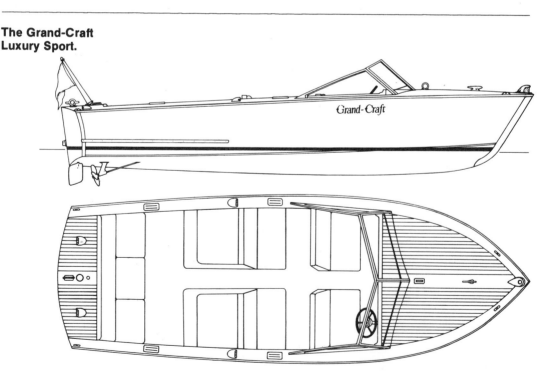

involved, and the wood used is Philippine mahogany, which is not the same as Honduras or African mahogany. Grand-Craft president Dick Sligh specifies dark mahogany, which is a more dense wood than some of the cheaper Philippine mahoganies like Luan, sands better, has greater strength, and takes stain more uniformly. Chris-Craft used it almost exclusively in the '30s.

"We order perhaps 20,000 feet at a time," says Sligh, "and then hand-select out of that what we feel we can use. After we weed out the defects or grain patterns that aren't suitable to us, we'll end up with 25% or 30% of what we started with. The rest gets sold to others to make billiard cue sticks or something else, or is thrown away.

"With the WEST System," Sligh goes on, "the mahogany won't warp and cup and change shape when the owner leaves the boat ashore for extended periods. All they have to do is cover the boat to protect the varnish; the wood will take care of itself."

After the hulls are constructed, they are sanded and varnished, a process in which Sligh takes particular pride. "After the sixth coat," he says, "we start looking for a finish. That might take eight or 10 or 12 coats. You just sand and apply, sand and apply, and keep going until the finish gleams." And it does.

The Grand-Craft 24 weighs 5,200 pounds, which is 10% or 20% heavier than the typical fiberglass 24-foot sport boat. But she'll do close to 50 m.p.h. with twin Chrysler 275 h.p. engines, or a bit less with a single. Even with twins, cruising at around 23 m.p.h. gives fuel economy of a surprising 3.8 m.p.g. That's great for twin engines.

Since the 24's beam is eight feet even, she's readily trailerable, and with a bunked rather than rollered trailer, the boat is simply driven up on the trailer with the engines. "We can't pull it up with a winch," says Sligh. "It would break the winch."

Grand-Crafts aren't cheap, and in fact the ultimate price for a "loaded" Grand-Craft can get up above a hundred grand. Even the base price on a 24 is upwards of $50,000. Thus, as you might expect, Grand-Craft boats appeal to people who want something distinctive and have the money to pay for it. Asked who buys his boats, Dick Sligh beams and answers: "Robert Redford is probably the most notable buyer. Margaret Thatcher's nephew, Paul Thatcher, bought a boat. And my mother-in-law is another example."

**Spec check:**
Length (LOA) ......... 24'0"
Beam ................ 96"
Weight ............. 5,200 lbs. (approx.)
Fuel capacity ........ 80 gallons
Power ............... 460 CID Chrysler V-8 (340 h.p.) inboard
                       is standard; twin 360 CID Chryslers
                       (275 h.p. each) are optional.
Fuel economy, ........ 3.8 m.p.g. at 23 m.p.h.
   maximum (twins)

Fuel economy, ........ 0.9 m.p.g. at 48 m.p.h.
    at top speed
Noise range .......... 72 to 101 dB
    operation

For more information contact:
Grand-Craft Corporation
448 West 21st Street
Holland, MI 49423
(616) 396-5450

## A pair of racing sloops

***Rod Johnstone's J/24.***  The J/24 fills the bill for several thousand small-boat racing enthusiasts who want something big enough to do a little cruising once in a while, small enough not to be imposing in terms of maintenance time and expense, and popular enough to find a racing fleet of them almost anywhere there's water.

The hulls, made in the U.S. by quality builder Tillotson Pearson (and by others elsewhere in the world), use a fiberglass and balsa-core sandwich construction that results in lightness combined with strength, stiffness, and durability. Fittings are first-quality (Harken, Barient, IMI spars), and safety in the design is given its due (lifelines, pulpit, etc.). The boat is fast, sensitive, and fun to sail. There are around 150 racing fleets scattered all over the U.S. In many locations the folks who race these boats are world-class experts, and this can be a little daunting for casual weekend sailors, but as in golf, if you play with somebody more adept at the sport than you are and stay alert, your own game will soon improve.

My family and I owned J/24 #3333 for four years, and never regretted it. Our two boys, then in their teens, probably got more use out of the boat than did Mom and Dad, but that didn't bother us at all. We didn't win many races, but then we hardly ever came in last either.

To me, one of the nice things about the J/24 is her trailerability. I still remember with pleasure the week's cruise the four of us took in Narragansett Bay, R.I. We towed the boat to Newport in half a day (versus three days if we had tried to sail the same distance). Once there, we quickly launched using the Fort Adams State Park electric hoist, and found a place to anchor overnight. On the couple of days it rained, we just jumped in the car and "cruised" by land for the day. The rest of the time we explored by boat. It was a great vacation.

New boats list for $25,000 to $30,000 with equipment, but used ones are beginning to appear at much lower prices. You'll find a choice of 1978 or 1979 models for under $10,000; a 1978 boat purportedly in good condition was advertised in the March 1991 *Soundings* for $4,995. But watch out for some problems in boats built between 1978 and 1980—such as leaky hull-to-deck joints, delamination of the main bulkhead, cracks developing in the mast around halyard openings, weak rudder

**The J/24.**

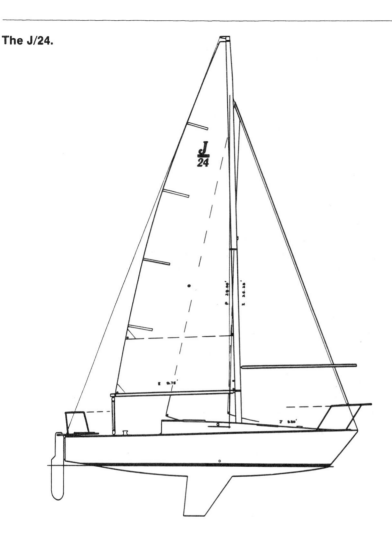

fastenings, and a loosening of the keel-to-hull joint, evidenced by the appearance of a crack along the joint. All of these problems are fixable, but do require spending time and money to do it. By the 1981 model year, most of the problems had been solved at the factory, and newer boats, we hear, are pretty much problem-free.

**Spec check:**

LOA ................. 24'0"
LWL ................. 20'0"
Beam ............... 8'11"
Draft ............... 4'0"
Displacement ........ 3,100 lbs.
Ballast .............. 950 lbs.
Sail area ............ 261 sq.ft.

For more information, contact:
J Boats, Inc.
Box 90
Newport, RI 02840
(401) 846-8410

***Charlie Morgan's Morgan 24.***  Way back in 1966, sailmaker Charlie Morgan, who had been dabbling with racing yacht design and had come up with a fantastic string of winners, conceived the Morgan 24. Designed to take full advantage of the then-popular MORC and CCA rating rules, like her bigger-boat predecessors she was an instant success. She has all the conveniences one could want in a small cruiser: galley sink, ice chest, marine toilet, 8-foot-long self-bailing cockpit with big sail lockers, shallow draft using an unusually high-aspect-ratio centerboard (which gives an unusually deep board-down draft of 7'), and good performance in most conditions, including heavy air. Now, a quarter of a century later, the old Morgan 24 continues to win her share of races. Early boats in reasonable condition can be had today for around $5,500—the same price that Morgan charged new in 1967.

In the 1970s, Morgan Yachts was taken over by a large "cookie-cutter" manufacturer and construction quality slipped a bit. If you're in the market for one of these babies, I'd advise sticking with the product from the 1960s.

Incidentally, the Morgan 24, which measures 24'11" end to end, was at some point renamed the Morgan 25. The 25 and the 24 are virtually identical except for the usual changes that take place between model years.

**Spec check:**
LOA ................. 24'11"
LWL ................. 21'0"
Beam ............... 8'0"
Draft, board up ....... 2'9"
      board down .... 7'0"
Displacement ........ 5,000 lbs.
Ballast .............. 1,900 lbs.
Sail area ............. 310 sq.ft.

For further information, see the sailboat classified ads, or your favorite yacht broker. One who specializes in selling "pre-owned" Morgans is:
Charles Morgan Associates
200 2nd Ave. South
St. Petersburg, FL 33701
(800) 922-4887 or (813) 894-7027

## A good maxi-trailerable power cruiser

***Chris Craft's new 252 Crowne.***  Venerable Chris-Craft (founded in 1874) has gone through several changes in ownership over the years, the most recent of which put it under the wing of the giant Outboard Marine Corporation (OMC). Since the OMC acquisition, Chris-Craft has committed to revitalizing the whole company, complete with an exciting new look to its product line. As of early 1991, 12 boats have been retooled under OMC's tutelage; more are to follow.

The 252 Crowne, introduced in 1990 in Miami, is one of these new beauties. I tested her for *MotorBoat* magazine in the fall of 1990, in a "shootout." We were comparing five maxi-trailerable power cruisers, that is, a boat small enough to be trailered, but big enough to qualify as a comfortable and practical weekend liveaboard cruiser. Specifically, a true trailerable maxi-cruiser must have:

- An enclosed cabin big enough to walk around in, with full standing headroom;
- Reasonably comfortable sleeping accommodations for at least two and preferably four adults;
- A dining area below, with table big enough for dinner plates, flatware, and beverage containers for two to four;
- A *real* galley, with sink, stove, electric refrigerator, and hot and cold pressure water, all preferably usable both at dockside and underway;
- An enclosed head big enough to include a built-in hot-water shower;
- A single-engine drive system sufficient to propel a party of four at a comfortable speed—30 m.p.h. or more—yet with acceptable fuel efficiency;
- A beam of no more than 8½ feet, so the boat can be towed without a special permit on most highways.

**The Chris-Craft 252 Crowne.**

Impossible to cram all those great features into just one boat, you say? Well, I found a number of boatbuilders who claimed otherwise. Five of them came to the *MotorBoat* test area in Sarasota Bay, Florida for a little show-and-tell. In my opinion, in terms of all-around features, the Chris 252 Crowne came out on top.

Why? First of all, I liked her unique white-on-white color scheme. Chris-Craft spokesman Mark Yunger says that most of the public likes the all-white effect too. Why? "Because darker hulls and decks generally need more upkeep. You tend to see more marks along the hull sides, and more chalking and fading. And many people feel that a boat looks cleaner with a white hull," says Yunger. In other words, because white is practical. But I think the aesthetics play a part too.

Another thing I liked is the rounded shapes sculpted into the 252's complex deck molding. Everything is round and smooth—even the two forward hatches and the companionway hatch are circular—and there are no bulky corners.

In the performance department, compared with the other test boats, the 252 Crowne was in the middle of the fleet in many of the tests. She was in the exact middle on top speed (39 m.p.h.), despite the fact that at 5,600 pounds dry, she was next to the heaviest boat. Her fuel economy was the second best of the group: 2.4 m.p.g. while cruising at 30 m.p.h. Cruising range with the 252's 70-gallon tank is 168 miles, virtually identical to the range for two of the other boats. Noise as measured on our decibel meter is better than average at low speeds, and not as good at high speeds, but in both instances is in the range where differences would be hard to notice without special instruments.

The classy instrument panel, with white instrumentation in a gothic arch cluster, reminded me aesthetically of the dashboard on a 1930s Bugatti racing car, brought up to 21st century standards.

I also liked the cockpit layout in the 252 Crowne, an uncomplicated 2-2-2 arrangement with an opportunity to set up an optional table to dine four al fresco in the stern. Another good idea is an optional set of filler cushions that make up into a sunpad, 4 feet across and 5 feet fore to aft, between the facing aft seats.

The themes of curves, roundness, and a clean sculpted white look on deck have been carried through in the cabin interior, from the semicircular white polyethylene entrance hatch that slides easily around to starboard on a curved plastic track, to the egg-shaped dinette table. The latter is 54 inches long and 28 inches wide, commodious enough to seat eight.

Headroom in the cabin area is a full 72 inches, under a ceiling nicely finished in foam padded olefin cloth—neater looking than the commonly used "monkey fuzz" in some other boats. The galley area, of molded fiberglass, is small but stylish, again repeating the theme of a curvilinear environment with a small (11½" diameter) round sink, a faucet in the shape of a swan's neck, and a curved, powder coated aluminum grabrail around the edge of the ogee-shaped countertop. Even the optional fridge is hidden behind a curved, sculpted fiberglass door.

Naturally, everything in the area is white, white, white, with a few accents of light tan or gray. The effect is great-looking, and the only things I'd change would be to add low fiddles around the V-berth shelves and the galley counter edge, and a slide-out shelf for more galley countertop space when needed.

The base price on the Chris-Craft in late 1990 was a bit over $34,000, and the price as tested was around $41,000. Chris-Craft calls this a mid-price-range boat, and in fact "as tested" it is the middle boat in the test group. Not a great bargain, but if you want to go in 21st century style, this could be the right boat for you.

**Spec check:**
Length (LOA) ......... 27'6"
Length ............... 25'0"
  (centerline)
Beam ............... 8'6"
Weight (dry) .......... 5,600 lbs.
Fuel capacity ........ 75 gallons
Power (base) .......... OMC 5.8 L Cobra (235 h.p.)
Power (as tested) ...... OMC 5.7 L Cobra (260 h.p.)
Power (options) ....... OMC 7.5 L King Cobra (340 h.p.), others
Fuel economy, ........ 2.4 m.p.g. at 30 m.p.h.
  maximum
Fuel economy, ........ 1.7 m.p.g. at 39 m.p.h.
  at top speed
Noise range .......... 62 to 90 dB
  in operation

For further information contact:
Chris-Craft
8161 15th St. East
Sarasota, FL 34243
(813) 351-4900

# Two sailboats you can build

***The 25' Black Skimmer.*** Phil Bolger designed the original *Black Skimmer* in 1974–75 for my friend Mike O'Brien, then proprietor of Mike's Boat Shop in Gloucester Point, Virginia, and now senior editor at *WoodenBoat* magazine. Mike wanted a cat yawl with very shoal draft, one that would be very easy to build and would have good performance. He liked some of Bolger's stock designs, but since there was nothing in the size he wanted—26 feet on deck—he asked Bolger to design a boat for him.

What resulted was a happy synthesis of some of Bolger's now-familiar trademarks: leeboards matched to a hard-chined, shallow-draft sharpie hull; jauntily raked free-standing masts utilizing sprits and snotters rather than conventional booms; a fold-up rudder; and a bow "cockpit" for handling the anchor, hoisting the main, or simply getting away from the crowd in the big cockpit aft. These individual features, seen separately on other less well-executed designs, sometimes come up short on practicality. But on Skimmer, they blend perfectly, helping make the boat a real pleasure to sail.

Under the auspices of *Boat Journal*, my wife and I had a chance to charter a Black Skimmer on Florida Bay. As it coincidentally turned out, the boat assigned to us by Key Largo Shoal Water Cruises was originally built by another friend of ours, Florida Bay Boat Company owner Reuben Trane, for his own use. Trane made a number of clever modifications to the original design, mostly, we think, for the better:

- The bowsprit and clipper bow were chopped off, and a traditional sharpie bow substituted;
- The mechanism for the leeboards was modified to make raising and lowering the boards an easy, one-hand operation and to prevent excessive chafe and premature failure of the original pivot mechanism (which was a piece of rope);
- The interior was fitted out with a propane stove, and cabinetry, shelves, drawers, and other storage appropriate to a comfortable cruiser;
- Ventilation and interior lighting was improved by the addition of an opening forward port plus larger, oval side ports, and an electrical lighting system. Also added was a solar panel to keep the battery charged.
- Some extra cleats were installed at strategic points around the boat. That particularly appealed to me, since I happen to be a "cleat nut." One cleat addition I particularly liked was at the bow, where Bolger's original plan called for a 1½-inch diameter belaying pin. Trane switched to twin ¼-inch bronze bars, installed side by side. What a pleasure when trussing her up in a slip, with springs and doubled bow lines going every which way!

The boat we chartered sails beautifully, is self-steering on most courses if properly balanced, and is easy to handle. Her shallow draft makes it relatively easy to get on board and off to beaches via the chine log, which juts out from the hull far enough to accommodate the toe end of a human foot. Her cockpit coamings are high enough to give good back support and a feeling of being protected. And, of course, her bow cockpit features a waist-high solid wall, offering the ultimate in security.

You should try her—and if you like her as much as I do, maybe you should build one for yourself.

**Spec check:**
LOA ................. 25'3"
LWL ................. NA
Beam ............... 7'0"

Draft, blades up ...... 10"
Draft, blades down .... 3'6"
Displacement ........ 2,800 lbs. (approx.)
Ballast .............. 500 lbs.

For further information contact:
Philip Bolger, Yacht Designer     Key Largo Shoal Water Cruises
29 Ferry St.                      Bareboat Charters
Gloucester, MA 01930              P.O. Box 1180
                                  Key Largo, FL 33037
                                  (305) 451-0083

**26' Norwalk Islands Sharpie.**  Bruce Kirby, designer of the extraordinarily popular 14-foot Laser sailboat (over 100,000 made and sold to date) has created a series of relatively easy-to-construct cruising sailboat designs for the home builder. The series starts with an 18-foot catboat and includes 23-foot, 26-foot, and 29-foot versions of a Norwalk Islands Sharpie, Kirby's modern counterpart of the traditional long, narrow, easy-to-handle workboats seen along the east coast in the late 19th and early 20th centuries.

**The Norwalk Islands Sharpie.**

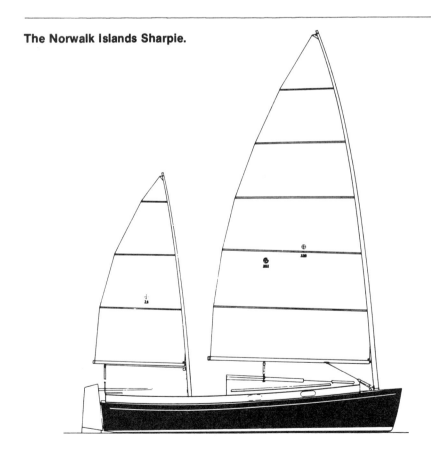

Features of the N.I.S. 26 include hard chine, flat-bottomed hull, giving a draft of only 10 inches with the board up—just the thing for cruising along beaches and exploring shallow coves. The sail area-to-displacement ratio is a little above 20, which combined with high ballast ratio, bendy masts and easily reefed full-battened sails, give her good performance in both light and heavy air.

Kirby has devised two different accommodations plans, one sleeping two and the other four. Couples usually opt for the two-sleeper version, which gives a bit more room to spread out; family groups may prefer the four-sleeper.

The hulls are constructed of marine plywood, bonded with epoxy resin and sheathed in fiberglass. Judging from Kirby's plans and construction notes, it looks like a relatively easy job for an amateur craftsman with a few power tools and some space to work in. The only finished boat I've seen (and sailed in) is the designer's own N.I.S. 26, *Exit 12*, which was built for Kirby in British Columbia by legendary yacht builder Bent Jespersen. It is truly a magnificent construction job.

An especially clever feature on *Exit 12* is the outboard motor arrangement. The motor bracket travels up and down on a vertical track, and is raised and lowered by hauling on a multi-part tackle. When in the "up" position, the prop is kept from fouling with weeds and barnacles, and a cover slides under the motor's skeg to make the bottom smooth and fair for minimum hull drag.

If you're looking for a small, fast, handy and trailerable cruising boat to build on your own, you'd be hard-pressed to do better than this little sharpie.

**Spec check:**
LOA ................. 26'3"
LWL ................. 22'6"
Beam ............... 7'11"
Draft, board up ....... 10"
      board down .... 5'10"
Displacement ........ 3,200 lbs.
Ballast .............. 1,500 lbs.
Sail area ............ 302 sq.ft.

For further information contact:
Norwalk Island Sharpies
213 Rowayton Ave.
Rowayton, CT 06853

# My all-time favorite sailboat (at the moment, anyway)

**The remarkable F/27 Trimaran.**  What constitutes the ideal cruising sailboat? Opinions may differ on details, but almost everyone would agree that the ideal cruiser should be fast, stable, and seakindly. In

**The F/27 Trimaran.**

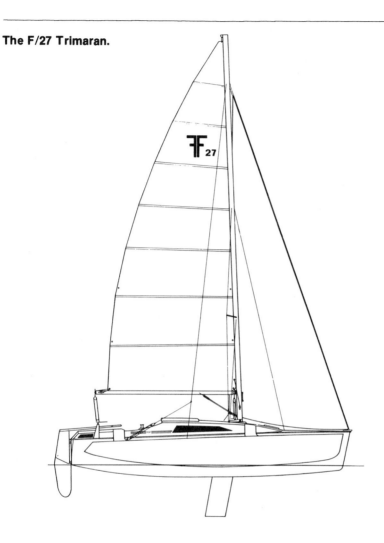

addition she should be easy to handle, preferably requiring only one person. And she should be roomy and have enough load-carrying capacity to permit two adults to live aboard comfortably for several weeks at a time. Accommodations for a family of four—let's say in two separate cabins for privacy—would be even better.

That's a pretty tall order to fill. Nevertheless to this basic list I'd add another half dozen "shoulds." First, she should be easily trailerable; that is, one person of average strength should be able to launch her, set up her rig, and sail her away. Second, she should be small enough to store and maintain on her trailer in the owner's backyard, thereby eliminating yard bills. Third, she should be light enough to tow behind an ordinary large station wagon with a towing capacity of 5,000 pounds, or even less. Fourth, she can be modern and functional but nevertheless should look reasonably "yachty." Fifth, her draft should be shoal enough to bring her right up to a beach without worry about stranding or hull damage. And sixth, she should be capable of carrying a small sailing dinghy on deck without obstructing the helmsman's vision.

To my knowledge, there is only one boat design in production today that meets and in fact surpasses all these criteria to the max: The F/27, a 27-foot, 2,600-pound folding trimaran from the board of Ian Farrier, produced by Corsair Marine.

The F/27 is truly fantastic. She'll do 25 knots in a stiff breeze, and her balance is so well-tuned that whether at 5 knots or 20 you can sail her with two fingers on the helm. She's extremely stable; and if you put her helm hard over, she'll turn tight, fast 360s until you bring the helm back, even if you ignore sheet trim.

She can be burdened with 1,000 to 1,200 pounds of people and gear before the weight noticeably slows down the boat. That's good enough carrying capacity for two people to sail her across the Atlantic (which she's done, in 33 days). She's also made several trips from California to Hawaii.

The F/27 has three berths in the main cabin plus a fourth "mini-double" in a separate aft cabin—great for the kids. You won't find standing headroom in this boat except in the galley area with the pop-top erected, but then, it wasn't on the above list of requirements either. Sitting comfort below and on deck is excellent.

Moreover, she's a trailer sailor's dream, with a rig that allows one person to raise or lower her mast. Trailering weight is under 4,000 pounds, even allowing for extra gear.

Although her appearance may take some getting used to, I think she looks good streaking through the water at 15 knots or so. Her 14-inch draft is perfect for beach-hopping. And a Dyer 8- or 9-foot sailing dink fits nicely in the wing nets. In fact, you can even carry two—one on each side!

In summary: If I had 50 or 60 grand earmarked for a new cruiser, it would be an easy job to decide where to spend it.

**Spec check:**
LOA ................. 27'1"
LWL ................. 26'3"
Beam, sailing ........ 19'1"
       folded ........ 8'5"
Draft (hull only) ...... 1'2"
Draft, board down .... 4'11"
Approx. weight ....... 2,600 lbs.
Sail area ............ 446 sq.ft.

For further information, contact:
Corsair Marine Inc.
150 Center St.
Chula Vista, CA 92011
(619) 585-3005

# A comfortable shoal-draft yawl

***Sparkman & Stephens' Tartan 27 yawl.*** Like the Morgan 24, the Tartan 27 was one of the hot new fiberglass boats of the 1960s. She won some important races early in her career, and that accelerated her popularity. I owned hull #310, built in 1967, for seven years and loved every moment of it (until my kids convinced me to sell her and buy a J/24, a move that a sailing buddy told me was "akin to divorcing Dagmar and marrying Twiggy").

When I bought her, she was a sloop, but in no time at all I had converted her to a yawl, my favorite rig. As originally designed, you could buy the Tartan 27 either way. The mainsail dimensions for the yawl were slightly different from the sloop on the official Sparkman & Stephens

**The Tartan 27.**

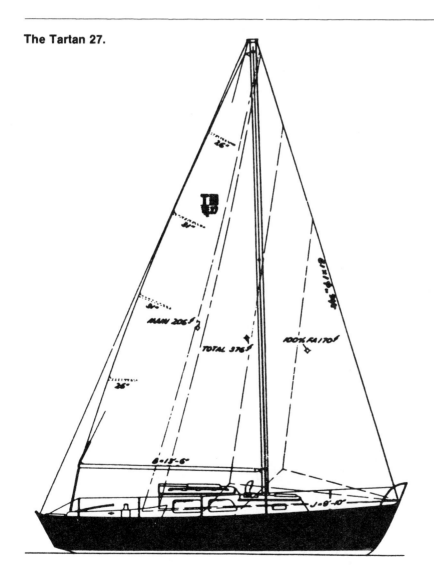

sailplans, but I found she balanced just fine as a yawl without changing the sloop mainsail configuration.

With my wife and I in our early 40s and the kids in their preteen years, the Tartan had everything we wanted at the time: standing headroom; sleeping accommodations for four, with a separate cabin with a door to close off the kids at night; an enclosed head, equally available to both forward and main cabins; a dinette layout with a big table that could be left in place for the kids to play; a full galley including a huge icebox into which you could conveniently load a hundred pounds of ice through a hatchway in the cockpit seat; shoal draft for exploring the gunkholes of New England; good performance in the light and medium air we usually encountered on Long Island Sound; the heft (7,400 pounds) to be a comfortable sea boat; enough sisterships to make us feel like we were entering the Brotherhood of Tartan 27 owners; and finally, the possibility of a yawl rig, the main benefits of which I have already enumerated in describing the South Coast 23 above.

Incidentally, the Tartan 27s I am talking about here were made from 1960 until 1976. In 1977, a "Mark III" version was introduced (beginning with hull #649), using the same hull mold but with a wholly new design for deck and interior. I like the looks and the layout of the pre-1977 version much better than the later models.

With more than 600 of these boats in circulation, there's a steady stream of used ones trading on the market. Selling prices range from around $5,000 to $18,000, depending on age, condition, etc. Very often you can get a lot for your money by buying a Tartan, particularly at the low end of this price range.

**Spec check:**
LOA ................ 27'0"
LWL ................ 21'5"
Beam ............... 8'7½"
Draft, board up ....... 3'2"
      board down .... 6'4"
Displacement ........ 7,400 lbs.
Ballast .............. 2,400 lbs.
Sail area, sloop ....... 376 sq.ft.
      yawl ........ 394 sq.ft.

# Three good 20-footers

**L. Francis Herreshoff's 28' Rozinante.** This is a boat for a cruise or daysail in peaceful solitude. She's the kind of boat in which many people wouldn't want to install a motor, let alone a microwave oven or a loran. If your aim is to get close to nature, this could be the perfect vehicle in which to do it.

She was designed by the great L. Francis Herreshoff to be built of wood, but there are several fiberglass versions around (though none being built at the moment to my knowledge). Cheoy Lee offered her as a production boat in a choice of all teak or fiberglass and teak in the 1960s; South Coast Seacraft offered a fiberglass kit boat in the early 1960s. (I almost bought one, but settled on the South Coast 23, described above, instead.) Used ones occasionally pop up in the classified for anywhere from $5,000 to $50,000.

To me, the great appeal of the Rozinante lies in her beauty of line and her simplicity . . . and in the many clever little touches L. Francis added to give her personality. For example, a thwart across the after end of the cockpit just abaft the mizzen mast is positioned three inches higher than the cockpit seats so the helmsman can see over the heads of his passengers. The cabin doors are stowed on special slides under the cockpit seats. Below, a folding canvas chair similar to a beach chair can be set up athwartships for reading and relaxing at the end of the day's journey. A sweep (an oar 10 feet long) stows along the cabin ceiling and, fitted into an oarlock in the cockpit coaming, permits the skipper to move the Rozinante along at 1 to 2 knots. Non-purists will find that a 4-h.p. outboard motor clamped to a removable bracket alongside will move her at around 5 knots.

Her masts are raked aft just the right amount to maximize her sex appeal—and to create a tack angle so that on a reach in a wild sea, the tips of the booms are in virtually no danger of sweeping through the water. And of course, her pointy canoe stern reeks of beauty. What a boat!

**Spec check:**
Length on deck ....... 28′0″
LWL ................. 24′0″
Beam ............... 6′4″
Draft .............. 3′9″
Displacement ........ 6,600 lbs.
Sail area ........... 348 sq.ft.

*The Cape Dory 28 Fly Bridge Cruiser.* In the Cape Dory 28 FB Cruiser, a traditional Down East semi-displacement hull form has been mated with a nicely joined teak-sheathed interior and an up-on-top helm station. The principal reason I like this boat is that she's a well-executed example of a lobsterboat, a type I just can't seem to keep my eyes off. But I also like the emphasis on comfort and simple elegance rather than the overstated glitter and gloss that many powerboat designers aim for. And I like the superb 360-degree visibility the fly bridge provides, and the big rectangular ports in the wheelhouse so all hands can see what's going on outside. This would be a fine minimum-size boat for a retired couple to use to explore coastal waters from Maine to Florida, or around the Great Lakes.

The boat is available with either a 275-h.p. Chrysler gasoline engine or (for quite a bit more money) a Volvo 200-h.p. diesel. If I could afford the extra $7,000 or $8,000 first cost, I'd take the diesel for long-term reliability and economy.

**The Cape Dory 28
Fly Bridge Cruiser.**

The layout thoughtfully puts the galley within hailing distance of the inside helm station, and locates an L-shaped settee and table near the helm too, so the skipper can swap sea stories with the passengers and crew while he (or she) mans (or womans?) the wheel. A big open cockpit aft would be a great place to add some canvas-backed deck chairs for watching the sunset at day's end. Can't you just picture yourself conning this one?

**Spec check:**
```
LOD ................. 27'11"
LWL ................. 25'11"
Beam ................  9'11"
Draft ...............  2'11"
Displacement ........ 8,000 lbs.
Fuel capacity ....... 76 gallons
Water capacity ...... 45 gallons
```

For further information contact:
Cape Dory Yachts, Inc.
160 Middleboro Ave.
East Taunton, MA 02718
(617) 823-6776

**Commodore Munroe's 28' Egret, a modified Sharpie.**   A few times each century, a boat comes along that is so perfect for its designed service, so elegant in its concept, so "right," that building replicas and near-replicas of the design gets to be a popular pastime. Captain Joshua Slocum's *Spray* was such a boat, as were John MacGregor's canoe yawl *Rob Roy* and Horace and Worthington Crosby's Cape Cod catboats. Now

**Commodore Munroe's** *Egret.*
**Courtesy of WoodenBoat**
**Publications.**

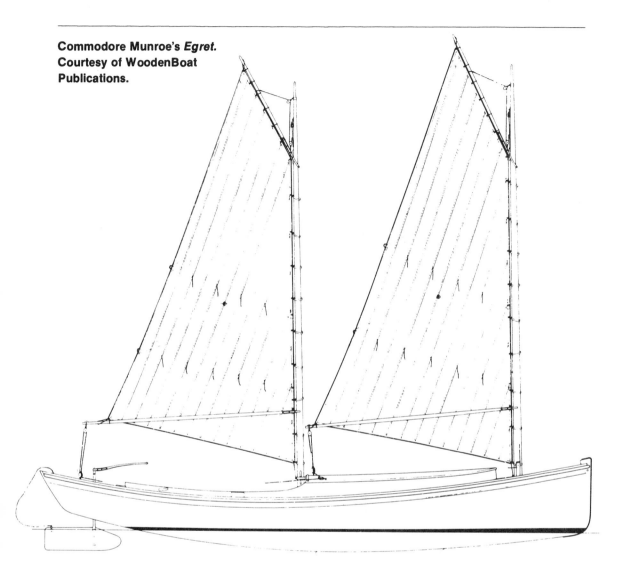

comes a new entrant in the replica sweepstakes: Commodore Ralph
Middleton Munroe's *Egret.*

By the time he designed the *Egret* at age 38, Commodore Munroe
(founder and first commodore of the Biscayne Bay Yacht Club) had
already started to make his mark, not only as a sailboat designer, but also
as an adventurer, entrepreneur, photographer, ecologist, and pioneer
resident on the virtually uninhabited south Florida coast of the 1880s. As
a dweller in these jungle-like lands, he was looking for a good way to
travel between his home in Coconut Grove (just south of Miami) and
other South Florida coastal settlements from Key West to Jupiter Inlet, a
stretch of shoreline encompassing some 240 miles. His problem wasn't
easy—there were neither roads nor railroad tracks through the densely

forested subtropical wilds, and the shoal waters along the coasts were cursed with constantly shifting sandbars, coral reefs, and treacherous inlets. To get away from Coconut Grove, you either had to walk the beach for days or weeks, or venture into the Atlantic in a very small-shoal draft boat, hoping for good weather. Coasting schooners could sail outside the bars and reefs, but had difficulty negotiating the inlets in anything except the calmest weather. Lighthouse keepers, mailmen, judges, jurors, tax collectors, and others whose work compelled them to travel in the area had a choice of hiking along the beach, risking their lives in small boats at sea, or staying home.

It was a made-in-heaven opportunity for the Commodore to create a new and different vessel, properly suited to the need, and that's just what he did. What he came up with, as he explained in his book, *The Commodore's Story*, was a "28-foot double-ended sharpie lifeboat, *Egret*, very strongly but lightly constructed . . . [to] make these trips and run the inlets in almost any weather. . . . She drew eight inches, and had only fifty to seventy-five bricks, laid under her floor, for ballast. She was fitted with all the appurtenances needed to keep the sea in almost any weather, and if necessary to be put on the beach without harm. That she fulfilled all requirements until the first road was opened, the older residents can testify. . . . She served me for several years without mishap as a dispatch boat between Biscayne Bay and Jupiter telegraph station, via the Gulf Stream, blow high or blow low, often making the trip comfortably when no other boats would attempt either the Stream or the surf in the shoal inlets."

Both the Commodore's *Egret* and his larger (41 feet LOA, 30-inch draft) *Presto* have captured the imagination of small-boat sailors in recent times. Starting in the 1930s, a steady stream of Egret-types of boats were built, and a recent resurgence has appeared in the 1980s, spurred by the publication by *WoodenBoat* magazine in 1983 of reconstructed plans for the original *Egret* herself.

Unfortunately, an exact replica, true to Munroe's original design in every respect, cannot be built, since the Commodore's only drawings and specifications for *Egret* were lost in a disastrous hurricane in 1926 that swept "The Barnacle," his Coconut Grove home and design office. However, diligent research by Munroe fans has, over the years, turned up enough photographs and other memorabilia to enable a reasonably close approximation in the reconstruction of *Egret*'s design.

The plans reveal a simple, almost primitive cabin arrangement, and the construction requires a good knowledge of boatbuilding technique. But for history buffs who want to enjoy the flavor of sailing in the 1880s, or for someone who's looking for shoal draft and trailerability to escape the noisy outboard boats and find peace and quiet away from the madding world, this could be a highly appropriate vehicle.

**Spec check:**
LOA ................. 28'2"
LWL ................. 22'8"

Beam ................ 7'2"
Draft, board up ....... 1'0"
          board down .... 3'6"
Displacement ........ 4,058 lbs.
Sail area ............. 229 sq.ft.

For further information contact:
WoodenBoat Publications, Inc.
P.O. Box 78
Brooklin, ME 04616
(800) 225-5205; in Maine, (800) 287-4651
(Full sets of plans are available from WoodenBoat.)

## Seven in the mid-range

**Bill Garden's 30' Mist of Lemolo.** When Garry Horder was 69 years old, he sold *Inisfail,* his 48-foot Arthur Robb cutter, and retired from blue-water racing and cruising. However, he wasn't ready to swallow the anchor altogether. Consequently, he decided to have built "an old man's single-hander," and turned to world-renowned designer William Garden to draw the lines. Garry's requirements were intriguing:

- His new boat should have shallow draft to explore gunkholes; she should be able to rest on her bottom without listing significantly because low tide would leave her home mooring virtually dry.
- Her hull and spars should be made of wood to give the look of a traditional yacht, but modern materials and methods should be employed to enhance strength, preserve beauty, and ease maintenance.
- She had to be narrow and light enough to trailer behind Garry's 1973 Chevy pickup to distant cruising grounds, but she also needed sufficient size and weight to make her comfortable while afloat, even in a rough seaway.
- Garry had been a top-ranked Star-class and ocean-racing sailor in his day, and he wanted his new boat to be lively, reasonably fast, but easy to handle. He wasn't, after all, getting any younger. Her rig, especially, had to be ultra-simple, easily controlled by sheets and halyards led to the cockpit. A cat-ketch rig with unstayed masts might be nice.

Bill Garden had designed literally hundreds of salty-looking and smart-sailing boats, several of which came close to meeting Garry's needs, but two of the requirements—trailerability and ultra-easy single-handing—needed special consideration.

What eventually emerged was *Mist of Lemolo,* big (30 feet) and heavy (8,000 lbs.) enough to provide a measure of seagoing comfort, but narrow (7'9") enough to put her well under the maximum trailer-load width.

**Bill Garden's *Mist of Lemolo*.**

*Mist*'s rig is one of her most unique features. Garry had used double-ply "twin Jeni Wings" on *Inisfail*, and he wanted a similar rig on his new boat. Garden came up with twin booms on "crabs," or pedestals, and a two-ply mainsail on one luff-rope. A special mainsheet arrangement controls both booms together on the wind and reaching, but it becomes two parts, each controlling one boom, on downwind runs. Downwind, the butterfly rig gives you the softest jibe you ever saw, since air compressed between the plies of the sail cushions the effect.

Other unusual features include two centerboards in tandem for excellent balance and tracking on various points of sail and easy, quick tacking; and an extremely modest interior layout. But, says Garry, "All we wanted was comfortable seating, dining, and sleeping. We did not want a 'quart in a pint pot,' a two-bedroom with kitchenette and TV room. When we go sailing, one object is to get away from the comforts and atmosphere of the modern-day home."

Bent Jespersen, who built Bruce Kirby's 26-footer (see above), also built *Mist.* Says Garry: "She's not everybody's cup of tea, but she's really an *ultimate* boat for a guy who's sailed a lot of boats, from a decked sailing canoe to IOR racers. The boat is a real delight. The net result is a really satisfied old sailor whose wife also loves the boat."

**Spec check:**
LOA ................. 30'0"
LWL ................. 29'0"
Beam ............... 7'9"
Draft, boards up ...... 2'0"
    boards down .... 4'9"
Displacement ........ 8,000 lbs.
Ballast .............. 2,500 lbs.
Sail area ............ 359 sq.ft.

For further information contact:
William Garden, Yacht Designer
2071 Kendall Avenue
Victoria, BC V8P 1R7
CANADA

*Clive Dent's Cape Dory 300 Motorsailer.*   This is a relatively rare breed of boat these days: a motorsailer that looks like a motorsailer and yet sails remarkably well. I tested one of the early CD 300s a few

**The Cape Dory 300 Motorsailer.**

years ago in Annapolis, and was amazed to be able to sail along at 3 or 4 knots in an 8-knot breeze, without "cheating" by turning on the engine. But it was comforting to know that if the wind died completely a 46-h.p. diesel would push the CD 300's heavy displacement hull (11,500 lbs.) at 7 to 8 knots.

This is the right boat for those marginal days, when the temperature is below 70, the cloud cover is stubbornly holding, and the forecast is for a 40% to 60% chance of rain. With this boat, you can throw caution to the winds and go out for an afternoon sail anyway. If it starts to rain, there's a warm and cozy pilothouse to retreat to—and if the sun comes out, you just slide open the side windows, flip up the twin port and starboard pilothouse roof hatches, and stroll aft to catch a few rays.

The CD 300's accessories are aimed at easy operation and convenience, from the anchor pulpit to the self-tacking jib on a boom to the fold-out bench seats in the cockpit to the swim platform aft. Main and jib sheets are led to the pilothouse, so you can tweak lines to your heart's content while tending the helm. With the optional remote reefing main and jib controls, you can even set, reef, and furl the sails without leaving the pilothouse. If I owned one of these beauties, I could almost see myself wishing for a chilly wind with rain and fog in the offing.

**Spec check:**
LOD ................. 29'10"
LWL ................. 26'6"
Beam ............... 11'5"
Draft .............. 3'11"
Displacement ........ 11,500 lbs.
Ballast ............. 4,500 lbs.
Sail area ........... 442 sq.ft.

For further information: see Cape Dory address on page 260.

***Frank Butler's Catalina 30.*** The Catalina 30 is one of the world's most popular mid-size cruising sailboats, with more than 6,000 made and sold since production started in 1974. Over the years the basic hull dimensions have remained pretty much unchanged, although the design has been gradually modified to keep up with new trends in styling and technology. For example, the Atomic Four gasoline engine has been replaced by a diesel, the traveler has been moved from the aft end of the cockpit to the cabintop, a winged keel option has reduced the shoal-draft model from 4'4" to 3'10" deep, and so on.

What makes the Catalina 30 so popular? One major attraction is a relatively low price (in the low $40,000 range for a new boat in 1991) combined with relatively good looks in a traditional vein, construction of reasonable quality, and a generous list of standard equipment. For example, included in the 1991 base price is a stainless steel gimballed propane stove with oven, twin stainless sinks, teak and ash trim in the cabin, a wheel rather than a tiller, and pulpit and lifelines.

Another attraction is the well-run Catalina owners' association. (See page 186 for more on this.)

Two hull configurations are available: The standard fin keel gives a draft of 5'3" and a shoal model utilizing a winged keel reduces draft to 3'10". The rig is also available in two versions, a standard sail rated at 446 square feet, and a tall rig (two feet higher, 10% more sail area) for light air regions.

**Spec check:**

LOA ................ 29'11"
LWL ................ 25'0"
Beam .............. 10'10"
Draft, standard fin. .... 5'3"
   shoal, wing ....... 4'4" or 3'10"
Displacement ........ 10,200 to 10,300 lbs.
Ballast ............. 4,200 to 4,300 lbs.
Sail area ........... 444 to 505 sq.ft.
Note: exact specs in some cases depend on model and year of manufacture.

For further information contact:
Catalina Yachts
P.O. Box 989
Woodland Hills, CA 91367
(818) 884-7700

***Thomas Gillmer's Seawind 31 Mark II ketch.*** Alan Eddy's *Apogee,* the first fiberglass boat to sail around the world, was a Seawind ketch. The original Seawind was built by Allied Boatbuilding Company (later the Wright Yacht Company) in Catskill, N.Y. from 1961 to 1974, at which point designer Thomas Gillmer came up with a "Mark II" version. The Seawind II is slightly bigger in all directions as compared with the original design. She has a larger rudder tucked under the counter rather than outboard, and her sailplan is bigger and laid out in a more efficient arrangement (e.g. larger foretriangle and higher-aspect-ratio main) than the earlier boat.

With her hefty (14,600 pounds) hull and spread out ketch rig, she is well adapted to long passages—though fitting a self-steerer onto the after deck would be tricky with the mizzen in the way. She is also a windy-weather boat; her scant sail area could not be relied upon to drive her at anything approaching reasonable cruising speeds in light-air regions like western Long Island Sound. Her standard engine was a 25-h.p. diesel; if you're considering acquiring this boat for use in light-air areas, installing a bigger mill might be a good idea.

Allied and Wright are gone from the scene, but Seawinds regularly appear in the used-boat classifieds for prices in the teens and up. Prospective world cruisers on a tight budget please take notice.

**Spec check:**

| | |
|---|---|
| LOA | 31'7" |
| LWL | 25'6" |
| Beam | 10'5" |
| Draft | 4'6" |
| Displacement | 14,600 lbs. |
| Ballast | 5,800 lbs. |
| Sail area | 555 sq.ft. |

***McLear & Harris' Allied Sea Breeze 35 yawl.*** Along with the Seawind described above, Allied Boatbuilding also built the Sea Breeze, a boat five feet longer overall and with a distinctly different hull form, with gracefully long overhangs fore and aft rather than the spoon bow and truncated stern of the Seawind. Thus the "bigger" boat's waterline length is actually shorter, by a full 18 inches, than the "smaller" boat. She is also lighter and carries less ballast.

Nevertheless the Sea Breeze is remarkably similar in many ways to the Seawind. For example, the Sea Breeze's beam is within 2 inches of the Seawind's, and her sail area is practically identical; her aft-galley-pilot-berth arrangement is a very close match (except that the sink has been taken out of the forward cabin and put back into the head compartment where it belongs).

There are lots of features I like about the Sea Breeze. She is a shoal-draft centerboarder, good for gunkholing (though admittedly 3'10" is getting up there); she can be had as a yawl; her cockpit is long enough to stretch out in, and has coamings providing good back support; she has space under the boom for a dinghy on her cabintop; and the engine is readily accessible through the cockpit lockers. Too bad Allied is not still around to build these beauties.

**Spec check:**

| | | |
|---|---|---|
| LOA | | 34'6" |
| LWL | | 24'0" |
| Beam | | 10'3" |
| Draft, board up | | 3'10" |
| | board down | 6'9" |
| Displacement | | 13,400 lbs. |
| Ballast | | 4,000 lbs. |
| Sail area, sloop | | 550 sq.ft. |
| | yawl | 575 sq.ft. |

***The Grand Banks 36 classic trawler yacht.*** Trawlers designed for use as yachts generally have heavy, rugged, comfortable, full-displacement hulls that feature large load-carrying capacity and outstanding fuel economy—and a relatively slow cruising speed. The Grand Banks 36 is no exception. She'll cruise at 8 to 8½ knots with a single 135-h.p. Ford Lehman diesel, and consume only 3 gallons of fuel per hour. At 8 knots, that's equivalent to a little over 3 land miles per gallon.

Most trawlers, including the Grand Banks 36, are available with either single or twin engines. The twins increase speed somewhat—usually a knot or two—but are seldom necessary for satisfactory performance in terms of speed, maneuverability, or reliability, and in most cases the expense of such redundancy is out of proportion to the benefits received.

The appeal of the Grand Banks line in general is its good basic design, very-high-quality construction, and an active, stable dealer network, all of which translates to good resale value. Specifically and personally, I like her no-nonsense, I-can-go-to-sea looks and I like her layout. She has:

- A big, open, airy saloon with port and starboard doors, excellent all-round visibility from the helm station, and galley and dining table adjacent to the inside helm station to promote skipper-crew togetherness;
- A separate owners' cabin aft with a choice of furniture layouts, an exit hatch to the aft deck, and its own private head and shower;
- A separate forward guest or crew cabin with *its* own private head;
- Space on deck for a good-sized sailing dinghy (chocks supplied), and aluminum mast and boom to launch and retrieve with;
- A flybridge with excellent all-round visibility at the upper helm station and seating for six or more;
- Plenty of stowage space everywhere;
- Enough fuel capacity (400 gallons) and water tankage (140 gallons) to remain away from civilization for weeks at a time.

Other than environmentalists requesting a switch from diesel-fueled engines to some kind of solar power, what more could a water person ask for?

**Spec check:**
LOA ................. 36'10"
LWL ................. 35'2"
Beam ............... 12'8"
Draft .............. 4'0"
Displacement ........ 26,000 lbs.

For further information contact:
Grand Banks Yachts Ltd.
563 Steamboat Rd.
Greenwich, CT 06830
(203) 869-9274

***Murray Peterson's 36' coasting schooner.*** Way back in 1978, when we were cruising with our preteenaged kids from western Connecticut to Cape Cod and Nantucket in our Tartan 27, we devised an

# THREE DOZEN OF MY FAVORITE BOATS

**Murray Peterson's 36'
Coasting Schooner.**

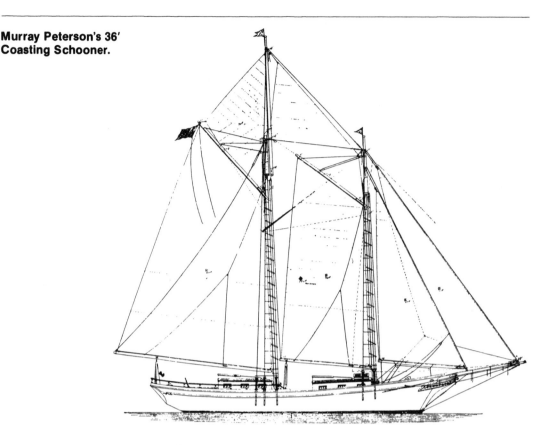

activity called "Boat of the Day." Everyone in the family would observe boats passed during our day's voyage, and the boats moored around us after we'd anchored for the night. Each of us would vote for our favorite-looking boat, and after discussion and politicking, one of the candidates would emerge as the top vote-getter and be given our "Boat of the Day" award. This would involve writing the name and other specifics of the winner in the ship's log, and (unless the best boat we could find that day was a real dog) taking photographs of the BOTD for posterity.

According to our records (which have been meticulously preserved), on August 26, 1978, in Edgartown harbor, we voted for a schooner named *North Star*. This boat turned out to be a sistership of the coaster described in Roger C. Taylor's neat book, *Good Boats*, published the previous year. We happened to have a copy of Taylor's book on board with us, so we rowed over to *North Star* in our Dyer with book in hand, explained about Boat of the Day and ooohed and ahhhed until we were invited to come aboard. After a tour of the schooner from stem to stern, we even got *North Star*'s owners, Bruce and Norman MacNeil, to autograph the coaster article for us in *Good Boats*.

What made *North Star* our BOTD? First of all, the mere sight of any well-designed, old-time, gaff-rigged, clipper-bowed schooner is almost guaranteed to catalyze most sailors with an ounce of romanticism in them into passionate enthusiasm, and this Murray Peterson-designed little ship was no exception. Then there was her construction (by Camden Shipbuilding Company in Maine in 1962) and finish, which was yacht quality. She sported a red bottom, white boottop, dark green topsides, and white cabin sides and bulwarks. Below she shone with butternut trim and white-and-buff painted panelling. She had gold-leafed traditional carvings on her trailboards and carved rope strands on her transom. Her combination gallows frame and dinghy davits blended in perfectly with the overall design, and her dinghy was named *Twinkle*. Perfect.

**Spec check:**

LOD ................. 36'5"
LWL ................ 29'8"
Beam ............... 11'2"
Draft .............. 5'9"
Sail area ............ 900 sq.ft.

**Bill Tripp's Hinckley Bermuda 40 Yawl.**

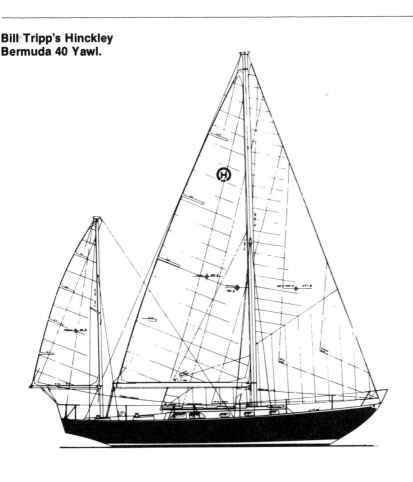

## Forty feet and above

***Bill Tripp's Hinckley Bermuda 40 yawl.*** If, by now, you're getting the idea that I like centerboard yawls, you're right. And the Bermuda 40 is a very good example of why I like them. With the B-40, besides shoal draft and all the advantages of the mizzen mast and sail previously enumerated, you get the strength and integrity of first-class materials and construction: Solid bronze centerboard, monel fuel tanks, stainless steel water tanks, masts stepped on the keel, carefully hand-laid up fiberglass lamination, solid teak sole inlaid with real holly, best quality joinery.... The list could go on and on.

You also get one of the late Bill Tripp's best designs. You get loads of extra space for all the goodies you might want to take on an extended cruise. You get the Hinckley organization's followup; they will treat your boat—and you—with tender loving care if you ask them for help. And you can look forward to selling your Hinckley, if and when the time ever comes, at a price that's perceptibly above the market for other craft in this range of size and type. (In the June 1991 issue of *Soundings*, Hinckley Yacht Brokers advertised a 1970 B-40 for $149,000, and a 1980 B-40 for $210,000.) Of course, when you buy, you almost always also *pay* a perceptibly higher price. But this may be one true example of the saying (not always accurate) that "you get what you pay for."

**Spec check:**

| | |
|---|---|
| LOA | 40'9" |
| LWL | 27'10" |
| Beam | 11'9" |
| Draft, centerboard up | 4'1" |
| centerboard down | 8'7" |
| Displacement | 19,500 lbs. |
| Ballast | 6,000 lbs. |
| Sail area | 741 sq.ft. |
| Fuel capacity | 48 gallons |
| Water tankage | 110 gallons |

For further information contact:
Henry R. Hinckley & Co.
Southwest Harbor, ME 04679
(207) 244-5531

***Ray Hunt's 40' Concordia yawl.*** Ray Hunt, the multi-talented designer who pioneered in developing the powerboat planing hull after World War II, drew the lines of the Concordia Yawl in 1939, when he was Waldo Howland's partner at The Concordia Company boatyard in South Dartmouth, Massachusetts. The boat was designed and built for Waldo's father Llewellyn, who wanted a 40-footer that would sail on her bottom, not her side, in heavy weather, and be fast under all weather conditions. Secondary were matters of space and comfort below.

**Ray Hunt's 40'**
**Concordia Yawl.**

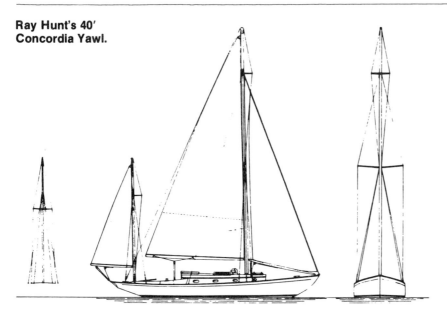

Hunt came up with a boat that is graceful yet powerful, stiff and dry, and pretty as a picture. She's also loaded with clever sea-going gadgets, such as fold-up slat-backed canvas berths (the design of which was frequently copied on other yachts and which acquired the name "Concordia berths"); flip-up backrests at the aft end of the cockpit; a hatch cover split athwartships that opens to form two seats; and a jibboom for easy self-tacking.

Llewellyn's boat, the *Java,* was much admired and started a trend of building sisterships and near sisters, finally totalling more than a hundred and collectively named "the Concordia yawls." They're great for the conditions for which they were designed (i.e. medium and heavy air), and for light air areas a bigger sail plan could be arranged via more mizzen area, bowsprit with extra jib, etc. These days used boats are available starting at around $40,000. Asking prices, of course, can go much higher.

## Spec check:

LOA ................. 39'10"
LWL ................. 28'6"
Beam .............. 10'3"
Draft .............. 5'8"
Displacement ........ 18,000 lbs.
Ballast ............. 7,700 lbs.
Sail area ............ 650 sq.ft.

For further information contact:
The Concordia Company
P.O. Box P-203
South Dartmouth, MA 02748
(508) 999-1381

***Philip Rhodes' 41' Reliant yawl.*** The Rhodes Reliant was made for a few years in the 1960s by Cheoy Lee Shipyards. She is no longer produced, but her classic lines never seem to go out of style, infused as they are with Phil Rhodes' eye for just the right sheer line and counter overhang and stem shape.

Cheoy Lee built a lot of boats in the 1960s of "Fiberteak," a combination of structural fiberglass for hull, deck and cabin trunk, with teak decks and cabin sides overlaid. The interiors are replete with ornately carved teak and fine joinery. That's a definite plus if you like elegance. On the other hand, as cruisers these boats are fairly heavy, narrow, and cramped compared with the broadbeamed, not to say bulbous, modern yachts of today. I wouldn't carry more than two couples cruising on the Reliant, and one couple would be better. And, before you bought, you'd want to consider the maintenance chore of varnishing all that teak. Still, for some, owning a Reliant would be worth these inconveniences.

On the used market, the boats currently sell for prices in the $40s and up. Vessels in unusually fine shape with major upgrades may go in the $70s. Two designs were offered, one a sloop, the other a yawl. You know which one I'd pick.

**Spec check:**
LOA ................. 40'9"
LWL ................. 28'0"
Beam .............. 10'9"
Draft .............. 5'9"
Displacement ........ 21,700 lbs.
Ballast ............. 8,240 lbs.
Sail area, yawl ........ 750 sq.ft.

***Ted Brewer's Whitby 42.*** If the Rhodes Reliant described above is a bit cramped in her accommodations, the Whitby 42, with practically the same LOA, is just the opposite. In fact, this design by cruising boat specialist Ted Brewer has just about the same amount of space as the beamy, airy, and comfortable Grand Banks 36 trawler.

As such, she'd make a wonderful liveaboard boat or a candidate for an extended cruise for four. The aft owner's cabin with its own head and separate hatchway to the cockpit is especially nice; so is the passageway past the engine room, great for rainy days when you want to roam between cabins.

Center cockpit boats often come out looking like floating wedding cakes, but somehow Brewer has produced one that's not half bad looking. Furthermore, her split rig makes sailing in varying wind conditions relatively easy, and her long, straight keel lets her rest along a quay for painting without major stability problems.

Whitby Boatworks, up in Ontario, seems to have slipped from the scene recently, but there are plenty of used Whitby 42s around. They're advertised for around $80,000 and up.

**Spec check:**

LOA ................. 42′0″
LWL ................. 32′8″
Beam ............... 13′0″
Draft ............... 5′0″
Displacement ........ 23,500 lbs.
Ballast .............. 8,000 lbs.
Sail area ............. 875 sq.ft.
Fuel capacity ........ 210 gallons
Water tankage ........ 290 gallons

*Jay Benford's 50′ Florida Bay Coaster.* Jay Benford's designs tend to lean toward the whimsical and cute. Whether his Florida Bay Coaster—or any 50-footer—can be considered "cute" may be arguable. But if cute is not the right word, it's not far off.

In any case, no one would call the Coaster "run of the mill." Basically, what we have here is a steel (not fiberglass) floating condo with a combination of features rarely seen on or off the water. For example, she has:

- An accommodations plan that can be customized, but generally includes what the company calls "a full-size kitchen, baths, laundry room, living room, bedrooms, and porches." A study can be worked in if you wish. All spaces generally have headroom over 6′6″, carpeted floors, and furniture just like you might have in your home.

**Jay Benford's 50′
Florida Bay Coaster.**

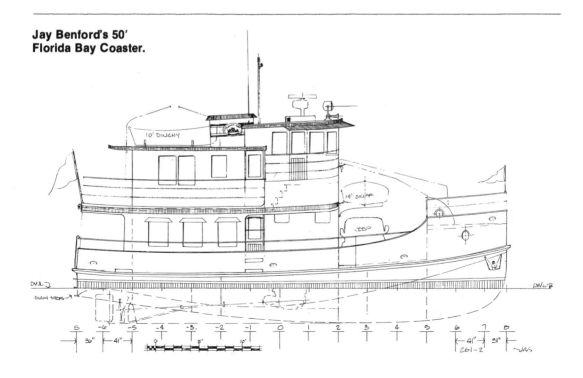

- A sizable pilothouse with a sheltered helm station a story and a half off the water, and outside bridge wings extending the full width of the vessel, not unlike an ocean liner's.
- An engine room like a ship's, with full standing headroom and space to move around. Twin diesels have access on all four sides, and virtually all the ship's mechanical systems are installed here, including one or two gen sets, batteries, pumps, strainers, fresh water and waste systems—with room left over for full-size washer and dryer, workbench, and tool and spares storage.
- Draft of about four feet (depending on load) and a cutaway forefoot that allows her to ease up to a riverbank, a beach, or sandbar. If the tide goes out, she's designed to rest firmly on the bottom without damage to hull or props.
- A well deck big enough to carry a small car, and a crane strong enough to lift the vehicle from boat to shore and back again, whether onto a wharf or while the boat is nosed into a riverbank.
- Space for a launch (such as the 13' Hobie Power Skiff mentioned earlier), in a swing-away cradle over the vehicle on the well deck. The launch may be put overboard and retrieved using the crane.

Of course, all this comes at a price—a base of about $425,000 for a new 50-footer—the price for a good-size waterfront house in Florida. The difference is that you can't move the house.

**Spec check:**
LOA ................. 50'0"
LWL ................. 49'6"
Beam ............... 18'0"
Draft ............... 4'0"
Displacement ........ 90,000 lbs.
Clearance ........... 20'0"
Fuel capacity ......... 1,000 gallons
Water tankage ........ 1,000 gallons

For further information contact:
Florida Bay Coaster Company
937 Bulkhead Rd.
Green Cove Springs, FL 32043
(904) 284-2230
or
Benford Design Group
P.O. Box 447
St. Michaels, MD 21663
(301) 745-3225

***Sparkman & Stephens' 51' Yankee, a world cruiser.*** The liveaboard ketch *Yankee* was designed by Olin Stephens in close collaboration with her owner, the celebrated Captain Irving M. Johnson. At the time of her conception, Johnson and his wife had already sailed nearly a half million miles and had completed seven circumnavigations, some of them in two earlier *Yankee*s. Johnson wanted his new boat "to negotiate canals and rivers and yet be a good sea boat and the biggest craft a man and his wife can handle under all conditions." Specifically, he had three primary requirements:

- On general layout: Abaft a center cockpit, he wanted space for a real home for himself and his wife, with a great cabin aft complete with windows in the transom. Forward of the cockpit, the boat should have separate and private guest quarters. She should also have two heads, one forward and one aft, each big enough to dress in as well as to shower.
- On inland cruising ability: She must be able to sail and motor across Europe, from the heights of Switzerland to the Low Countries, via the European river, canal, and lock systems. That meant shallow draft, centerboards, folding masts, quick-turning ability under power, and special oil-filled, stainless steel shod rubrails to protect her topsides when navigating in narrow canals and locks.
- On seaworthiness and strength: She must be able to cross any ocean and meet any storm; to withstand shipwreck and sail away unhurt; and to be so shaped that she wouldn't roll over when grounded in the strong river currents sometimes found in European waterways. This resulted, among other things, in construction using extra-strong, extra-thick Cor-Ten steel.

These requirements, and many other secondary ones, were met nicely, and the Johnsons did not only what they set out to do, but wrote a book about it (*Yankee Sails Across Europe*) and made a videotape as well that still pops up every once in a while on public television. The Johnsons had a dream and made it come true; with some thought and energy, you can too.

## Spec check:

| | |
|---|---|
| LOA | 50'7" |
| LWL | 49'6" |
| Beam | 18'0" |
| Draft, boards up | 4'6" |
| Sail area | 1,125 sq.ft. |
| Fuel capacity | 940 gallons |
| Water tankage | 1,200 gallons |

# APPENDIX 2

# Where To Find Information When You're Learning About, Shopping For, Buying, Time-Sharing, Insuring, Financing, Equipping, Using, and Selling a Boat

Start with the phone book. If you live near water, your local Yellow Pages may have entries under the following headings: boat brokers; boat builders & yards; boat chartering; boat covers, tops, & upholstery; boat cushions; boat dealers; boat equipment & supplies; boat insurance; boat marinas; boat motors; boats for rental & charter; boat repairing; boat storage; boat trailers; boat transporting; boat & yacht designers; boating associations; boating instruction; marinas; marine documentation; marine electronic equipment & supplies; marine engines; marine hardware; marine paint; marine railway; naval architects; sailing schools; ship & yacht appraisals; ship & yacht brokers; yacht & boat designers; yacht brokers; yacht chartering; and yacht stations.

To find a basic, advanced, or boardsailing school near you, call 800-447-4700. This is a free referral service of the National Sailing Industry Association. It provides you with the name, address, and phone number of the school nearest to your zip code.

## Names and addresses of boating periodicals

### Powerboat magazines
*Boating,* 1633 Broadway, 45th Floor, New York, NY 10009; 212-767-6000.
*Canoe,* P.O. Box 3146, Kirkland, WA 98083; 206-827-6363.
*MotorBoat,* 475 Park Avenue South, New York, NY 10016; 212-689-3600.
*Power and Motoryacht,* 475 Park Avenue South, New York, NY 10016; 212-689-3600.
*Powerboat,* 15917 Starthern St., Van Nuys, CA 91406; 818-989-1820.
*Powerboat Reports,* Box 2626, Greenwich, CT 06836-2626; 203-661-6111.
*Waterski,* Box 2456, Winter Park, FL 32790; 305-628-4802.

### Sailing periodicals

*American Sailor*, c/o USYRU, Box 209, Newport, RI 02840; 401-849-5200.
*Cruising World*, 5 John Clarke Rd., Newport, RI 02840; 401-847-1588.
*Practical Sailor*, Box 819, Newport, RI 02840; 401-849-7438.
*SAIL*, 275 Washington St., Newton, MA 02158-1630; 617-964-3030.
*Sailing*, 125 East Main St., P.O. Box 248, Port Washington, WI 53074;
    414-284-3494.
*Sailing World*, 5 John Clarke Rd., Newport, RI 02840; 401-847-1588.
*Multihulls*, 421 Hancock St., Quincy, MA 02171; 617-328-8181.
*Windrider*, P.O. Box 2456, Winter Park, FL 32790.
*Wind Surf*, P.O. Box 561, Dana Point, CA 92629.

### Periodicals offering both sail and powerboat information

*Boat Journal*, 2100 Powers Ferry Road, Atlanta, GA 30339; 404-955-5656.
*Chartering*, P.O. Box 11356, Marina del Rey, CA 90292; 213-827-4678.
*Motor Boating & Sailing*, 224 West 57th St., New York, NY 10019.
*Ocean Navigator*, P.O. Box 569, Portland, ME 04112-0569; 207-772-2466.
*Soundings*, Pratt St., Essex, CT 06426-1122; 203-767-3200.
*Trailer Boats*, 20700 Belshaw Ave., Carson, CA 90746-3510; 213-537-6322.
*WoodenBoat*, P.O. Box 78, Brooklin, ME 04616; 207-359-4651.
*Yachting*, 2 Park Avenue, New York, NY 10016; 212-779-5300.

### Periodicals devoted to fishing

*Bassin'*, 15115 S. 76 East Ave., Bixby, OK 74008.
*Bassmaster*, One Bell Road, Montgomery, AL 36141; 205-272-9530.
*California Angler*, 1921 East Carnegie St., Suite N, Santa Ana, CA 92705.
*Field & Stream*, 2 Park Ave., New York, NY 10016; 212-779-5000.
*Fins and Feathers*, 318 West Franklin Ave., Minneapolis, MN 55404;
    612-879-0226.
*Fishing World*, 51 Atlantic Ave., Floral Park, NY 11001.
*Florida Sportsman*, 5901 SW 74th St., Miami, FL 33143; 305-661-4222.
*Marlin*, P.O. Box 12902, Pensacola, FL 32576; 904-434-5571.
*Outdoor Life*, 2 Park Ave., New York, NY 10016; 212-779-5000.
*Salt Water Sportsman*, 280 Summer St., Boston, MA 02210.
*Southern Salt Water*, One Bell Road, Montgomery, AL 36141; 205-272-
    9530.
*Sport Fishing*, P.O. Box 2456, Winter Park, FL 32790; 305-628-4802.
*Sports Afield*, 250 West 55th St., New York, NY 10019; 212-649-4014.

### Regional boating periodicals

*Coastal Cruising*, P.O. Box 157, Beaufort, NC 28516; 919-728-2233.
*Eastern Boating/Southeast Boating*, P.O. Box 159, Newtown, PA 18940;
    215-860-0774.
*Great Lakes Sailor*, 2132 East 9th St., Cleveland, OH 44115; 216-861-1777.
*HeartLand Boating*, P.O. Box 1067, Martin, TN 38237-1067; 901-587-6791.
*Lakeland Boating*, 1600 Orrington Ave., Ste. 500, Evanston, IL 60201;
    312-869-5400.
*Latitude 38*, P.O. Box 1678, Sausalito, CA 94966; 415-383-8200.

*Offshore*, P.O. Box 817, Needham Heights, MA 02194; 617-449-6204.

*Pleasure Boating*, 1995 N.E. 150th Street, North Miami, FL 33181.

*Santana*, 5132 Bolsa Ave., Suite 101, Huntington Beach, CA 92649; 714-893-3432.

*Southern Boating*, 1766 Bat Rd., Miami Beach, FL 33139-1414.

*Western Boatman*, 20700 Belshaw Ave., Carson, CA 90749-5427; 213-537-6322.

### Foreign boating periodicals

*Australian Sea Spray*, Box 662, Manly, NSW 2095, Australia.

*Bateaux*, Socpresse, 8-10 rue Pierre Brossolette, 92300 Levallois Perret, France.

*Canadian Yachting*, 227 Front St. East, Toronto, Ontario, CANADA M5A 1E8.

*Die Yacht*, Siekerwall 21, Postfach 4809, 48 Bielefeld, Germany.

*Kazi*, 2-17,1 Chome, Hamamatsu-cho, Minato-ku, Tokyo, Japan.

*Modern Boating*, c/o Sydney Morning Herald, 21st floor, 1500 Broadway, New York, NY 10036; 212-398-9494.

*Multihull International*, 53 High St., Totnes, Devon, TQ9 5NP, ENGLAND.

*New Zealand Powerboat*, 15 Augustus Terrace, Parnell, New Zealand.

*Neptune Yachting*, 6 Rue Ancelle, 92200 Neuilly-sur-Seine, France.

*Race & Cruising SEGLING*, Hasselstigen 1, 13300 Saltsjobaden, Sweden.

*Sailing Canada*, 1200 Eglinton Ave. East, Ste. 404, Don Mills, Ontario M3C 1H9, CANADA.

*Seahorse*, c/o The Observer, Chelsea Bridge House, Queenstown Rd., London SW8 ENGLAND.

*Sea Spray*, 15 Augustus Terrace, Parnell, New Zealand.

*Seilas & Batliv*, Postboks 25, Bygdoy 0211 Oslo 3 Norway.

*Yachting Monthly*, King's Reach Tower, Stamford St., London SE1 9LS ENGLAND.

*Yachting World*, Prospect House, 9-13 Ewell Rd., Cheam, Surry, SM1 4QQ ENGLAND.

*Yachts & Yachting*, 196 Eastern Esplanade, Southend-on-Sea, Essex SS1 3AB ENGLAND.

*Yate Y Motonautica*, Haymarket, S.A. Aribau, 168-170, 08036 Barcelona, Spain.

## Boat-choosing annuals, catalogs, and books

Some of the following may be out of print; try your local used-book store or library.

*Cruising World* Annual (combined with October regular issue); 5 John Clarke Rd., Newport, RI 02840; 401-847-1588.

*SAIL*'s Sailboat & Equipment Directory; 275 Washington St., Newton, MA 02158-1630; 617-964-3030.

*Sailing World* Annual (bound in December regular issue); 5 John Clarke Rd., Newport, RI 02840; 401-847-1588.

*Boat Trailers & Tow Vehicles*, Steve Henkel; International Marine Publishing, 1991.

*Dinghies and Daysailers*, Butch and Rita Wilcox; Barca De Vela Publishing, 1987.

*Practical Boat Buying*, by the editors of *Practical Sailor*; Englander Communications, 1984.

*A Field Guide to Sailboats*, Richard M. Sherwood; Houghton Mifflin Co., 1984.

*Fifty Wooden Boats*, by the editors of *WoodenBoat* magazine; Wooden-Boat Publications.

*The Proper Yacht*, Arthur Beiser, Second Edition; International Marine Publishing, 1978.

*Sailboat Buyer's Guide*, Alan Chappel; Sea Shore Publications, 1983.

*Skene's Elements of Yacht Design*; Dodd, Mead & Co., 1981.

*Ted Brewer Explains Sailboat Design*, Ted Brewer; International Marine Publishing, 1985.

*What Shape Is She In?*, Allan H. Vaitses; International Marine Publishing, 1985.

# Good sources for many other books on boats and boating

The following offer free catalogs:

Dolphin Book Club, A Division of Book-Of-The-Month Club, Camp Hill, PA 17012.

International Marine Publishing, P.O. Box 220, Camden, ME 04843; 1-800-822-8158.

W. W. Norton & Company Inc., 500 Fifth Avenue, New York, NY 10110; 212-354-5500.

Sailors Bookshelf, P.O. Box 643, Hillside, NJ 07205; 201-964-4620.

### Boat ad sources

(in addition to boating periodicals listed above)

Admax Boatowners Multiple Listing Service, P.O. Box 21046, Ft. Lauderdale, FL 33335, and 1430 Arroyo Way, Walnut Creek, CA 94596, 1-800-327-9630. More than 15,000 boats listed, charges for both sellers and buyers.

American Boat Listings Ltd., P.O. Box 660, Oceanside, NY 11572; NY 516-764-0420, FL 305-760-9209. Over 3,000 boats listed, charges for sellers, sometimes for buyers.

Marine Trader, 2444 Solomons Island Rd., Annapolis, MD 21401; 301-266-6672.

New Boats & Brokerage Magazine, 4051 Glencoe Ave., Suite 14, Marina del Rey, CA 90292; 213-306-5038.

*The New York Sunday Times* (classifieds in sports section); and many other Sunday newspaper classified sections.

Best Boat Buys (power and sail), Stack Pub., Box 449, North Falmouth, MA 02556.

Yacht Broker Buyer's Guide, P.O. Box 3156, Bloomington, IL 61702; 309-829-5214.

## Surveyors

See your local Yellow Pages listings, or contact:

National Association of Marine Surveyors ("NAMS"), 305 Springhouse Lane, Moorestown, NJ 08057; 1-800-822-6267 (609-722-5515 in New Jersey).

## Boat enthusiasts' associations

American Canoe Association, 8580 Cinderbed Road, Suite 1900, P.O. Box 1190, Newington, VA 22122-1190.

American Water Ski Association, P.O. Box 191, Winter Haven, FL 33882; 813-324-4341.

American Powerboat Association, P.O. Box 377, East Detroit, MI 48021; 313-773-9700.

American Sailing Association, 13922 Marquesas Way, Marina del Rey, CA 90292; 213-822-7171.

Antique Boat Society, Manset, ME 04656; 207-244-5015.

Antique & Yacht Club, 114 East 32nd St., Suite 1405, New York, NY 10016; 212-683-9197.

Antique & Classics Boat Society Inc., P.O. Box 831, Lake George, NY 12845.

Boat/US, 880 South Pickett Street, Alexandria, VA 22304; 703-823-9550.

Classic Yacht Association, 3248 East Willow St., Signal Hill, CA 90806; 213-426-2488.

The Corinthians, Box 3224, Grand Central Station, New York, NY 10017.

Seven Seas Cruising Association, P.O. Box 1598, Ft. Lauderdale, FL 33302.

Traditional Small Craft Association, P.O. Box 350, Mystic, CT 06355; 203-536-6342.

United States Power Squadron, 1504 Blue Ridge Road, P.O. Box 30423, Raleigh, NC 27622; 919-821-0281, or in Canada, 1-800-268-3579. For closest USPS contact, call 1-800-336-BOAT (1-800-245-BOAT in Virginia).

USYRU (United States Yacht Racing Union), P.O. Box 209, Newport, RI 02840; 401-849-5200.

For yacht clubs in your area, see Lloyd's Register of American Yachts (now out of print but available in many public libraries).

For marinas and possibly clubs in your area, see your local Yellow Pages listings under "Associations," "Marinas," and "Yacht Stations."

## One-design class sailing associations

A Class Catamaran Association
W.H. Beadling
4570 S.E. Rocky Point Way
Stuart, FL 33494

US "A" Division Catamaran Association
Frank W. Miller
320 1st Ave. S
Teirra Verde, FL 33715

National "A" Scow Class Association
Brad Robinson, President
20614 Linwood Circle
Excelsior, MN 55331

International Abbott 33 Class Association
Harold Hoffman
4232 Elmway Dr.
Toledo, OH 43614

U.S. Albacore Association
Daphne Byron, President
13701 Beauwick Court
Silver Spring, MD 20906

Aqua Cat Association
P.O. Box 366
Ladson, SC 29456

Atlantic Class Association
Wilma Lauricella
255 Milbank Ave.
Greenwich, CT 06830

Bandit 15 Class Association
Ray Hoffman
1028 S. 7th Ave.
West Bend, WI 53095

Banshee Class Association
Henry R. Hinckley
P.O. Box 699
Southwest Harbor, ME 04679

Barnett 1400 Class
Gerry Hudlund
534 Commercial Ave.
Green Lake, WI 54941

New England Beetle Cat Boat Association
Dorothy M. Davis
195 Rosemary St., #4
Needham, MA 02194

Bermuda 40 Association
Henry R. Hinckley
P.O. Box 699
Southwest Harbor, ME 04679

Blue Jay Class Association
Julie A. Dunbar
P.O. Box 651
Mantoloking, NJ 08738

Buccaneer Class Association
Linda Schmida
3385 Pine Ridge Lane
Brighton, MI 48116

Bullseye Class Association
Emily L. Wick
37 Atlantic Ave.
Rockport, MA 01966

National Butterfly Association
Jim Barrett, President
4503 N. Orange Blossom Trail
Orlando, FL 32804

C & C 35 Association
7 N. Graitiot, Suite 201
Mount Clemens, MI 48043

International C Class Catamaran Association
Charles Manning
306 S. Vinedo Ave.
Pasadena, CA 91107

National "C" Lark Association
c/o Terry Foren
22470 Bennette Rd.
McMinnville, OR 97128

National "C" Scow Class Association
Tom Keenan, President
1983 Ridge Rd.
Highland, MI 48031

National "C" Scow Sailing Association
David B. Bohl, President
21 South Quincy St.
Hinsdale, IL 60521

Cal 20 Class Association
Martin Burke
533 Paseo de la Playa
Redondo Beach, CA 90278

Cal 25 Class Association
Bob Kirstine
15-68th Pl.
Long Beach, CA 90803

Cal Owners Association
O'Day Boat
100 Franklin St.
Boston, MA 02110

# WHERE TO FIND INFORMATION

Cape Cod Frosty Class Association
Jennifer Kano
P.O. Box 652
Cataumet, MA 02534

Capri 14.2 National Association
Leslie Gallo
2352 Pima Lane
Ventura, CA 93001

Capri 18 Class Association
Catalina Yachts
P.O. Box 989
Woodland Hills, CA 91367

Capri 22 National Association
Franke Burke
5255 E. Orchid Lane
Paradise Valley, AZ 85253

Capri 25 National Association
Catalina Yachts
P.O. Box 989
Woodland Hills, CA 91367

Capri 30 National Association
Steve Hathaway
P.O. Box 989
Woodland Hills, CA 91367

Capri National Association
Catalina Yachts
P.O. Box 989
Woodland Hills, CA 91367

Catalina 22 National Sailing Association
Joyce Seale
2646 E. Marilyn Rd.
Phoenix, AZ 85032

Catalina 25 National Association
Christy Morgan
5011 Revere Ave. N.W.
Massillon, OH 44646

Catalina 27 Association
Mark Pickard
P.O. Box 1389
Sunset Beach, CA 90742

Catalina 30 Class Association
Doris Goodale
9141 Mahalo Dr.
Huntington Beach, CA 92646

Catalina 34 National Association
Richard Barck, Commodore
285 Silvia Court
Los Altos, CA 94024

Catalina 36 Association
Allan Elliot, Commodore
13900 Panay Way, M120
Marina del Rey, CA 90292

Catalina 38 Association
Bill Huber
5076 Bordeaux Ave.
Irvine, CA 92714

Celebrity Class Yacht Racing Association
Theodore B. Conklin
Box 1408
Westhampton Beach, NY 11978

Cheetah Cat Catamaran Association
Edme H. Deschamps
9901 Corinthian Dr.
Stone Harbor, NJ 08247

Comet Class YRA
Jim Walter, Jr.
915 Pines Lake Dr. W.
Wayne, NJ 07470

International Contender Class Association
Paul Powers
53 62nd Pl. "C"
Long Beach, CA 90803

Coronado 15 Class Racing Association, Inc.
Ted Stoker
5157 El Roble
Long Beach, CA 90815

Crescent Sloop Class Association
Ken Gust
1490 Iroquois
Detroit, MI 48214

D C 10 Class Association
c/o Dr. Carol L. Reinisch
45 Marvin Circle
Falmouth, MA 02540

D-Class Catamaran Association
Alan O'Driscoll
1166 Richardson Ave.
Los Altos, CA 94022

Dart Catamaran Association
Judy Fondrk
37 Frederick Rd.
Vernon, CT 06066

Day Sailer Association
Patricia Skeen
1936 Danebo
Eugene, OR 97402

Designer's Choice Class Association
Robert Jones
c/o Homar Boats
Box 7112
Edison, NJ 08118

National Dolphin Senior Class Association
Bob Fink, Commodore
5817 Seminole Ct.
Oklahoma City, OK 73132

American International Dragon Association
Murray Hestley
49 Fairfax Rd.
Rochester, NY 14609

Duster Class YRA
Chris Van Kirk
38 Oak St.
Bloomingdale, NJ 07403

U.S. DYAS Class Association
Gary Baun
878 Lochmoor
Grosse Point, MI 48236

National Class "E" Scow Association
Sherri Campbell
122 Laurel Ave.
Toms River, NJ 08753

18 Square Meter Sailing Association
Richard Lemke
1460 West 17th
Hastings, MN 55033

El Toro International YRA
Helga Wolff
39673 Catamaban Ct.
Freemont, CA 94538

Ensign Class Association
Ed Terrell
23772 Amesbury Dr.
North Olmsted, OH 44070

Enterprise Association of the U.S.
Malcolm Dickinson, President
1731 Yale Station
New Haven, CT 06520

Ericson Association
Rick Black
29 Harvest Hill Rd.
Simsbury, CT 06092

International Etchells 22 Class Association
Pamela P. Smith
HCR 33, Box 30, Route 102A
Bass Harbor, ME 04653

U.S. International Europe Class Association
USYRU
P.O. Box 209
Newport, RI 02840

Evelyn 26C Association
Formula Yachts
P.O. Box 9176
Groton, CT 06340

Express 27 National Class Association
Skip Shapiro, President
113 Lois Lane
Palo Alto, CA 94303

Express 34 Association
Alsberg Brothers
702 Sunset Dr.
Capitola, CA 95010

Express 37 Class Association
Rod Sievers
4249 Clover Knoll Ct.
Carmichael, CA 95608

F-27 Class Association
David Hahn
150 Center St.
Chula Vista, CA 91911

U.S. International Finn Class Association
James Davis, President
6425 Bellac St.
Corpus Christi, TX 78414

U.S. International Fireball Association
Scott Rovanpera
P.O. Box 3973
Walnut Creek, CA 94598

International 5.5 Metre Class
Bruce Chandler
1600 S. Bayfront
Balboa Island, CA 92662

International 505 Class Yacht Racing
Association
Ellen Ablow
22 Ridge Court
Woodside, CA 94062

U.S. Flying Junior Class Association
David Wallace, President
15218 South 16th Pl.
Phoenix, AZ 85044

## WHERE TO FIND INFORMATION

International Flying Dutchman Class
  Organization
  Guido Bertocci, President
  160 Overbrook Dr.
  Freehold, NJ 07728

Flying Scot Sailing Association
  Maryann Eubanks
  3008 Millwood Ave.
  Columbia, SC 29205

San Francisco Bay Folkboat Association
  Bill Du Moulin
  5850 Birch St., #4
  Oakland, CA 94618

Folkboat Association
  Scandinavian Yachts
  22 Severn Ave.
  Annapolis, MD 21404

Force 5 Class Association
  Peter Young
  145 E. 15th St.
  New York, NY 10003

Formula 500 Class Association
  Serge Pond, President
  110 Esplanade
  Capitola Beach, CA 95010

International 470 Association
  Alan Beckwith, President
  54 Royal St., Apt. 2
  Allston, MA 02134

U.S. International 420 Class Association
  Ron Breault, President
  162 Four Mile River Rd.
  Old Lyme, CT 06371

Freedom 21 Class
  Freedom Yachts International
  1 Harbor View Dr.
  Newport, RI 02840

Frers 33 Class Association
  Paul Zabetakis
  130 E. 77th St.
  New York, NY 10021

"G" Cat 5 Meter Class Association
  Karl S. Wehr
  625 - 115th Ave.
  Treasure Island, FL 33706

"G" Cat 5.7 Meter Class Association
  Karl S. Wehr
  625 - 115th Ave.
  Treasure Island, FL 33706

Geary 18 International YRA
  Ken Northfield, President
  P.O. Box 1746
  Port Orchard, WA 98366

Gemini Owners Association
  Pat and Jim Godfrey
  3122 Bryant Lane
  Webster, TX 77598

Grandstand Sailing Association
  Ted Watts
  P.O. Box 14925
  Surfside Beach, SC 29587

International H-Boat Class Association
  Herb Marshall
  Finnyacht USA
  P.O. Box 231
  Barnstable, MA 02630

"H" Class Association
  William G. Harding
  Box 1
  Cataumet, MA 02534

Hampton One Design Association
  Harvey T. Walsh, Jr.
  2245 Leeward Shore Ct.
  Virginia Beach, VA 23451

Hawkfarm One Design Class Association
  John Siegel
  115 C Southampton Lane
  Santa Cruz, CA 95062

Highlander Class Association
  Gordon Stafford
  4920 Marybrook Dr.
  Kettering, OH 45429

Hobie World Class Association
  Doug Skidmore
  P.O. Box 1008
  Oceanside, CA 92054

Holder Class Association
  Doug Skidmore
  P.O. Box 1008
  Oceanside, CA 92054

Hotfoot 27 Association
  3475 Ripon Rd.
  Victoria, B.C.
  CANADA

Hunter 23 Association
  Robin A. Gustavson
  1419 Monica St.
  Austin, TX 78758

International "DN" Ice Yacht Racing
Bob Dill
21 Marian St.
Burlington, VT 05401

Ideal 18 Class Association
Frank R. Shumway, Jr.
100 Pattonwood Dr.
Rochester, NY 14617

U.S. Illusion Class Association
Dave Forsman
326 Shawnee Dr.
Erie, PA 16505

Impulse 21 Class Association
Belinda Bates Owens
10610 Metric Dr., #145
Dallas, TX 75243

Impulse 26 Association
Impulse Marine
10610 Metric Dr., #145
Dallas, TX 75243

National Interclub Frostbite Dinghy
Association
Marianne Borowski, President
47 Bartlett Pky.
Winthrop, MA 02152

Interlake Sailing Class Association
Clark Chapin
974 Church St.
Plymouth, MI 48170

U.S. International 14 Association
Dennis Williams
7032 13th Ave., NW
Seattle, WA 98117

International 210 Class Association
James R. Robinson, President
38 Searing Rd.
Hingham, MA 02043

U.S. Isotope Class Association
Rhoda Meldau
2212 S. Miami Blvd.
Durham, NC 27703

J/22 Class Association
Carolyn Freeman
P.O. Box 843, 1st & Main
Franklin, TN 37064

International J/24 Class Association
Richard L. Tillman
P.O. Box 372578
Satellite Beach, FL 32937

J/27 Class Association
Ronald A. Sebring, President
2329 Highway 34
Manasquan, NJ 08736

J/29 Class Association
Joel Hamburger
95 Penn Hill Dr.
Schnecksville, PA 28078

J/30 Class Association
Bill Raney
107 N. Second St.
Wilmington, NC 28402

J/35 Class Association
Thomas Petkus
1 North LaSalle St.
Chicago, IL 60602

J/40 Class Association
J Boats
P.O. Box 90
Newport, RI 02840

J/44 Class Association
Bob Johnstone
24 Mill St.
Newport, RI 02840

Javelin Class Association
Fred Lange, Commodore
4850 Lindsey Lane
Cleveland, OH 44143

Jet 14 Class Association
Mary Ungemach
26 Pontiac Dr.
Wayne, NJ 07470

JY15 Class Association
Peter Freeman/Jessica Jonestone P.
P.O. Box 452
East Haddam, CT 06423

San Francisco Bay Knarr Association
P.O. Box 2125
San Francisco, CA 94126

North American Land Sailing Association
2100 W. Gaylord St.
Long Beach, CA 90813

International Laser Class Association
Allan Broadribb
P.O. Box 600
Aylmer, P.Q.
CANADA J9H 6L1

# WHERE TO FIND INFORMATION

Laser "II" Class Association
Allan Broadribb
P.O. Box 600
Aylmer, P.Q.
CANADA J9H 6L1

U.S. Olympic Lechner Class
Lynn Hornosky
P.O. Box 1412
Newport, RI 02840

Lido 14 International Class Association
P.O. Box 1252
Newport Beach, CA 92663

International Lightning Class Association
Donna Foote
808 High St.
Worthington, OH 43085

National "M" Scow Class Association
Garry Winter, President
1017 Janet Ave.
Darien, IL 60559

M-20 Sailing Association
Robert R. Witt
2881 Merritt Terrace
Port St. Lucie, FL 34952

Manhasset Bay One Design
George N. Grof, Jr.
55 Farmview Rd.
Port Washington, NY 11050

U.S. Mariner Class Association
Andrew Jackson
1209 Cropwell Rd.
Cherry Hill, NJ 08003

Marshall 22 Association
Marshall Marine
P.O. Box P-266
S. Dartmouth, MA 02748

MC Class Sailboat Racing Association
Curt Bradley
1620 Timberlane N.E.
Grand Rapids, MI 49505

Mercury Class YRA
Jim Bradley
54 Lakewood Ave.
San Francisco, CA 94127

Merit 22 Association
Merit Marine
13541 Desmond St.
Pacoima, CA 91331

Merit 25 Association
Hartney Plastics
1641 Fiske Pl.
Oxnard, CA 93033

U.S. International Mini 12 Meter Class
Association
Vivienne Anderson, President
1605 Main St., Ste. 800
Sarasota, FL 34236

U.S. Mirror Class Association
John M. Borthwick
5305 Marian Dr.
Lyndhurst, OH 44124

Mistral Class Association
Scott Steele
7222 Parkway Dr.
Dorsey, MD 21076

Mobjack Class Association
Tara Lytle
2421 Boissevain Rd.
Richmond, VA 23229

Moore 24 National Association
3135 Indian Way
Lafayette, CA 94549

Moore 30 Association
Moore Sailboats
1650 Commercial Way
Santa Cruz, CA 95065

International NACRA Class Association
Jack Young
1810 E. Borchard St.
Santa Ana, CA 92705

Narrasketuck One Design Association
c/o Donna Johnson
81 Jean Rd.
West Islip, NY 11795

National One-Design Class Association
Jolly Booth
1225 E. Bronson St.
South Bend, IN 46615

New York 36 Association
68 Westover Lane
Stamford, CT 06902

Nonsuch Class Association
Johnathan Ayers
317 Bay Ave.
Huntington, NY 11743

North American 40 Association
John Martin
112 Vendome Rd.
Grosse Pt. Farms, MI 48236

North American Hobie Class Association
31700 Middlebelt Rd., Ste. 100
Farmington Hills, MI 48334

O'Day Owners Association
Hanify King
100 Franklin St.
Boston, MA 02110

U.S. OK Dinghy Association
Matt Mikkelborg
14555 Hwy. 303
Poulsbo, WA 98370

Olson 25 Association
Bill Riess
6144 Wood Dr.
Oakland, CA 94611

Olson 30 Class Association
Mark Folkman
3301 Gibson Pl.
Redondo Beach, CA 90278

International One-Design Class Association
Tony Leggett
28 Old Fulton St.
Brooklyn, NY 11201

One Design Fourteen Class Association
Peter Johnstone
P.O. Box 736
Newport, RI 02840

110 Class Yacht Racing Association
Jim Stone
935 Indiana Dr.
Macatawa, MI 49434

U.S. Optimist Dinghy Association
Ken Slater
118 School St.
Manchester, MA 01944

Optimist Pram Association
Ellie's Sailing Shop
1300 N. Betty Lane
Clearwater, FL 33515

Pearson 30 Association—Chesapeake Bay
Jennifer Coe
2 Brice Rd.
Annapolis, MD 21401

Penguin Class Dinghy Association
Mark Kastel
Rt. 3, Box 129
Cashton, WI 54619

Phantom Class Racing Association
Andrew Beaton
c/o Howmar Boats
Box 7112
Edison, NJ 08818

Prindle Class Association
Todd Smith
10965 Rochester Ave., #303
Los Angeles, CA 90024

Ranger 20 Class Association
Phil Rousseau, Commodore
1912 Walker Park Rd.
Shelton, WA 98585

Ranger 23 Class Association
Ed Marks
3 Conservation Way
Scituate, MA 02066

National Rebel Class Association
Peggy Quiniff
421 Amherst
Des Plaines, IL 60016

Rhodes 18 Class Association
c/o Richard D. Marchand
Box 245
Barnstable, MA 02630

Rhodes 19 Class Association
William K. Henze, President
168 Wednesday Hill Rd.
Durham, NH 03824

Rhodes Bantam Class Association
Kathy Burlitch
806 Hanshaw Rd.
Ithaca, NY 14850

S2 7.9 Meter Class Association
Doug Slade
533 Avalon Ten, S.E.
Grand Rapids, MI 49503

S2 9.1 RC Association
S2 Yachts
725 E. 40th St.
Holland, MI 49423

International Naples Sabot Association
Peggy Lenhart
690 Senate St.
Costa Mesa, CA 92627

# WHERE TO FIND INFORMATION

U.S. Sabot Class Association
  Kyle Stonecipher
  5269 Colony #12
  Agoura Hills, CA 91301

San Juan 21 Class Association
  Rick Ashworth
  1204 Perry Loop
  Kennewick, WA 99336

San Juan 24 Class Association
  Mark Nerheim, Commodore
  P.O. Box 70163
  Seattle, WA 98107

Santa Barbara Sea Shell Association
  P.O. Box 3075
  Santa Barbara, CA 93130

Santa Cruz 50 Association
  Bill Lee Yachts
  3700B Hilltop Rd.
  Soquel, CA 95073

Santana 20 Class Association
  L. Gene Proffitt, President
  893 Lakeshore Dr.
  Klamath Falls, OR 97601

Santana 30/30 Association
  W.D. Schock
  23125 Temescal Canyon Rd.
  Corona, CA 91719

Santana 35 Fleet of San Francisco
  Shelley Graham
  581 Seaver Dr.
  Mill Valley, CA 94941

Saroca Class Association
  Saroca
  27 Hedly St.
  Portsmouth, RI 02871

Schock 35 Class Association
  Richard Dorfman, President
  3251 Tilden Ave.
  Los Angeles, CA 90034

U.S. Sea Spray Association
  Victor Kohfal
  241 South Wilson, #103
  Pasadena, CA 91106

Long Beach Sea Spray Association
  John Janus
  245 Ave. Santa Barbara, Apt. C
  San Clemente, CA 92672

American Shark Association
  John Lennon, Secretary
  P.O. Box 303
  Canadaigua, NY 14424

U.S. Shark Class Association
  Charles Obersheimer
  1884 Niagara St.
  Buffalo, NY 14207

National Shields Class Association
  Chris Withers, President
  50 Bliss Mine Rd.
  Newport, RI 02840

U.S. Sidewinder Association
  Chris Pisczek
  312 Second St.
  Conemaugh, PA 15909

U.S. International Six Metre Association
  The Sailing Foundation
  7001 Seaview Ave., N.W.
  Seattle, WA 98107

Snipe Class International Racing Association
  Thomas Payne
  4096 Chestnut Dr.
  Flowery Branch, GA 30542

Sol Cat Class Association
  Ed Quillen
  10618 Huntington Point
  Houston, TX 77099

U.S. Soling Association
  Rose A. Hoeksema
  1615 N. Cleveland, #3N
  Chicago, IL 60614

Sonar Class Association
  Janet Drumm
  4 Pinecliff Dr.
  Marblehead, MA 01945

International Star Class YRA
  Doris Jirka
  1545 Waukegan Rd., #8
  Glenview, IL 60025

Stiletto Class Association
  P.O. Box 20606
  Sarasota, FL 34238

North American Stingray Association
  R. Ruediasale
  11008 W. Bayshore
  Traverse City, MI 49684

U.S. Sunfish Class Association
  Terry Beadle
  P.O. Box 128
  Drayton Plains, MI 48330

Superay Class Association
  1150 19th St. N
  St. Petersburg, FL 33713

Supercat Race Association
Dianne Haberman
118 Hickory St.
Mahtomedi, MN 55115

Sweet 16 Sailing Association
Tom Mallinger
8 E. 117 Terrace
Kansas City, MO 64114

Interstate Swing Keel Association
Charles M. Wollert
12123 Swords Creek Rd.
Houston, TX 77067

Tanzer 16 Class Association
David Lenat
P.O. Box 26003
Raleigh, NC 27611

Tanzer 22 Class Association
Barbara Charters
P.O. Box 22
St. Anne e Bellevu, P.Q.
CANADA H9X 3L4

Tanzer 26 Association
Tanzer International
P.O. Box 67
Dorion, P.Q.
CANADA J7V 5V8

Tartan 10 Class Association
Paul Lady, President
35 Lakecrest Lane
Grosse Pointe Farms, MI 48236

North American Tasar Association
Zigmond Burzycki
3190 West 43rd
Vancouver, B.C.
CANADA V6N 3J5

U.S. International Tempest Association
James O'Hara
2115 White Oaks Dr.
Alexandria, VA 22306

The Ten Class Association
James R. Melton, President
3635 West 132nd St.
Cleveland, OH 44111

Thistle Class Association
Honey Abramson
1811 Cavell Ave.
Highland Park, IL 60035

Thunderbird Class Association
Ray Ilich
P.O. Box 1033
Mercer Island, WA 98040

U.S. Tornado Association
Patricia Zitkus
23361 Robert John
St. Clair Shores, MI 48080

International Tornado Association
Paul Standley
32 Pint Point Rd.
Rowayton, CT 06853

National Triton Association
David Bradley, President
Bayview Heights
Chesebro Lane
Stonington, CT 06378

Twelve Class Association
Viena H. Melton
3635 West 132nd St.
Cleveland, OH 44111

International Twelve Metre Class Association
A. R. G. Wallace, M.D.
Aquidneck Medical Center
Newport, RI 02840

Udell Class Association
Robert B. Christie
c/o Hagerty Gra.
141 W. Jackson, Rm. 1280
Chicago, IL 60604

Ultimate 30 Class Association
Joe Evans
c/o Hamilton Yacht
P.O. Box 3349
Annapolis, MD 21403

U.S. 1 Class Association
Continental Sail Craft
P.O. Box 182015
Casselberry, FL 32817

Vega One Design Chesapeake Association
Sidney A. Rosen
10615 Whitman Cir.
Orlando, FL 32821

Wabbit Class Association
North Coast Yachts
2100 Clement Ave.
Alameda, CA 94501

U.S. Wayfarer Association
Robert Frick
4765 Crescent Pt.
Pontiac, MI 48054

Wayler Sailboard One Design Association
R. Lepman
608 Winthrop
Addison, IL 60101

Wianno Senior Class Association
  Carter S. Bacon
  6 Curve St.
  Sherborn, MA 01770

Windmill Class Association
  Don Malpas
  2212 Blue Ridge Blvd.
  Birmingham, AL 35226

Windsurfer Class Association
  Diane Schweitzer
  2030 E. Gladwick St.
  Dominguez Hills, CA 90220

National "X" Boat Class Association
  Milton Haeger, President
  7747 Van Buren St.
  Forest Park, IL 60130

American Y-Flyer YRA
  Paul C. White
  7349 Scarborough Blvd. E. Dr.
  Indianapolis, IN 46256

N. American Yngling Association
  Bill Tomlinson, President
  440 Union Pl.
  Excelsior, MN 55331

## Co-op boating clubs and yacht time-sharing organizations

The Manhattan Yacht Club, 207 Front St., New York, NY 10038; 212-619-3656; shared fleet of J/24 sailboats.

Sailaway Club, P.O. Box 204, City Island, NY 10464; 1-800-221-4326 or 212-885-3200; has 65 members and is growing, with bases on Tortola, BVI, Captiva Island, Pleasant Bay, Cape Cod, and City Island; fleet is Solings and Lasers. Unlimited use of boats for $795/person membership fee (less per person for families).

Olympic Circle Sailing Club, 1 Spinnaker Way, Berkeley Marina, Berkeley, CA 94710; 415-843-4200; pay-as-you-go fleet of sailboats.

Florida Yacht Club, 1290 5th St., Miami Beach, FL 33139; 1-800-537-0050; low-cost charters and social events; sail only.

Myacht Club, c/o Steve Adams, Capital Corp., 235 N.E. 17th Street, Miami, FL 33132; 305-525-9255; offers $2,500/year time-shares in yacht *Pasha*, a $1.2 million, 75-foot luxury motoryacht staffed with captain and 3-man crew.

## Free mail order discount catalog sources

BOAT US (catalog free after joining and paying membership fee), 880 South Picket Street, Alexandria, VA 22304; 1-800-336-2494.

Coast Navigation, 1934 Lincoln Drive, Annapolis, MD 21401; 1-800-638-0420.

Consumers Marine and Electronics, 20 South Concourse, Neptune, NJ 07753; 1-800-332-2628 or 201-774-9025.

Continental Marine, 36 Temple Hill Road, New Windsor, NY 12550; 1-800-992-4872 or 203-637-3144.

Defender Industries, Box 820, New Rochelle, NY 10801; 914-632-3001.

Eastern Marine, 1064 Sun Valley Drive, Annapolis, MD 21401-4927; 1-800-222-9440.

E & B Marine, Box 3138, Edison, NJ 08818; 201-287-3900.

Goldberg's, 202 Market St., Philadelphia, PA 19106; 1-800-262-3900.

JSI Discount Sailing Source, Box 20926, St. Petersburg, FL 33742; 1-800-577-3220 (mail flyers only).

International Marine Electronics, 234 Sumac Rd., Wheeling, IL 60090; 1-800-323-3500.

Marine Buyer's Co-op, P.O. Drawer 130, Hingham, MA 02043; 1-800-225-5244.

Marine Center, Box 9968, Seattle, WA 98109; 206-284-2000.

Marine Exchange, 128 Newbury St., Peabody, MA 01960; 508-535-3212.

M & E Marine, Box 601, Camden, NJ 08101; 609-858-0400.

MMOS, 15219 Michigan Avenue, Dearborn, MI 48126; 313-582-9480.

Neptune Trading Corp., 240 Halstead Ave., Harrison, NY 10528; 1-800-637-0660 or 914-835-1505.

Sailorman, 350 East State Road 84, Fort Lauderdale, FL 33316; 1-800-523-0772 or in Florida, 1-800-331-5359.

Supermarine Inc., 651 East Egret Bay Blvd., League City, TX 77573; 1-800-558-0063 or 713-332-1515.

West Marine Products, Box 5189, Santa Cruz, CA 95063; 1-800-538-0775.

## Major insurance companies that underwrite marine insurance

### *Marine insurers selling through brokers and independent agents*

Note: There are many companies that offer marine insurance through a nationwide network of agents and brokers. The following list is a sample only, and is not all-inclusive. See your local Yellow Pages for agents in your area who deal with these insurance underwriters.

Chubb Insurance

Commercial Union

INA-Aetna (CIGNA)

New Hampshire Insurance

Royal Insurance (Canada)

State Farm Mutual

Travelers Insurance

### *Marine insurers that are "direct writers," selling through captive agents*

Allstate (many local agents; see your Yellow Pages)

BOAT/US (Boat Owner's Association of the United States), 880 South Pickett St., Alexandria, VA 22304; 703-823-9550.

National Marine Underwriters, Annapolis, MD; 1-800-262-8467.

Ocean Underwriters, Cocoa, FL 32922 (sailboat insurance only).

### *Marine insurers that specialize in "difficult-to-find" coverage (see Chapter 15 for details)*

Hagerty Marine Insurance, Box 87, Traverse City, MI 49685; 616-941-7477.

Jefferson Insurance, 511 East Arcadia Ave., Waukesha, WI 53186.

C. L. McCabe Insurance Agency, Annapolis, MD, 301-268-9055.

## Sources of boat industry and government information on boating

U.S. Coast Guard, 2100 Second St., SW, Washington, DC 20593; 202-267-2992.

National Marine Manufacturer's Association, 401 N. Michigan Ave., Chicago, IL 60611; 312-836-4747.

## Reference guides on boat prices

ABOS Blue Books, Intertac Publishing, P.O. Box 12901, Overland Park, KS 66212.

Antique & Classic Boat Society, P.O. Box 831, Lake George, NY 12845.

BUC International, 1314 N.E. 17th Court, Ft. Lauderdale, FL 33305.

NADA, Official Boat Guide, National Automobile Dealers Used Car Guide Co., 8400 Westpark Drive, McLean, VA 22102-9985; 1-800-544-6232. Subscription costs $70 for three issues, one every four months.

National Boat Book, National Market Reports, Inc., 300 West Adams St., Chicago, IL 60606.

# What Boat Loans Cost

The table below shows the monthly payment and total interest cost of a $1,000 boat loan at annual percentage rates ("APR") of 8% to 15% and loan durations of 1 to 10 years. To figure the total monthly payment or total interest for your loan, simply multiply the cost per $1,000 below times the number of thousand-dollar increments of your loan.

For example, for a $15,000 loan, multiply the numbers below by 15 to get the monthly payment and the total finance charge. Example: the monthly payment on a 10-year 10% loan is $13.22 for $1,000, or $13.22 × 15 = $198.30 for $15,000. The total finance charge for the same loan is $585.81 × 15 = $8,787.15. The total amount paid over the 10 years will be $23,787.15: $15,000 of principal plus $8,787.15 of interest.

**Monthly payment on
a $1000 boat loan**

| | ANNUAL PERCENTAGE RATE | | | | | | | |
|---|---|---|---|---|---|---|---|---|
| NUMBER OF YEARS | 8% | 9% | 10% | 11% | 12% | 13% | 14% | 15% |
| 1 | 86.99 | 87.45 | 87.92 | 88.38 | 88.85 | 89.32 | 89.79 | 90.26 |
| 2 | 45.23 | 45.68 | 46.14 | 46.61 | 47.07 | 47.54 | 48.01 | 48.49 |
| 3 | 31.34 | 31.80 | 32.27 | 32.74 | 33.21 | 33.69 | 34.18 | 34.67 |
| 4 | 24.41 | 24.89 | 25.36 | 25.85 | 26.33 | 26.83 | 27.33 | 27.83 |
| 5 | 20.28 | 20.76 | 21.25 | 21.74 | 22.24 | 22.75 | 23.27 | 23.79 |
| 6 | 17.53 | 18.03 | 18.53 | 19.03 | 19.55 | 20.07 | 20.61 | 21.14 |
| 7 | 15.59 | 16.09 | 16.60 | 17.12 | 17.65 | 18.19 | 18.74 | 19.30 |
| 8 | 14.14 | 14.65 | 15.17 | 15.71 | 16.25 | 16.81 | 17.37 | 17.95 |
| 9 | 13.02 | 13.54 | 14.08 | 14.63 | 15.18 | 15.75 | 16.33 | 16.92 |
| 10 | 12.13 | 12.67 | 13.22 | 13.78 | 14.35 | 14.93 | 15.53 | 16.13 |

# WHAT BOAT LOANS COST

**Total interest cost
(finance charge) on a
$1000 boat loan**

|  | ANNUAL PERCENTAGE RATE | | | | | | | |
|---|---|---|---|---|---|---|---|---|
| NUMBER OF YEARS | 8% | 9% | 10% | 11% | 12% | 13% | 14% | 15% |
| 1 | 43.86 | 49.42 | 54.99 | 60.58 | 66.19 | 71.81 | 77.45 | 83.10 |
| 2 | 85.45 | 96.43 | 107.48 | 118.59 | 129.76 | 141.00 | 152.31 | 163.68 |
| 3 | 128.11 | 144.79 | 161.62 | 178.59 | 195.72 | 212.98 | 230.39 | 247.95 |
| 4 | 171.82 | 194.48 | 217.40 | 240.59 | 264.02 | 287.72 | 311.67 | 335.88 |
| 5 | 216.58 | 245.50 | 274.82 | 304.55 | 334.67 | 365.18 | 396.10 | 427.40 |
| 6 | 262.39 | 297.84 | 333.86 | 370.45 | 407.61 | 445.34 | 483.61 | 522.44 |
| 7 | 309.24 | 351.48 | 394.50 | 438.28 | 482.83 | 528.12 | 574.16 | 620.93 |
| 8 | 357.12 | 406.42 | 456.72 | 508.00 | 560.27 | 613.50 | 667.66 | 722.76 |
| 9 | 406.02 | 462.63 | 520.50 | 579.59 | 639.90 | 701.39 | 764.04 | 827.83 |
| 10 | 455.93 | 520.11 | 585.81 | 653.00 | 721.65 | 791.73 | 863.20 | 936.02 |

# Present Value of $1,000 At Various Rates of Return

| NUMBER OF YEARS FROM NOW | AVERAGE RATE OF RETURN AVAILABLE ON MONEY | | | | | | | |
|---|---|---|---|---|---|---|---|---|
| | 0% | 2% | 4% | 6% | 8% | 10% | 12% | 14% |
| 0 | $1000.00 | $1000.00 | $1000.00 | $1000.00 | $1000.00 | $1000.00 | $1000.00 | $1000.00 |
| 1 | 1000.00 | 990.10 | 980.60 | 971.30 | 962.30 | 953.50 | 944.90 | 936.60 |
| 2 | 1000.00 | 970.70 | 942.90 | 916.30 | 891.00 | 866.80 | 843.70 | 821.60 |
| 3 | 1000.00 | 951.70 | 906.60 | 864.40 | 825.00 | 788.00 | 753.30 | 720.70 |
| 4 | 1000.00 | 933.00 | 871.70 | 815.50 | 763.90 | 716.40 | 672.60 | 632.20 |
| 5 | 1000.00 | 914.70 | 838.20 | 769.40 | 707.30 | 651.20 | 600.50 | 554.50 |
| 6 | 1000.00 | 896.80 | 806.00 | 725.80 | 654.90 | 592.00 | 536.20 | 486.40 |
| 7 | 1000.00 | 879.20 | 775.00 | 684.70 | 606.40 | 538.20 | 478.70 | 426.70 |
| 8 | 1000.00 | 862.00 | 745.20 | 646.00 | 561.50 | 489.30 | 427.40 | 374.30 |
| 9 | 1000.00 | 845.10 | 716.50 | 609.40 | 519.90 | 444.80 | 381.60 | 328.30 |
| 10 | 1000.00 | 828.50 | 688.90 | 574.90 | 481.40 | 404.40 | 340.70 | 288.00 |
| 11 | 1000.00 | 812.30 | 662.40 | 542.40 | 445.70 | 367.60 | 304.20 | 252.60 |
| 12 | 1000.00 | 796.30 | 637.00 | 511.70 | 412.70 | 334.20 | 271.60 | 221.60 |
| 13 | 1000.00 | 780.70 | 612.50 | 482.70 | 382.10 | 303.80 | 242.50 | 194.40 |
| 14 | 1000.00 | 765.40 | 588.90 | 455.40 | 353.80 | 276.20 | 216.50 | 170.50 |
| 15 | 1000.00 | 750.40 | 566.30 | 429.60 | 327.60 | 251.10 | 193.30 | 149.60 |
| 16 | 1000.00 | 735.70 | 544.50 | 405.30 | 303.30 | 228.30 | 172.60 | 131.20 |
| 17 | 1000.00 | 721.30 | 523.50 | 382.30 | 280.90 | 207.50 | 154.10 | 115.10 |
| 18 | 1000.00 | 707.10 | 503.40 | 360.70 | 260.10 | 188.60 | 137.60 | 101.00 |
| 19 | 1000.00 | 693.30 | 484.00 | 340.30 | 240.80 | 171.50 | 122.90 | 88.60 |
| 20 | 1000.00 | 679.70 | 465.40 | 321.00 | 223.00 | 155.90 | 109.70 | 77.70 |
| 21 | 1000.00 | 666.30 | 447.50 | 302.90 | 206.40 | 141.70 | 98.00 | 68.10 |
| 22 | 1000.00 | 653.30 | 430.30 | 285.70 | 191.20 | 128.80 | 87.50 | 59.80 |
| 23 | 1000.00 | 640.50 | 413.80 | 269.50 | 177.00 | 117.10 | 78.10 | 52.40 |
| 24 | 1000.00 | 627.90 | 397.80 | 254.30 | 163.90 | 106.50 | 69.70 | 46.00 |
| 25 | 1000.00 | 615.60 | 382.50 | 239.90 | 151.70 | 96.80 | 62.30 | 40.30 |
| 26 | 1000.00 | 603.50 | 367.80 | 226.30 | 140.50 | 88.80 | 55.60 | 35.40 |
| 27 | 1000.00 | 591.70 | 353.70 | 213.50 | 130.10 | 80.00 | 49.60 | 31.00 |
| 28 | 1000.00 | 580.10 | 340.10 | 201.40 | 120.50 | 72.70 | 44.30 | 27.20 |
| 29 | 1000.00 | 568.70 | 327.00 | 190.00 | 111.50 | 66.10 | 39.60 | 23.90 |
| 30 | 1000.00 | 557.60 | 314.40 | 179.30 | 103.30 | 60.10 | 35.30 | 21.00 |
| 31 | 1000.00 | 546.60 | 302.30 | 169.10 | 95.60 | 54.60 | 31.50 | 18.40 |
| 32 | 1000.00 | 535.90 | 290.70 | 159.50 | 88.50 | 49.70 | 28.20 | 16.10 |
| 33 | 1000.00 | 525.40 | 279.50 | 150.50 | 82.00 | 45.20 | 25.10 | 14.10 |
| 34 | 1000.00 | 515.10 | 268.80 | 142.00 | 75.90 | 41.10 | 22.40 | 12.40 |
| 35 | 1000.00 | 505.00 | 258.40 | 134.00 | 70.30 | 37.30 | 20.00 | 10.90 |

Note: above present value factors were calculated using mid-year convention.

# Compound Interest Table

**$1,000 compounded
annually at a percentage
rate of . . .**

| YEARS | 2% | 4% | 6% | 8% | 10% | 12% | 14% | 16% | 18% | 20% |
|---|---|---|---|---|---|---|---|---|---|---|
| 1 | 1020 | 1040 | 1060 | 1080 | 1100 | 1120 | 1140 | 1160 | 1180 | 1200 |
| 2 | 1040 | 1082 | 1124 | 1166 | 1210 | 1254 | 1300 | 1346 | 1392 | 1440 |
| 3 | 1061 | 1125 | 1191 | 1260 | 1331 | 1405 | 1482 | 1561 | 1643 | 1728 |
| 4 | 1082 | 1170 | 1262 | 1360 | 1464 | 1574 | 1689 | 1811 | 1939 | 2074 |
| 5 | 1104 | 1217 | 1338 | 1469 | 1611 | 1762 | 1925 | 2100 | 2288 | 2488 |
| 6 | 1126 | 1265 | 1418 | 1587 | 1772 | 1974 | 2195 | 2436 | 2670 | 2986 |
| 7 | 1149 | 1316 | 1504 | 1714 | 1949 | 2211 | 2502 | 2826 | 3185 | 3583 |
| 8 | 1172 | 1369 | 1594 | 1850 | 2144 | 2476 | 2853 | 3278 | 3759 | 4300 |
| 9 | 1195 | 1423 | 1689 | 1999 | 2358 | 2773 | 3252 | 3803 | 4435 | 5160 |
| 10 | 1219 | 1480 | 1790 | 2159 | 2594 | 3106 | 3707 | 4411 | 5233 | 6192 |
| 11 | 1243 | 1539 | 1898 | 2332 | 2853 | 3479 | 4226 | 5117 | 6176 | 7430 |
| 12 | 1268 | 1601 | 2012 | 2518 | 3138 | 3896 | 4818 | 5936 | 7288 | 8916 |
| 13 | 1294 | 1665 | 2132 | 2720 | 3452 | 4363 | 5492 | 6886 | 8599 | 10699 |
| 14 | 1319 | 1732 | 2260 | 2937 | 3797 | 4887 | 6261 | 7987 | 10147 | 12839 |
| 15 | 1346 | 1800 | 2397 | 3172 | 4177 | 5474 | 7138 | 9265 | 11974 | 15407 |
| 16 | 1372 | 1873 | 2540 | 3426 | 4595 | 6130 | 8137 | 10748 | 14129 | 18488 |
| 17 | 1400 | 1948 | 2693 | 3700 | 5054 | 6866 | 9276 | 12468 | 16672 | 22186 |
| 18 | 1428 | 2026 | 2854 | 3996 | 5560 | 7690 | 10575 | 14462 | 19673 | 26623 |
| 19 | 1457 | 2107 | 3025 | 4316 | 6116 | 8613 | 12056 | 16776 | 23214 | 31948 |
| 20 | 1486 | 2191 | 3207 | 4661 | 6727 | 9646 | 13743 | 19461 | 27393 | 38337 |
| 21 | 1516 | 2279 | 3400 | 5034 | 7400 | 10804 | 15667 | 22574 | 32324 | 46005 |

# Typical Equipment and Costs

| ITEM, TYPE, QUANTITY & SIZE | TYPICAL PRICE FOR ONE ITEM | | TOTAL COSTS FOR VARIOUS SIZES OF BOATS (1) | | |
|---|---|---|---|---|---|
| | *list* | *discount* | *Small boat (2)* | *Medium boat (3)* | *Large boat (4)* |
| **Safety Equipment** | | | | | |
| Anchor, Danforth "std" .... 1-4# | $20 | $15 | $15 | — | — |
| 1-8# | 31 | 20 | 20 | $20 | — |
| 1-13# | 49 | 31 | — | 31 | $31 |
| 1-18# | 69 | 43 | — | — | 43 |
| 1-22# | 84 | 55 | — | — | 55 |
| Anchor rode, nylon 3-strand twist | | | | | |
| $5/16'' \times 150'$ | 30 | 23 | 46 | — | — |
| $3/8'' \times 150'$ | 50 | 37 | — | 75 | — |
| $1/2'' \times 150'$ | 75 | 50 | — | — | 150 |
| Anchor chain (American-made, proof coil type) | | | | | |
| $1/4'' \times 6'$ | 8 | 5 | 5 | — | — |
| $5/16'' \times 8'$ | 18 | 12 | 12 | 12 | 12 |
| $3/8'' \times 10'$ | 24 | 16 | — | 16 | 16 |
| $1/2'' \times 12'$ | 48 | 32 | — | — | 32 |
| Anchor light, 21-day w/battery ... | 49 | 36 | — | 36 | 36 |
| Cushions, floatable, four at ...... | 12 | 9 | 36 | 36 | 36 |
| Distress signal kit .............. | 50 | 29 | 29 | 29 | 29 |
| Fender, 8" × 22" ............... | 42 | 26 | 26 | 52 | 104 |
| Fire extinguisher, Type 1A10BC ................ | 31 | 18 | 36 | 54 | 72 |
| First-aid kit .................... | 32 | 24 | 24 | 24 | 24 |
| Flashlight ..................... | 9 | 5 | 5 | 10 | 10 |
| Freon fog horn, handheld ....... | 45 | 31 | 31 | 31 | 31 |

*continued*

# TYPICAL EQUIPMENT AND COSTS

| ITEM, TYPE, QUANTITY & SIZE | TYPICAL PRICE FOR ONE ITEM | | TOTAL COSTS FOR VARIOUS SIZES OF BOATS (1) | | |
|---|---|---|---|---|---|
| | *list* | *discount* | *Small boat (2)* | *Medium boat (3)* | *Large boat (4)* |
| Harness & safety line ........... | 105 | 78 | — | 156 | 156 |
| Life ring & launcher, Forespar ... | 80 | 52 | — | 52 | 52 |
| Man-overboard pole with strobe .................. | 295 | 188 | — | — | 188 |
| EPIRB for offshore passages .... | 350 | 183 | — | 183 | 183 |
| Life vests, Omega Gran Prix, Type III ..................... | 55 | 39 | 78 | 78 | 78 |
| Life vests, kapok-filled, Type II ..................... | 10 | 7 | 14 | 28 | 42 |
| Radar reflector ................. | 30 | 25 | — | 25 | 25 |
| **Navigational and Electronic Equipment** | | | | | |
| Alarm clock, Tozaj, quartz, battery ...................... | 9 | 6 | — | 6 | 6 |
| Autopilot, Navico, Model 1800 tiller .............. | 500 | 330 | — | 330 | — |
| Model 5000 wheel............. | 1,000 | 630 | — | — | 630 |
| Compass, Aquameter Gemini Model ................. | 173 | 100 | 100 | 100 | 100 |
| Charts for area being navigated..................... | 42 | 42 | 42 | 42 | 42 |
| Parallel rule, 12″ ................. | 5 | 4 | — | 4 | 4 |
| Cruising guide for area being navigated.............. | 45 | 35 | — | 35 | 35 |
| Depth sounder, Standard Horizon ..................... | 500 | 180 | — | 180 | 180 |
| Loran, Micrologic portable model ....................... | 600 | 310 | — | 310 | 310 |
| Radar, Apelco ................. | 1,690 | 1,300 | — | — | 1,300 |
| AM/FM radio, portable ......... | 28 | 20 | 20 | 20 | 20 |
| VHF radio, Standard Eclipse..... | 339 | 180 | — | 180 | 180 |
| Wind Meter, Dwyer hand-held ................... | 10 | 8 | 8 | 8 | 8 |
| **Utility and Galley Gear** | | | | | |
| Bilge pump—22 GPM manual, with hose ........... | 125 | 92 | 92 | 92 | 92 |
| Boat hook, 8′, soundings marked in feet ................ | 20 | 17 | 17 | 17 | 17 |
| Buckets, two at $4 .............. | 12 | 8 | 8 | 8 | 8 |
| Sponges, 4 at $3 ................ | 18 | 12 | 12 | 12 | 12 |
| Ditty bag for rope and canvas work, with nylon whipping thread, marline, etc........... | 20 | 15 | 15 | 15 | 15 |

*continued*

| ITEM, TYPE, QUANTITY & SIZE | TYPICAL PRICE FOR ONE ITEM | | TOTAL COSTS FOR VARIOUS SIZES OF BOATS (1) | | |
|---|---|---|---|---|---|
| | list | discount | Small boat (2) | Medium boat (3) | Large boat (4) |
| Dock lines, cut and spliced by boat owner; | | | | | |
| ³/₈″ nylon × 100′ .............. | 56 | 38 | 38 | 38 | 38 |
| ¹/₂″ nylon × 150′ .............. | 85 | 57 | — | 57 | 57 |
| Ice carrier (nylon bag) ......... | 16 | 12 | 12 | 12 | 12 |
| Ice chest, Igloo 52-quart ........ | 46 | 40 | 40 | 40 | 40 |
| Storage battery, deep cycle ..... | 100 | 75 | — | 150 | 150 |
| Stove, two-burner Origo alcohol ..................... | 305 | 185 | — | 185 | 185 |
| Swim ladder ................... | 40 | 30 | 30 | 30 | 30 |
| Tool box, tools & supplies (WD-40, oil can, etc.) ......... | 100 | 80 | 80 | 80 | 80 |
| Galley china, cutlery, utensils, cookware..................... | 80 | 50 | — | 50 | 100 |
| **Personal gear** | | | | | |
| Binoculars, 7 × 50, low-priced type......................... | 80 | 50 | 50 | 50 | 50 |
| Foul-weather suits, per suit, jacket ....................... | 135 | 75 | 150 | 150 | 150 |
| pants....................... | 95 | 55 | 110 | 110 | 110 |
| Sleeping bags .......... per bag | 60 | 55 | 110 | 110 | 110 |
| Sun glasses, Polaroid.............. per pair | 12 | 9 | 18 | 18 | 18 |
| **TOTAL OF ABOVE** ............. | | | **$1,291** | **$3,422** | **$5,544** |

1. Costs exclude any installation services. Total cost shown may be a multiple (e.g. double or triple) the listed discount price for a single item, when spares are desirable, such as for anchors and batteries. Both new and used boats generally come with at least some (but seldom all) of the gear listed, at no extra cost.

2. "Small boat" assumes a runabout or daysailer, 12′ to 20′ long, for day use in protected lakes and harbors.

3. "Medium boat" assumes a 20′ to 34′ powerboat or sailboat for day use and occasional overnights in inshore areas.

4. "Large boat" assumes a powerboat or sailboat 34′ or longer used for occasional one-week or longer cruises and offshore passages.

5. General note: this listing is only a starting point for assembling required gear; it is not intended to be all-inclusive. Each boat and service has its own requirements, which the boatowner is advised to think through carefully before completing a final shopping list for needed gear. The brands shown were chosen for economy, and are not necessarily recommended by the author (though most are known and used by him with satisfactory results).

# Index

# Index

# Index